William Sadlier

Sadlier's excelsior studies in the history of the United States

William Sadlier

Sadlier's excelsior studies in the history of the United States

ISBN/EAN: 9783741111723

Manufactured in Europe, USA, Canada, Australia, Japa

Cover: Foto ©ninafisch / pixelio.de

Manufactured and distributed by brebook publishing software (www.brebook.com)

William Sadlier

Sadlier's excelsior studies in the history of the United States

EXCELSIOR SERIES OF CATHOLIC SCHOOL-BOOKS.

SADLIER'S EXCELSIOR STUDIES

IN THE

HISTORY

OF THE

UNITED STATES

FOR SCHOOLS.

BY THE
AUTHOR OF SADLIER'S ELEMENTARY HISTORY.

NEW YORK:
WILLIAM H. SADLIER.
11 BARCLAY STREET.

PREFACE.

THE principal motive which induced the preparation of the present volume, was to provide for American youth, (so far, at least, as could be done in so small a compass), a correct narrative of our country's history.

If it be true, as has been remarked by a celebrated modern writer, that European history has long been a vast "conspiracy against truth," it is equally certain that American history, or, at least, text-books on the subject, have also been in league against truth. It is simply wonderful how the part enacted by Catholics on our soil, from the days of Columbus to the present time, has been persistently and coolly ignored by writers of text-books; so that, from this very silence, a child of even ordinary intellect could not fail to infer that Catholicity has done little, or nothing, for our country; whereas, the reverse is singularly and emphatically the case.

Catholics have been here from the earliest dawn; and, as was pithily observed by Archbishop Hughes, "*Neither the first page, nor the last page, nor the middle* page of our history would have been where or what it is without them." The discovery, exploration, and, to some extent, the colonization of our country were undertaken by Catholics, with Catholic aims, and with Catholic aid. The only systematic and successful attempts to civilize and Christianize the Indians were made by Catholic missionaries, than whose lives and deaths few records of the human race will be found more sublime. "*Before the fire of the trapper's gun struck down his woodland game, before the edge of the exile's axe had caught a ray of western sunshine, a mild and steady light is perceptible in the primitive forest; and by its friendly aid we discover the Indian kneeling before the pine-tree cross, while the Black-robe pours on his humbled head the waters of regeneration.*" Lastly, the independence of the United States was, in a great degree, secured by Catholic blood, talent, and treasure. If our country's history be truly told, Catholicity must be met, willingly or unwillingly, at every step.

A second motive was the desire to give to our schools, a text-book at once brief, clear, and interesting; one which would make the story of our country's growth what it ought to be, to young and old, singularly attractive.

The "*dryness*" of United States History, is, at present, proverbial with teacher and pupil. This ought not so to be; for, certainly, there is richness enough of material to make it otherwise. Nevertheless, such an accumulation of statistics and data of various kinds is presented in the majority of school-books on the subject, as to make the youthful learner shrink in dismay from the mass he is expected to commit to memory. Moreover, the absence in such works, of a clear and well-defined plan, and the unnecessarily intricate interweaving of times, and places, and events, make it almost impossible for the pupil to gain anything like a definite outline of our history as a whole. Only the student already familiar with the subject could derive any benefit therefrom.

In the present volume, these objections have been avoided, the plan pursued being essentially the same as that of the "Excelsior Elementary History," a plan which, for its almost mathematical clearness and simplicity, has received the highest commendations.

According to Horace,—and his idea is endorsed by all intelligent educators,—"*the teacher to be successful, must blend the useful with the agreeable.*" Hence, the charms of poetry, anecdote, and brief but well-selected quotations from standard authors, together with the finest maps and choicest illustrations, have here been brought into service, to lend fascination to the study.

How far the ends proposed have been attained, the work of the class-room, the experience of teacher and pupil, must prove. This is the true, the only crucial and final test.

With special love and sympathy for the youthful members of the Church, who are so dear to the Heart of Christ, and with earnest good wishes for their success in the pursuit of learning and piety, "THE EXCELSIOR BRIEF STUDIES IN THE HISTORY OF THE UNITED STATES" is respectfully submitted by

THE AUTHOR.

POINTS TO BE SPECIALLY NOTED
IN
SADLIER'S BRIEF STUDIES IN THE HISTORY OF THE UNITED STATES.

1. The work is divided into *five sections*, each, except the first, embracing the events of one century. Each *Section* is divided into as many *Studies* as may be necessary, care being taken not to make any *study* too long.

2. Each section is followed by "*Biographical Sketches*" of the principal personages mentioned therein; by Tables of American and European Chronology, and Contemporary Popes; and by a Geographical Index. These matters, at the will of the teacher, may either be committed to memory, or simply read over by the pupil.

3. Where there is sufficient material, each study is concluded by a description of the manners, customs, etc., of the country or time.

4. The last or fifth section contains an account of the inventions, discoveries, etc., of the XIXth Century; also a *Study* giving some idea of the state of our literature.

5. Interesting anecdotes are freely interspersed, that "the useful and the agreeable" being thus intermingled,

the pupil may, even in spite of himself, be won to study.

6. To this end also, appropriate poetical and prose quotations from standard authors are, to a limited extent, introduced.

7. The Revolution and the Civil War, the details of which teachers find it so difficult and well-nigh impossible to impress upon the memory of their pupils, are, as far as possible, condensed. A crystallizing process is thus promoted in the mind of the student, whereby accessories and details group themselves around the main facts and ideas of the narration. The true glory of a nation lies, after all, in peace and true moral progress rather than in war.

8. Catholics, so far as could be in this brief outline, are assigned their proper place in the annals of our land.

9. Lastly, to lead to a more independent use of the book, as also to the topical mode of study and recitation, questions have been placed at the close of the work, rather than at the bottom of each page.

A. M. D. G.

CONTENTS.

SECTION I.

		PAGE
STUDY No. 1.	—America previous to 1492......................	1
STUDY No. 2.	—Discovery of America by Columbus	9
STUDY No. 3.	—Columbus, (Continued).—The Cabots...........	18
	Biographical Sketches.........................	22
	Chronological Review, Fifteenth Century........	25
	Geographical Table No. 1.....................	26

SECTION II.
A. D. 1500 TO A. D. 1600.

STUDY No. 1.	—Declining Years of Columbus.—Successors of the Great Admiral........................ ...	28
STUDY No. 2.	—Missions in the South.—St. Augustine Founded.	36
STUDY No. 3.	—English Explorations.—Unsuccessful Attempt to Colonize Virginia.........................	42
	Biographical Sketches.........................	47
	Chronological Review, Sixteenth Century.......	54
	Geographical Table No. 2.....................	56

SECTION III.
A. D. 1600 TO A. D. 1700.

STUDY No. 1.	—Virginia......................................	59
STUDY No. 2.	—Virginia, (Continued).........................	66
STUDY No. 3.	—New England.....	71
STUDY No. 4.	—New England, (Continued)................	80
STUDY No. 5.	—New England, (Continued).................	87
STUDY No. 6.	—Early Jesuit Missionaries at the North..........	91
STUDY No. 7.	—Missionaries at the North, (Continued)..........	102
STUDY No. 8.	—New York.....................................	111
STUDY No. 9.	—Maryland........................	121
STUDY No. 10.	—Pennsylvania.—Delaware.................. ..	126
STUDY No. 11.	—The Carolinas................................	130
STUDY No. 12.	—King William's War, (1689-1697)..............	133
	Biographical Sketches.........................	137
	Chronological Review, Seventeenth Century. ...	146
	Geographical Table No. 3.....................,	149

x   CONTENTS.

SECTION. IV.
A. D. 1700 TO A. D. 1800.

		PAGE
STUDY No. 1.	—The American Colonies during the First Half of the Eighteenth Century...............	151
STUDY No. 2.	—French and Indian War......................	159
STUDY No. 3.	—Causes of the American Revolution, and its First Battles...........................	170
STUDY No. 4.	—Campaigns in New York. New Jersey, and Pennsylvania, (1776–1777).................	185
STUDY No. 5.	—Alliance with France —Campaign at the South..	195
STUDY No. 6.	—Events of the War at the North.—The Final Campaign, (1778–1781)...............	207
STUDY No. 7.	—The Constitution Accepted.—Administrations of Washington and Adams................	218
STUDY No. 8.	—Occupations, Manners, Education, etc...........	227
STUDY No. 9.	—Catholicity and the Revolution...............	233
	Biographical Sketches.........................	239
	Chronological Review, Eighteenth Century......	249
	Geographical Table No. 4...................	252

SECTION V.
A. D. 1800 TO A. D. 1890.

STUDY No. 1.	—Administration of Jefferson and Madison.—War of 1812.................................	255
STUDY No. 2.	—Madison's Administration, (Continued).—War with England, (Continued)...............	262
STUDY No. 3.	—Monroe.—John Quincy Adams.—Jackson........	272
STUDY No. 4.	—Van Buren.—Harrison.—Tyler.—Polk..........	281
STUDY No. 5.	—Taylor.—Fillmore.—Pierce.—Buchanan.......	290
STUDY No. 6.	—Lincoln.—First Year of the Civil War..........	299
STUDY No. 7.	—Lincoln.—Second Year of the Civil War, (1862)..	306
STUDY No. 8.	—Lincoln.—Third Year of the Civil War, (1863)...	318
STUDY No. 9.	—Lincoln.—Fourth Year of the Civil War, (1864)..	325
STUDY No. 10.	—The Last Year of the War.—Johnson...........	337
STUDY No. 11.	—Grant.—Hayes.	350
STUDY No. 12.	—Garfield.—Arthur.—Cleveland.—Harrison	360
STUDY No. 13.	—Occupations, Arts, Literature, etc.............	364
STUDY No. 14.	—Religion	370
	Biographical Sketches.........................	380
	Chronological Review, Nineteenth Century.....	393
	Geographical Table No. 5.....................	397
	Review Questions.............................	401

Declaration of Independence.................................. 415
Constitution of the United States............................. 418
Amendments to the Constitution.............................. 426
Table of the Presidents 429
Table of States... 430

SECTION I.
A.D. 1492 TO A.D. 1500.

STUDY NO. 1.
AMERICA PREVIOUS TO 1492.

1. First Inhabitants of America.—America was peopled probably from Asia, by way of Behring Strait.[5]* At this point only, do the two continents approach each other; moreover, the earliest inhabitants found here by Europeans bore a striking resemblance to the Tartars of Eastern Asia. The Indians as found by Columbus were not, however, its earliest inhabitants. They had been preceded by a race much more civilized and skilled in the arts, of which extensive remains are to be seen throughout the whole length of the Mississippi Valley, and even as far north as the copper region of Lake Superior.[35]

It is a singular coincidence that, in Asiatic Tartary, are to be found remains indicating that it, too, was once the seat of a civilization far superior to that of its present inhabitants.

2. The Mound Builders.—This earlier race in America is known as the Mound Builders, from the great number of mounds, or earthworks, which they erected On the terraces of the Mississippi Valley, and in the forests bordering on the Mexican Gulf, may be seen a succession of such works, mainly defensive in character. In connection with these, are found others apparently of a religious origin.

* These numbers refer to Geographical Table, at close of Section.

Some of the mounds arrest our attention by their geometrical regularity of form; others, by their great size. One of this description on the plain of Cahokia, Illinois, opposite to the city of St. Louis, is 700 feet long by 500 feet broad, at the base, and 90 feet high. It occupies an area of 8 acres, and its contents number 20,000,000 cubic feet.

In Adams County, Ohio, is a curious earthwork, representing an immense serpent, about one thousand feet long. It appears to hold in its mouth an egg-shaped mound, one hundred and sixty feet in length; and its tail is twined into a triple coil.

Sixteen miles east of Little Rock, Arkansas, are two mounds, the larger of which is over two hundred and fifty feet in height.

MOUNDS NEAR LITTLE ROCK, ARKANSAS.

3. **Contents of the Mounds.**—In a single mound, are sometimes discovered elaborate carvings in stone; pottery, often of elegant design; articles of use or ornament in metals; silver, and native copper from Lake Superior; mica from the Alleghanies,[1] and shells from the Gulf of Mexico. In the sepulchral mounds, which are the most common monuments of the Mississippi Valley, are occasionally found two or more skeletons; but generally only one. The idea that they contain vast heaps of slain and are memorials of great battles, is unsupported by facts.

4. Antiquity of the Mounds.—The age of the mounds is a matter of conjecture. From various facts and circumstances connected with these monuments, some antiquarians deduce for most of the earthworks of the Mississippi Valley an age of not fewer than two thousand years. Certain it is, that, upon them, the largest forest trees are often found growing. On a mound near Marietta, Ohio, there are trees which must have seen at least eight centuries.

5. What became of the Mound Builders?—The fate of these ancient architects is unknown. Whether they migrated to some more genial climate, or sank beneath the victorious arms of an alien and hostile race, or were exterminated by the ravages of some direful epidemic, are questions which, in all probability, will remain forever unanswered here below. Their works alone remain to tell the tale.

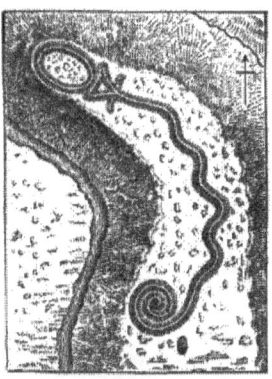

THE SERPENT MOUND, OHIO.

> "A race that long has passed away
> Built them; a disciplined and populous race
> Heaped with long toil the earth, while yet the Greek
> Was hewing the Pentelicus to forms
> Of symmetry, and rearing on its rock
> The glittering Parthenon."—BRYANT.

6. The Indians.—The Indians who succeeded the Mound Builders, and who, at the time of Columbus, numbered about 400,000 souls, were by far their inferiors in civilization. Their highest achievement in art was the building of a wigwam, the carving out of a birch canoe,* or

---

* The frame of the canoe was made of white cedar. Over this, was stretched the bark of a birch tree. The edges were sewed with thongs cut from the roots of the

4   EXCELSIOR HISTORY.

the framing of a snow-shoe.* In one little section only of the country, on the borders of the Gila[11] and Rio Grande, the people manufactured a native cotton and a rude pottery, and lived in houses of unburnt bricks.

7. War was, with them, the chief occupation; and next to it, ranked hunting and fishing. They had no written language, though they sometimes used a species of hieroglyphics, or picture writing. Schoolcraft gives a copy of a drawing made

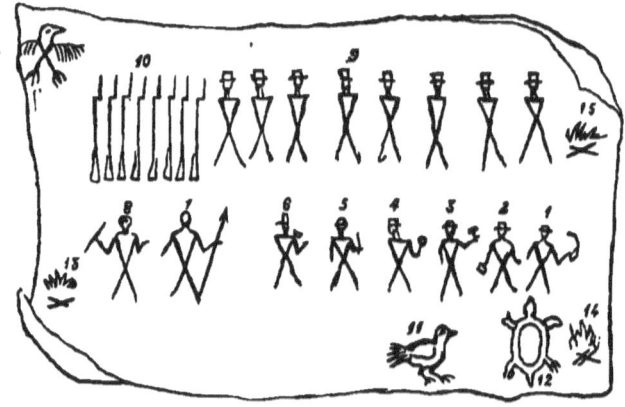

INDIAN PICTURE WRITING.

No. 1 represents the commanding officer, sword in hand; No. 2, with the book, the secretary; No. 3. carrying a hammer, the geologist; Nos. 4, 5, and 6, attendants; Nos. 7 and 8, Indian guides, known as such because without hats; 10, muskets carried by the party; 11 and 12, a prairie hen and a tortoise which had been eaten by the party; 13, 14, 15, show that there had been three camp-fires; and the inclination of the pole indicates the direction of the proposed march.

cedar, and were then covered with pitch made from the gum of trees. The largest of these canoes were about 30 ft. long; and each could carry ten or twelve Indians.

* The snow-shoe consisted of a maplewood frame, three or four feet long, curved and tapering, and filled in with a net-work of deer's hide. It was fastened by thongs to the foot, which was thus supported on the surface of the snow. An Indian could travel forty miles a day upon snow-shoes, and could easily overtake the deer and the moose, whose pointed hoofs cut through the snow crust.

by his Indian guides, on a piece of birch bark, to inform their comrades that a party of fourteen whites and two Indians had encamped at that place.

8. Woman was considered by them a degraded being, in fact, a slave. She did all the drudgery, raised the crops and carried the burdens. "*Their women*," says Champlain, "*are their mules.*" Here, as elsewhere, Christianity first raised woman to her rightful position.

NORTH AMERICAN INDIANS.

9. Their religion was a species of devil-worship. "*Pure unmixed devil-worship,*" says John Gilmary Shea,* "*prevailed throughout the length and breadth of the land.*" No word in any Indian dialect had an equivalent for the word God. All

---

* **Shea, John Gilmary** (1824–), a well-known American author, noted for his researches into early American history. His best known works are "History of the Catholic Missions among the Indian tribes of the United States," "Discovery and Exploration of the Mississippi Valley," also a translation of Charlevoix' "New France," in 6 volumes, with copious notes.

events, in their estimation, were brought about by *manitous* (*spirits*).

There were manitous, as they thought, in everything; in animals, lakes, rivers, hills, valleys, winds, and stars. In this connection they cherished many wild fancies, some of which have been embodied in Longfellow's *Hiawatha*.

Catholic missionaries, certainly, had terrible obstacles to surmount before they could christianize these dusky children of the forest · but the Church that had tamed and civilized the fierce tribes that overran the Roman Empire, was not to be appalled at new difficulties. The divine command of Christ was with them; " *Go teach all nations.*" We shall see, in the sequel, their success with the poor Indian.

10. Voyages of the Northmen.— Iceland was visited by the Irish, in the ninth century, or earlier; and the continent of North America was discovered by the Norwegians, or Northmen, in the tenth.

NORMAN SHIP.

In the year 1000, Catholic missionaries found their way to Greenland, and before long its churches and convents began to compare favorably with those of the mother country.*

---

* This much at least is certain : that sixty-five years previous to the discovery of Iceland by the Northmen in the 9th century, Irish emigrants had visited and inhabited that island ; that about the year 725, Irish ecclesiastics had sought seclusion

11. The hardy Northmen continued their explorations southward, in all probability, as far as Narragansett Bay.[13] It is certain, that, in 1120, Eric,* who subsequently became bishop of Garda in Greenland, visited that portion of our country known as Vinland. This was situated, probably, in the vicinity of Rhode Island. At Newport,[14] † have been found, and still exist, Scandinavian ruins bearing a striking resemblance to the relics of the Northmen in Greenland [15] and Iceland,[16] and wholly unlike any known remains of Indian workmanship.

TOWER AT NEWPORT.

12. Fate of the Greenland Colony.—In the fourteenth century, the colony of Greenland was ravaged by a plague, which with famine and the attacks of a hostile native tribe, completely destroyed the settlement. The voyages of the Northmen were soon forgotten, even in their own land; while, of the existence of a continent beyond the Atlantic, the people of Southern Europe did not even dream.

Hence these early expeditions do not at all detract from the glory of Columbus.‡

upon the Faroe Islands; that in the 10th century, voyages between Iceland and Ireland were of ordinary occurrence; and that, in the 11th century, a country west from Ireland and south of that part of the American continent which was discovered by the adventurous Northmen in the preceding age, was known to them under the name of White-man's Land, or Great Ireland.—BEAMISH.

* Bishop Eric must not be confounded with Eric the Red, who, some time before, had discovered and settled Greenland.

† The ancient "tholus" (or tower) in Newport, the erection of which seems to be coeval with the time of Bishop Eric, belonged to a Scandinavian church or monastery, where, in alternation with Latin Masses, the old Danish tongue was heard seven hundred years ago.—*Memoirs of the Royal Society of Antiquarians.*

‡ "We come to regard Columbus himself in a new light. We may not admire him so much as an original discoverer, but as one who repeated and established the

13. Other Supposed Expeditions.—There are several traditions relating to other voyages to the Western World, during the interval between the tenth and fifteenth centuries. Of these, the most remarkable concerns Madoc, a Welsh Prince.

14. Madoc.—According to the legend, Prince Madoc, the son of Owen Gwynneth, being obliged by civil disturbances to leave his native country, set sail, with a small fleet, on a voyage of discovery. Having steered directly west from Ireland, he, after a voyage of some weeks, reached a country of exceeding fertility, whose inhabitants differed greatly from those of Europe. Having returned to England, he shortly afterwards, with a considerable colony, again set sail for the same lands. Of his after-fate, no tidings ever reached Europe. Humboldt refers to this tradition, and Southey has made it the subject of a poem.

accredited discoveries of his predecessors, in a most heroic and glorious style of experiment. Thus was the ancient Syrian and Pythagorean system of astronomy revived, restored and developed by Copernicus and Newton. Their immense merit consisted in the examination, accumulation and demonstration of antique theories, that had been well nigh consigned to oblivion. And this, in our estimation, requires a loftier and wider range of intellectual science than original discovery itself.

"Original discovery, as it is called, is often the result of chance, accident, the spirit of contradiction, and even the rashness of desperation. Original discoveries are often struck out in an instant, to the astonishment of their inventors, who had no anticipation of them. Not so with the profound truth-searcher, who, knowing that what is true is not new, and that what is new is not true, searches back through the recondite annals of our planet for the golden links of the sole philosophy. For this man, what perseverance is required, what subtlety, what fine perception of analogies, what a critical analysis of all the elements which constitute probability! Such men, if not original discoverers, are discoverers of a still higher order. They lay hold of the neglected germ which original discovery had flung on the harsh rocks of incredulity, and develop it into an august and glorious system of demonstrated verity. They seize the little spark of Promethean fire which was just about to perish in the fogs of forgetfulness, and by it they rekindle the universe into a blaze of exulting hope.

"If, therefore, we admire Columbus less as the hardy adventurer (who with a dogged and desperate resolution, hoping against hope, launched forth on the Atlantic to discover he knew not what), we reverence him more than ever as the keen-sighted and philosophic truth-searcher, who, from the accumulated history of ages, in the haughty independence of conscious genius, moulded a most refined yet demonstrable theory of facts."—*Dublin Review.*

1

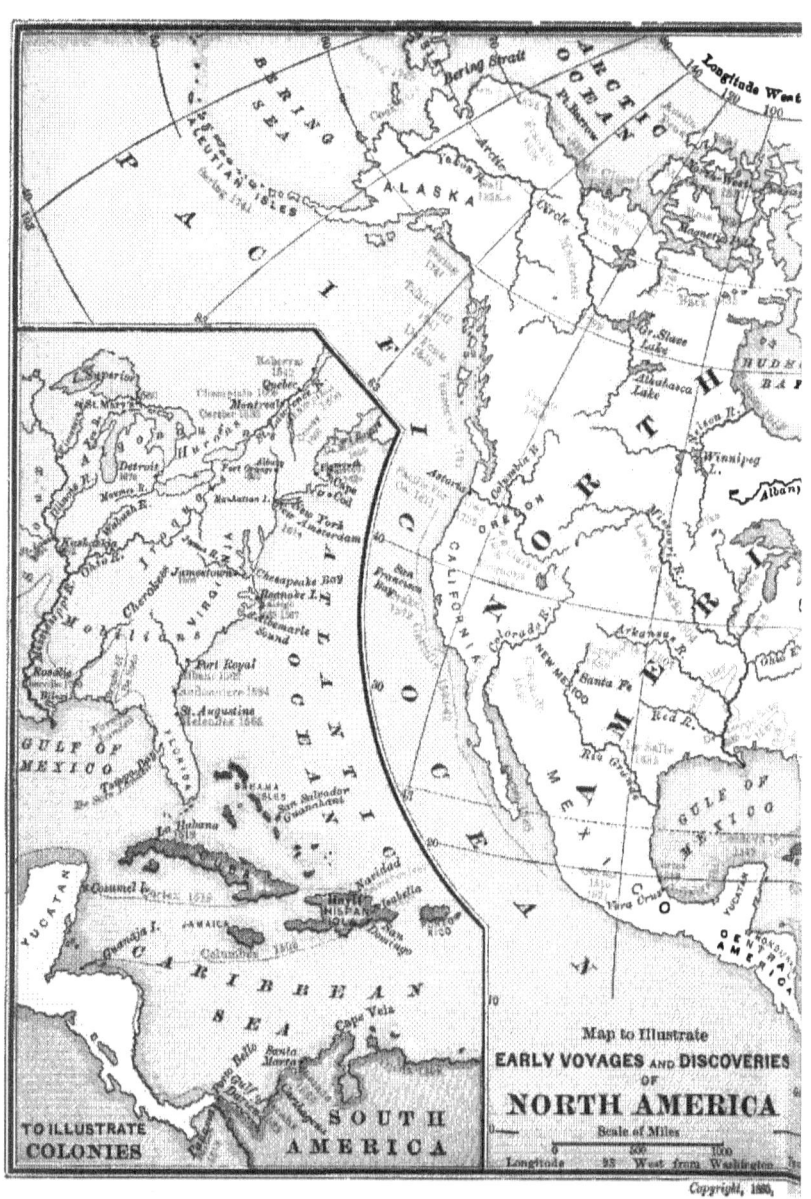

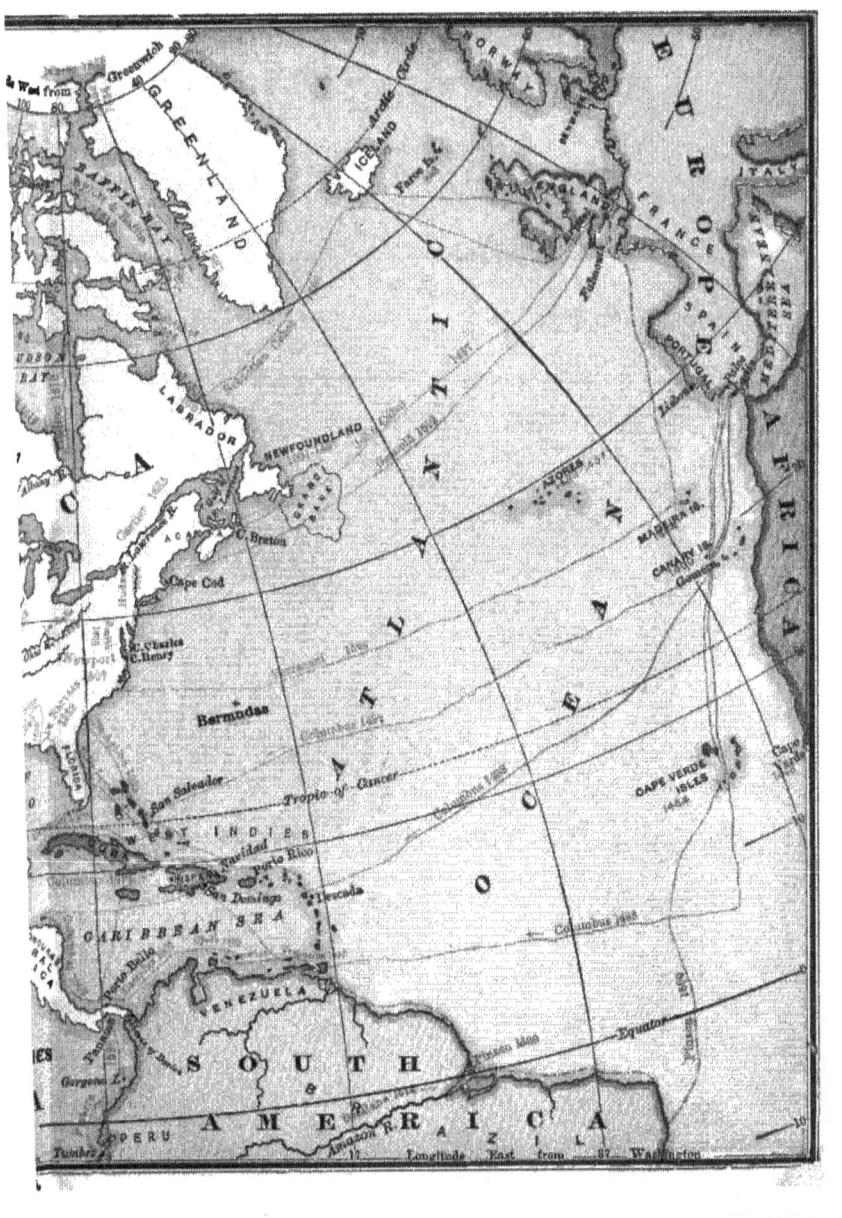

STUDY NO. 2.

DISCOVERY OF AMERICA BY COLUMBUS

1. America Four Centuries Ago.—Four hundred years ago, our beautiful country was a wilderness. Where now stand our busy cities and thriving villages, then primeval forests or rolling prairies alone were to be seen. Our noble lakes and majestic rivers, now alive with magnificent steamers and large sailing vessels, were then burdened by no better craft than the Indian's frail canoe. The whole country was occupied by an immense number of comparatively small, but hostile, Indian tribes, many of whose names still linger on our lakes and rivers.

> "You say they all have passed away,
>   That noble race and brave,
> That their light canoes have vanished
>   From off the crested wave;
> That 'mid the forests where they roamed
>   There rings no hunter's shout;
> But their name is on your waters,
>   You may not wash it out.
>
> "'Tis where Ontario's billow
>   Like ocean's surge is curled,
> Where strong Niagara's thunders make
>   The echo of the world;
> Where red Missouri bringeth
>   Rich tributes from the West,
> And Rappahannock sweetly sleeps
>   On green Virginia's breast.
>
> "You say their cone-like cabins,
>   That clustered o'er the vale,
> Have fled away like withered leaves
>   Before the autumn gale;

But their memory liveth on your hills,
 Their baptism on your shore;
 Your everlasting rivers speak
 Their dialect of yore.

"Old Massachusetts wears it
 Within her lordly crown,
And broad Ohio bears it
 Amid her young renown;
Connecticut hath wreathed it
 Where her quiet foliage waves,
And bold Kentucky breathes it hoarse
 Through all her ancient caves."—SIGOURNEY.

2. The World Four Centuries Ago. — Europe, meanwhile, was ignorant even of the existence of this vast continent.

THE WORLD AS KNOWN IN 15TH CENTURY.

In truth, the world, as known at that time, was a very small one. Take away the two American continents, Southern and Central Africa, and Australia, together with Northeastern Asia (not any of which places were then known to Europeans), and we cannot but be amazed at the comparatively small space in which the then known history of the world had been transacted.

3. Maritime Science.—Just at this epoch, however, geographical and maritime science received a powerful impulse in the desire to discover a new and easier route to the Indies.* Finally, Christopher Columbus, a native of Genoa,[10] in Italy, convinced of the sphericity of the earth, proclaimed that by sailing westward over the Atlantic, he could reach the eastern shores of Asia.

* The trade with India was a source of great wealth to Southern Europe. At this time, the traders, in order to reach India, were obliged to go by way of the Mediterranean and Red Seas, and then overland by caravans. This was a very expensive way of transporting goods.

DISCOVERY OF AMERICA. 11

4. Precursors of Columbus.—Among the precursors of Columbus in geographical attainments, three persons deserve to be especially mentioned: Cardinal D'Ailly of France, Prince Henry of Portugal, and Paul Toscanelli of Florence.[9]

5. Cardinal D'Ailly is considered by Humboldt as the restorer of geographical science. His celebrated work, (*Imago Mundi*) is supposed to have been of service to Columbus. A copy of the same, bearing marginal notes in the great discoverer's own handwriting, is still preserved.

6. Prince Henry of Portugal erected an observatory on his palace at Cape St. Vincent,[24] entertained there teachers of every art, and studied under them as humbly as any of his dependants. Under his auspices, the Azores[3] were discovered and Africa was partially circumnavigated. It was from the enterprise of this illustrious man that the genius of Columbus took fire. Indeed, Prince Henry was hardly less a personage than Columbus himself.

7. Toscanelli had obtained from the canons of the Church of St. Mary, at Florence, the use of their tower as an observatory; and here, raised far above the noise and tumult of the world, he wrote encouraging letters to Columbus, and devised that conjectural chart of the Atlantic which the 'Admiral took with him on his first voyage.*

8. Columbus.—Columbus having in vain applied to his native State, to Venice,[26] France, England, and Portugal, for aid to carry out his plans, at length (in 1484) repaired to Spain. Although here he met with a more favorable reception, still many years elapsed before he obtained the desired assistance.

* On this map, the eastern coast of Asia was depicted in front of the western coasts of Africa and Europe, with a moderate space of ocean between them, in which were placed, at convenient distances, Cepango, Antilla, and other islands.—IRVING.

FATHER PEREZ PLEADING WITH ISABELLA.

9. Father Juan Perez.—About the year 1484, while on a short journey, Columbus accidentally stopped for refreshment at the monastery of Santa Maria de la Rabida, about half a league from Palos.[21] Here he found a warm friend and powerful advocate, in the person of the prior Juan Perez. This good Franciscan, struck by the noble appearance of the stranger, entered into conversation with him, soon appreciated his genius, and beholding in Columbus the marks of a providential election, devoted himself to his interest, with an ardor which ceased only with life.

10. When, in 1491, Columbus was about to leave Spain in despair, Juan Perez restored him to confidence and hope. Saddling his mule at midnight, the good monk privately

departed for the court. "He journeyed," says Irving,*
"through the conquered countries of the Moors, and rode
into the newly-erected city of Santa Fe,[28] where the sovereigns
were superintending the close investment of the capital of
Granada."[12] Here he pleaded so earnestly and eloquently the
cause of Columbus, that the noble and generous Isabella
charged Father Perez to summon Columbus to her presence
without delay.

11. Isabella's Generosity.—After another disappointment, caused by the interference of some influential persons still opposed to the project of Columbus, Isabella gave utterance to that magnanimous and oft-repeated sentence: "*I undertake the enterprise for my own crown of Castile,[7] and will pledge my jewels to raise the necessary funds.*" Thus did Isabella become the protectress of Columbus and the earthly patroness of the New World.

12. Santangel, the royal treasurer, always a warm friend of Columbus, assured the queen that she would not be obliged to pledge her jewels, as he himself would advance the necessary sum from the funds of Arragon.

13. Preparations for the Voyage.—Three small vessels were soon fitted out, named respectively, the Santa Maria, the Pinta, and the Niña. Columbus and his crew devoutly prepared themselves for the dangers of the deep by the reception of the Sacraments of Penance and Holy Eucharist, at the monastery of La Rabida, and then marched in procession to the vessels. Father Perez gave them his parting blessing, and promised to pray earnestly for the success of the undertaking which he had already

* **Irving, Washington** (1783-1859), a classical American prose writer, surnamed the American Goldsmith, was born in New York city. Among his first and most successful works was his humorous History of New York. Later appeared "The Life and Voyages of Christopher Columbus," a charmingly written work. Irving, however, being a Protestant, failed to appreciate fully the Catholic hero. He died at Sunnyside, on the Hudson, at an advanced age.

so materially aided. As they started on their perilous voyage, we can imagine how the men and women of Palos watched the white specks of sail vanishing in the west; and how, as each frail bark disappeared from view, mothers and sisters turned weepingly away, as if from the last farewell at the grave of their sailor kinsmen.

COLUMBUS DEPARTING FROM PALOS.

14. **The Voyage.**—Days and weeks passed, and at length they found themselves where never before (at least to their knowledge) had mariner found himself, in mid-ocean. All things seemed new and strange; new constellations appeared in the heavens, the needle of the compass varied, and the hearts of the sailors sank within them; but

DISCOVERY OF AMERICA. 15

Columbus seemed to know no fear. The standard of the cross floated from the mast, and every evening the crew chanted in common "*Ave Maris Stella.*" The trust of Columbus, says Knight,* was "in the guiding hand of God and in a '*Star of the Sea*' shining from a higher Heaven than eyes of the body could reach."

15. As time wore on and still the desired land appeared not, the crew became mutinous. They overwhelmed their brave commander with reproaches, refused to go further, and threatened to throw him overboard. Columbus, however, remained firm, declaring that *he had started for the Indies, and, with the help of God, thither he would go.*

16. Land.—The patience and perseverance of Columbus were at length rewarded. At daybreak, on the morning of Friday, Oct. 12th (1492), the joyful sound of "Land! Land!" resounded from the little vessels ; and, before them, clothed in all the luxuriant vegetation of the south, lay the beautiful island of San Salvador. Columbus sank upon his knees, chanting the "Te Deum." His men responded, with hearts full of gratitude to God, and of sorrow for their previous ungenerous treatment of their commander.

17. As the day grew bright, the natives, more astonished than even Columbus and his crew, were seen gazing in wondering curiosity at the huge white birds, which they imagined the ships to be, and at the strange beings who, they supposed, must have descended from the skies. Three small boats having been lowered, Columbus rowed to the land, and with tearful eyes and grateful heart, stepped ashore. Kneeling, he kissed the ground he had so long desired to see, and then uttered aloud that short but beauti-

* Rev. A. G. Knight, S. J., an English Jesuit, author of a recent "Life of Columbus," of great merit and beauty.

COLUMBUS TAKING POSSESSION.

ful prayer which, after him, all Catholic discoverers were wont to repeat.

"O Lord God, Eternal and Omnipotent, who by thy Divine Word hast created the heavens, the earth, and the sea! Blessed and glorified be thy Name, and praised thy Majesty who hast deigned by me, Thy humble servant, to have that sacred Name made known and preached in this other part of the world!"

18. Then rising with majesty and displaying the standard of the Cross, he solemnly offered to God the first fruits of his discovery, named the island San Salvador (Holy Saviour),[2] and gave orders for a large cross to be constructed. Supposing that he had reached the islands off the east coast of Asia, he called the country the West Indies, and the natives Indians. The cross being completed, it was solemnly

DISCOVERY OF AMERICA.   17

exalted while the "*Vexilla Regis*" was chanted. At the conclusion of the ceremony, Columbus again intoned the Te Deum.

19. The Spaniards and the Natives.—The Spaniards now distributed among the natives various trifles. The latter, on their part, were charmed with the wonderful

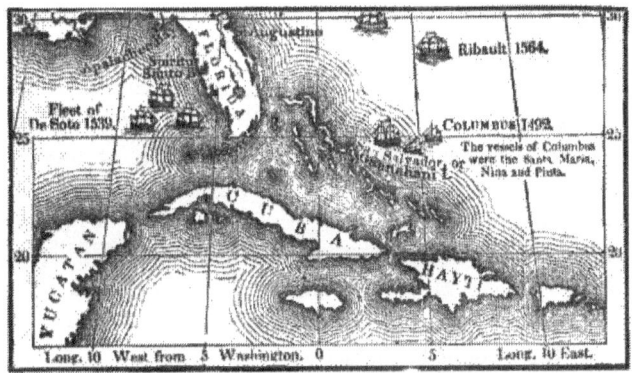

SAN SALVADOR AND THE ADJACENT ISLANDS.

strangers,* and regarded as precious everything that came from their hands,—even pieces of broken glass being valued as treasures. Seven of the Indians were easily induced to go with Columbus, and though one of them deserted, others were afterwards added from Cuba[8] and St. Domingo.[15] It was the pious intention of Columbus to present them to Ferdinand and Isabella, to have them instructed in the faith, and then sent back to help in the conversion of their countrymen.

* The idea that the white men came from Heaven was universally entertained by the inhabitants of the New World. When, during subsequent voyages, the Spaniards conversed with the cacique Nicaragua, he inquired how they came down from the skies, whether by flying, or whether they descended on clouds.—*Herrera.* Ah! had all Europeans but used their influence aright, with what comparative ease might the Indians have been made Christians!

STUDY NO. 3.

COLUMBUS, Continued.—THE CABOTS.

1. Further Discoveries.—Columbus, anxious to continue his discoveries, did not long remain in one place. Proceeding southward he discovered an island, or rather a group of islands, to which he gave the name of Santa Maria de la Conception. Shortly afterwards, he discovered Cuba and Hayti, or Hispaniola, called also San Domingo.[15] San Domingo is a central point, not only of the West Indies, but of the Western Hemisphere, and therefore most fortunately located for the further progress of discovery and conquest.

2. The Return Home.—On the 4th of January, 1493, Columbus again set sail for Spain. The homeward voyage was most tempestuous. Fearful of shipwreck, Columbus wrote on parchment a brief account of his voyage, and enclosing it in a cake of wax, committed it to the sea in a cask. He hoped that, even if all else were lost, this, at least, might be picked up by some stray mariner, and his discoveries thus revealed to the world.*

3. His Vow.—In the moment of greatest danger, his Catholic heart prompted him to invoke the succor of Our Lady. He accordingly vowed to make, on landing, a pilgrimage to her nearest shrine. This vow, on reaching Palos in safety, he faithfully fulfilled; and it fell to the lot of good Father Perez to offer up the Mass of Thanksgiving.

---

* Martin Alonzo Pinzon, one of his first companions, had wilfully parted company with Columbus on the coast of Cuba, covetousness being probably the cause of this most undutiful proceeding.

4. His Reception in Spain.—The court being at Barcelona,⁵ Columbus immediately repaired thither; and his progress through the country was like the march of a victorious conqueror. The king and queen received him with the highest honor,* listened with respectful attention to his recital, and loaded him with favors. These honors were in strange contrast to the neglect, treachery, and injustice of which he was afterwards the victim. We shall see later that, as in the case of his Divine Master, these hosannas envy soon changed into clamors for his imprisonment.

5. The Egg.—Even then, at a banquet given in honor of Columbus, a shallow courtier remarked that any one might have done what the admiral had done. Columbus made no direct reply, but taking an egg, requested those present to make it stand on end. All tried, but in vain. Columbus then struck it on the table, breaking the shell, but leaving it upright. "*Any one could do that!*" again exclaimed the courtier. "*Yes,*" replied Columbus, "*when the way has once been pointed out.*"

6. Second Voyage of Columbus, — Columbus speedily (Sept. 25th, 1493) set out on a second voyage; and now, by order of the Sovereign Pontiff, he was accompanied by a number of Dominican missionaries, destined to labor for the conversion of the Indians.† Some say that Father Perez also accompanied the mariners. Among the noted personages who engaged in the expedition, was Don Alonzo de Ojeda, who afterwards colonized Darien. They reached the West Indies towards the close of the year 1493; and, on

---

* As Columbus approached, the sovereigns arose, as if receiving a person of the highest rank. Bending his knees, he offered to kiss their hands; but there was some hesitation on their part to permit this act of homage. Raising him in the most gracious manner, they ordered him to seat himself in their presence; a rare honor in this proud and punctilious court.—IRVING.

† "This pious mission," says Irving, "was provided with all things necessary for the dignified performance of its functions, the queen supplying from her own chapel the ornaments and vestments to be used on all solemn occasions."

the Festival of the Epiphany (Jan. 6th, 1494), the first Catholic church in the New World was dedicated at Isabella,* in Hayti.⁷

7. Other Voyages of Columbus.—The great discoverer made two other voyages to the New World, and in 1498 he discovered the island of Trinidad,† and soon after the continent of America, near the mouth of the Orinoco River.

8. The Cab'ots.—The brilliant career of Columbus induced many daring men to brave the dangers of the deep. He had borne the "*heat and burden*" of the day; they were to reap the reward of his labors. The earliest of these were John and Sebastian Cabot.

9. In 1497, John Cab'ot, an Italian in the service of England (which was still Catholic),‡ set sail for this country. He was accompanied by his son Sebastian. After a prosperous voyage, they reached Labrador and sailed along the coast for some distance. On his return to England he was received with signal honor and was styled "The Great Admiral."

10. Sebastian Cab'ot continued his father's discoveries; and, the following year (1498), he explored the Atlantic coast from Labrador to Florida. He sailed as far north, probably, as the 60th degree of north latitude, where great ice-fields impeded his progress. Seeing no prospect of an open sea further north, Cabot sailed back, and discovered a large island, which he called Newfoundland (*nu'-fund-land*). Hav

---

* "A plan of the city was formed; and, Columbus having determined its proportions, laid, in the name of the Most Holy Trinity, the foundation-stone of it, giving it the name of Isabella. The service of God surpassing, in his estimation, all other considerations, the first edifice to be erected was the church. This was pushed with such activity, that on the 6th of January, the anniversary of the entrance of the Spanish sovereigns into Granada, High Mass was therein solemnly celebrated."—*Life of Columbus, by De Lorgnes.*

† So named in honor of the Holy Trinity.

‡ Protestantism commenced about the year 1517.

ing observed the abundance of codfish in the adjacent waters, he, on his return to Europe, made known this fact; whereupon hardy fishermen from France and England soon found their way to these shores.

11. The Discoveries of the Cabots* laid the foundation to the English claim in North America. Sebastian Cabot was one of the most extraordinary men of his day. "*He gave to England a continent,*" says Bancroft, "*yet no one knows his burial-place.*" Sad comment on the gratitude of nations!

12. The Name America.—In 1499, Amerigo Vespucci (*ah-mā-rē'-go ves-poot-chee*), a Florentine, accompanied an expedition to South America. Having returned home, he published a glowing account of his discoveries. This having fallen into the hands of a German writer on Geography, the country received from him the name of America.

13. Spirit of the Discovery.—The discovery of America was pre-eminently a Catholic enterprise. In fact, Protestantism did not as yet exist. The voyage was made under the protection of the Blessed Virgin, and for truly Catholic motives, namely: first, to carry the light of Christianity to pagan lands; secondly, to raise funds sufficient to defray the expense of equipping a large army to rescue the Holy Sepulchre from the hands of the Turks. Such were the motives of Columbus.

14. To make it, if possible, still more Catholic, the reigning Pontiff, Alexander VI, issued a Bull (May 9th, 1493) in which he laid it as an obligation on the Spanish sovereigns, to send to the newly-found islands and continent "*tried men who fear God, learned, and skilful, and expert, to instruct the inhabitants in the Catholic faith, and teach them good morals.*"

---

* Little attention was, at first, paid to these discoveries; because, about that time (1498), Vasco de Gama, a Portuguese, had rounded the Cape of Good Hope, and opened for ships the long-desired route to the East.

BIOGRAPHICAL SKETCHES.

OF THE PRINCIPAL PERSONAGES MENTIONED IN THE PRECEDING SECTION.

Cabot, John, an Italian (probably a Genoese), at the time of the discovery of America, resided in England. In the spring of 1497, he with his son Sebastian, embarked for the New World in a single vessel, and discovered the North American Continent, more than a year before the mainland of South America was seen by Columbus. He called the land Prima Vista, or *First Seen*, and the adjoining island St. John, in honor of the day (June 24). John Cabot made no second voyage to the New World. The time and place of his death are unknown.

Cabot, Sebastian [1475–1560 (?)], son of the preceding. In 1498, he sailed on a second voyage to the New World, and explored the Atlantic coast from Labrador to Florida. On the death of Henry VII of England, Sebastian Cabot was invited to Spain by Ferdinand, and was appointed one of the council for the New Indies.

In 1548, however, he returned to England, where his merits and nautical skill brought him to the notice of the boy-king, Edward VI, who settled upon him a handsome pension. In 1553, a company of merchants of which he was the head, projected an expedition to find a northwest passage to the Indies. One of the ships was frozen up in a Lapland harbor, and all on board perished; the other discovered Archangel, and opened a commerce between England and Russia. England thus owes to him her first mercantile connection with Russia.

The time of his death is uncertain. The last authentic record of him is in May 1557, at which time he received a new grant of a pension.

Columbus, Christopher (1435–1506), a native of Genoa, in Italy. His father was a wool-comber, also the owner of a small cloth factory. At the age of ten, Columbus was sent to the University of Pavia, where he laid the foundation of that scientific knowledge in which he afterwards excelled. Two years later, he was withdrawn by his father, probably from inability to meet the attendant expense. At the age of fourteen, he commenced his sea-faring life, which he continued almost uninterruptedly till his death. He himself said: "*Wherever ship has sailed, there have I voyaged.*" In 1492, his little fleet having been fitted out by Ferdinand and Isabella of Spain, he discovered America. This was a source of great glory and immense wealth to the Spanish crown. Later, he made three other voyages to the New World; but the sovereign whom he served treated him with the basest ingratitude and injustice. He died poor and unhonored, in a small inn at Valladolid, May 20th, 1506. His last words were: "*Into thy hands, O Lord, I commend my spirit.*" Columbus was a man of uncommon talents, lofty aspirations, and profound piety.

"*The finger of the historian,*" says Prescott, "*will find it difficult to point to a single blemish in his moral character. Whether we contemplate it in its public or private relations, in all its features it wears the same noble aspect. It was in perfect harmony with the grandeur of his plans and their results; more stupendous than those which Heaven has permitted any other mortal to achieve.*"

D'Ailly, Cardinal Peter (1350-1420), surnamed the Eagle of the Doctors of France, was born of poor parents, but started early on the way of renown, by a devoted application to study. Having chosen the priesthood as his vocation, he was made bishop of Cambrai in 1398, and cardinal in 1411. He was also almoner to Charles VI. Notwithstanding his many cares, he found time to pursue his favorite studies, and his work, the *Imago Mundi*, is supposed to have been of service to Columbus.

Eric, Bishop of Garda. He was of Norwegian birth, and having been ordained priest, his apostolic spirit prompted him to give his life and labors to the Greenland Mission. Later, he proceeded to Vinland. In 1120, having returned to Europe to represent the necessities of the American Church and to bring about the establishment of a bishopric, he himself was chosen to fill the see. He was consecrated in Denmark in 1121, by Archbishop Adzar. After his return to this country, he devoted himself especially to the church in Vinland, and finally resigned his mitre that he might end his days as a simple missionary. The date of his death is uncertain.

Gama, Vasco da, was born at the small seaport town of Sines, in Portugal. Of the date of his birth and the circumstances of his early life, little is known. Being in the service of Emmanuel, king of Portugal, he was appointed commander of an expedition which was to seek its way to India by sailing around the southern cape of Africa. Accordingly, having set sail from Lisbon in July, 1497, he doubled the cape about the middle of November, reached India the following May, and in September, 1498, was again at Lisbon, where he was received with great honor. In 1524, Gama was appointed viceroy of India; and in 1525, he died. He was noted alike for his public and private virtues.

Henry, Prince of Portugal, surnamed "The Navigator" (1394-1463), was the third son of John I of Portugal and Philippa, daughter of John of Gaunt, Duke of Lancaster. He was distinguished for his mathematical and geographical learning; and he founded at Sagres an observatory, and a school in which young noblemen were taught the sciences connected with navigation. The first use of the compass in European navigation,—and, in part, the invention of the astrolabe,—are attributed to him. Under his auspices, various explorations and discoveries were made. He was noted for his learning, valor, generosity, and piety. He died at Sagres.

Isabella, the Catholic, queen of Castile and Leon (1451-1504). She was the daughter of John II. of Castile and Isabella of Portugal, and was therefore descended, through both houses, from John of Gaunt, Duke of Lancaster. At the age of nineteen, she married Ferdinand, king of Aragon, and thus the two crowns were united. Their reign is one of the most brilliant in history. Ferdinand made war upon Granada, the last Moorish kingdom in Spain, and after a long siege, the Alhambra, a renowned Moorish fortress, was captured. From this time the power of the Moors, or Saracens, in Spain declined. In the same year (1492), America was discovered by Columbus.

Isabella was remarkable for beauty, intelligence, and fervent piety. "*Isabella of Spain,*" says Irving, "*is one of the purest and most beautiful characters on the pages of history.*" She died in 1504, almost two years before Columbus.

Perez, Father Juan, a kind-hearted, learned and zealous Franciscan, Superior of the Monastery of La Rabida, near Lisbon. He had been Confessor to Queen Isabella; but disliking exceedingly a court life, he petitioned to be allowed to return to his cell. He had a great taste for science, and had erected on the roof of his monastery a kind of observatory, wherein he spent much of his leisure time. He proved, as we have seen, the faithful friend and counsellor of Columbus, and is supposed to have accompanied him on his second voyage to the New World.

Toscanelli, Paul, a celebrated mathematician and cosmographer of Florence. He was familiarly admitted into the pontifical court during his visits to Rome, and the king of Portugal consulted him on all subjects connected with geography and navigation. About the year 1474, he entered into correspondence with Columbus; and, to prove the feasibility of reaching India by sailing westward, he sent to the latter, a map projected partly according to Marco Polo and partly according to Ptolemy.

Vespucci, Amerigo (1451-1512), a native of Florence. He was in Spain when Columbus returned from his first voyage; and, having occasionally met the great admiral, he began to think of embracing a nautical career. He having, subsequently, made several voyages to the New World, and having written concerning the same, the name America was, as early as 1507, applied by a German geographer to this continent. It does not appear that Vespucci himself desired to take the honor from Columbus, with whom he was on friendly terms.

CHRONOLOGICAL REVIEW.

FIFTEENTH CENTURY.

1432.—The Azores were discovered.
1435.—Columbus was born.
1463.—Prince Henry of Portugal died.
1484.—Columbus applied to the government at Genoa.
1484.—Columbus met Father Juan Perez.
1486.—Columbus applied to the court of Spain.
1491.—Columbus was about to leave Spain in despair.
1492.—Columbus sailed from Palos (Aug. 3d).
1492.—Columbus discovered America (Oct. 12th).
1493.—Second voyage of Columbus.
1493.—Date of the Bull of Pope Alexander VI, concerning America (May 9th).
1494.—First Catholic church dedicated at Isabella (Hayti).
1497.—The Cabots discovered Newfoundland.
1498.—Third voyage of Columbus; he discovered South America.
1498.—The Cabots discovered the Atlantic Coast.
1499.—Amerigo Vespucci visited the coast of South America, which Columbus had discovered in 1498.

CONTEMPORARY CHRONOLOGY.

1400.—The "War of the Roses" began in England.
1428.—Joan of Arc raised the siege of Orleans.
1440.—Printing was invented by Guttenburg, at Strasburg.
1485.—End of the "War of the Roses" and succession of Henry VII.
1486.—The Cape of Good Hope discovered by the Portuguese.
1491.—St. Ignatius of Loyola born.
1497.—The Portuguese, under Vasco de Gama, doubled the Cape of Good Hope and sailed to the East Indies.

CONTEMPORARY POPES.

Innocent VIII. (Reign 1484-1492.) Alexander VI. (1492-1503.)

GEOGRAPHICAL TABLE NO. 1.

(OF PLACES MENTIONED IN PRECEDING SECTION.)

(1.) **Alleghanies,** or Appalachian Mountains, the great mountain chain or system which extends southwesterly, nearly parallel to the Atlantic coast, along the southeastern side of the North American continent.

(2.) **Atlantic Ocean,** one of the five great divisions of water upon the globe. It is bounded by Europe and Africa on the east, and by North and South America on the west. Its extreme breadth is about 5,000 miles, and its area about 25,000,000 square miles.

(3.) **Azores,** a series of islands, of volcanic origin, in the North Atlantic Ocean. St. Michael, the largest, is about 50 miles long and from 5 to 12 broad.

(4.) **Bahama Islands,** a group of about five hundred islands, or rocky islets, lying northeast of Cuba and east of the coast of Florida. The Gulf Stream passes between them and the mainland.

(5.) **Barcelona,** a seaport on the northeastern coast of Spain, and the chief seat of manufactures and commerce. The principal public edifice is the cathedral, the origin of which dates from the first ages of Christianity. Barcelona is said to have been founded by the Carthaginians under Hamilcar Barça, hence its name.

(6.) **Behring Strait,** the channel which separates Asia and America at their nearest approach to each other, and connects the Arctic with the Pacific Oceans.

(7.) **Castile,** a former kingdom of Spain, occupying the great central table-land of the peninsula.

(8.) **Cuba,** the largest of the West India Islands.

(9.) **Florence,** a brilliant city of northern Italy, on the river Arno. It is noted for its literary establishments, libraries, museums, and galleries of painting and sculpture. It is hence called "The Athens of Italy."

(10.) **Genoa,** a famous fortified seaport city of northern Italy, on the coast of the Mediterranean. Its origin is said to be more remote than that of Rome.

(11.) **Gila River,** a considerable river in the southeastern part of the United States. It flows from east to west through Arizona.

(12.) **Granada,** an old province, and formerly a kingdom in southern Spain. It was the last possession of the Moors in that country, and from it they were driven by Ferdinand and Isabella in 1492.

(13.) **Greenland,** a vast island, or group of islands united by fields of ice, situated northeast of North America. At present it is chiefly inhabited by Esquimaux.

(14.) **Havana,** the capital of the island of Cuba, and the greatest commercial port of the West Indies.

(15.) **Hayti,** a rich and beautiful island, the second in size of the West Indies; discovered by Columbus, December 5th, 1492, and named by him Hispañola (*i. e.*, Little Spain).

(16.) **Iceland,** an island belonging to Denmark, and situated between the North Atlantic and Arctic Oceans.

(17.) **Isabella,** a port on the north coast of Hayti, 36 miles from Santiago (Hayti). At the present day the original site is almost all overgrown with forest; but there are still to be seen standing the pillars of the church, part of the residence of Columbus, and remains of other buildings, all of hewn stone.

(18.) **Narragansett Bay,** a large body of water extending north from the Atlantic into the State of Rhode Island. It receives several considerable rivers, and contains a number of beautiful islands.

(19.) **Newport,** on the island of Rhode Island, is one of the capitals of the State, and a noted watering place. Its harbor is one of the best on the United States coast.

(20.) **Pavia,** a city of northern Italy, nineteen miles south of Milan, on the left bank of the Ticino. From its numerous public edifices it was once called "The City of a Hundred Towers;" but its magnificence and fame belong to a former age.

(21.) **Palos,** a port on the northwest coast of Spain.

(22.) **San Salvador,** one of the Bahama Islands, called by the natives Guanahani (*gwah-nah-hah'-ne*).

(23.) **Santa Fe,** a town of Spain, 7 miles west of Granada. It was built by Ferdinand and Isabella during the siege of Granada, and the deed of surrender was signed here. In 1806 it was much injured by an earthquake.

(24.) **St. Vincent, Cape,** the southwestern point of Portugal.

(25.) **Superior, Lake,** the most westerly and most elevated of the North American chain of lakes, and the largest expanse of fresh water on the globe.

(26.) **Trinidad,** the largest and most valuable of the British West Indies, except Jamaica. It belonged successively to the Spaniards and French, but capitulated to the British under Abercrombie, in 1797. Port of Prince, on the northwest side of the island, is the capital.

(27.) **Venice,** a beautiful city, built on 72 islands at the head of the Adriatic Sea. It was formerly, for many centuries, the first maritime and commercial city of the world. Its origin dates as far back as 452.

SECTION II.
A. D. 1500 TO A. D. 1600.

STUDY NO. 1.

DECLINING YEARS OF COLUMBUS.—SUCCESSORS OF THE GREAT ADMIRAL.

1. Columbus a Prisoner.—The sixteenth century dawns on a sad sight,—Columbus in chains. Slanderers had injured his reputation at the court of Spain; and in the fall of 1500, the hero who had given to Castile and Leon a new world, was sent back to Europe a prisoner. The commander of the vessel respectfully proposed to remove the fetters during the homeward voyage; but Columbus replied: "*No; I will wear them until their majesties, the sovereigns of Spain, command them to be removed; and then I shall preserve them as memorials of the reward I have received.*" "*I saw them always hanging in his cabinet,*" says his son and biographer, Fernando.

2. Death of Columbus.—On the arrival of Columbus in Spain, Isabella, pained beyond description at the ill-treatment he had received, hastened to break his fetters, and to load him with new favors. In 1502, Columbus made his fourth and last voyage to the New World. He returned to Europe in 1504, only to find the pious and noble queen, his faithful friend and protectress, on her death-bed. Three weeks later, she peacefully expired (Nov. 26th). After this,

DEATH OF COLUMBUS. 29

Ferdinand treated Columbus with marked injustice and neglect; and on the Festival of the Ascension, May 20th, 1506, the great Admiral himself died, poor and unhonored, in a small inn, at Valladolid.[20] * At his bedside were his two sons, and a Franciscan Father. His last words were: "*Into thy hands, O Lord, I commend my spirit!*"

How impressive a lesson is conveyed by the closing scenes of the life of this great man! How eloquently they speak of the vanity of human glory and the ingratitude and injustice of human friends!

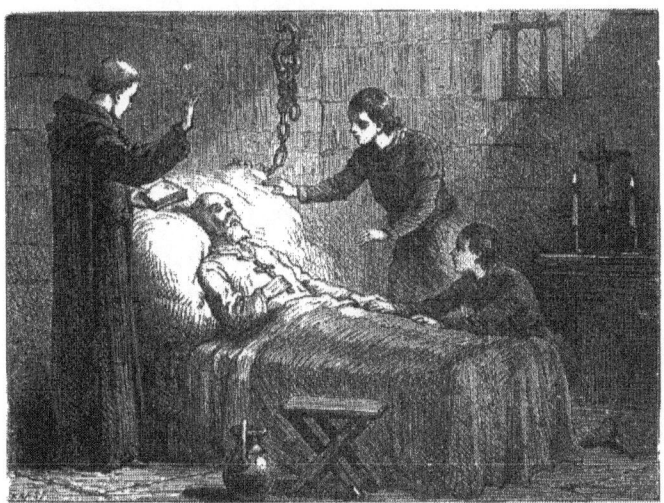

DEATH OF COLUMBUS.

3. Lands Occupied by the Spaniards.—By this time, (1500), the Spaniards had already occupied the islands of Cuba, Porto Rico, Hispaniola, and Jamaica.[8] From these points, it was easy to reach the mainland in different directions.

4. The Portuguese.—The king of Portugal, regret-

* These figures refer to the Geographical Table, at close of Section.

ting his rejection of the offers of Columbus, now readily favored an expedition for northern discovery, and Gaspar Cortereal (*kor-tay-ray-al*), was appointed commander. In the year 1500, he explored the American coast for five or six hundred miles, being stopped by ice in the Gulf of St. Lawrence.[27] He seized a number of the natives as slaves, and hence called the country Labrador (*laborer*). This name has since been transferred to a more northern coast. Cortereal undertook a second expedition, but never returned.

5. Las Casas.—In 1502, the celebrated Dominican missionary, Las Casas, afterwards Bishop of Chiapa [4] (*che-ah'-pah*), came to the New World, and during the ensuing sixty years, labored with untiring and apostolic energy for the welfare of the Indians.

6. Darien Settled.—In 1510, Ojeda (*o-hāy'-dah*), one of the companions of Columbus, sailed south from Cuba and settled the Isthmus of Darien.[6]

7. Florida Discovered.—Two years later (1512), Ponce de Leon (*pone-thay-dāy-lay-on*), also a companion of Columbus, sailed from Porto Rico on a voyage of discovery, and soon came in sight of Florida. Some say he was in search of a fountain of perpetual youth. Having landed, he took possession of the country in the name of his sovereign, and called it Florida or the "*Land of Flowers*," from the Spanish name of Palm Sunday, the day on which he had first descried land.

8. The Pacific Discovered.—The next year (1513), Balboa, the governor of a Spanish colony on the Isthmus, discovered the Pacific Ocean. When, from a peak of the Andes,[2] he beheld for the first time, the grand expanse of waters glittering in the morning sun, he sank upon his knees in thanksgiving. Then, having descended, he waded into the waters with the cross in one hand, and the banner of Castile in the other, thus taking solemn possession of its shores for the crown of Castile.

9. Cordova and Grijalva (*grĕ-hal'-vah*).—In 1517, Cordova sailed from Cuba and explored the north coast of Yucatan.²¹ In 1518, a second expedition, under Grijalva, explored the southern coast of Mexico, and verified the belief in the existence of a rich empire in the interior.

10. Cortez in Mexico.—In 1519, Hernando Cortez, at the head of a small body of men, penetrated into the interior of Mexico.¹⁰ After a severe struggle, he overthrew the empire of the Aztecs,* and brought it under the dominion of Spain. It so remained for three centuries, from 1521 to 1821.

11. Narvaez (*nar-vah'-eth*) **and Bishop Juarez** (*hoo-ah'-reth*).—In 1528, Narvaez, a Spaniard, with about four hundred men, sailed from Cuba on an expedition to Florida. He expected to find another rich empire like that of Mexico; but in this he was disappointed. The adventurers suffered terribly; were defeated by the Indians, and afterwards shipwrecked, only four of their number escaping. Narvaez was accompanied by several Franciscan missionaries, the superior of whom, Father John Juarez, had already been consecrated Bishop of Florida. He was, therefore, the first Bishop who held jurisdiction within the present limits of the United States.

---

* The earliest inhabitants of Mexico, of whom we have any knowledge, were the Toltecs, a people of considerable culture. After a period of about five hundred years (from the seventh to the twelfth century), the Toltecs, having been diminished probably by war and pestilence, migrated southward. They left after them as monuments of their skill, massive columns, aqueducts, pyramids, and temples. The Toltecs were succeeded by the Aztecs, who, having extended their sway over the adjacent tribes during a period of three hundred years, were the ruling people when the Spaniards arrived. The Aztecs were inferior in civilization to the Toltecs, though much superior to the more northern tribes.

12. French Explorations, Verrazani (*vay-rat-sah'-ne*).—The attention of France had already been turned to the New World. We learn from Charlevoix, that, within seven years after the discovery of America, the fisheries of Newfoundland were known to the hardy seamen of Brittany and Normandy. At length, in 1524, Francis I. of France employed Verrazani, another Florentine, to explore the new regions. This navigator reached the coast of Carolina in safety, and proceeding north, examined the shores and harbors as far as Nova Scotia.[16] The harbor of New York especially attracted his attention; and in that of Newport,[15] he remained fifteen days. Here he found vines and grapes, just as the Northmen had described them centuries before. Verrazani gave to the country the name of New France, and erected crosses at various points. He returned to Europe in July of the same year.

His narrative of the voyage contains the earliest original account, now extant, of the coast of the United States.

13. Cartier (*kar-te-ay*).—Ten years later, James Cartier, a mariner of St. Malo,[23] was sent out by the same king, to make further discoveries. In the spring of 1534, he entered the Gulf of St. Lawrence, sailed around the Island of Newfoundland, erected a cross thirty feet high on the shore of Gaspé Bay,[7] and then passed on to the River St. Lawrence,[26] which he ascended until he could see land on either side. His kindness to the natives was such that a chief allowed his two sons to accompany the party to France, on condition that the youths should be brought back the following year.

14. The next year (1535), Cartier made a second voyage. He now ascended the great river, (which he named St. Law-

FRENCH EXPLORATIONS. 33

rence, in honor of the martyr,) as far as the Indian village of Hochelaga (*ho-she-láh-ga*), the present site of Montreal.[12]

The town was pleasantly situated at the foot of a mountain; and Cartier, in company with a Huron chief, having climbed to its summit, was so charmed with the view that he called it Mont Réal (*mong-ray-al*) Royal Mountain. After a severe winter, he returned to France.

CARTIER AND THE INDIAN CHIEF ON ROYAL MOUNTAIN.

Cartier's second voyage was the means of procuring much useful information. It made known parts of America far inland, but which could be reached through a great river navigable by the largest ships of those days. It is believed also that, when at Montreal, Cartier was told of other parts, still further distant, where there were great lakes, and beyond which another great river flowed towards the south.

15. In 1541, Cartier, accompanied by a band of colonists, made a third voyage to the St. Lawrence. He built a fort near the present site of Quebec,[19] and here they passed the winter. The next spring, however, they returned dissatisfied to France.

16. De Soto Discovers the Mississippi River.[11]—About the same time, (1539), De Soto, governor of Cuba, with an army of nearly one thousand men, all fully equipped for a long expedition, sailed from Havana. Their intention was to conquer Florida and explore the interior.

DE SOTO DISCOVERING THE MISSISSIPPI.

They were accompanied by a number of missionaries, secular and regular, to convert and instruct the conquered nations; for none doubted of success. Having landed at Tampa Bay,[29] De Soto pressed onward, amid incredible hardships and frequent encounters with the natives, during a period of more than two years. At length, having traversed what is now Georgia, Alabama, and Mississippi, he reached the banks of the Mississippi River in the spring of 1541.

17. The Indians supposed the Spaniards to be children of the sun, and the blind were brought into their presence to be healed by these sons of light; but De Soto said to them, "*Pray only to God who is in Heaven for what you need.*"

ROUTE OF DE SOTO.

18. Death of De Soto.—Early in the year 1542, overcome by weariness, labor and disease, on the banks of the great river he had discovered,—beneath the shadow of the cross he had planted, De Soto died. He had the consolations of religion on his deathbed; and over his remains was chanted the first requiem ever heard in those wild regions. To conceal his death from the Indians, his body was wrapped in a mantle, and in the stillness of midnight was silently sunk in the middle of the stream.

'*He fell in the wilderness*," says McGee, "*and the sorrowing Mississippi took him in pity to her breast.*"

"*He had crossed a large portion of the continent*," says Bancroft, "*and found nothing so remarkable as his burial place.*"

19. A wretched remnant of the once brilliant expedition afterwards reached a Spanish settlement on the Gulf of Mexico; but, before this, every priest had perished.

STUDY NO. 2.

MISSIONS IN THE SOUTH.—ST. AUGUSTINE FOUNDED.

1. Franciscan Missions in New Mexico.—In the same year, (1539), in which De Soto started on his memorable expedition, another took place, to which the mind can turn with sentiments of purest pleasure and admiration. Father Mark, an Italian Franciscan, whose zeal had been aroused by the accounts of a survivor of the expedition of Narvaez, resolved to carry the Gospel 'to the inland tribes. Having traveled many hundred miles, over deserts and mountains, he, at length, reached New Mexico,[14] and planted a cross at the Indian city of Cibola. The entire region he named San Francisco, in honor of his beloved patron.

"*The kingdom of San Francisco,*" says Shea, "*lives but in his narrative; yet, as if to realize his wish, a city of that name is now the Carthage of the Pacific.*" [21]

2. The next year, (1540), five Franciscans, all eager to labor for the salvation of the Indians, accompanied an expedition to New Mexico, under Coronado. He, dissatisfied with the result, returned to Mexico; but two of the missionaries, Father John de Padilla and Brother John of the Cross, with heroic courage, remained in the country and taught the doctrine of Christ, until they were slain during an incursion of stranger savages.

In 1544, Father Olmas, another Franciscan, amid untold hardships, established a successful mission among the Indians of Texas. Having made himself master of their language, he composed or translated many works for their use.

MISSIONS IN FLORIDA. 37

3. Dominicans in Florida.—In 1549, Father Cancer, a holy Dominican, and friend of Las Casas, unarmed and unattended, visited Florida in the hope of converting the natives. Soon after his arrival, he was scalped by the Indians, thus falling a martyr to his zeal. Two others shared his fate. Father Tolosa also, who had landed at a different spot, found a speedy martyrdom.

4. In 1559, an attempt was made to plant a colony in Alabama, by the Spaniards under Tristan de Luna. After various disasters and a short trial of the country, the plan was abandoned (1560). This expedition was also accompanied by a number of Dominican Missionaries. Two Fathers reached the countries of the Creeks and Natchez; but the baptism of a few dying infants and adults was all that repaid their zeal. To them, however, the salvation of a single soul was ample reward.

5. The Huguenots.[*]—The Huguenots, under the auspices of Coligni, resolved to form a settlement, and a colony was accordingly sent out in 1562, under John Ribaut (*ree-bo*). This having proved a failure, another under Laudonnière (*lo-don-yare*), was dispatched to the New World in 1564. The settlers reached the mouth of the St. John River,[25] and there built a fort called Carolina, but they were improvident and mutinous. Some, at length, turned pirates and captured several Spanish vessels. The others had determined to abandon the colony, when Ribaut arrived with supplies.

6. Arrival of Melendez (*may-len-deth*).—Just at this juncture, five Spanish vessels appeared in the harbor. They were commanded by Melendez, the greatest admiral of

---
[*] French Protestants, or Calvinists.

the day, who had been sent from Spain to colonize Florida. He had lately lost his only son, who was believed to have been wrecked on the coast of Florida; but the father still clung to the hope of finding him, either with French pirates or among the Indians. This had induced Melendez to accept the commission of colonizing Florida.

7. Ribaut set out to sea to attack the Spanish, but was soon after wrecked. Melendez proceeded against Fort Carolina, and put the garrison to the sword, only Laudonnière and a few others escaping. He soon after massacred nearly all those who had escaped shipwreck.

8. "Whether in this treatment of the French Huguenots, he regarded them as pirates, or as parties, perhaps, in the death of his son, or acted in obedience to the orders of Philip, or to his own persecuting spirit, can never be known; but in no point of view can his conduct be justified."—SHEA.

9. **St. Augustine**[34] **Founded.**—Melendez now (1565) laid the foundations of a colony which, in honor of the day on which he had first descried land, he called St. Augustine. This is the oldest town in the United States. Missionaries, several of whom had accompanied Melendez, immediately began to labor among the Indians of the Everglades; and from the Franciscan monastery of St. Helena, the benign light of Christianity began to diffuse itself over the peninsula.

10. **Jesuits in Florida.**—Melendez applied to St. Francis Borgia, then general of the Jesuits, for some missionaries of that order. In response to this appeal, Father Martinez and two other priests, in June, 1566, started for the New World. Father Martinez, on his arrival, was almost immediately put to death. His companions, however, escaped, and having spent the winter studying the Indian language, were ready in the spring to commence missionary labor. One

MISSIONS IN FLORIDA. 39

of these, Father Roger, may be regarded as the founder of the Florida mission.

11. In 1568, their number was increased by the arrival of several other Jesuits; and though, for a long time, the field remained unpromising, still, all eyes were turned towards it with intense interest. Even the Holy Father, St. Pius V., issued a brief to the governor of Florida (Melendez), to excite his zeal in the cause (1569). We shall see later that all this care was repaid with interest, and that the Florida missions gained many souls for Heaven.

12. **Father Segura.**—In 1570, Father Segura and four other Jesuits, together with a converted Indian chief, and several Indian youths who had been educated at Havana, penetrated to the north, as far as Chesapeake [3] or St. Mary's Bay. Here they hoped to found a mission, far from any Spanish settlement. But the chief apostatized, and the whole party, after having endured grievous hardships for several months, were massacred. One of the Indian boys, Alonzo, alone escaped.

13. Two years later, Melendez, who had just returned from Europe, sailed northward to the Chesapeake, in search of the murderers of Father Segura and his companions. Eight were seized and executed, all of whom, under the instructions of the saintly Father Roger, embraced Christianity and died blessing God.

14. **Franciscans in Florida.**—In 1573, a band of Franciscans arrived in Florida, and in 1593, still another; thus, though colonization was tardy, the missions still went on. For some years, converts continued to be gathered into the fold, and Florida seemed an Eden of peace.

About this time, Father Pareja, a Franciscan, drew up in the

Yemassee tongue, an abridgment of the Christian doctrine, the first ever published in any Indian language.

15. In 1597, however, Father Da Corpa was slain at the foot of the altar, by the companions of a young chieftain

DEATH OF FATHER CORPA.

whom he had reproved for his vices. Nearly all the mission stations were then destroyed, and the missionaries put to death. Father Avila was taken captive and sold in a neighboring village. Having been a year a prisoner, and having undergone great hardships and cruelties, he was finally exchanged for an Indian captive at St. Augustine. Thus closed the sixteenth century in Florida.

The spot sanctified by the death of Father Corpa, is now the cemetery of St. Augustine.

16. **Franciscans in New Mexico.**—Previous to this (in 1581), three Franciscans who had attempted a mission in New Mexico, had there met a martyr's death.

MISSIONS IN NEW MEXICO. 41

In 1583, Espego (*es-pāy'ho*), a Spanish nobleman, at the head of a band of soldiers, and accompanied by missionaries, founded the city of Santa Fé,[23] the second oldest city in the United States. In a short time, this mission proved astonishingly successful, though not without having encountered many difficulties. Long before the English had made any permanent settlement on our shores, whole tribes on the Rio Grande[20] had been converted and civilized, and many a red man of the forest had even learned to read and write.

17. God's Warriors.—With the successors of Columbus, it is true, came the cannon and the sword; but there came also the Gospel, and the Sacraments. There came the thirst for dominion, for lands and for gold; there came cruelty, bloodshed, and all the vices of civilization; but with them, as unharmed by the contact as the sun-ray touching the mire, came self-sacrifice, devotion, zeal for souls, love of God and of man for Christ's sake. They that took the sword perished by the sword, winning only blood-stained names as a reward; but the warriors of God won souls for Heaven; and even if they died in the conflict, their blood spoke louder than their voices had done.

" To fight the battle of the Cross, Christ's chosen ones are sent,—
Good soldiers and great victors,—a noble armament.
They use no earthly weapon, they know not spear or sword,
Yet right, and true, and valiant is the army of the Lord.

' The soul ox every sinner is the victory they would gain;
They would bind each rebel heart in their Master's golden chain;
Faith is the shield they carry, and the two-edged sword they bear
Is God's strongest, mightiest weapon, and they call it Love and
Prayer."—PROCTER.

STUDY NO. 3.

ENGLISH EXPLORATIONS.—UNSUCCESSFUL ATTEMPTS TO COLONIZE VIRGINIA.

1. Frobisher.—Between the years 1576 and 1579, Martin Frobisher, an English navigator, made three voyages to the New World. Their only result was the discovery of several bays, inlets, and islands on the Northern Coast of America. He had hoped to discover a Northwest passage to India, but in this he was disappointed; and the supposed gold ore with which he loaded his vessels, on two of the return-voyages, proved to be but worthless stones.

SIR FRANCIS DRAKE.

2. Sir Francis Drake.—In 1579, Francis Drake, another English sea-captain, reached the Pacific Ocean by way of Magellan Strait.[9] Having pillaged the Spanish settlements in Peru and Chili, he sailed northward and explored the coast of California. He then spent several weeks in the Bay of San Francisco,[2] and afterwards returned to England by way of the Cape of Good Hope, thus completing the *second circumnavigation of the globe*.

3. On his arrival in England, Queen Elizabeth partook of a splendid banquet given by him, on board his vessel, *"The*

Pelican," in Plymouth [18] harbor. The food was served on silver dishes, and the wine in golden goblets, all the fruit of plunder. At the close of the banquet, the queen conferred upon Drake the honor of knighthood.

After this, Drake's exploits on the sea were numerous and daring. Although he is honored for his enterprise and the glory he won for England, and is regarded as the founder of the Royal Navy, still he was only a pirate on a large and legalized scale.

4. Sir Humphrey Gilbert.—In 1583, the year in which Santa Fé was founded, Sir Humphrey Gilbert attempted an English settlement at Newfoundland.[18] The enterprise proved unsuccessful. Gilbert, on his way home, was shipwrecked, and all on board perished.

5. Sir Walter Raleigh (*raw-ly*).—Gilbert's half-brother, Walter Raleigh, who had been deeply interested in Gilbert's enterprise, now obtained a patent for himself. In 1584, he sent to America two ships under the command of Amidas and Barlow. They explored Albemarle[1] and Pamlico[17] Sounds, and visited

SIR WALTER RALEIGH.

Roanoke Island, where the Indians received them with great kindness. They then returned home with cargoes of furs and woods, and gave a glowing account of the country. Elizabeth, in her own honor, bestowed upon it the name of Virginia, and declared that its acquisition was one of the greatest glories of her reign. As a reward for his services, she knighted Raleigh.

6. Raleigh's first step towards Elizabeth's favor depended upon a very slight circumstance. Having met the queen

44   EXCELSIOR HISTORY.

one day as she was walking with her maids of honor, and having observed a wet spot on her path, he took from his shoulders a rich velvet mantle, and bowing gracefully, spread

RALEIGH MEETING ELIZABETH.

it upon the ground for the royal feet to tread upon. After this, Raleigh was immediately admitted to court and speedily rose in the favor of the queen.

7. Raleigh's First Attempt at Colonization. —The next year (1585) Raleigh sent out a colony, with Ralph Lane as governor. They landed at Roanoke Island, but instead of tilling the ground, they hunted for gold. Distress and want soon followed. They were, therefore, only too glad to be taken back to England by Drake, who, having pillaged and burned St. Augustine during a cruise against the Spaniards, stopped at Roanoke on his homeward voyage. They brought tobacco back with them ; and the custom of "*drinking tobacco*" as it was called, soon became fashionable.*

8. Raleigh's Second Attempt.—In 1587, Raleigh sent out another colony consisting of families. John White was appointed governor. A grand-daughter of White, named Virginia Dare, born soon after their arrival, was the first offspring of English parents on the soil of the United States.

9. White, at the entreaty of the settlers, soon went to England for supplies.† He left behind him eighty-nine men, seventeen women, and two children. Three years elapsed before his return (1590), ‡ and then no vestige of the colony was to be seen. On the trunk of a tree, was carved the word "*Croatan.*"⁵ The fate of the "lost colony of Roanoke," to this day, remains a mystery. Among the Indians, there is a tradition that these colonists were adopted by the Hatteras tribe, and that they became mingled with them. The idea receives further confirmation from the physical

---

* On one occasion, when Sir Walter was smoking, his servant entered the room with a tankard of ale. On beholding, for the first time, the smoke issuing from his master's mouth and nostrils, he in great alarm dashed the liquor into his face, and ran to inform the household that Sir Walter was on fire.

On another occasion, Sir Walter was conversing with the queen on the various properties of tobacco, and he assured her that he could tell the exact weight of smoke in any quantity consumed. The incredulous queen dared him to a wager. Having accepted it, Raleigh weighed the tobacco, smoked it, and then having carefully weighed the ashes, stated the difference. The queen laughingly acknowledged that he had won, and added that she "had before heard of turning gold into smoke, but he was the first who had turned smoke into gold."

† On his way, he touched at Ireland, where he left some potato plants, the first ever seen in Europe.

‡ The English were at this time putting forward all their resources to repel the invasion of the Spanish Armada; but Raleigh, by great exertions, sent White back with supplies the following year (1588). The latter, however, delayed on the way.

character of the tribe, in which the English and Indian races seem to have been blended.

DESERTED COLONY OF ROANOKE.

10. The season being late, White, fearful of the storms which, he knew, prevailed on the coast at that period, returned to England. Raleigh, for a long time, cherished the hope of finding the lost colonists; and it is said that, at his own expense, he five different times sent persons in search of them; but no traces could be found. At length, discouraged by failure, he transferred his patent to the London Company.

11. At the close of the sixteenth century, there was not a single English town in any part of America. The only permanent settlements were St. Augustine and Santa Fé, both Spanish Catholic missions.

BIOGRAPHICAL SKETCHES

OF REMARKABLE PERSONAGES MENTIONED IN THE PRECEDING SECTION.

Balboa, Vasco Nunez de (1475-1517), a Spaniard of noble lineage but small fortune, who came to the New World in 1501. Various circumstances contributed to make him governor of the new settlement of Santa Maria, in Darien (1512), and his humane conduct won for him the friendship of the Indians. In 1513, while exploring the isthmus, he discovered the Pacific Ocean. Later, he was obliged to undergo many severe trials. Through the intrigues and jealousy of a rival, he was charged with treason, subjected to a mock trial and finally executed. He died protesting his innocence and loyalty, having previously received the Sacraments of Penance and Holy Eucharist.

Cancer, Father Louis, a Spanish Dominican, who came to America in 1514. Having labored a considerable time with the illustrious Las Casas, he, in 1547, determined to proceed to Florida. Scarcely had he reached the wished-for shore, when he was martyred by the Indians (1549).

Cartier, James (1494-1555), a French navigator, born at St. Malo. Between the years 1535 and 1542, he made three voyages from his native port to the St. Lawrence. Some say he made also a fourth voyage; but of this we have no certain accounts. Like most of the early captains, Cartier was a man of profound piety. This he evinced in all his proceedings. Before starting on a voyage, he always besought the blessing of the Church on his undertaking, and received the Blessed Sacrament; and during the voyage, he caused religious services to be regularly held, on the ships under his command. Towards the close of his life, he retired to the suburbs of St. Malo, where an estate still bears his name.

Cordova, Francis de, a Spanish navigator born in the latter part of the fifteenth century. In 1517, having sailed from Havana at the head of a small expedition, he discovered Yucatan. On his way home, he touched at Florida, and his reports led to the expedition of Grijalva. He died the following year (1518).

Coronada, Francis de, an explorer of New Mexico and the countries on the Gila River. On the return of Father Mark from his first expedition, a second was fitted out under the command of Coronada (1540). He passed up what is now the State of Sonora, to the River Gila; visited many towns somewhat similar to the existing villages of the Pueblo Indians, and then proceeded eastward to the Rio Grande. On his homeward route (1542), he met with an accident which proved fatal.

Cortereal, Gaspar, a Portuguese navigator of distinguished family. In 1500, he commanded an expedition sent out to explore the northern coasts of North America. He freighted his vessels with fifty-seven Indians, whom, on his return, he sold as slaves. The name Labrador (*laborer*), afterwards transferred further north, is a memorial of this visit. Later, Cortereal set out on a second voyage, from which he never returned.

Cortez, Ferdinand (1485-1547), a native of Spain and conqueror of Mexico. At the age of fourteen, he was sent to the university of Salamanca to study law. Here he remained two years. In 1504, he sailed for the New World and was received with great favor by the governor of Hispaniola. Having been appointed commander of an expedition to Mexico, he, in 1518, set out for that country. Having reached the coast, he laid the foundation of Vera Cruz, and destroyed his ships to make retreat impossible. After a severe struggle, he overthrew the Mexican, or Aztec empire, and reduced it to the dominion of Spain. His victories caused him to be dreaded by some, and envied by others. At length, disgusted with the treacherous conduct of many around him, he returned to Spain. Here he was coldly received by the emperor, Charles V., and after a time, he fell so low in the royal favor that he could not obtain an audience. He finally withdrew from court, and died in solitude in the sixty-third year of his age.

Da Corpa, a Spanish Franciscan, who, with three companions, labored, about the year 1592, to Christianize the Indians inhabiting what is now called Georgia. Though they had to endure untold hardships, they were amply repaid by the numerous converts who gathered round them. At length, Father Da Corpa, having found it necessary to reprove the son of a chief for a grave scandal, the young Indian and his companions revengefully resolved to put the missionary to death. The murderers reached the mission chapel amid the silence of the night, and found the faithful priest at his devotions before the rude altar. Here he sank in death beneath the tomahawk of the chief. After this, they ravaged all the adjoining missions; and Father Corpa's companions had the glory of sharing with him the crown of martyrdom (1597).

De Soto, Fernando (1497-1542), a celebrated Spanish explorer of noble but reduced family, who came to the New World in 1519.

BIOGRAPHICAL SKETCHES.

Having explored the coasts of Guatemala and Yucatan, he, in 1532, joined Pizarro in his expedition into Peru. Here, he distinguished himself for his bravery, especially at the capture of Cuzco. After this, he returned to Spain; but, in 1538, he projected the conquest of Florida; and with this intent, he again set sail for the New World, accompanied by 600 men, 24 ecclesiastics and 20 officers. They landed at Tampa Bay in the spring of 1539. After a weary and toilsome march, they reached the Mississippi three years later. Here De Soto died. His wife, on hearing his fate, survived the intelligence only three days.

Drake, Sir Francis (1545–1596), a famous English naval officer. He made three predatory voyages to the West Indies and captured more than one hundred vessels. On a land expedition, he seized a convoy of mules laden with gold and silver, and hastening back with it to England, declared that he had obtained it by barter with the natives. About the year 1577, while on another tour, he crossed the Atlantic, passed the Strait of Magellan, after many dangers doubled the Cape of Good Hope and returned to England. Though on the way he had been guilty of many misdeeds, they were forgotten in the glory of having circumnavigated the globe. In 1596, having failed in an attack on Panama, he died of chagrin.

Gilbert, Sir Humphrey, an English gentleman, half-brother of Sir Walter Raleigh. Having received from Queen Elizabeth the grant of a large tract of country on this continent, he, in 1583, sailed to America, and in her name took possession of Newfoundland. On the return voyage he was lost.

Grijalva, Juan de, a Spanish navigator, born in the latter part of the fifteenth century. He was sent by his uncle Velasquez, first governor of Cuba, to complete the discoveries made by Cordova in Yucatan. He coasted along the peninsula, and his intercourse with the natives proved both friendly and profitable. He afterwards settled in Nicaragua, where, in 1527, he was slain by the Indians.

Juarez, Right Rev. John, a Spanish Franciscan, first Bishop of Florida. He was one of twelve Franciscans who, in 1524, founded a mission in Mexico. Later, being appointed by the Holy See, Bishop of Rio de las Palmas in Florida, he accompanied thither the unfortunate expedition of Narvaez (1528). Towards the close of the same year, having undergone great hardships, he, with Brother John de Palos, perished either by hunger, or at the hands of the Indians.

Las Casas, Bartholomew (1474–1566), a celebrated Dominican missionary, born at Seville, Spain. Having pursued his studies with brilliant success at the University of Salamanca, he afterwards entered the Dominican order, and in 1502 was sent as a missionary to the New World. He was ordained priest at St. Domingo in 1510, and during the remainder of his life devoted himself with untiring and apostolic energy to the welfare of the Indians. In his efforts to convert and civilize them, he traversed the wilderness in various directions, sparing not time, or labor, or life itself when their interests were concerned. To vindicate their wrongs, he made several voyages to Spain, and even wrote many volumes. He has been deservedly styled the "Protector of the Indians." Having, in 1539, declined the rich bishopric of Cuzco, he, the next year, accepted the much poorer one of Chiapas. In 1551, he returned to Spain and retired to the monastery at Valladolid. Here he composed his great work, "*The General History of the Indies*," which, however, has not been published. Here, also, he breathed his last, at the advanced age of ninety-two.

Mark, Father, of Nice, an Italian Franciscan, who came to America in 1531, and labored first in Peru and afterwards in Mexico. Inflamed with zeal for the conversion of the Indians in the interior of the country, (chiefly through the accounts gleaned from the survivors of the ill-fated expedition of Narvaez), he, in 1539, set out from Mexico, and amid incredible hardships, traversed a vast extent of territory to reach the Indian city of Cibola. Here he planted a cross but made no converts. His glowing though mistaken accounts, however, led the way to new expeditions, the first of which he himself accompanied. This he did not long survive, his toilsome journeys and wearing labors having completely shattered his health.

Martinez, Father Peter, a Spanish Jesuit of great learning and sanctity, who, with Father Roger and Brother Villareal was sent to the Florida mission, by St. Francis Borgia in 1565. On the eve of his departure, he said to the celebrated Franciscan, Father Lobo, "*Oh, Father! how I long to shed my blood at the hands of the savages for the Faith, and to bathe with it the shores of Florida!*" His words were prophetic; for scarcely had he reached the scene of his intended labors, when he was put to death by the Indians near St. Augustine (1566). His companions retired for a time to Havana to study the Indian languages. Father Martinez was noted for his rare abilities, great learning, humility and love of suffering; and his death was an immense loss to the Florida mission. He was the first Jesuit who entered the territory now embraced by the United States.

Melendez, Pedro (1519-1574), a Spanish admiral, and the colonizer of Florida, was born at Avila. Under Philip II., he had risen to the highest rank in the Spanish navy. In 1554, he commanded the vessel which bore his king to England to marry Queen Mary; and in 1561, he commanded the great treasure fleet of galleons from Mexico to Spain. During this voyage, the vessel on which his son sailed was lost. On his arrival in Spain, he asked permission to return in search

BIOGRAPHICAL SKETCHES.

of the missing ship, but was refused. Later, however, his request was granted on condition that he should explore and colonize Florida. Here, having encountered and defeated the French under Ribaut, he laid the foundations of St. Augustine (1565). By the conditions of the charter he had received, he was to bring out twelve Franciscans and four Jesuits to labor for the spiritual welfare of the Indians. Missionaries were accordingly settled along the coast from Cape Carnaveral to the Chesapeake. The progress of the colony was, however, retarded by the absence of Melendez, who was repeatedly called to Spain to command her fleets. In 1574, while preparing the Armada for the invasion of England, he died. This event was a fatal blow to the prosperity of Florida. His son he had never recovered.

Narvaez, Pamfilo de (1480–1528), a Spanish explorer who came to America about the year 1501. Having served some time in San Domingo, he passed to Cuba, where he soon stood next in rank to the governor. In 1527, he obtained a grant of Florida and sailed thither with a large force. Hoping to find rich cities and great empires, he pressed on through tangled everglades during a period of eight weeks. Finally, he reached the great capital his imagination had pictured in glowing colors, and found it to be a wretched village of forty huts. Having continued their march, Narvaez and the whole party, with about four exceptions, perished. The treasurer De Veca, almost alone, made his way on foot, passing from tribe to tribe, until, after a period of eight years, he reached a Spanish port on the Pacific.

Ojeda, Alonzo de, a Spanish cavalier who accompanied Columbus on his second voyage. He made also several other voyages, and in 1510, settled the isthmus of Darien. He was noted for his daring and heroic courage, his many and remarkable adventures, and, not least, his fervent piety. At length, worn out by labors and misfortunes, he expired at St. Domingo. One historian says that he became a monk in the monastery of St. Francis, where he died. Certain it is, that with his last breath, he entreated that his body might be buried at the portal of that monastery, in humble expiation of his past pride, "*that every one who entered might tread upon his grave.*"

Olmas, Father Andrew de, a Spanish Franciscan who came to America, in 1528, with Bishop Zumarraga. He soon became complete master of several Indian languages, and in the same year wrote several works, chiefly spiritual. In 1544, he penetrated into Texas and there converted so many Indians, that he formed a *Reduction*, or civilized and Christian Indian village. He closed a life of arduous labor and eminent sanctity, in 1571.

Raleigh, Sir Walter (1552–1618), is famous as a courtier, adventurer, and writer. He was born in Devonshire, studied at Oxford,

and served as a volunteer in France and the Netherlands, for several
years. In 1581, he was made governor of Cork ; and during his term of
office he permitted the cold-blooded massacre of the garrison of Smer-
wick. From the year 1589, he rose rapidly in the favor of the queen,
was knighted, and appointed to various high and lucrative offices.
Having received letters-patent empowering him to colonize unoc-
cupied territories in North America, he made several unsuccessful
attempts at colonization. Under James I. he was charged with conspiracy, and he was imprisoned from 1604 to 1616. During his captivity
he composed his celebrated "*History of the World.*" Being released
on condition that he should open a gold mine in Guiana, he attempted
to accomplish this feat, but was again unsuccessful. The old charge
being a second time revived, he was executed (1618). .

Ribaut, a French navigator born at Dieppe. In 1562, being sent
by Coligni to Florida in command of two vessels, he built a fort near
the present site of Beaufort. Soon after, having left twenty-six
colonists to keep possession of the country, he returned to France for
supplies. The colonists, however, were soon reduced almost to starvation, and the few survivors having set sail for their native country,
were picked up by an English ship. A second colony, sent out under
Laudonnière in 1564, was also on the point of sailing for France, when
Ribaut returned with supplies. Scarcely, however, had he cast
anchor, when Melendez appeared at the head of a considerable Spanish fleet. After various encounters, Ribaut and the greater number
of his men were put to death.

Roger, Father John, a Spanish Jesuit, companion of Father
Martinez on the Florida mission. He labored first among the Creeks,
and then spent some time in Havana, to inaugurate a school for the education of Indian children from Florida. Later, he returned to Florida,
and having penetrated into the interior, labored with untiring energy,
but with little success, among the native tribes. He accompanied
Melendez on the expedition in search of the murderers of Father
Segura. Eight having been captured, Father Roger anxiously endeavored to procure their pardon, as they had been led on and prompted
by the perfidious Indian, Don Luis. Having failed in this, he procured a respite, and had the happiness of converting and baptizing
them before their execution. He died in Mexico, in 1581.

Segura, Father John Baptist, a Spanish Jesuit, who, with
ten companions, soon after the death of Father Martinez, was chosen
by Saint Francis Borgia for the Florida mission (1568). Having spent
some time in Cuba. studying the language and manners of the natives,
he, with several Jesuits, some Indian youths educated at Havana, and
Don Luis, a converted Indian chief, proceeded towards the shores of

Chesapeake Bay. This part of the country was at that time called Upper Florida. Here he intended to found a new mission far from Spanish settlements, so that new converts might not be scandalized at the sight of Spanish vice. The Indian chief, however, proved false; and after having toiled through a vast wilderness, and endured great hardships, the whole party, with the exception of an Indian boy, were massacred (1570).

St. Francis Borgia, (1510-1572) Duke of Gandia, and third general of the Society of Jesus. He was grandson of the king of Naples, and was closely allied to all the sovereigns of Europe. Having completed his studies at Saragossa, he was sent by his father to the court of the Emperor Charles V. Here he led the life of a saint, fulfilling every duty with scrupulous fidelity. On the death of his father, he became Duke of Gandia, and, as such, filled many high offices in the state. He was one of the most honored at the court of Elizabeth of Spain; and, on her death, was the grandee selected to attend the body to Granada. Here it became necessary for him, according to the custom of the realm, to open the coffin to identify the body. The awful change a few days had wrought in her, one of the most powerful sovereigns of the time, showed him the true value of earthly greatness, and he resolved to abandon the world, resigning all its dignities. In 1547, he entered the Society of Jesus; and, in 1565, was chosen general of the order. He was much interested in the American missions, and sent, as we have seen, many excellent laborers to that field. He was noted for his humility, mortification, and ardent zeal, as well as for his practical wisdom. He died at Rome in 1572, and was canonized by Clement XI. in 1716.

St. Pius V. (1504-1572) was born of a noble family at Bologna. He pursued his studies under the care of the Dominicans, and at the age of fifteen entered that order. Having, at the canonical age, been ordained priest, he taught philosophy and theology in Northern Italy for many years. In 1556, he was raised to the episcopal dignity, and one year later, to the cardinalate. Finally, in 1565, he became Supreme Pontiff. He was distinguished for his firmness, humility, piety and charity, as well as for his remarkable intellect. In 1569, he addressed a brief to Melendez in behalf of the Florida missions; and in 1570, he wrote to the imprisoned Mary Stuart, consoling her in her captivity, and exhorting her to new constancy and devotion to her religion. He also extended his assistance to the Knights of Malta in their protracted struggle against the Turks; and during his pontificate, was fought the famous battle of Lepanto (1571). St. Pius V. died in the sixty-ninth year of his age, and one century later was beatified by

Clement X. He was canonized in 1712, and is classed among the greatest and best of the successors of St. Peter.

Verrazani, John (1485-1527), a native of Florence. At an early age he went to France, where he found employment as a navigator. In 1524, he commanded an expedition sent out by Francis I. of France, and explored the Atlantic coast from Maine to North Carolina. The magnificent harbor of New York especially attracted his attention. He embarked also on a subsequent expedition, from which he never returned.

CHRONOLOGICAL REVIEW.
SIXTEENTH CENTURY.

1500.—Columbus in chains.
1500.—Cortereal explored the Atlantic coast.
1502.—Las Casas came to America. Fourth Voyage of Columbus.
1504.—Isabella died, (Nov. 26th).
1506.—Columbus died, (Ascension Day, May 20th).
1510.—Ojeda settled Darien.
1512.—De Leon discovered Florida.
1513.—Balboa discovered the Pacific.
1517.—Cordova explored the north coast of Yucatan.
1518.—Grijalva explored the south coast of Mexico.
1520.—Magellan's voyage.
1521.—Cortez conquered Mexico.
1524.—Verrazani explored the coast of North America.
1528.—Expedition of Narvaez. Bishop Juarez and his companions perished.
1534.—Cartier discovered the Gulf and River St. Lawrence.
1539.—Father Mark penetrated into New Mexico.
1540.—Coronada penetrated into New Mexico.
1541.—De Soto discovered the Mississippi.
1544.—Father Olmas founded a mission in Texas.
1549.—Fathers Cancer and Tolosa martyred in Florida.
1559.—Tristan de Luna attempted a settlement in Alabama.
1562.—The Huguenots under Ribault attempted a settlement in Florida.
1565.—St. Augustine founded, (Sept. 8th).
1566.—St. Francis Borgia sent Jesuit missionaries to Florida. Father Martinez martyred.
1569.—The Holy Father, Saint Pius V., issued a Brief concerning the Florida missions.

CHRONOLOGICAL REVIEW.

1570.—Father Segura and companions martyred.
1573.—Franciscans in Florida.
1579.—Drake explored the coast of California.
1583.—Santa Fé founded; the Franciscans evangelize New Mexico.
1583.—Sir Humphrey Gilbert attempted a settlement in Newfoundland.
1584.—Sir Walter Raleigh received a grant of territory in the New World. Expedition under Amidas and Barlow.
1585.
1587. } Unsuccessful attempts to settle Virginia.
1597.—Father De Corpa and companions martyred in Florida.

CONTEMPORARY CHRONOLOGY.

1500.—Brazil was discovered by the Portuguese.
1509.—Henry VIII. of England commenced his reign.
1515.—Francis I. of France commenced his reign.
1516.—Charles I. of Spain (Charles V. of Germany) commenced his reign.
1517.—Martin Luther apostatized.
1529.—Lutherans first called Protestants at Spire.
1534.—England separated from the See of Rome.
1534.—Order of the Jesuits founded.
1543.—Copernican system introduced.
1545.—The Council of Trent opened.
1571.—Battle of Lepanto.
1572.—Massacre of St. Bartholomew's day.
1587.—Execution of Mary Queen of Scots.

CONTEMPORARY POPES.

Pius III. (reign 1503-1503); Julius II. (1503-1513); Leo X. (1513-1522); Adrian VI. (1522-1523); Clement VII. (1523-1534); Paul III. (1534-1550); Julius III. (1550-1555); Marcellus II. (1555-1555); Paul IV. (1555-1559); Pius IV. (1559-1566); St. Pius V. (1566-1572); Gregory XIII. (1572-1585); Sixtus V. (1585-1590); Urban VII. (1590-1590); Gregory XIV. (1590-1591); Innocent IX. (1591-1592); Clement VIII. (1592-1605).

GEOGRAPHICAL TABLE NO. 2.

(1.) **Albemarle Sound** is situated in the northeast part of North Carolina, and extends from the Atlantic westward about 60 miles.

(2.) **Andes Mountains,** a range of mountains of such vast extent as to render it one of the most remarkable physical features of the globe. It commences at Cape Horn and extends, nearly parallel to the Pacific coast, throughout the entire length of South America to the isthmus of Panama, a distance of about 4500 miles. From this point, the range continues, and, under different names, traverses the whole North American continent from South to North, terminating in Barrow Point on the Arctic Ocean. Its total length is about 9000 miles.

(3.) **Chesapeake,** the largest bay in the United States. It enters Virginia between Capes Charles and Henry, and extends into Maryland. It receives the waters of several fine rivers and affords vast advantages for navigation.

(4.) **Chiapa,** a town of Mexico on the Tobacco River, 20 miles northwest of Ciudad Real.

(5.) **Croatan,** an island in Chesapeake Bay. Here lived Manteo, an Indian chief friendly to the whites, who, by order of Raleigh, was created "Lord of Roanoke."

(6.) **Darien (or Panama),** Isthmus of, a neck of land joining North and South America. As one of the routes of communication between the Atlantic and Pacific Oceans, it is of considerable importance. From a mountain-top on this Isthmus, Balboa first saw the Pacific.

(7.) **Gaspe Bay,** an inlet of the Gulf of St. Lawrence.

(8.) **Jamaica,** one of the West India islands, about 90 miles south of Cuba. It was originally colonized by the Spaniards in 1508, and remained subject to the Spanish crown until 1655, in which year it was taken by an English fleet. Since then, it has remained a British possession.

(9.) **Magellan Strait** separates the continent of South America from the island of Terra del Fuego. It is upwards of 300 miles long, and is of difficult navigation.

(10.) **Mexico,** formerly called New Spain, extends, in a gradually contracting manner, from the frontier of the United States on the north, to the narrow tract of Central America on the south, the Pacific

EXCELSIOR HISTORY.   57

Ocean bounding it on the west, and the great Mexican Gulf on the east. It was conquered by Cortez in 1521, and remained a possession of Spain until 1810, when it became independent. It is by nature one of the most beautiful and productive regions of the globe.

(11.) **Mississippi River,** the most important river of North America, and with the Missouri, its principal branch, the longest in the world. It rises in Minnesota, and flowing in a generally southerly course, empties into the Gulf of Mexico.

(12.) **Montreal,** a city of British America, situated on the south side of the island of Montreal, in the St. Lawrence River. It was founded in 1640 under the name of Ville Marie, on the site of the Indian village of Hochelaga.

(13.) **Newfoundland,** an island of large size, lies on the east side of the Gulf of St. Lawrence and closely approaches the coast of Labrador at its north extremity. It is noted for its fisheries, more cod being taken on its banks and near the adjacent shores, than on any other part of the globe.

(14.) **New Mexico,** a territory in the southwestern part of the United States, crossed by various parallel ranges of the Rocky Mountains. From the elevation of its surface, it has a temperate climate. Gold, silver, and copper are abundant; but the mines have not been developed to any extent.

(15.) **Newport,** a port of entry and semi-capital of the State of Rhode Island. It is situated on the west shore of the island of Rhode Island, about five miles from the ocean. Its harbor is one of the best on the Atlantic coast; and its fine sea-air and varied scenery have rendered it one of the most celebrated watering-places in New England.

(16.) **Nova Scotia,** a long narrow peninsula connected with New Brunswick by an isthmus only 15 miles wide.

(17.) **Pamlico Sound,** a shallow body of water on the east coast of North Carolina. It communicates with Albemarle Sound on the north, and receives the Neuse and Pamlico Rivers at its west extremity.

(18.) **Plymouth,** a seaport town and naval station, at the head of Plymouth Sound, on the southwestern coast of England. The entrance into the sound is guided by the celebrated Eddystone light-house, which stands on a large cluster of rocks in the channel.

(19.) **Quebec,** situated on the left bank of the River St. Lawrence, is the most strongly fortified city in America and the oldest in Canada.

(20.) **Rio Grande,** an important river of North America. It rises in Colorado, flows in a generally southeasterly direction, and empties into the Gulf of Mexico. It forms the boundary between Texas and Mexico.

GEOGRAPHICAL TABLE.

(21.) **San Francisco**, the most commercial city of California, and the queen city of the far west, is situated on the west shore of San Francisco Bay.

(22.) **San Francisco Bay**, a magnificent land-locked harbor in which the combined navies of Europe and America might move, is situated on the Pacific coast of the United States, in the State of California. The entrance to the bay is called the "Golden Gate."

(23.) **Santa Fe**, the capital of New Mexico. It stands on a plateau elevated about 7,000 feet above the sea, and is a short distance from the base of a snow-capped mountain which rises 5,000 feet above the level of the city.

(24.) **St. Augustine**, a city of Florida, and the oldest in the United States, is situated 200 miles southeast of Tallahassee. The mildness of the climate and the refreshing breezes from the sea, render this a famous winter residence for invalids.

(25.) **St. John's River**, Florida. It has its source in a marshy tract in the central part of the peninsula. The country through which it passes consists chiefly of pine barrens and cypress swamps.

(26.) **St. Lawrence River**, the principal river of Canada, and the outlet of the great lakes.

(27.) **St. Lawrence Gulf**, a large inlet of the Atlantic Ocean, in North America. It is surrounded by Canada East, New Brunswick, Cape Breton and Newfoundland. It contains Anticosti, Prince Edward, the Magdalen and many other islands.

(28.) **St. Malo**, a fortified seaport of France, on the English channel. It is situated on a peninsula connected by a causeway with the mainland, and is defended by strong walls and a castle. It was the birthplace of Cartier, also of Chateaubriand.

(29.) **Tampa Bay**, (formerly *Espiritu Santo* Bay), is situated on the west side of the peninsula of Florida, and opens into the Gulf of Mexico. It is about 40 miles long, and forms a good harbor for large vessels.

(30.) **Valladolid**, a city of Spain on the left bank of the Pisuerga River. In the fifteenth century, it was considered the finest town in Castile; but on the removal of the court to Madrid, it began to decline.

(31.) **Yucatan**, a peninsula, bounded on the east by the Caribbean Sea; northeast by the Channel of Yucatan; north and west by the Gulf of Mexico. The ruins of numerous towns and villages, which have excited much antiquarian research, are found in different parts of the country. Many of them display great architectural skill, and exhibit in their ornaments a tolerably advanced state of art.

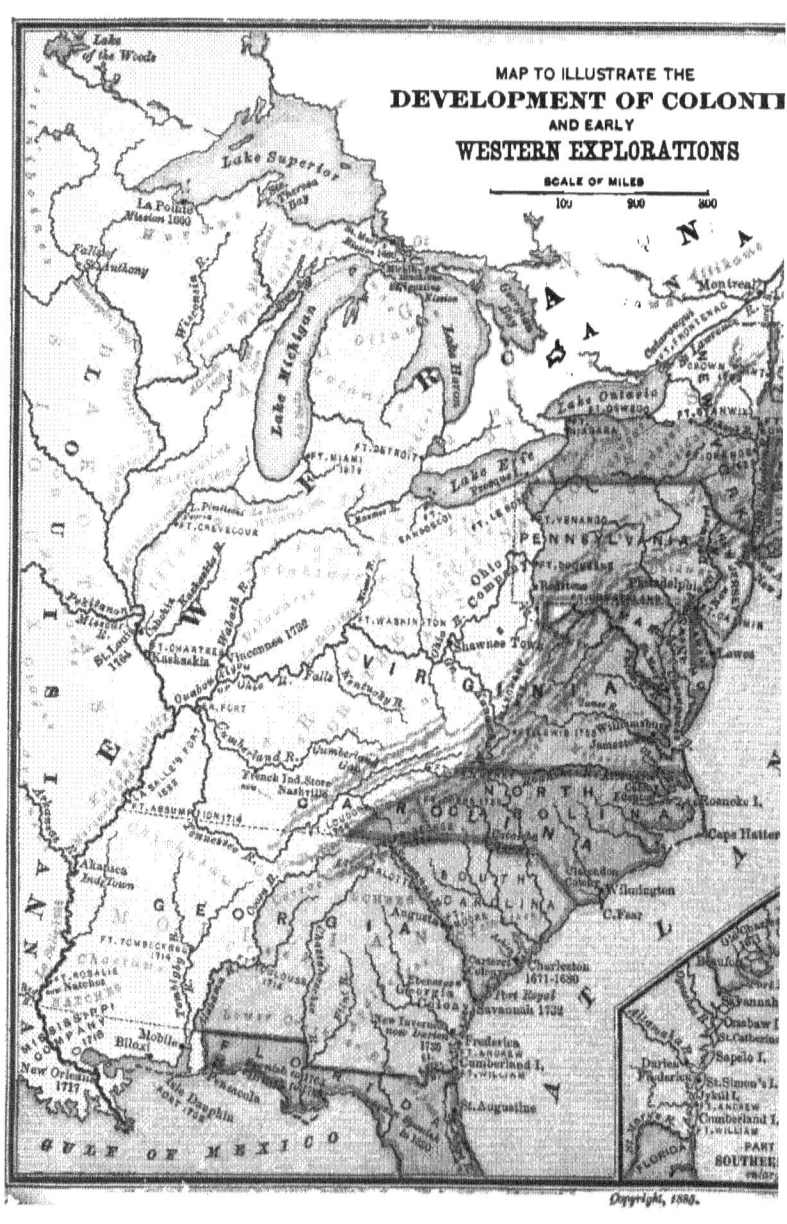

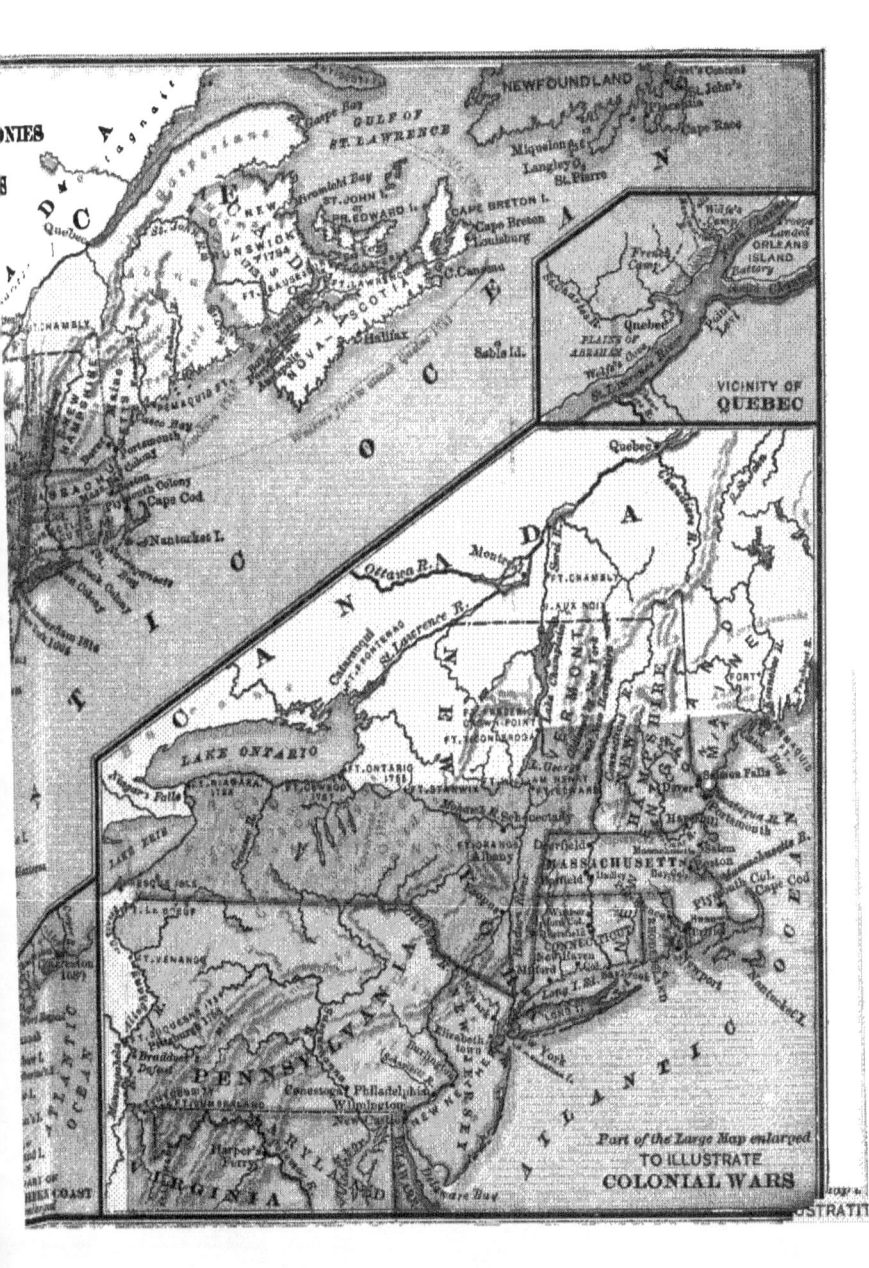

SECTION III.
A. D. 1600 to A. D. 1700.

STUDY NO. 1.
VIRGINIA.

1. Bartholomew Gosnold's Voyage.—Not discouraged by previous failures, the English still clung to the idea of colonizing Virginia. Accordingly, in 1602, Bartholomew Gosnold attempted a settlement on Cuttyhunk Island,[1]* in Buzzard's Bay,[2] Massachusetts. After a few weeks, however, the colonists returned to England. They loaded their vessels with sassafras-root, then much valued as a medicine; furs gathered by traffic with the Indians; cedar-wood, and other products. During his stay, Gosnold had explored the coast from Boston to Newport; and had given its name to Cape Cod,[3] because of the great numbers of codfish seen near its shores.

SEAL OF VIRGINIA.

2. Martin Pring's Voyage.—The next year another voyage was undertaken by Martin Pring, a friend of Raleigh and Gosnold. He also returned laden with furs and sassafras. The favorable reports of these voyages brought about the formation of the Plymouth and the London Company, under whose auspices explorations and settlements were to be made.

* These figures refer to the Geographical Table at the close of section.

3. Jamestown Settled.—Several expeditions sent out by the Plymouth Company failed; but, in 1606, the London Company despatched to the New World three small vessels under the command of Captain Christopher Newport, and bearing one hundred and five emigrants or colonists. A severe storm carried them beyond the former settlement of Raleigh; and they entered the magnificent bay,[8] over whose waters Father Segura and his companions had sailed *thirty years before*. The Capes at its entrance, they named Charles[1] and Henry,[1] in honor of the sons of James I.; and their first settlement they called Jamestown,[2] in honor of the king. This was the third permanent settlement made in the United States by Europeans, and the first by Englishmen.

JAMESTOWN AND VICINITY.

4. Character of the Colonists.—Among the colonists there were but few mechanics, and only twelve laborers. The greater number were useless gentlemen and pardoned criminals, people wholly unsuited to the foundation of a settlement. They refused to work, and before autumn half their number had perished.

5. The First Charter.—Under the first charter, the

VIRGINIA. 61

colony was governed by two councils; one resident in England, the other in the colony. Although Wingfield was appointed president, Smith was in reality the most able man among them; and to him, they were frequently obliged to turn for advice. At length, Wingfield was deposed for misconduct, and Smith was chosen to succeed him.

6. John Smith.—Smith now became the master-spirit and preserver of the colony, and is justly styled "THE FATHER OF VIRGINIA." He maintained discipline, caused the erection of houses and suitable defences, and endeavored to induce the *idle gentlemen* to work.

Smith, at different times, made expeditions along the coast, as far north as Maine. He visited the Isles of Shoals⁰ in New Hampshire,

SMITH SHOWING HIS COMPASS TO THE INDIANS.

which were formerly called "*Smith's Isles*," and on which a monument is now erected to his memory. He, also, first gave the name of New England to that part of the country.

He, moreover, made many journeys into the interior. During one of these, being surprised by a party of Indians, he was severely wounded. However, seizing one of his Indian guides, he bound him to his left arm as a shield; then, alternately firing and retreating, he would probably have escaped had he not unexpectedly sunk into a swamp. He was now taken prisoner; but, not at all daunted, he surprised and interested his captors by showing them a pocket compass, and telling them many things concerning the earth and stars. He was borne about as a curiosity, from tribe to tribe, over the peninsula since rendered famous by McClellan's campaign, and was finally brought before Powhattan, the chief, who was to decide his fate. Having been condemned to death, his head was already upon the block, when his life was saved through the intercession of Pocahontas, the gentle daughter of Powhattan.* The Indian maiden continued ever after the firm friend of the colonists, and was often seen with her companions bringing baskets of corn to the garrison.

7. Smith, on his return from this expedition, found the colonists in a wretched condition. He had been absent but three weeks, yet their number was reduced to forty men. Some were about to leave the colony and become pirates, when Captain Newport arrived with supplies and emigrants. Unfortunately, the new comers were of the same stamp as the former. They would neither build nor plant, but preferred to spend their time searching for gold. At length, Smith made a rule that all able-bodied men should work, at least, six hours a day. "*He that will not work,*" said the President, "*shall not eat.*" †

8. **The Starving Time.**—In 1609, Smith being accidentally injured by an explosion of gunpowder, was obliged to return to England for surgical aid. His departure was followed by a season of misery. The colonists, no longer controlled by an acknowledged authority, refused

---

* This story is doubted by many.

† "*When you send again,*" wrote Smith about this time, "*I entreat you rather send but thirty carpenters, husbandmen, gardeners, fishermen, blacksmiths, masons, and diggers of tree-roots well provided, than a thousand such as we have.*"

to work, the Indians became hostile, the provisions were rapidly consumed, and the horrors of famine ensued. A band of thirty, having seized a ship, left the colony and became pirates. The winter of 1609–10 was long known as the *Starving Time.* Out of nearly five hundred left by Smith, only sixty were alive at the end of six months; and these appeared more like spectres than living men.

9. At last, they determined to flee from the wretched place; and they had nearly reached the mouth of the James River, when they met a fleet coming to their aid. On board, was Lord Delaware, who had just been appointed governor for life. All returned to the homes they had deserted; and from this period, the colony prospered. Labor was exacted from all, new forts were erected as a defence against the Indians, and measures were taken to procure supplies.

10. **Argall's Treachery.**—In 1613, Pocahontas, the ever-faithful friend of the whites, was treacherously purchased from a tribe she had been visiting, by Argall, an infamous Virginia sea-captain. The price paid was a copper kettle. Argall expected to obtain from her father, Powhattan, a considerable quantity of corn and other articles as her ransom; but the chief rejected with scorn the proposals of the pirate, and prepared for war.

11. **Marriage of Pocahontas.**—Just at this juncture, however, John Rolfe, a young Englishman, desired to make the Indian maiden his wife. Her father's consent was easily obtained; Rolfe instructed her in the doctrines of Christianity; she received baptism, and they were soon after married. By this event, peace was once more cemented between the Indians and the whites.

12. **Her Death.**—Three years later, Pocahontas, with her husband, sailed for England, where "*the Lady Rebecca,*"

POCAHONTAS.

as she was called, was received with kindness and distinction. At court, she was treated with the ceremonious respect due to the daughter of a monarch. Shortly after, as she was preparing to return to the New World, at the early age of twenty-two, she fell a victim to the English climate. She left one son, Thomas Rolfe, who was educated by his uncle, and from whom are descended some of the leading families of Virginia.

13. Further Exploits of Argall.—A few months after the kidnapping of the gentle benefactress of the young colony at Jamestown, Argall sailed northward, and destroyed a French missionary settlement on Mount Desert Island, Maine. One of the missionaries, the Jesuit Brother Du Thet, was killed; and several of the colonists, including one Jesuit, were turned adrift, in an open boat, to the mercy of the waves. Fathers Biard and Quenten, with twelve others, were borne captives to Virginia. Here the governor, Sir Thomas Dale (who had succeeded Delaware), was inclined to hang them all. He relented, however, and the prisoners, having undergone a long captivity and many hardships, at length reached France. During the same year, (1613), Argall destroyed another French settlement at Port Royal, Nova Scotia.

14. Argall, Governor.—In 1617, Argall was made deputy governor; and, while he continued in office, the condition of Virginia was intolerable. He defrauded the Company and oppressed the colonists; and martial law being in force, life itself was hardly secure in his hands. His misdeeds, at length, brought about the appointment of a new governor; but before the arrival of the latter, Argall had withdrawn, taking with him his ill-gotten wealth (1619). Nevertheless, in 1623, he was knighted by King James I.

15. Tobacco.—The cultivation of tobacco commenced in 1615, and soon became the general pursuit. Even the streets of Jamestown were planted with it. As coin was scarce, it passed for currency, the money value of a pound of tobacco being fixed at about seventy-five cents. Taxes, salaries, and all private debts, were payable in tobacco. Even legacies were left by will, to be paid in the same plant.—The production of this staple greatly increased the demand for labor.— At first, "*apprenticed servants*" were sent over from England and bound out to the planters for a term of years. Later, however, the work was performed by negroes.

TOBACCO.

STUDY NO. 2.

VIRGINIA—Continued.

1. The First Colonial Assembly.—After some years of tyranny and misrule under Argall, Virginia received for its governor, George Yeardly [*yard'-ly*]; and from this period the real progress of the colony dates (1619). Within a few months after his appointment, a colonial assembly was convened. This was known as "*The House of Burgesses,*" and constituted *the first representative body ever known in America*. It consisted of delegates from each of the eleven plantations, who met at Jamestown.

2. Slavery.—About this time (1620), a Dutch trading vessel from Africa, sailed up the James River, and landed twenty negroes, who were sold as slaves to the planters. Thus was *slavery* introduced into the colonies.

3. Family Ties.—During the same year, were sent out to the colony, nearly one hundred virtuous girls, who soon found husbands able and willing to pay the expenses of their passage. Domestic ties were thus formed, and the colonists having homes, became *Virginians*.

4. Indian Troubles.—Virginia now seemed on the high road to prosperity, when Opecancanough (*o-pe-kan-kan'-o*),* who had succeeded his brother Powhattan, and had witnessed with sorrow the decline of his race, formed a plan for the extermination of the whites. Accordingly, on

---

* It is related of Opecancanough that, a house having been built for him after the English fashion, he was so charmed with the lock and key, that he would lock and unlock the door a hundred times a day.

VIRGINIA.

the 22d of March, 1622, the Indians suddenly attacked all the settlements on the James River; and in one hour, three hundred and forty-seven men, women and children were massacred. Jamestown was saved through the timely warning of a friendly Indian. A war now ensued, in which the Indians were so severely punished that they remained quiet for twenty years. Then (1644) another massacre took place, which was followed by the total expulsion of the Indians from that region.*

5. Virginia a Royal Province.—In 1624, King James took away the charter, and Virginia became a royal province. It thus continued, with brief intermission, until the Revolution. When the English civil war broke out (in 1642), Virginia remained true to the royal cause, and was hence called "*The Old Dominion.*" †

6. The Navigation Acts.—In 1660, the English Parliament passed certain laws called *the Navigation Acts*. By these, the colonists were required to carry on all their commerce in English vessels, to ship all their tobacco to England, and to purchase all their goods in that country. These laws bore heavily on the Virginians, and proved a cause of great discontent.

7. Bacon's Rebellion.—About the year 1676, an Indian war breaking out on the borders of Maryland, the Virginians armed themselves for defence, under the leadership of a young and patriotic lawyer named Nathaniel Bacon. Berkely, the governor, mistrusted Bacon and denounced him

---

* We see here, and as our history progresses, shall often see again, that the general policy of the English with regard to the Indians, has been *extermination*.

† When Charles II. came to the throne, he did not forget the loyalty of the Virginians. He caused the arms of that province to be quartered with those of England, Ireland, Scotland, as an independent member of his empire. From this circumstance Virginia received the title of Old Dominion. Coins with these quarterings were struck as late as 1773.

as a rebel. In the contest which ensued, (the real cause of which was an ill-feeling between the people and the aristocratic party,) Berkely was driven out of Jamestown, and the village itself burned to the ground. In the midst of his success, Bacon died.

8. The insurgents were treated with the utmost severity by Berkely, twenty-two being hanged. The principal men were hunted down with most fero-

BERKELY RECEIVING DRUMMOND.

cious zeal. When William Drummond, one of these, was brought in, Berkely, bowing low, remarked ironically, "*I am more glad to see you than any other man in Virginia. You shall be hanged in half an hour.*" Drummond was condemned at once, and hanged at four o'clock the same day.

Soon after this, Berkely was recalled to England, where he died in disgrace. He who, in his young manhood, had been noted as a prudent and able governor, had become, in his old age, an unwise and cruel oppressor. Jamestown was never rebuilt. At present no vestige of it remains, but the crumbling, ivy-clad church tower, and a few monuments in the graveyard near it.

9. White Slaves.—Much of the labor in Virginia was performed by convicts and other exiles from the British Isles. Bancroft writes:

"White servants came to be a usual article of traffic. They were sold in England, and in Virginia were resold to the highest bidder."

"In Ireland, the crowded exportation of Irish Catholics was a frequent event, and was attended by aggravations hardly inferior to the African slave-trade."

RUINS OF JAMESTOWN.

Father Thébaud, in his magnificent work, "*The Irish Race*," alluding to the wholesale transportation of that people, during the time of Cromwell, says:

"Nearly all the British colonies then existing in America received their share of this emigration. Several ship-loads of the exiles were certainly sent to New England, at the very time that New Englanders were earnestly invited by the British government to '*come and plant Ireland.*' Virginia, too, paid probably with tobacco for the young men and maidens sent there as slaves."

10. Manners.—The Virginians were social, hospitable, and not so constrained in their manners as the New England colonists. As there were but few books and little education in those early times, amusement was often sought in horse-racing, fox-hunting, and other out-door sports.

FIELD-SPORTS OF THE SOUTH—FOX-HUNTING.

11. Education.—Education at first received but little attention. Berkely, in 1671, wrote: "*I thank God there are no free schools nor printing; and I hope we shall not have them these hundred years.*" However, in 1693, William and Mary's College was established.

12. Religion.—The established religion in Virginia was the Episcopalian. All had to contribute to its support; and attendance at its service was compulsory, a fine of twenty pounds being imposed upon all absentees. All Catholic priests were to be sent out of the colony within five days after their arrival.

STUDY NO. 3.

NEW ENGLAND.

1. Attempted Settlement in Maine.—The first settlement in New England was made during the summer of 1604, by the French under De Monts [*mong*] and Champlain [*shamplane*]. It was located on Boone Island* in the St. Croix [*krwah*] River, near the present site of Calais, Maine. Various buildings were erected, including a small chapel; and here they spent a severe winter. During the fall, Champlain explored the coast of Maine, visited and named Mt. Desert Island, and entered the mouth of the Penobscot River.

CHAMPLAIN.

2. Explorations.—On the arrival of spring, (1605) De Monts determined to look for a more favorable site for his colony; and with him, Champlain again sailed along the New England shores, "landing daily, holding conference with the Indians, giving and receiving gifts," until they

---

* "In 1783, the River St. Croix, by treaty, was made the boundary between Maine and New Brunswick. But which was the true St. Croix? In 1798, the point was settled. De Monts Island was found; and, painfully searching among the sand, the sedge, and the matted whortleberry bushes, the commissioners could trace the foundations of buildings long crumbled into dust. For the wilderness had resumed its sway, and silence and solitude brooded once more over this ancient resting-place of civilization."—*Parkman*.

had passed Capes Cod and Malabar.* On the latter point, Champlain erected a cross, and took possession in the name of his royal master. Here provisions failing, they returned to St. Croix.

3. Acadia.—Having seen no spot suitable for the location of a settlement, they transferred the St. Croix Colony to Port Royal (now Annapolis) on the opposite shore of the Bay of Fundy. The entire region, they called Acadia. This, as claimed by the French, embraced Maine, New Brunswick, and Nova Scotia.

4. Saint Saviour's, Maine.—In 1613, another French missionary settlement was founded on Mt. Desert Island. The colonists numbered about forty, including four Jesuits. Buildings had been erected, laborers had commenced to till the ground, and Father Biard had visited and made a favorable impression upon the neighboring Indians,† when the colony was suddenly cut down.

5. Saint Saviour's a Ruin.—Argall, (in Virginian annals famous for tyranny and craft,) appeared off the coast

---

* "Champlain, who, we are told, delighted marvellously in these enterprises, busied himself, after his wont, with taking observations, sketching, making charts, and exploring with an insatiable avidity the wonders of the land and the sea. Of the latter, the horse-shoe crab awakened his especial curiosity, and he describes it at length with an amusing accuracy.

"With equal truth he paints the Indians, whose round, mat-covered lodges they could see at times thickly strewn along the shores, and who, from bays, inlets, and sheltering islands, came out to meet them in canoes of bark or wood. They were an agricultural race. Patches of corn, beans, tobacco, squashes, and esculent roots lay near all their wigwams. Clearly, they were in greater number than when, fifteen years afterwards, the Puritans made their lodgment at Plymouth, since, happily for the latter, a pestilence had then more than decimated this fierce population of the woods."—*Parkman.*

† While the workmen were employed at the buildings, Father Biard had crossed to the mainland, and hearing plaintive cries in the distance, he penetrated still further. Presently, he beheld a number of Indians uttering the deepest lamentations, and in the centre a stalwart brave, apparently a chief, holding in his arms a dying infant. Having approached nearer, the good father endeavored to offer words of consolation. Then, touched with compassion, he baptized the babe, and knowing the good impression its recovery would make, he besought God to heal the child. His prayer was answered and the whole tribe was jubilant. Thus was the first sacrament administered in the present State of Maine.

in an armed ship, attacked. the settlement, and killed several of the colonists, among the number Du Thet, a Jesuit lay brother. To prevent further bloodshed, the French now surrendered. Argall having treacherously seized the papers of the commander, turned some of the colonists adrift in an open boat, to make their way as best they might to Port Royal. The rest, including three Jesuits, he carried with him to Virginia. Thus did the English put an end to the first mission in the present diocese of Portland. (*See page* 64.)

6. Arrival of the Puritans.—Seven years after the destruction of St. Saviour's, on a stormy day in fall (1620), an English vessel, the *Mayflower*, cast anchor in the vicinity of Cape Cod. It bore a band of English Puritans who, fleeing from religious persecution in their own country, sought to settle in the New World. Having explored the coast for some time, they finally determined to land at *Plymouth*, as it was called on Smith's chart.

SEAL OF MASSACHUSETTS.

The rock on which they first stepped ashore is still held in veneration by the people of New England.

PLYMOUTH ROCK.

7. Their First Winter. — Owing to the severity of the season their sufferings were intense, and before spring

GREETING OF THE INDIANS TO THE PLYMOUTH SETTLERS.

half their number, including Governor Carver, had perished. Wm. Bradford was elected the second Governor. For several years, they suffered much from famine. At one time their provisions were reduced to a pint of corn, which, being distributed, gave to each individual only *about five kernels.* At another, they were saved from famishing, only by the kindness of fishermen off the coast.

8. The Indians.—Fortunately, the Indians among whom they found themselves proved friendly. Early in the spring of 1621, they were visited by Massasoit [*mas-sas'o-it*], the chief of the Wampanoags [*wom-pa-no'ags*], who made with them a treaty of peace and alliance. This was sacredly kept for more than half a century. Canonicus, the chief of a tribe at variance with the Wampanoags, once sent to

NEW ENGLAND.

Governor Bradford, a bundle of arrows wrapped up in the skin of a rattlesnake. This was in token of hostility. The Governor returned the skin filled with powder and shot; and the chief, understanding the significant hint, molested them no more.

9. Progress of the Colony.—The progress of the colony was slow. At the end of ten years, it numbered only three hundred individuals; still, it led to the foundation of other and larger settlements in New England.

10. The Massachusetts Bay Colony.—In 1629, a party of Puritans under John Endicott, settled at Salem, and commenced the *Massachusetts Bay Colony*. Others followed and settled at Charlestown. Finally, in the summer of 1630, fifteen hundred Puritans arrived, with John Winthrop as Governor. They founded Dorchester, Cambridge, Lynn, Roxbury, Boston, and other places.

GOVERNOR WINTHROP.

11. Religious Intolerance.—Though the Puritans had been the victims of religious persecution in the Old World,—in the New, they themselves proved equally intolerant. They established odious religious tests, and persecuted or banished all those who ventured to worship God in a manner different from their own.

12. Roger Williams.—In consequence of this state of things, Roger Williams, a young minister who favored the opinions of the Baptists, was banished from the colony (1635). Men were sent to arrest him and put him on board a vessel bound for England; but he was fore-warned in time to escape. For more than three months, in the depth of a New England winter, he wandered through the wilderness. At length he was kindly received by the friendly Massasoit, and afterwards by Canonicus.

ROGER WILLIAMS.

13. Rhode Island Settled. — In the following spring (1636), Williams bought from the natives, a tract of land on Narragansett Bay; and here he commenced a settlement which, in gratitude for his preservation, he named Providence. Thus was laid the foundation of Rhode Island. In 1638, another party driven from

ROGER WILLIAMS RECEIVED BY CANONICUS.

Massachusetts on account of religion, settled Portsmouth on the Island of Rhode Island; and in 1639, a portion of these founded Newport. For some years the colony of Providence remained a pure democracy, transacting its public business in town meetings; but, in 1643, Williams went to England and procured for it a Charter which united the settlements into one Colony.

14. Mrs. Hutchinson. — During the same year, (1636), a woman named Anne Hutchinson created much excitement by her religious doctrines. She instituted meetings of her own sex to discuss religious matters,—claimed to have received private revelations from Heaven, and denounced the authority of the clergy. Among her followers were Vane, Cotton, Wheelwright, and the whole Boston Church except five members. Being summoned before the general court, after a trial of two days, she and some of her adherents were sentenced to banishment. The remainder were deprived of arms, lest they *might, upon some revelation, make a sudden insurrection.*

SEAL OF RHODE ISLAND.

15. Mrs. Hutchinson, for a time, joined the colony of Roger Williams. She still continued to preach, and indeed became so popular that, by some of the people of Massachusetts, she was suspected of *witchcraft*. Later, she and her family removed to New York, near the site of the present New Rochelle, and here she perished during an Indian insurrection.* Wheelwright and some others proceeded to New Hampshire, and founded Exeter.

* All the members of her family excepting a grand-daughter about eight years of age, were murdered. Her house and barns were burned, her cattle butchered, and the little girl taken captive. The captor, a young Indian brave, spared the child's life, and treated her kindly. Four years later, in accordance with the terms of a treaty, she was delivered to the Dutch governor at New Amsterdam, to be sent to her friends at Boston. She had then forgotten her own language, and was anxious to remain with her Indian friends.

16. New Hampshire Founded.—The first settlements in New Hampshire were made at Portsmouth and Dover, in 1623, by a party in the service of Gorges [*gor-jez*] and Mason, the proprietors. In 1629, Gorges and Mason dissolved partnership, and Mason then obtained a new grant for the territory between the Merrimack and the Piscataqua. This he named New Hampshire, from Portsmouth, Hampshire, England, of which place he had been governor. About the year 1641, owing to various Indian and other troubles, the people of New Hampshire put themselves under the protection of Massachusetts. Affairs remained thus until 1680, when New Hampshire was made a separate *royal province*. In 1690, they were again united, but a final separation took place in 1741.

17. Quakers Persecuted.—Twenty years after the banishment of Mrs. Hutchinson a number of Quakers* having found their way into Massachusetts, severe laws were passed against them (1656). Those who entered the colony were condemned to lose their ears, to be branded on the shoulder, to have their tongues bored with red-hot irons, and, on a second offence, to be hanged. Four were executed; but, soon after, a milder penalty was substituted.

18. In 1643, a Union of the Colonies of Plymouth, Massachusetts Bay, New Haven, and Connecticut, was formed, under the title of the *United Colonies of New England*. Their object was mutual protection; and the union lasted forty years.

---

* The Quakers or Friends are a religious sect founded in England, by George Fox, about the middle of the 17th century. They disavow all ceremonies, have no liturgy, no stated form of prayer, no regular preaching, and, of course, no Sacraments. —At their meetings, all remain in silence until some one feels moved to address the audience.—It is said that, at one period, *a whole year elapsed, and yet no one spoke.* —They profess to believe in the fundamental doctrines of Christianity as professed by Protestants generally. In the United States, where they now number about 100,000, a rupture in the society occurred about the year 1827. They were subsequently divided into *Orthodox* and *Hicksites*.

NEW ENGLAND.

19. Jesuits in Maine.—In the early part of the century, the French Jesuits had commenced and firmly established their missions in Canada. Subsequently, at various times, the Abnaki of Maine (among whom the St. Saviour Mission had been projected in 1613) visited the Christian Indian settlement near Quebec, and not a few became converts. These now persuaded their clansmen to ask for a *Black-gown*.* In response to this appeal, in 1646, —the same year in which Father Jogues was sent to the Mohawk,—Father Druillettes† [*drwee-yet*] was chosen to commence a mission on the Kennebec. (See p. 98.)

20. Through his labors and those of the Fathers who succeeded him, the conversion of the whole tribe was effected. They proved fervent Christians; and, on all occasions, acted as brave and faithful allies of France. During our revolution, they fought on the American side under their noble chief Orono. Even to this day, the remnants of this powerful tribe who still occupy several villages in Canada and Maine, are all Catholics, as, during the two preceding centuries, their forefathers were.

* The name by which the Jesuit missionaries were known to the Indians.

† In 1650, Father Druillettes was sent by the Canadian government to effect a negotiation with the New Englanders. Notwithstanding the existing laws against Jesuits, he was hospitably received by the Governors at Plymouth, Boston, and other places. In this, however, we must remark, they regarded him rather as a national envoy, than as a Catholic priest.

STUDY NO. 4.

NEW ENGLAND—Continued.

1. King Philip's War.—In 1675, an Indian War broke out, known as King Philip's. On the death of the ever-friendly Massasoit, the chieftainship devolved upon his son Alexander, who was soon after put to death by the whites. King Philip, the second son of Massasoit, pierced with grief, resolved to avenge this and other wrongs of his nation. Before his plans were matured, however, he was, on mere suspicion, summoned before a Puritan tribunal. At this indignity to their chief, the anger of the tribe broke forth, and they speedily murdered the Indian informer who had betrayed him. The murderers were seized in turn, by the whites and hanged; the Indians again retaliated, and thus the war began. The contest, which lasted for more than a

KING PHILIP.

year, was noted for great cruelties on both sides,* and at its close, the Wampanoags were almost exterminated.

2. The Swamp Fight.—The principal battle, known as *the Swamp Fight*, took place in an almost inaccessible swamp

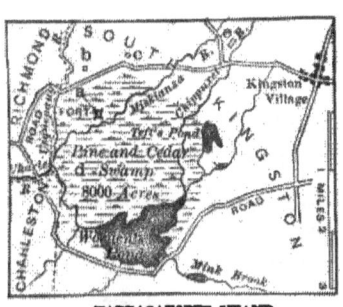

NARRAGANSETT SWAMP.

in South Kingston, R. I. After a desperate struggle, the Indians were defeated, and their wigwams, filled with winter stores, were burned to ashes. Philip was now left almost alone. Hunted from place to place, he was at length shot by a faithless Indian (Aug. 1676). His head was cut off by Captain Church and sent to Plymouth, where it was hung on the palisades of the town. Philip's son, a boy nine years of age, the only heir to his father's dignity, was sold into slavery, to wear out his life under the burning sun of Bermuda. Thus perished the family of Massasoit.

3. The Narragansetts had made with the colonists a treaty of neutrality, and had promised to deliver up hostile Indians; they, nevertheless, gave shelter to such of the fugitive Wampanoags as had escaped destruction. In consequence of this, a party of New Englanders, headed by Captain Winslow, entered the territory of the Narragansetts and devastated all before them. Their wigwams were burned, and their aged men, their women and their children perished by hundreds in the fire.

* Captain Church was the most noted man on the English side; and, if his own account is to be believed, he committed the most savage brutalities and cruelties on the poor Indians. From June to October 1676, this gallant Captain slaughtered from 700 to 1000 Indians, while most of those who were taken prisoners were sold into bondage.

4. "Then indeed," says Bancroft, "was the cup of misery full for these red men. Without shelter and without food, they hid themselves in a cedar swamp, with no defence against the cold but boughs of evergreen trees. They prowled the forest and pawed up the snow, to gather nuts and acorns; they dug the earth for ground nuts; they ate remnants of horse-flesh as a luxury; they sank down from feebleness and want of food."—After this, of the once prosperous Narragansetts scarcely one hundred men remained.—Thus did England pursue her policy of extermination.*

5. The Charter Abolished.—The Navigation Acts which bore so heavily on Virginia, crippled also the trade of the New England colonists; but the latter evaded the laws as much as they could. In consequence of this, their charter was abolished by James II., who sent out Edmund Andros as Governor. Six years later King William gave to Massachusetts a new charter, by which toleration was granted to all Christians *except Roman Catholics.*

6. Salem Witchcraft Delusion (1692).—Toward the close of the century a remarkable delusion known as the *Salem Witchcraft,* created great excitement in Massachusetts. The idea originated in the house of Mr. Parris, a Puritan minister at Salem, whose children were supposed to be the victims of the spells of a witch. The mania spread like wild-fire. Numbers of innocent persons, generally the crazy, the afflicted, the aged, or the homely, were accused and cast into prison. Even the wife of the Governor, Lady Phipps, did not escape the accusation.

7. The delusion in its greatest violence lasted about six months, but was not fully allayed till the end of the year.—

---

* Several hundred Abnakis of Maine were treacherously seized and sold into slavery by Captain Waldron; but he suffered dire revenge during King William's War. (See page 69.)

During this "reign of terror" twenty persons were hanged, fifty-five tortured, and one hundred and fifty imprisoned. All mutual confidence was suspended and the noblest sentiments of human nature forgotten. Members of the same family sometimes became the accusers of one another, one man being executed on the testimony of his wife and daughters; while rapacity, malice, or revenge often impelled persons to accuse the innocent.

8. This extraordinary episode in the history of Massachusetts astonished the civilized world, and made a most unfavorable impression on the neighboring Indians. The latter could not but contrast a religion which permitted such cruel fanaticism, and whose ministers had acted so prominent a part in the fearful tragedy, with that of the mild, devoted and self-sacrificing Jesuit missionaries of Maine and the frontier.—Henceforth the Indians attached themselves to the French. When, a few years later, Governor Phipps visited the tribes at Bristol Bay, Maine, to secure their alliance, they steadily refused, saying: "The French have driven witchcraft from among us and we do not care to associate with those who cherish it."

9. **Character of the Colonists.**—The Puritans were industrious, sober, enterprising, and religious in their own way; but they were also narrow-minded, exclusive, and short-sighted in character, cruel to the Indians, and bigoted and persecuting toward all creeds except their own. "Seldom," says Parkman, "has religious tyranny assumed a form more oppressive than among the Puritan exiles. New England Protestantism appealed to liberty and then closed the door against her. Their attention, however, was early turned to the subject of education. Harvard College was founded in 1637, and two years afterwards a printing-press was set up.

10. Manners.—Their religious ideas being severe and gloomy, the manners of the colonists naturally partook of the same cast. Amusements were prohibited, and gayety was deemed sinful. In the first year of the Massachusetts Bay Colony, Endicott broke up a settlement at Merrymount near Boston, because the people there led gayer and idler lives than the Puritans approved. Among other misdemeanors, they had erected a May-pole.—

THE STOCKS.

No one under twenty was allowed to use tobacco; those over that age could smoke once a day, but only at a distance of ten miles from any dwelling.

11. Private morals were carefully watched by the authorities of church and state. For shooting fowl on Sunday, a man was whipped. The swearer was usually made to stand in a public place with his tongue in a cleft stick. Sometimes he was fined or set in the stocks, or imprisoned,—and in some instances even his tongue was bored

A SCOLD GAGGED.

through with a hot iron. The unhappy housewife whose temper got the better of her wisdom, was not overlooked. Scolds were gagged and obliged to stand at their doors at certain hours, that passers-by might see their disgrace. Those who remained outside of the meeting-house on Sundays were admonished by the constables, and on a second offence, they were set in the stocks. Such was the severe spirit of the laws at that time.

12. The houses of the first settlers were simply log cabins, with an immense chimney built externally at the side. The chinks between the logs were "daubed," as the term was, with a mortar of clay and straw.

After about thirty years, a better class of dwellings began to be more common. They were usually made of heavy oak frames, put together in the most solid manner, and made secure at night by massive wooden bars. The foundations of the large old stone chimneys were about twelve feet square. Forest logs, four feet in length, were piled upon the ponderous andirons, and on occasions, a big "back log" was drawn into the house by a horse, and rolled into the fireplace with handspikes. "Blazing hearth-stones" then had a literal meaning wholly unknown in our day.

13. Occupations.—Trade, agriculture, etc., were the main employments of the people. Money was scarce, and trade was carried on chiefly by barter, a coat for a cow, or a barrel of sugar for a pile of boards. In 1635, bullets were given instead of farthings; but in 1652, a mint was set up, and for thirty years all the coins bore the same date. They are known as the pine-tree shillings, sixpences, etc., from the fact that they bore on one side the inscription "*Massachusetts*," with a pine-tree in the centre. All men from sixteen to sixty years of age were expected to prepare themselves to bear arms; hence all were required to participate in the general drill. There does not appear to have been on these occasions any uniform dress, or any music except that of the drum. Military titles were much reverenced, for a long time that of "*Captain*" being the highest given.

TRAINING DAY IN THE OLDEN TIME.

14. Religion.—The prescribed religion was Puritanism. No other was tolerated, not even any of the other Protestant sects. Roman Catholics and Quakers were held in special abhorrence; and even after the laws against the latter had been abolished, those against the former remained in force. Jesuits were forbidden to enter the colony; and, in case of a second transgression, the penalty was death. In their desire to avoid all observance of any Catholic Festivals, it was even deemed wrong to eat mince-pie on Christmas day; and Endicott, in his zeal, cut the cross out of the British flag, because it seemed indicative of Catholicity.

STUDY NO. 5.

NEW ENGLAND,—Continued.

1. Connecticut Explored by the Dutch.—The coast of Connecticut was first explored in 1614, by Adrian Block, a Dutch navigator. He was also the first European to sail through that dangerous whirlpool of the East River, called *Hurlgate*. Block Island in the Atlantic, south of the State of Rhode Island, still bears the name of the bold mariner. Other Dutch navigators afterwards sailed up the Connecticut River, and claimed its banks and the whole shore of Long Island Sound, as far as Cape Cod. In 1631, they bought of the Indian chief, Sassacus, the land on which Hartford now stands, and there built a trading-house.

SEAL OF CONNECTICUT.

2. Connecticut Settled by the English.—But the English also claimed the valley of the Connecticut, in virtue of a grant from their king; and, in 1633, a party of traders from Plymouth built a fort at Windsor. Two years afterwards, the foundations of Hartford and Wethersfield were laid. These settlements were at first under the protection of Massachusetts, and were called the Connecticut Colony.

3. The Pequod War.—Scarcely were the settlers established in their new home, when a war broke out with the Pequod Indians. About this time, a Massachusetts trading-vessel was captured, and the commander killed near Block Island, by the Indian allies of the Pequods, who had already shown signs of hostility.

4. The authorities of Massachusetts having determined to punish these misdeeds, Endicott led a force into Connecticut, and burned two Pequod towns. On this, the natives flew to arms; and, had it not been for the kind mediation of Roger Williams, the Narragansetts would have joined their brethren of the forest. He, at the risk of his life, went to the Indian council, and after a three days' struggle, prevailed upon the Narragansetts to side with the whites.

5. Although Massachusetts had involved the colonists in this war, she was too much occupied with the religious disputes of Mrs. Hutchinson, to lend immediate aid. Accordingly, a party of Connecticut colonists, under Captain Mason, prepared to attack the Pequod stronghold on the Mystic River, near the present towns of Stonington and New London. They reached the fort at daybreak (June 4th, 1637), while the unsuspecting Indians, after a night of revel, were stilled wrapped in slumber. The barking of a dog aroused the sleeping sentinels, who speedily shouted, "*Owanux! Owanux!*" (the Englishmen); but it was too late. The troops were already within the palisades.

6. The Indians made a fierce resistance; but Captain Mason having seized a burning firebrand, hurled it among the wigwams, and in one hour *seven hundred men, women and children*, had perished in the flames. As Mason marched towards the coast, he encountered a second body of Pequods, under their chief Sassacus, who were also defeated. The next month, another force from Massachusetts entered the Pequod territory and captured or destroyed almost the

entire remnant of the tribe. Sassacus fled to the Mohawks, but was there murdered, and his scalp was sent to Boston. *The tribe was exterminated.* At the close of the war, New Haven was founded by a party of Puritans from England (1638).

7. The Charter Oak.—In 1662, Charles II. granted to the Connecticut colonies a charter allowing them to elect their own governor and representatives. About twenty years later, this charter was annulled by James II. In 1687, Andros, who had been appointed royal governor of New England, went to the assembly at Hartford to seize the precious document. A protracted debate ensued; and, during the excitement, the lights were suddenly extinguished. When they were re-lighted, the members were seated in perfect order, the charter was gone. Captain Wadsworth had seized it, escaped through the crowd, and hid it in the hollow of a tree famous ever after as *the Charter Oak.** Andros, however, put an end to the self-government of the colony, and ruled like a despot. At length his tyranny became unendurable, and he was deposed. Then the *Charter Oak* gave back its faded but valued treasure.†

THE CHARTER OAK.

* This incident is denied by some. Contemporary documents seem to prove that no such event occurred; that Andros really took possession of the original charter, and that a duplicate had been concealed some time previous.

† "*The Charter Oak*" remained vigorous, bearing fruit each year, until a little after midnight in August, 1856, when it was prostrated by a storm of wind. It stood in a vacant lot on the south side of Charter street, a few rods from Main street, in the city of Hartford.

8. Blue Laws of Connecticut. — Whether the name "Blue Laws" originated from the fact that the first printed edition thereof had *blue covers*, or that the laws themselves were deemed intrinsically *blue* is undecided. They were a harassing system of legislation which regulated not alone those matters which ordinarily come under the jurisdiction of the state, but even a man's religion, the very cut of his hair, the fashion of his dress, and the particular occasions on which a mother might kiss her child.* Twelve offences were punishable by death ; and, for crimes not capital, the rack, the stocks, the whipping-post, and the branding-iron were frequently called into requisition.

9. Although the accounts of these laws† may be somewhat exaggerated, and although the statutes themselves have been modified or repealed, still the fact that they were once in force must forever remain a blot on the fame of New England. While in point of scourging, branding, banishing and hanging heretics and witches, Massachusetts takes the lead,—with regard to *Blue Laws*, Connecticut deserves the palm.

* We subjoin the following specimen laws taken from *Barber's Antiquities of New Haven:*
"21. No one shall run on the Sabbath day, or walk in his garden, or elsewhere, except reverently to and from meeting."
"22. No one shall travel, cook victuals, make beds, sweep house, cut hair, or shave, on the Sabbath day."
"23. No woman shall kiss her child on the Sabbath or fasting day."
"26. No one shall read Common Prayer, keep Christmas, or Saints' days, make mince pies, dance, play cards, or play on any instrument of music except the drum, trumpet, or jewsharp."
"44. Every male shall have his hair cut round according to a cap."
The following is also found among the laws of Connecticut :
"10. No priest shall abide in this dominion ; he shall be banished and suffer death on his return. Priests may be seized by any one without a warrant."

† Some have attempted to disprove the existence of these laws ; but the testimonies to their reality still stand.

STUDY NO. 6.

THE EARLY JESUIT MISSIONARIES AT THE NORTH.

1. An Impressive Theme.—To the truly Christian mind, there is nothing more impressive, nothing more fascinating in the whole range of our country's history, than that portion which chronicles

FATHER MARQUETTE AMONG THE INDIANS. (Page 108.)

the labors of the early missionaries on our soil. We have seen, in the two preceding centuries, how amid the tropical heats of the South, they braved danger, hardship, and even death in the cause of their Master. We have now to behold them amid the snows of the North; and the heart that does not thrill at the history of a Brebœuf (*brĕ-buf*), a Jogues, or a Marquette (*-ket*), must be hardened indeed.

2. Explorations of the Missionaries.—It so happens, moreover, that the missionaries were the pioneers not alone of the Cross and of religion, but of discovery and exploration, of colonization and civilization. Of white men, they were the first to sail over our great rivers and great lakes, as well as the first to traverse our magnificent woodlands. More than one, in his apostolic journeys, passed from the mouth of the St. Lawrence to the Mississippi and Texas, and returned by sea, thus making the circuit of what the entire United States were, as late as a century ago. Every great exploration was followed by a map and a memoir describing the physical geography of the country. This of itself was invaluable.

3. Discoveries and Improvements made by the Missionaries.—They discovered the salt-springs of New York and the oil-springs of Pennsylvania; drew attention to the cotton-plant and mulberry-tree of the Mississippi Valley; introduced the sugar-cane from New Orleans, and wheat and the plough into the prairies; and planted the peach in Illinois. They first made wine from the native grape, wax from the wild laurel, and incense from the gum-tree; and were the first to work the copper-mines of Lake Superior. But these useful discoveries and improvements were only incidental, and dwindle into insignificance, when compared with their labors for the salvation of souls.

4. Franciscan Missionaries in Canada.—In the year 1608, Champlain, who had already made more than one

MISSIONARIES AT THE NORTH. 93

voyage to the New World, founded the city of Quebec. His first care, as soon as colonization commenced, was to provide missionaries for the many tribes whose friendship he had won. Accordingly, at his invitation, in 1615, three Franciscan priests, (*Récollets*) and one lay brother, came to Canada. One Father gave himself to the Hurons; the others devoted themselves to the Algonquin and other tribes on the St. Lawrence. In 1625, at the entreaty of the Franciscans, three Jesuits, (one being Father Brebœuf [*brĕ-buf*]), came to their assistance. After this, the two orders labored conjointly until 1629, when Quebec was taken by the English. The missionaries were then sent back to Europe. In the same year in which the Jesuits arrived, Father Viel [*ve-ell*], a Franciscan, through the treachery of an Indian guide, was drowned in the Rapids near Montreal. The spot has since been called Sault au Récollet [*sote-o-ray-col-ay*], or the Recollects Rapid.

5. The Missions Resumed.—In 1633, on the restoration of Canada to the French, and just one year before the settlement of Maryland, the Jesuits resumed the work already commenced. From this period, Quebec became the grand centre from which missionaries went forth to discovery, to spiritual conquest, or to martyrdom. "Not a cape was turned, or a river entered, but a Jesuit led the way." Among the first to arrive, were Fathers Brebœuf [*brĕ-buf*], Davost, [*dav-o*], and Daniel. The three priests almost immediately commenced a mission in the Huron country; and there they erected a log-house which, being divided off, served both as dwelling and chapel.

This edifice and its furniture were a source of never-ceasing wonder to the Indians. A striking-clock possessed by the Fathers, in particular excited their admiration; and for hours, they would sit in expectant silence, waiting to hear it strike. It was, they felt sure, some strange animal from the East; though how it lived without eating, was a subject long debated by the sages of the tribe.

6. Brebœuf. [*brĕ-buf*].—After years of toil and hardships of every kind, the labors of the missionaries were crowned with success, and almost the whole Huron nation embraced the Faith. Brebœuf, whom Parkman styles "*the Ajax* of the Mission*," and Archbishop Spauld-

THE INDIANS AND THE CLOCK.

ing, "*the Xavier of North America*," was their great Apostle. At his death, the Christian Hurons numbered eight thousand, and their missionaries included eighteen Jesuits.

7. Jesuits in Michigan.—In 1641, the Jesuits received an invitation to visit the Chippewas at Sault [*so*] St. Mary.²⁵ For this expedition, Fathers Raymbault [*bo*]†

* The bravest of all the Greeks in the Trojan War.

† Father Raymbault was well versed in the Algonquin customs and language, and Father Jogues was an adept in the Huron tongue.

and Jogues were selected. After a voyage of seventeen days, they reached the falls, where they addressed an assembly of two thousand souls. The Chippewas earnestly pressed the missionaries to remain among them; but, owing to the scarcity of priests, the establishment of a permanent mission at that time, was impracticable. On this occasion, the Jesuits heard of the far-famed Sioux [*soo*], who dwelt eighteen days further west, warlike tribes with fixed abodes, cultivators of maize and tobacco, and of an unknown race and language.

8. The Iroquois. [*e-ro-kwoi'*].—The present State of New York was, at that time, occupied by the Iroquois, the bravest, handsomest, most powerful, and most blood-thirsty of the Indian clans of North America. They were divided into five nations; the Senecas, Cayugas, [*ki'-oo-gas*], Onondagas [*on-on-dah'-gas*], Oneidas [*o-ni'-das*], and Mohawks. Of these, the Mohawks were the most cruel. The Five Nations were regarded by the other tribes with terror and distrust. When the French arrived, the Hurons and Iroquois were at deadly enmity; and the French proving friendly to the former, became for a long time the objects of the hostility of the latter.

9. Father Jogues in New York.—One year after his return from Michigan (1642), Father Jogues was taken captive by a band of roving Mohawks, and carried by them to their castles in New York. With him were also captured his companion, the gentle René Goupil, and about forty Christian Hurons. Father Jogues was now subjected to all the horrors of Indian cruelty. He was wounded, bruised, and burned. His nails were torn out, his hands and feet dislocated and mutilated, his left thumb hacked off; but, as if by a miracle, his life was spared. During his long captivity of fifteen months, however, he was enabled to effect many baptisms and hear many confessions, chiefly among the prisoners of the Indians, sometimes even amid the flames which surrounded them.*

10. Alluding to the captivity of Father Jogues, Bancroft writes: "*Roaming through the stately forests of the Mohawk*

FATHER JOGUES.

Valley, he wrote the name of Jesus on the bark of the trees, graved the cross, and entered into possession of these countries

---

* On one occasion, being anxious to bestow baptism upon a convert who desired it, Father Jogues was unable to obtain water. Just at that moment, a passing Indian flung at his feet an ear of Indian corn, upon which the morning dew still glistened in large drops. Gathering the precious element in his hands, he baptized the Huron upon the spot.

On another occasion, he was compelled to witness a human sacrifice in honor of the heathen gods. A woman was the victim. The savages formed a line around the stake, and each one did his share in cutting, burning, or otherwise torturing the unhappy creature. But behold the benign Providence of God! Father Jogues had previously instructed her in the Faith. Now, availing himself of an opportunity, he pressed forward, and even amid the very flames of the heathen sacrifice, poured the waters of regeneration upon her head.

Thus were the Sacraments first administered in the State of New York!

in the name of God, often lifting up his voice in a solitary chant. Thus did France bring its banner and its Faith to the confines of Albany."

11. At length, in the summer of 1643, he was humanely ransomed by the Dutch governor at Albany, and by him sent to New

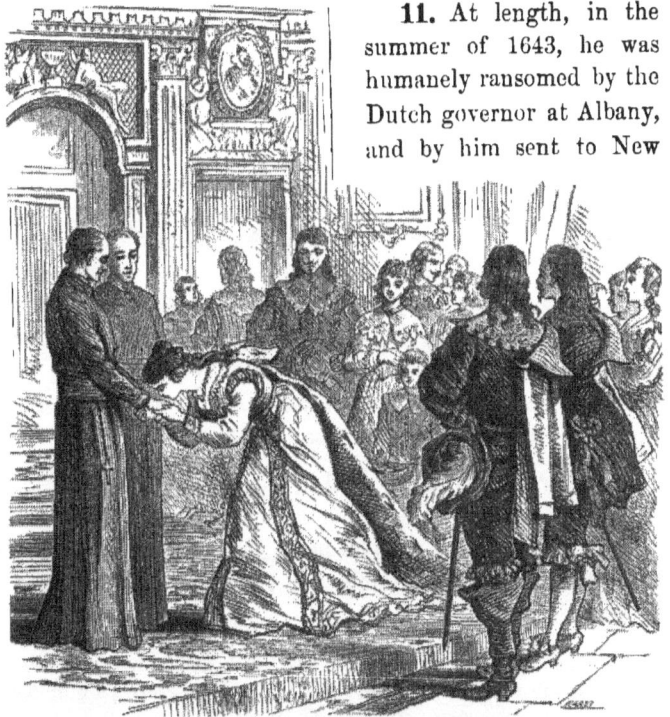

ANNE OF AUSTRIA KISSING FATHER JOGUES' HANDS.—(See note p. 98.)

York, then New Amsterdam.* Here he was treated with the utmost kindness by Governor Kieft, who provided him with suitable clothing, and, soon after, secured his pas-

* The present monster city then consisted of a little fort garrisoned by sixty men, a governor's house, a church, and about four or five hundred dwellings scattered over the island. Father Jogues' description of the New Netherlands, was presented to the University of New York, by the Rev. Father Martin, Superior of the Jesuits in Canada.

sage to France.* His heart, however, was with the Indians; and in the spring of 1645, he returned to Canada. Having projected a mission among the dreaded Iroquois, he once more entered the State of New York, and near Caughnawaga, the scene of his former sufferings, he gained what he had long coveted, a martyr's crown (1646).

12. Other Missionaries.—The same year, Father Druillettes [*drwee-yet*] made the long and painful journey from the St. Lawrence to the sources of the Kennebec, to commence his labors among the Abnakis of Maine. In February, 1646, Father de Noué [*noo-ay*], after years of zealous toil, was frozen to death amid the snows of Canada. They found him kneeling upright, his crucifix clasped to his breast, and his calm eyes open and fixed on Heaven. Two years later, Father Daniel, surrounded by his Huron converts, and clad in his vestments, was killed at the foot of the altar, amid the horrors of an Iroquois massacre.

13. Brebœuf and Lalemant.—In the spring of 1649, the renowned Father Brébœuf and the gentle Lalemant received the crown of martyrdom at the hands of the same fierce tribe. Their sufferings are thus described by John Gilmary Shea:

"The hands of Brebœuf were cut off; while Lalemant's flesh quivered with the awls and pointed irons thrust into every part of his body."

---

* After a series of trials and disasters, he reached a college of his order at Rennes. As soon as it was known that he came from Canada, the Fathers pressed around him to ask if he brought any tidings of Father Jogues. When he disclosed his name and showed the marks of his sufferings, great was the joy and gratitude throughout the community.

Everywhere the missionary was received with honor; princes and nobles vied in showing him courtesy; the Queen-mother, the stately Anne of Austria, felt privileged on being allowed to kiss his deformed and mangled hands; and the reigning Pontiff, Urban VIII, granted him a special dispensation to offer the Holy Sacrifice, saying: "*It were unjust that a martyr of Jesus Christ should not drink the blood of Jesus Christ!*"

MARTYRS IN THE NEW WORLD.

"Amid the din rose the voice of the old Huron missionary consoling his converts, denouncing God's judgments on the unbeliever, till his executioners crushed his mouth with a stone, cut off his nose and lips, and thrust a brand into his mouth, so that his throat and tongue, burnt and swollen, refused their office."

"They tore off his scalp, and thrice, in derision of baptism, poured the water over his head, amid the loud shout of the unbelievers. The eye of the martyr was now dim, and the torturers, unable from first to last, to wring from his lips one sigh of pain, were eager to close the scene. Hacking off his feet, they clove open his chest, took out his noble heart and devoured it."

"Thus, after three hours of frightful torture, expired Father John de Brebœuf, a man such as the Catholic Church alone could produce."

14. "Gabriel Lalemant had cast himself at the feet of Brebœuf to kiss his glorious wounds; but he had been torn away, and after being wrapped in pieces of bark, left for a time. When his superior had expired, they applied fire to this covering; as the flame curled around him, Father Lalemant, whose delicate frame, unused to toil, could not resist the pain, raised his hands on high and invoked the aid of Heaven. Gratified by this expression of pain, his tormentors resolved to prolong his agony; and through the long night added torture to torture to see the writhing frame, the quivering flesh of the young priest."

"He, too, saw his flesh devoured before his eyes, or slashed off in wanton cruelty. Every inch of his body, from head to foot, was charred and burnt; his very eyes were put out by the hot coals forced into them. At last, when the sun had risen, on the 17th of March, 1649, they closed his long martyrdom by tomahawking him, and left his body a black and mangled mass."

15. The Roll of Martyrdom (Continued).—In December of the same year (1649), Father Garnier, pierced by three Iroquois musket-balls, dragged himself along the blood-stained ground to minister to an expiring Christian Indian. As he gave the last absolution, an Iroquois tomahawk clove his skull. The next day (Dec. 8th), Father

MISSIONARIES AT THE NORTH.   101

Chabanel received his death-blow from the axe of an apostate Huron.*

16. Thus closed the crimson record of the first half of the seventeenth century, in the north. Meanwhile, the news from the American missions had excited the greatest zeal and enthusiasm in Europe. Young men left camp and court to enter the Jesuit order, in hopes of sharing the toil and merit of the missionaries. Among these, was the young Marquis de Gamache [*gam-ash*], who also gave his ample fortune to endow the first college at Quebec.† The hospital nuns and the Ursulines left home and country, to minister to the spiritual wants of the Indians.

17. The advent of these ladies is thus described by Bancroft: "As the youthful heroines stepped on shore at Quebec, they stooped to kiss the earth which they adopted as their country, and were ready, in case of need, to tinge with their blood. The governor, with the little garrison, received them at the water's edge; Hurons and Algonquins, joining in the shouts, filled the air with yells of joy; and the motley group escorted the new-comers to the church, where, amidst a general thanksgiving, the *Te Deum* was chanted. Is it wonderful that the natives were touched by a benevolence which their poverty and squalid misery could not appall? Their education was also attempted; and the venerable ash-tree still lives, beneath which Mary of the Incarnation, so famed for chastened piety, genius, and good judgment, toiled, though in vain, for the culture of the Huron children."

* Some of the Fathers who labored on the American mission during the first half of the 17th century, were afterwards dispersed. One, Father Grelon, was sent to China. Years after, when traveling through the plains of Tartary, he met a Huron woman whom he had known in the wilds of America. She had been sold from tribe to tribe and had finally reached the interior of Asia. This fact led to the discovery of the near approach of America to Asia.

† The foundations of this, the oldest university north of Mexico, were laid in 1635, shortly before the death of Champlain.

STUDY NO. 7.

MISSIONARIES AT THE NORTH—Continued.

EXPLORATIONS IN THE NORTH-WEST.—THE MISSISSIPPI EXPLORED.

1. Peace with the Iroquois.—On the death of Father Jogues, the war broke out anew. The fierce Iroquois desolated the lands of the Hurons, drove the northern Algonquins from the shores of the lakes, and slew the French and their allies, under the very walls of Quebec. At length, weary of the war-path, they themselves sued for peace. The Onondagas were the first to ask for missionaries, and to them was sent (1655) Father Le Moyne, an old and tried veteran in the field. The blood of Father Jogues was about to be avenged.

2. Salt Springs of New York discovered.—At a small fishing village near the mouth of the Oswego, Father Le Moyne began his mission; thence he proceeded to Onondaga;[20] and it was on this occasion he discovered New York's apparently inexhaustible salt-springs.* He was soon followed by Fathers Dablon and Chaumonot † [*sho-mo-no*], and in November, 1655, was commenced the first chapel in the present State of New York. "*By the zeal of the natives,*" says Bancroft, "*it was finished in a day; and there, in the heart of New York, the solemn services of the Roman Church were chanted as securely as in any part of Christendom.*"

---

* These springs are situated chiefly in and around Syracuse in Onondago County, which annually yield from 4,000,000 to 5,000,000 bushels of table-salt.

† About this time, the Onondagas were to meet the Eries in battle. The former, inspired by a converted Indian chief, vowed, like Clovis of old, that if the God of the Christians would grant them victory, henceforth they would serve Him alone. The Onondagas were victorious; and, though all did not prove true to their vow, still a goodly number remained faithful, and thus formed a nucleus of converts.

MISSIONARIES AT THE NORTH. 103

3. Garacontie [*gar-a-kon-tee-ay*]. — The success of this mission excited the anger of the pagan Iroquois, and

BAPTISM OF GARACONTIE.

after three years of flourishing existence, it came to a temporary end. War was renewed; but, through the influence of Garacontie, a wise and eloquent chief, the greatest Iroquois of his time, peace was restored in 1660. Garacontie, though not as yet a Christian, had listened with attention to the instructions of the missionaries; grace touched his heart, and he at length resolved to embrace the Faith. He was accordingly baptized with great solemnity in the Cathedral at Quebec (1669). After this, he always remained faithful to his religion, and continued the warm friend of the French and the protector of the missions.

4. Jesuits in the North-West.—In 1656, a projected mission to Michigan was frustrated through the cruelty of some pagan Iroquois. Thither, however, in 1660, at the entreaty of the Algonquins, was sent Father Menard, a survivor of the Huron mission and the companion of Jogues and Brebœuf. His hair was white with age, and his face scarred with the wounds he had received at Cayuga; for he, too, had been in Central New York. Having established a mission station one hundred leagues west of Sault St. Mary (probably at Keweenaw[12]), he lost his life in an attempt to reach the Indians dwelling on, or near, the Noquet Islands in Green Bay[9] (1661).

5. Four years later, Father Allouez [*al-way*], undismayed by the fate of Father Menard, penetrated into the west, and founded a mission at the further extremity of Lake Superior. Here he met the sun-worshipping Pottowattomie, the Sac and Fox, the gentle Illinois, and the proud Dacota warriors.* Having resided for two years chiefly on the southern margin of Lake Superior, and connected his name imperishably with the progress of discovery in the west, Allouez was joined by Fathers Marquette [*mar-ket*] and Dablon, and together they founded (1668) the mission of St. Mary, the oldest European settlement within the present limits of Michigan. For suc-

* On one of his journeys, he met the Sioux (*soo*), and from them he again heard of *the great river*. In writing of it, he called it *the Mesipi*.

ceeding years, "the illustrious triumvirate," Marquette, Allouez, and Dablon, were employed in evangelizing the vast regions that extend from Green Bay to the head of Lake Superior. Green Bay, (Wisconsin), was founded by Father Allouez, in 1669, and Mackinaw by Father Marquette, in 1671. One year later, their number was increased by the arrival of Fathers Druillettes and André.

6. Marquette's Exploration of the Mississippi.—Early in the summer of 1673, Marquette, having placed the expedition under the protection of the Blessed Virgin, with Joliet [*jo-lee-ay*], a French trader, and five other Frenchmen for his companions, set out on his voyage of discovery. Having embarked on the broad Wisconsin and glided down its current, amid vine-clad isles and by wooded shores, they, after seven days, reached the *Great River*, the "River of the Immaculate Conception," as Marquette called it.

7. Onward they floated, between the wide plains of Illinois and Iowa, until on the 25th of June, Marquette and Joliet disembarked for a time near the mouth of the Des Moines [*day-mwan*] River. They were thus the first white men who trod the soil of Iowa. Here dwelt the Illinois, a mild, dignified, and hospitable race whom Marquette had long desired to see. Their chief inferring the character of the missionary from his attire,* came forth to meet and welcome them. His greeting is beautifully given in Longfellow's "*Hiawatha*":

> "From the farthest realms of morning
> Came the Black-Robe chief, the Prophet,
> He, the Priest of Prayer, the Pale-face,
> With his guides and his companions.

* The name and fame of the French Black-gown, who taught concerning the Great Spirit, had gone abroad, and were now known to distant tribes who had never seen a white man.

Then the joyous Hiawatha
Cried aloud and spake in this wise:
'Beautiful is the sun, O strangers,
When you come so far to see us!
All our town in peace awaits you,
All our doors stand open for you;
You shall enter all our wigwams,
For the heart's right hand we give you.'"

MARQUETTE PARTING WITH THE ILLINOIS.

With these friendly red-men, Marquette lingered six days to preach the gospel. They besought him to remain longer, but as this he could not then do, they furnished him with provisions for his journey, and a *calumet* * for his defence.

* The *Calumet* is a large Indian pipe for smoking tobacco. It is also the emblem of peace. Its bowl is usually of soft red stone, and the tube a reed ornamented with feathers. To accept the calumet was to agree to terms of peace, and to refuse it was to reject them. The calumet of peace was used to seal or ratify contracts and alliances, to receive strangers kindly, and to travel with safety. Indian legend represented it as the gift of the Great Spirit.

He, on his part, promised, if his life were spared, to return and found a mission among them.

8. Marquette in Arkansas.—Having re-embarked, the voyagers went onward, past the perpendicular rocks, the mouth of the swift Missouri, and the primeval forest which then crowned the site of St. Louis; past the Kaskaskia and the Ohio, the St. Francis and the Arkansas rivers, until they reached a land "where the inhabitants never see snow, and never know winter save by the rain which falls oftener than in summer." They were in Arkansas. Having disembarked for a time, and learned all that he wished to know, namely, that the Mississippi has its mouth in the Gulf of Mexico, Marquette turned the prow of his canoe, and began to ascend the river (July 17th).

CALUMET.

9. Marquette's Return.—On his way home, Marquette again stopped to preach the Faith to the Illinois and Peorias. At length, after a voyage, on foot or in a birch canoe, of *two thousand seven hundred and sixty-seven* miles, he reached his mission at Green Bay (September, 1673). The results of this expedition were to affect the destinies of nations; the triumph of the age was complete; the whole valley of the Mississippi, the richest, most fertile, and accessible territory of the New World was thrown open to France. Joliet proceeded to Canada to convey the news; but the humble and saintly Marquette remained at his mission, to recruit his shattered health and renew his labors among the Indians.

10. In the fall of 1674, the eagerly desired orders reached him to go to the Illinois. Though still feeble, he joyfully departed, and, after much suffering, arrived at the Indian town of Kaskaskia. Here he was received as an angel from Heaven. For several days, he went from wigwam to wigwam, instructing and exhorting; and, at length on Thursday of Holy Week, he spoke to all in public.* His auditors listened with breathless attention† to the pale and wasted missionary, whose heart was burning to make them know and love Jesus Christ. The seed fell on good ground ; the Mission of the Immaculate Conception was founded; Marquette's work was done.

11. Feeling that his days were numbered, and hoping to reach the Jesuit station at Mackinaw, he once more bent his course northward ; but on the borders of a small stream that flows into Lake Michigan, he was obliged to pause. His companions laid him upon the shore, and stretched some birch bark upon poles above him. Here, like St. Francis Xavier, his beloved mission-model, he breathed his last, thanking God for the privilege of dying in the wilderness, a missionary of Jesus, and alone. His remains were carried to the Isle of Mackinaw.[15]

> "And when fierce storms the lake provoke,
> And angry waves dash high,
> The boatmen still his aid invoke,
> As of a spirit nigh."

12. **La Salle's Voyage.**—The next great explorer of the Mississippi was La Salle, a French fur-trader, at the time of Marquette's discovery Governor of Kingston (Canada). Filled with great projects of exploration and colonization, he underwent many disappointments and hardships in endeavoring to carry out his plans. Having previously navigated

---

* On this occasion, he addressed five hundred chiefs and seniors, who formed the first circle ; fifteen hundred young warriors who gathered behind them ; lastly, the women and children who formed the outer ring. (See p. 91.)

† Father Marquette had a remarkable talent for languages. He spoke with fluency, at least six Indian dialects.

MISSIONARIES AT THE NORTH. 109

Lakes Erie, St. Clair, Huron, and Michigan, he in 1682, found himself launched on the Mississippi. With him, were several Franciscan priests, twenty-three Frenchmen, and eighteen Indians.

13. Having sailed southward, for more than two weeks, he encamped, for a time, near the Chickasaw bluffs, and visited some of the Arkansas villages, where the Franciscans endeavored to make known the true God. Resuming his voyage, he passed the sites, now historic, of Vicksburg and Grand Gulf, and kept on until the river divided. He, with his party, then explored the three channels; and, at last, "*the great Gulf opened on his sight, tossing its restless billows, limitless, voiceless, lonely, as when born of chaos, without a sail, without sign of life.*"

LA SALLE AT THE GULF OF MEXICO.

14. La Salle and his companions now chanted the Te Deum, and planted a cross; then, in the name of the king of France, amid a volley of musketry, they took possession of the whole country. In the royal honor, it was called Louisiana.* On his way north, La Salle commenced Fort St. Louis, at *Starved Rock*,⁸⁷ on the Illinois. In November 1683, he reached Quebec. Later (1685), he attempted a settlement on Matagorda Bay in Texas, where he built another Fort St. Louis. He was killed (March 19, 1687) near a southern branch of the Trinity, (Texas), by one of his own unworthy followers. Although La Salle was not a priest, and possessed not the disinterested and self-denying devotion of the Jesuit missionary, still he was a sincere Catholic, and as such, undertook nothing without fortifying himself by religion.

"He stands," writes McGee, "sword in hand, under the banner of the cross, the tutelary genius of those great states which stretch away from Lake Ontario to the Rio Grande. Every league of that region he trod on foot, and every league of its waters, he navigated in frail canoes or crazy schooners. Above his tomb, the northern pine should tower; around it, the Michigan rose and the southern myrtle should mingle their hues and unite their perfumes."

15. The Cross in the West.—The Illinois missions inaugurated by Marquette, were continued by Fathers Allouez, Rasle, and others. In 1683, the modern Kaskaskia was founded by Father Gravier. Mary, the daughter of the chief of the Kaskaskias, became a fervent Christian, and her influence aided much in the conversion of the tribe. Here Gravier remained until 1699.

Other missions in the Mississippi Valley followed, and before the close of the 17th century, Catholicity had made the circuit of the country, from Maine to Florida, from Michigan and Wisconsin to Louisiana and Texas.

---

* The Louisiana of La Salle stretched from the Alleghanies to the Rocky Mountains; from the Rio Grande and the Gulf, to the furthest sources of the Missouri.

STUDY NO. 8.

NEW YORK.

1. Henry Hudson.—The harbor of New York was first visited by Verrazani in 1524. After that, history records no voyage of white man over its waters, until 1609. In the autumn of that year, Henry Hudson, an Englishman, in the service of Holland, while on a cruise in search of a northwest passage, penetrated *the Narrows*,¹⁹ crossed the Bay, and sailed up the beautiful stream which now bears his name.

HENRY HUDSON.

A few months earlier, Champlain, on an expedition into the Iroquois country, had entered the State from the north, and had discovered Lake Champlain.⁵

2. Ten days were spent by Hudson in exploring the river. When his little bark, "*the Half Moon*," had sailed some miles beyond the site of the present city of Hudson, the water became shallow, and he sent a boat as far as Albany. Then he retraced his course to the Bay; and on the 4th of October, about the time of Smith's return to England, he also set sail for Europe. Hudson never again beheld that beautiful river;

SEAL OF NEW YORK.

HALF MOON ASCENDING THE HUDSON.

but legends of the daring sailor still linger among the old Dutch families, and when thunder booms over the Palisades, they say: "*Hendrick Hudson and his crew are playing ninepins now!*"

Staten Island was so named by Hudson, in honor of the Dutch government, *Staaten* being Dutch for *States*.

3. **The Dutch in New York.**—On account of these discoveries, Holland laid claim to the shores of the Hudson, and called the whole territory New Netherlands. Soon after, (1614), a Dutch trading post was established on the southern extremity of Manhattan Island, and another on Castle Island, near Albany. In 1623, the Dutch East India Company sent out a number of colonists, who commenced

the first regular settlement, called New Amsterdam, on Manhattan Island.

4. The Patroons.—To encourage emigration, the company offered to grant lands and extraordinary privileges to any of its members who, within four years, would plant a colony of fifty adults in any part of New Netherland outside of Manhattan Island. Such proprietors were called *Patroons* (*patrons*), and they governed their respective domains like feudal lords.

The lands of each colony were limited to sixteen miles along one shore of a navigable stream, or to eight miles if they occupied both shores. One of these large manorial estates (the Van Rensselaer Manor on the Hudson) existed, with some of its privileges, until late in the present century. The famous anti-rent difficulties grew out of such titles. (p. 288.)

5. Dutch Governors.—Between the years 1626 and 1664, the New Netherland was ruled successively by four Dutch governors. The first, Peter Minuit [*min′u-it*], purchased Manhattan Island from the Indians for the sum of $25. Owing to troubles between the Company and the *Patroons*, Minuit was recalled in 1633. He thereupon offered his services to the Swedes, and soon after (1637) established a colony of that nation on the banks of the Delaware. The second governor, Wouter Van Twiller, was chiefly noted for his inactivity and incapacity. Of him, Irving, in his History of New York, has given a spirited caricature. His administration lasted four years, and the colony flourished in spite of him.* The third governor, Sir William Kieft [*keeft*], on account of his hot temper surnamed *William the Testy*, was noted for his cruelty to the Indians and the severity of his rule. His kindness to Fathers Jogues

* Of Van Twiller there is a slight memorial in the present Nutten Island, in New York Bay, which he purchased, and which is known as "*Governor's Island*."

(p. 100) and Bressani throws a pleasing gleam of light on an otherwise repulsive character. His unpopularity* at length led to the appointment of Peter Stuyvesant [sti've-sant], often called *Hard Koppig Piet,* or *Headstrong Peter,* the last and best of the Dutch governors.

GOVERNOR STUYVESANT.

6. Peter Stuyvesant. —The Dutch had had various troubles with the Puritans of Connecticut, the Swedes on the Delaware, and the neighboring Indians. All these difficulties, however, were overcome during the administration of Stuyvesant, who was decidedly an able and strong-minded man. Unfortunately, however, he was inclined to be despotic. Though brave and honest, he hated democratic institutions, and refused to yield to the spirit of liberty which began to prevail among the people. He even threatened to make "*a foot shorter*" any one who appealed from his decisions.

7. Surrender of New Amsterdam to the English.—Accordingly, when in 1664, a hostile English fleet appeared before New Amsterdam, the inhabitants were but too ready to surrender. Stuyvesant stamped about on

---

* The vessel on which Kieft returned to Europe was laden with ill-gotten wealth. It was wrecked on the coast of Wales, and there the governor and his treasure perished.

his wooden leg, and tore into pieces the letter of the English commodore demanding submission; but the people made him put it together again, and accept the terms offered. From that time forth, with the exception of a brief interval, the colony remained in possession of the English. The name of the whole territory, as well as that of the town on Manhattan Island, was changed to New York, in honor of the Duke of York, afterwards James II. To him, the region from the Connecticut to the Delaware had been granted by the king.

The Duke of York being also Duke of Albany, the latter name was given to Fort Orange.

8. English Governors.—Nicolls, the first English governor, ruled wisely; Lovelace, the second, with mildness. In 1674, however, Major Edmund Andros, who subsequently became noted as the oppressor of New England, was made governor. He ruled eight years, during which period he justly acquired the title of "*tyrant.*" He was at length recalled, and in his stead came Thomas Dongan, an Irishman and Roman Catholic.* Dongan called together (1683) the first legislative assembly of the State, one of the first acts of which was to proclaim *liberty of conscience.* † In 1686, Dongan still further signalized himself by granting the famous *Dongan Charter,* which to this day, forms the basis of the

* Governor Dongan had his private chapel, in which he and his household, as well as all the Catholics of the province could attend mass. The chaplain was a Jesuit Father who had accompanied him from England.

† The first General Assembly of the Province of New York was composed of seventeen representatives. It sat thirteen weeks, and passed fourteen acts, all of which were assented to by the Governor and his Council. The first of these was entitled, "*The Charter of Liberties and Privileges, granted by his Royal Highness, to the inhabitants of New York and its dependencies.*" It declared that supreme legislative power should forever be and reside in the Governor, Council, and people, met in General Assembly; that every freeholder and freeman should be allowed to vote for representatives without restraint; that no freeman should suffer but by judgment of his peers; that all trials should be by a jury of twelve men; that no person professing faith in God, through Jesus Christ, should at any time be in any way molested or disquieted for any difference of opinion.

laws, rights, and privileges of New York city. Dongan was a man of marked ability, great prudence, and tireless energy. By his vigorous prosecution of various measures, he incurred the displeasure of James II, by whom in 1688, he was removed from office.

9. Missions in New York.—After the peace brought about by Garacontié, the missions among the Iroquois were renewed, and by the year 1668 the cross towered over every Indian village from the Hudson to Lake Erie. The savage Iroquois had become as gentle as a child; and Caughnawaga (*kaw-na-wa'ga*), on the Mohawk, the scene of the death of Father Jogues, and now the chief mission-centre, had its schools and its church. Here too lived Catharine Tegahkwita (*te-gak-we'tah*), surnamed "*the Lily of the Mohawks,*" an Indian maiden distinguished for sanctity.

10. Catholicity Proscribed.—The English Revolution of 1688, which hurled James II from his throne, was not unfelt in the colonies. The New York Assembly of 1691 declared null and void the acts of the Assembly of 1683, and Catholicity was proscribed. Many Catholic Iroquois then emigrated to Canada,* where, at this day, several

* "Although the field was laid waste, the fruit had been gathered. In thirty-five years from the capture of Father Jogues, *two thousand two hundred and twenty-five Iroquois* were baptized,—many children, but many noble women and the choice of the sachems and orators; *Garacontié*, '*the Advancing Sun*,' the grandest statesman of the Five Nations, the bulwark of Christianity for a quarter of a century; *Kryn*, the high chief of the Mohawks, who, when his tribe would not listen to his pleadings, raised his wild war-cry for the last time in the streets of the village, gathered forty devoted followers, and, kneeling down amid the graves of their fathers, poured forth a prayer for his nation, then rose, and with streaming eyes led his braves away forever from the fires of their people to the Christian settlement at La Prairie; *Catherine Ganeakten*, the Erie by birth, the Oneida by adoption, the foundress of La Prairie, on the banks of the St. Lawrence; *Mary Tsawenté*, '*the Precious*,' the saint of the Onondagas; *Stephen te Gannonahoa*, who suffered purely for the faith, and was cut to pieces almost with knives before they threw him into the fire; *Ourehouharé*, the war chief of the Cayugas, who, when listening on his death-bed to the story of the Passion, cried out, like Clovis, '*Oh, had I been there, they never would so have treated my God!*' These, and many another like them, form the crown of the Iroquois missionary in Heaven. But, brightest and sweetest flower in the Indian coronal of Mary, was *Catharine Tegahkouita*, '*the saint of the Iroquois.*'"—MACLEOD.

Iroquois villages exist, preserving at once their nationality and their faith.

11. When the news of William and Mary's accession reached New York, there was a popular uprising, headed by a German citizen named Leisler (*lice'ler*). The people seized the fort, and Leisler put himself at the head of the colony,— "for the preservation of the Protestant religion," (1689). The next year, Colonel Sloughter (*slaw'ter*) was appointed governor. Leisler was tried and executed for high treason. The accession of William of Orange to the English throne led to a war between England and France, in which the colonies, especially New York, were involved. (See *King William's War*, p. 133.) From this time until the Revolution, New York remained a Royal Province, ruled by King's governors.*

12. New Jersey.—When New Netherland passed into the hands of the Duke of York, he sold the portion between the Hudson and the Delaware, to Lord Berkely and Sir George Carteret. This tract took the name of Jersey, in honor of Carteret, who had been governor of the island of Jersey in the British Channel. The first settlement, a cluster of four houses, was called Elizabethtown,³ after his wife. In 1674, Lord Berkely sold his share of West Jersey to a company of *Friends or Quakers*. Of this purchase, the celebrated William Penn was made manager.

SEAL OF NEW JERSEY.

---

* Towards the close of the seventeenth century, British commerce suffered greatly from the swarms of pirates that infested the Atlantic Ocean. At length, Captain William Kidd, a New York shipmaster, was appointed to go in search of them. He, however, turned pirate himself, and became the most noted of them all, his very name becoming a terror on the seas. Having returned from a guilty cruise, he was captured in Boston, taken to England, tried and executed.

Eight years afterwards, Carteret also sold his portion of East Jersey to Penn and a number of partners. In 1702, the two Jerseys were united into one *royal province*, under the name of New Jersey.

13. Manners.—The Dutch of New York were thrifty, tidy, honest, and hospitable. Their dress,* furniture, and equipage were extremely simple. Carpets were hardly known before 1750, and each housekeeper prided herself on the purity of her white sanded floor. While the Connecticut matron spun, wove, and stored her household linen in crowded chests, the Dutch dame scrubbed and scoured her polished floor and woodwork. The family breakfasted at dawn, dined at eleven, and retired at sunset. A fashionable tea-party of those days has been inimitably described by Irving.

14. The houses were of wood, with gable-ends built of small black and yellow bricks brought over from Holland. Each house had many doors and windows, and was often surmounted by a weathercock. Many of the citizens had also their country houses, called "*boweries*," with large porches or stoops, on which the men loved to sit and smoke their pipes. Clocks and watches were unknown, and the time was told by hour-glasses and sun-dials.

15. That exceptional class, *the patroons*, occupied a position not unlike an English baron with feudal retainers. Their social customs were simply those of the best European society of the day. They lived in a

---

* The women wore close white muslin caps, beneath which their hair was put back with pomatum. Their gayly-striped linsey-woolsey petticoats reaching to the ankle, exposed to view blue, red, or green stockings of their own knitting. From each one's girdle depended a huge patch-work pocket, a pincushion and pair of scissors. The men wore broad-skirted coats of linsey-woolsey, with large buttons of brass or silver; several pairs of knee-breeches, one over another, long stockings, with great buckles at the knees and on the shoes. Their hair was worn long, and put up in an eel-skin cue.

princely way on their large estates, which passed from father to son for more than a century. When the Revolution broke out, many of them sided with the king; thus their lands became confiscated, and their names ceased to exist in the ruling offices of the country.

DUTCH MANSION.

16. Religion.—By the charter of 1640, Protestantism was proclaimed the religion of the colony; but we do not read of any cases of persecution during the Dutch rule. During Governor Dongan's administration, a Catholic college was opened in New York city; and between the years 1683 and 1690, three priests were stationed there. By the New York Assembly of 1691, Catholicity was proscribed.

STUDY NO. 9.

MARYLAND.

1. Lord Baltimore.—Maryland was settled by persecuted English Roman Catholics. Lord Baltimore (*George Calvert*) had obtained from Charles I. the promise of a grant of territory in the New World, but he died before the document was executed. His eldest son, Cecil Calvert, the second Lord Baltimore, carried out his father's plans. On receiving the desired charter, he prepared to send out a colony. It was, at first, his intention to accompany the emigrants; but deeming it more to their interests that he should remain in England, he confided the colony to his brother, Leonard Calvert, whom he appointed governor.

LORD BALTIMORE.

2. The Ark and the Dove.—Early in the spring of 1634, two vessels, the Ark and the Dove, sailed up the

Potomac, and cast anchor near an island which they called *St. Clements*. On board, were about three hundred colonists, including four Jesuits (Fathers Altham and White, with two lay brothers). Having landed on the Festival of the Annun-

LANDING OF THE MARYLAND PILGRIMS.

ciation, Mass was celebrated for the first time in that wild region. A large cross was also erected as a symbol of Christianity, which had now taken possession of those shores. Two days later, the town of St. Mary's was founded, nearer the mouth of the river.

3. Progress of St. Mary's.—Unlike the Plymouth settlers, the Maryland pilgrims were not obliged to contend with inclemency of weather or scarcity of food. Around them, the country lay smiling in all the verdure of a Southern spring; and the Indians, won by the gentle and friendly manners of the strangers, readily gave them all the assistance in their power, even bestowing upon them half of an Indian village, with corn-fields already planted. The Indian women taught the wives of the English how to make bread of maize, and the savage warriors instructed the men where to find game. "Within six months," says Bancroft, "the colony had advanced more than Virginia had done in as many years."

4. Treatment of the Indians.—The Maryland colonists treated the Indians with the greatest kindness and charity. The missionaries, who were soon joined by others of their order, immediately commenced to labor among them, and the red men well responded to their zeal. Before long, Father White had the consolation of baptizing King Chilomacon, his family, and a part of his tribe (1640). This example was soon after followed by the young queen of the Potopacos and the principal braves of the tribe.

Soon after the arrival of the colonists, Governor Harvey of Virginia paid them a visit. He was received on board the *Ark* with great ceremony by Governor Calvert, who had prepared a grand banquet. Several chiefs were invited, and the Indian King of the Patuxents sat at table between the two governors. So delighted was this warrior with the kind treatment he received, that before departing for the Patuxent, he thus addressed the Indian braves present: "*I love the English so well, that if they were just about to kill me, and I had breath enough to speak, I would command that my death should not be avenged; for I know they would not do anything of the kind except through my own fault.*"

MARYLAND.

5. Religious Freedom.—The distinctive feature of this colony was *full toleration in religious matters*. Here the Catholic persecuted in England or the colonies, the Puritan expelled from Virginia, and the Quaker or the Baptist exiled from Massachusetts, found an asylum and a home. Peace and religion reigned alike in the wigwam of the Indian and the town of St. Mary. Maryland already well merited the title afterwards bestowed upon it, namely, "The Land of the Sanctuary." *

6. Clayborne.—About the time of Calvert's arrival, William Clayborne, an Englishman who had received a royal license to trade with the Indians in that part of the country, had located himself on Kent Island, in Chesapeake Bay. He and his adherents refused to submit to the authority of Lord Baltimore, and they prepared to resist by force of arms. Though defeated for the time, he continued to harass the settlers during a period of ten years, and he is not inappropriately styled "*the evil genius of the colony.*" During this insurrection, Father White and the other missionaries were ruthlessly seized and sent back to England in irons, to be prosecuted as "*Jesuits.*"

7. The Toleration Act and its Repeal.—In 1649 was passed the celebrated *Toleration Act*, which pro-

---

* "The happiness of the colony was enviable. The persecuted and the unhappy thronged to the domains of the benevolent prince. If Baltimore was, in one sense, a monarch—like Miltiades at Chersonesus, and other founders of colonies of old—his monarchy was tolerable to the exile who sought for freedom and repose. Numerous ships found employment in his harbors. The white laborer rose rapidly to the condition of a free proprietor; the female emigrant was sure to improve her condition, and the cheerful charities of home gathered round her in the New World. Affections expanded in the wilderness, where artificial amusements were unknown. The planter's whole heart was in his family; his pride in the children that bloomed around him, making the solitudes laugh with innocence and gayety."

"Emigrants arrived from every clime, and the colonial legislature extended its sympathies to many nations as well as to many sects. From France came Huguenots; from Germany, from Holland, from Sweden, from Finland, I believe from Piedmont, the children of misfortune sought protection under the tolerant sceptre of the Roman Catholic."—*Bancroft.*

vided that all Christian denominations should be protected in Maryland. Only five years later, the Protestants in the colony obtained control of the Legislature, and by an act of the Assembly, Catholics were declared not entitled to the protection of the laws of Maryland. Thus were the founders of the colony excluded from its rights and privileges, and treated with base ingratitude by those to whom, in an hour of need, they had extended a helping hand.

8. Civil War.—The result was a civil war (1655), in which the Catholics were defeated. Maryland continued in confusion and turmoil until 1661, when Lord Baltimore was restored to his rights as proprietor. After this, for about thirty years, peace and harmony reigned throughout the province.

9. On the dethronement of James II. (1689), religious bigotry broke out anew. The Protestants, under a wicked and designing man named Coode, seized the government and oppressed the Catholics. Two years later, the colony was made a *royal province;* and in 1699, the capital was removed from St. Mary's to Annapolis. Catholics did not recover their rights until the Revolution.

10. Manners.—Apart from religion, the manners and occupations of the Maryland colonists much resembled those of the Virginians. There were few large towns, and the people generally lived on plantations, and raised tobacco. Indian corn and the sweet potato were cultivated at an early period, and the waters of the Bay furnished much-prized delicacies, in the oyster and the canvas-back duck. There was no regular post,

SEAL OF MARYLAND.

letters being sent by private hand. Traveling was performed on horseback by land, and in canoes or other small boats by water. It was a delightful termination to a day of weary journeying, when the bridle was loosed before an inviting country home, and the gentlemanly host came forth to offer his courteous welcome. Free, generous, a prince in hospitality, the southern gentleman kept open house for all respectable strangers who might desire food or lodging.

11. On the low verandas and balconies, climbed in wild luxuriance, the yellow jasmine, sweet honeysuckle, or the trumpet flower; while the soft air was fragrant with the breath of scented shrubs, which sprang from the warm moist earth. Within the dwelling, the music of the harpsichord was oftener heard than the hum of the spinning-wheel, though the southern matron had, too, her own peculiar round of duties. Black slaves performed all the domestic labors; but the heart of the kind mistress was mindful of the wants of her large, and, in many respects, dependent household, in which she found sufficient employ.

12. A short distance from the family residence stood the kitchen, which, like the laundry, was always separate from the mansion. Conveniently retired might be found the negro quarters; a cluster of wooden cabins, each with its own little garden and poultry yard, and with numbers of black babies gamboling in the sunshine. The southern planter had, in his retinue of servants, artificers of all kinds: tailors, shoemakers, carpenters, smiths, and so on through all the needful trades of ordinary life.

13. Religion.—Under Catholic rule, all Christian religions were protected by law; but when Protestants rose to power, a spirit of intolerance unhappily prevailed.

STUDY NO. 10.

PENNSYLVANIA.—DELAWARE.

1. First Settlements. — The first settlement in Delaware was made by the Swedes, at New Sweden, near Wilmington (1638); in Pennsylvania, by people of the same nation, near Philadelphia. These settlements were subsequently conquered by the Dutch.

2. Pennsylvania Founded.—In 1681, the colony of Pennsylvania was founded by William Penn, an English Quaker, as an asylum for his persecuted English brethren. Penn had already become much interested in American colonization, through his connection with the Quakers in the Jerseys. The English government, moreover, at this time owed to his deceased father a large sum of money, and Penn agreed to take in payment thereof, a grant of territory in the New World. This tract lying west of the Delaware River, Penn named *Sylvania* (forest land), but the king insisted that it should be called PENNSYLVANIA. To this grant, the Duke of York afterwards added the territory included in the present State of Delaware. In the autumn of 1681, a large body of emigrants, chiefly Quakers, sailed from England for their new home. The next year Penn himself arrived.

SEAL OF PENNSYLVANIA.

PENNSYLVANIA. 127

3. Philadelphia.—Though on the conquest of New Sweden by the Dutch, such of the inhabitants as refused allegiance to Holland were sent back to Europe, many thrifty Swedes remained. From these, (1683), Penn purchased a tract of land extending from the high banks of the Delaware, fringed with pines, to those of the Schuylkill; and here, in the same year in which Father Gravier founded Kaskaskia, he laid out a city which he called *Philadelphia*, (*brotherly love*). Within a year, it contained one hundred houses; and in two years, it numbered one thousand inhabitants.

4. Penn's Treaty with the Indians.—Emulating

PENN'S TREATY TREE.

the example of Lord Baltimore, Penn treated the Indians with the greatest kindness and humanity. In consequence of this, Pennsylvania was long free from Indian warfare. Soon after his arrival, Penn met a number of the Indian Sachems (*say-hems*) under a wide-spreading elm near Philadelphia. With them, he entered into a treaty of friendship and alliance, which was ever afterwards sacredly kept. The savages, delighted with his gentle words and kindly bearing, exclaimed: "*We will live in love with William Penn and his children, as long as the sun and moon shall endure.*"

5. Penn's Return to England.—In 1684, Penn went back to England, leaving the settlers prosperous and happy. He remained absent fifteen years, during which time various dissensions arose in the colony. "*The three counties on the Delaware* becoming discontented, Penn gave them a deputy-governor and an assembly of their own. Delaware and Pennsylvania, however, remained under one government until the Revolution. After the accession of William and Mary (1689), Penn was thrice arrested on false charges of treason and conspiracy, growing out of his friendship for the deposed monarch, James II. Dishonest agents involved him in debt, and, on one occasion when he requested a moderate loan from the assembly of his colony, he was refused.

6. Penn's Last Years.—In 1699, Penn again came to the New World and granted to his colony a new charter. This gave the people much additional power. It remained in force until the Revolution. The colonists of Pennsylvania were unwilling to pay the rents by which Penn sought to reimburse himself for his heavy outlay. They, moreover, constantly sought to weaken the authority of the proprietor. Seeing this, Penn sorrowfully returned to his native land, where he died in want and obscurity (1718).

7. Mason and Dixon's Line.—Lord Baltimore's grant and Penn's covered, in part, the same ground; hence, the boundary line between Maryland and Pennsylvania was long disputed. The point was finally settled in 1767, when two surveyors, Charles Mason and Jeremiah Dixon, ran the line since famous as "*Mason and Dixon's.*" It was marked by placing at the end of every mile, a stone with the letter *P* and the arms of the Penns on the north, and the letter *M* with the escutcheon of Lord Baltimore on the south side.

Till a recent day, this line marked the boundary between the free and the slave States.

8. After Penn's death, his heirs became proprietors of the colony he had established. At the Revolution, the State of Pennsylvania purchased their claims for the sum of about half a million of dollars.

9. **Occupations and Manners.**—The early inhabitants of Pennsylvania were a thrifty and industrious people. They lived by farming, commerce, and ship-building. The great coal mines were not then discovered, but iron furnaces were early established. The houses were generally of brick or stone, and surrounded by gardens and orchards. Most of the English settlers preserved the simplicity of Quaker manners. Theatrical exhibitions were at first forbidden, and some other laws were made resembling those of the Puritans; but there was no religious persecution, and only one trial for witchcraft.

10. **Religion.**—Though William Penn granted religious toleration throughout his colony, still in maintaining it towards Catholics, he was bitterly opposed by his own people. In 1686, he mentions *an aged priest* among the inhabitants. The first chapel in which the Holy Sacrifice was offered, in 1686, was a wooden building on the northwest corner of Front and Walnut streets.

11. **Delaware.**—When New York passed into the hands of the Duke of York, Delaware formed a part of his possessions. For this reason he was able to grant the territory of Delaware to Pennsylvania.

SEAL OF DELAWARE.

STUDY NO. 11.

THE CAROLINAS.

1. First Permanent Settlements.—As early as 1562, the French had given the name of Carolina to the region south of Virginia; but they failed to colonize it permanently. About the middle of the seventeenth century, a party of persons who had been suffering in Virginia on account of their religion, migrated further south and commenced a settlement near Albemarle Sound. It was hence called "*The Albemarle Colony.*"

SEAL OF NORTH CAROLINA.

2. The Clarendon Colony.—Soon after, (1663), Charles II. gave to Lord Clarendon and others, a grant of all the land between Virginia and Florida. Two years later, a settlement was made near the mouth of the Cape Fear River, by a party of emigrants from Barbadoes (*bar-ba-doze*). This was called "*The Clarendon Colony.*"

3. The Carteret Colony.—In 1670, a third settlement called "*The Carteret Colony,*" was made at *Old Charleston*, on the south side of the Ashley River.[1] Ten years afterwards, these colonists removed to a

SEAL OF SOUTH CAROLINA.

THE CAROLINAS.   131

point of land between the Ashley and Cooper Rivers, and there laid the foundation of the present city of Charleston.⁶

4. The Grand Model.—The colonies suffered considerably from the Indians and from bad government. The English proprietors of Carolina engaged the philosopher Locke to draw up a plan of government for the province. He called it "*The Grand Model*," but it was entirely unsuited for America.* After a trial of some years it was abandoned.

THE TAX-GATHERER DRIVEN AWAY.

5. The attempt to enforce obedience to the new form of government, oppressive taxation, and the commercial restrictions imposed by the English navigation laws, produced general discontent. An agent of the government appeared

---

* According to the "*Grand Model*," all the vast territory embracing the present States of North and South Carolina, Georgia, Tennessee, Alabama, Mississippi, Louisiana, Arkansas, Florida, Missouri, and a large part of Texas and Mexico, was to be divided into counties, each containing four hundred and eighty thousand acres. Over each county there were to be a landgrave and two caciques or barons. They were to hold one-fifth of the land and the proprietors one-fifth, leaving the balance to the people. No one owning less than fifty acres could vote, while tenants were to be merely serfs, and slaves were to be at the absolute will of their masters.

who demanded a penny for every pound of tobacco sent to New England. The people resisted, the tax-gatherer was often rude, and frequent collisions were the result.

On one occasion, he attempted to drive away a steer in compensation for the unpaid tax on the tobacco of a planter, when the sturdy wife of the yeoman drove him off with a mop-stick.

6. John Archdale.—In 1695, John Archdale, a Quaker, became governor of the two Carolinas. Under his mild and wise administration, the colonies made considerable progress. He healed dissensions, established equitable laws, cultivated friendly relations with the Indians, and set the example of Christian toleration in religious matters.

7. With the Spaniards at St. Augustine, Archdale also maintained friendship. Four Indian converts of the Spanish missionaries having been taken prisoners by the Yemmasees and exposed for sale as slaves, were ransomed by Archdale and sent to the governor of St. Augustine. "*I shall endeavor to show reciprocal kindness,*" was the reply of the latter, "*and shall always observe a friendly correspondence with you.*" When, afterwards, an English ship was wrecked on the coast of Florida, the Spaniards joyfully returned the kind charity of Archdale.

8. Rice.—In 1694, the captain of a ship from Madagascar[16] gave to the governor a bag of seed rice, remarking that, in Eastern countries, it was much esteemed for food. Having been planted in different soils, it lived, thrived, and afterwards became an important staple.

9. Occupations.—In South Carolina the people lived on large isolated plantations, as in Virginia. In the north, the settlers dwelt still further apart, oftentimes in the woods, where there were no roads, and where they could only travel by paths *blazed* through the forest, by notches made here and there upon the trees. The general occupations in North Carolina were the cutting of timber, the making of tar and turpentine, hunting the bear and trapping the beaver.

STUDY NO. 12.

KING WILLIAM'S WAR (1689-1697).

1. Result of the Accession of William of Orange.—The accession of William of Orange to the English throne led to a war with France, where the exiled king, James II, had taken refuge. In this contest, the colonies became involved. William, as Prince of Orange, headed at that time, a Protestant league of several powers against Louis. England now joined the coalition and declared war against France. The latter nation, anxious to avoid the horrors of Indian warfare, offered neutrality in America; but this was rejected, and for the first time Canada was seen arrayed against the English colonists.

2. Massacre of Lachine.[13]—The Indians of Canada and Maine sided with the French. The English were aided by the *Five Nations* of New York. The latter, whom Dongan had already supported against the French, were now urged on by the Leisler (*lice-ler*) and Bayard parties into which the colony was divided (p. 117). Shortly after Leisler's usurpation, a party of 1500 pagan Iroquis fell at midnight (Aug. 4) upon the village of Lachine, on the island of Montreal, and in one hour inhumanly massacred two hundred of the inhabitants. They then approached the town of Montreal, took about two hundred prisoners, and at length made themselves masters of the island and the fort, of which they maintained possession until October.

3. Frontenac.—Just at this juncture, the celebrated Frontenac was a second time made governor of Canada.

From the French king, he had received instructions to invade New York and to punish the English for their constant aid to the Iroquois. He accordingly planned three expeditions; the first against Albany, the second to strike at the border settlements of New Hampshire, the third to attack those of Maine.

4. In the east, blood was first shed at Dover, N. H., (June 27). Here thirteen years before, three hundred unsuspecting Indians had been treacherously seized by Major Waldron and shipped for Boston, to be sold into foreign slavery (p. 82). The memory of this act had not faded away, and it was now to be avenged. The Penacook Indians of Maine took the town, massacred Waldron and twenty others, and returned to the wilderness with twenty-nine captives.

5. Massacre of Schenectady.[a]—At the dead of the night, one of the French and Indian parties sent out by Frontenac reached Schenectady, the farthest outpost of the colony of New York. The town was taken by surprise and sixty-three of its inhabitants massacred. The few who escaped fled half-clothed, through the blinding snow, to Albany.

Another French and Indian party destroyed Salmon Falls, N. H., and a third forced Casco (now Portland) to surrender.

6. Regret and Alarm of the English.—The English colonies, thoroughly alarmed, now bitterly regretted their rejection of the proffered neutrality, and began, with reason, to tremble for their own liberties. At a *Congress* held in New York (May 1st, 1690), it was determined to attempt the conquest of Canada, by attacking Quebec and Montreal.

7. Acadia Reduced.—A fleet was immediately sent out under Sir William Phipps, to conquer Acadia. Port Royal and other places were taken, and considerable booty obtained (May, 1690).

8. Attack on Quebec.—In October, 1690, the same Phipps proceeded up the St. Lawrence to attack Quebec. He had with him thirty-five vessels and about two thousand colonial militia.* Frontenac defended the place with indomitable courage and skill; and Phipps, after an unsuccessful siege of eight days, sailed down the river.

9. Late in November, Phipps reached Boston crestfallen and humiliated. One by one, the rest of his fleet came straggling after him, battered and weather-beaten. To celebrate Frontenac's success, a medal was struck at Paris; and in the lower town of Quebec, in memory of the event, a church was named, "*Our Lady of Victory.*"

10. Expedition against Montreal.—While Phipps was besieging Quebec, the English and Indian forces destined to attack Montreal were marching onward, by the borders of the Hudson and Lake Champlain; but on reaching the latter place, they paused. The officers quarreled, the Iroquois became discontented, small-pox broke out, provisions failed, and the expedition was at an end.

---

* When Frontenac received from a messenger the letter sent by Phipps, demanding, in the English king's name, a surrender of the city, he replied: "*Tell your general that I do not recognize King William; and that the Prince of Orange, who so styles himself, is a usurper, who has violated the most sacred laws of blood in attempting to dethrone his father-in-law. I know no king of England but King James. Your general ought not to be surprised at the hostilities which he says that the French have carried on in Massachusetts; for as the king, my master, has taken the king of England under his protection, and is about to replace him on his throne by force of arms, he might have expected that his Majesty would order me to make war on a people who have rebelled against their lawful prince.*"

The messenger, astonished and startled, asked if Frontenac would give his answer in writing. "*No,*" replied the governor, "*I will answer your general only by the mouths of my cannon, that he may learn that a man like me is not to be summoned after this fashion.*"

11. These two failures caused a cessation of hostilities, except in the east, where the French recovered Port Royal, and, by their Indian allies, kept the English frontier in a state of siege. The exhausted English colonies, repulsed from Canada, now attempted little more than a defence of their own borders.

12. In the summer of 1691, Major Schuyler, of Albany, with three hundred Mohawks, passed Lake Champlain, and at La Prairie[14] engaged eight hundred French troops. After a severe conflict, a number equal to that of his own forces being slain, he effected a safe retreat.

In January, 1692, a party of French and Indians burst upon the town of York, and gave its inhabitants no choice but captivity or death.

In England, the conquest of Canada was determined on, but the fleet destined to effect it, after a repulse at Martinique, reached Boston freighted with yellow fever, which destroyed two-thirds of the mariners and soldiers on board.*

13. Peace.—The peace of Ryswick (*riz'wik*),[23] 1697, put an end to the war.

14. Before the close of the 17th century, settlements had been made at Detroit, Michigan, by the French (1670); at Vincennes,[28] Indiana, by the French (1690); at Bexar, Texas, by the Spanish; and in Mississippi, by the French (1699).

---

* In March, 1697, Haverhill, Mass., was attacked. Mr. Dusten was at work in the field. Having hurried home, he brought out his seven children, and bidding them "run ahead," he slowly retreated, keeping the Indians back with his gun. His little flock thus reached a place of safety.

His wife, who was unable to escape with him, was dragged into captivity. After a weary march of one hundred and fifty miles, she and her Indian captors reached an island in the Merrimac. Here she resolved to escape. A white boy, who had previously been taken prisoner, found out from his master, at Mrs. Dusten's request, how to strike a blow that would produce instant death, and how to scalp. Having learned these facts, she in the night awoke the boy and her nurse, and arranged their parts. Having each taken a tomahawk, they struck vigorously and with wise division of labor. Soon ten Indians were killed; one squaw only escaped. Having scalped the bodies, in order to prove her story on reaching home, she hastened to the bank of the river, and in a bark canoe the three descended the Merrimac to the English settlements.

BIOGRAPHICAL SKETCHES

OF REMARKABLE PERSONAGES MENTIONED IN THE PRECEDING SECTION.

Allouez, Father Claude, (1620-1690), one of the earliest Jesuit missionaries and explorers of the northwestern part of our country, was a native of France. He reached America in 1658, spent some time at the Algonquin missions on the St. Lawrence, became a perfect master of that tongue, and gained some knowledge also of the Iroquois. At length, in 1665, he was sent to his long desired mission in the West, and in this field he labored until his death. For years "*The Illustrious Triumvirate,*" Allouez, Dablon, and Marquette, evangelized the vast regions that extend from Green Bay to the head of Lake Superior. In 1676, he was appointed to the Illinois mission begun by Marquette. The latest scene of his labor was among the Miamis, on the St. Joseph River. Here he died. Allouez's contributions to the Jesuit "*Rélations,*" are among the most valuable records of the ideas and manners of the Indians at that time.

Andros, Edmund, (1637-1713), an English colonial governor, born in London. He was brought up at court, his father being an officer of the royal household. In 1674, he became governor of the province of New York. After a rule of seven years, he was recalled to England, where he received the honor of knighthood. In 1686, he was made governor of New England; and in 1688, New York and New Jersey were added to his jurisdiction. He was notorious for tyranny, and his arbitrary conduct finally induced the people to take up arms against him. He was imprisoned and sent to England with a committee of accusers; but was acquitted without a formal trial. In 1692, he was made governor of Virginia, and after a rule of six years, was removed. He died in England.

Argall, Samuel, (1572-1639), an English adventurer, born in Bristol. He arrived at Virginia several years after its settlement, and his first public exploit was the kidnapping of Pocahontas, in 1612. During the administration of Governor Dale, (1613), he reduced and plundered Port Royal, N. S., and destroyed the French settlement of St. Saviour, on Mt. Desert, I. In 1617, he became deputy-governor of Virginia; but he demeaned himself so tyrannically that, in 1619, he was recalled. On the death of Lord Delaware, he took charge of his estate, and letters of Lady Delaware, still extant, accuse him of the most flagrant peculation. Argall was a man of ability, but was also unscrupulous and grasping.

Bacon, Nathaniel, (1630–1677), an eloquent and talented young lawyer, celebrated as the leader of Bacon's Rebellion, in Virginia, was born in England. He emigrated to the New World in 1675, and soon became very popular among the Virginians.

In 1676, the Indians having invaded the frontier of Virginia, and no efficient measures having been provided for the relief of the colony, Bacon assumed the command of the people. Though condemned as a rebel by Governor Berkely, his bravery restored quiet and confidence to the colonists. Having put an end to the Indian war, he was about to besiege Governor Berkely, when death closed his career.

Baltimore, Lord, (*Sir George Calvert*), (1582–1632), the founder and lawgiver of Maryland, was born in Yorkshire. Having graduated at Oxford, he was sent abroad to travel, and on his return was knighted. Soon after, he was made one of the principal secretaries of state. Although brought up in the English Church, the cruel persecution then waged against Catholics, touched his heart, and induced him to make a profound examination into the old Faith. The result was that, in 1624, he resigned his position as secretary and entered the Church. "*I am now a Roman Catholic,*" said he, "*and would be obliged either to violate my conscience in the discharge of that office, or be wanting to my trust.*" James I, nevertheless, retained him in the privy council, and made him Baron of Baltimore, in the Irish peerage. Calvert's great desire now was to found in the New World, a colony for his persecuted brethren in the Faith. After an unsuccessful attempt at a settlement in Newfoundland, his attention was drawn to the shores of the Chesapeake. From Charles I, he received a grant of territory including what now forms the states of Maryland and Delaware, and with his own hand he drew up a liberal charter, which he also submitted to the king. Before the papers were duly executed, Lord Baltimore died. His title and privilege descended to his eldest son, who carried out his father's designs. "*Calvert deserves to be ranked,*" says Bancroft, "*among the most wise and benevolent lawgivers of all ages.*"

Baltimore, Lord, (*Cecil Calvert*), (1613–1676), the eldest son of the first Lord Baltimore, was the first proprietor of Maryland. He never resided in Maryland, but appointed as his lieutenant, his brother Leonard, who arrived in the New World, in 1634, with about two hundred colonists, chiefly Catholics of gentle birth. Cecil Calvert discharged his duties to the colonists in a most liberal spirit, and died at an advanced age.

BIOGRAPHICAL SKETCHES. 139

Berkely, Sir William, (–1677), was born near London. He was educated at Oxford, and, in 1641, was appointed Governor of Virginia. During the Civil War, he sided with Charles I, and maintained the royal authority in Virginia until the death of the king. In 1651, he submitted to Cromwell, and then retired from office. Eight years afterwards, he was again appointed governor of Virginia; but he rendered himself very unpopular by his failure to protect the settlers from Indian raids. After "*Bacon's Rebellion*," he treated the insurgents with extreme severity. Being recalled to England, he is said to have died of chagrin.

Calvert, Leonard, (1606–1647), the first governor of Maryland, was a younger son of George Calvert. He governed Maryland from 1634 until his death.

Charlevoix, (*shar-le-vwah*), **Pierre Francis Xavier de,** (1682–1761), a French historian, critic, and traveler, born at St. Quentin. At the age of sixteen, he entered the Society of Jesus; and, while still a scholastic, was sent to Quebec. Here, he was employed four years in teaching. Later, he became professor of Belles-lettres in France. Having published a "*History of Christianity in Japan*," he returned to Quebec to write his most celebrated work, "*The History of New France.*" He remained for some time at Sault St. Louis, where his room is still shown. Then, having reached the Mississippi by way of the Illinois, he descended to New Orleans, and returned to France by way of Santo Domingo. In 1724, he published the "*Life of Mother Mary of the Incarnation*," the first superioress of the Ursulines at Quebec; and, in 1744, the *History of New France*, which had been completed almost twenty years before. This work, though of immense value, remained untranslated until recently, when an English edition was brought out in New York by John Gilmary Shea. Charlevoix's last work was the "*History of Paraguay.*" He died in France.

Champlain, Samuel de, (1567–1635), a French navigator, the founder of Quebec, and first governor of Canada, was born at Brouage, France. For services in the West Indies, during the war against the Spaniards, he was pensioned by Henry IV, under whose auspices he made his first voyage to Canada, (1603). In 1604, with De Monts, he began a settlement on the island of St. Croix, in a river of the same name, between Maine and New Brunswick. Between the years 1604–6, Champlain explored the coast as far south as Cape Cod, making careful surveys and maps; and, in 1607, he returned to France. Renewing his enterprise the next year, he ascended the St. Lawrence to the site of Quebec, and there planted a colony, (1608). In 1610, he discovered the lake which bears his name; and, in 1620, was appointed governor of Canada. He now set himself to labor energetically for the welfare of the colony, ever proving himself the faithful friend of the Indians and the kind patron of the missions. In 1629, the colony met with a severe blow, Quebec being taken by the English, and Champlain carried to England. In 1632, Canada was restored to the French, and Champlain reinstated. He did not, however, long survive, his death occurring on Christmas Day, 1635. Champlain was remarkable for his sagacity, penetration, and earnestness of character, as well as for his indomitable perseverance and sincere piety. More than two and a half centuries ago, during his sojourn in the West Indies, he conceived the plan of a ship-canal across the isthmus of Panama, "*by which,*" he says, "*the voyage to the South Sea would be shortened by more than fifteen hundred leagues.*" His piety is shown by the opening words of his journal: "*The salvation of a single soul is worth more than the conquest of an empire.*"

Dongan, Hon. Thomas, (1634–1715), belonged to an ancient and noble Irish Catholic family, and was born in Kildare. His father was Sir John Dongan of Castledown, and one of his maternal uncles was the famous Richard Talbot, *Earl of Tyrconnell*, who figured so conspicuously during the reign of James II. Having chosen a military career, he spent some time in the service of Louis XIV, and later received an appointment in the the English army. As the administration of affairs under Andros, in New York, at this time, produced great discontent, the Duke of York transferred the government to Colonel Dongan. This governor reached the New World in 1683, and in the fall of the same year, convoked *the first General Assembly of New York,* which granted the celebrated "*Charter of liberties.*" Dongan made many improvements in the City of New York, then the capital and seat of government; settled the boundary line between New York and Connecticut; and made an important treaty with the Iroquois in Western New York. Having at length incurred the displeasure of James II, his office was withdrawn from him, and he retired to his estate on Staten Island. Later, he succeeded to the titles and estates of his brother, thus becoming Earl of Limerick. He died in London.

Frontenac, Count Louis de, (1620–1698), came of an ancient and noble Basque family. His father held a high post in the household of Louis XIII, who became the child's godfather and gave him his own name. At the age of seventeen, he entered the army, and afterwards served in Italy, Flanders, Germany, and Candia. He was at length appointed governor-general of Canada, by Louis XIV, and reached that country in 1672. He built Fort Frontenac on the present site of Kingston, on Lake Ontario, to keep the Iroquois in check, and became the constant patron of La Salle in his various explorations. Having become involved with the intendant Duchesneau (*du-shay-no*), and with the ecclesiastical authorities who opposed the liquor trade among the Indians, he was recalled, (1682). When, however, in 1689, from various causes Canada had been brought to the verge of ruin, he was again made governor. He now planned and carried out three expeditions against the English Colonies, and completed his vigorous campaign by the repulse of Sir Wm. Phipps, before Quebec, 1690. After this he restored Fort Frontenac, and revived the French influence among the Indians. Having thus restored the fallen fortunes of France in the New World, he soon after died, and was buried in the Church of the Franciscans, to whom he was greatly attached. Frontenac was a man of marked ability and indomitable courage, but of impetuous disposition and haughty manners, and, hence, apt to be arbitrary and prejudiced. *"A more remarkable figure, in its bold and salient individuality and sharply marked light and shadow, is nowhere seen in American history."*

Joliet, Louis (1645-1700), was born at Quebec. Having completed his studies at the college in that city, he started westward to seek his fortune in the fur trade. He soon acquired a knowledge of the Indian languages and of western topography, which led the government to select him as the explorer of the Mississippi. Father Marquette and he studied over the route, and drew up maps from their own knowledge and Indian reports, laying down rivers, tribes, and natural features. In the summer of 1673, they made the celebrated voyage which has immortalized their names. On his return, Joliet lost all his papers in the rapids above Montreal. His report from memory was necessarily brief, and his map less accurate than that of Father Marquette. He was not rewarded as he deserved, his modest merits being soon thrown into the shade by the exploits of La Salle. In 1680, the island of Anticosti was given to him, and here he built a fort, a dwelling for his family and houses for trade. In 1690, Phipps on his way to attack Quebec made a descent on Joliet's establishment, burnt his buildings, and took prisoners himself, his wife and his mother-in-law. His property was a total loss; but he recovered his liberty when the English retired from Quebec. In 1697, he obtained the seigneury of Joliette, which still belongs to his family. He died apparently poor, and was buried on one of the islands of Mignon.

La Salle, Robert Cavelier de, (1635-1687), one of the most illustrious explorers of our country, was born at Rouen, France. In early youth he entered the Society of Jesus; but after some years of study he left the order, and started for Canada to build up his fortune, his own patrimony having been forfeited by the unjust provisions of the French law. In 1666, he sailed for Canada, and obtained from the Sulpitians a large tract of land near Montreal, which he named *La Chine*. In the winter of 1670, he started on an expedition towards the southwest, discovered the Ohio River, and sailed down as far as the site of Louisville. Having been appointed Governor of Fort Frontenac, he was encouraged by Colbert to pursue the discoveries and explorations which his own genius suggested. He built a vessel on Lake Erie, began his voyage in August, 1679, and passed through Lakes Huron and Michigan. At Peoria, having heard that his vessel *The Griffin*, had been wrecked, he built a fort called *Crève Cœur* (*the Broken Heart*), and returned by land to Kingston, (1680). In 1682, with a large party, he renewed his enterprise, and descended the Mississippi in canoes from the Illinois River to the Gulf of Mexico, (April, 1682). The next year he went to France, and having obtained a commission to plant a colony in Louisiana, he undertook a voyage to that region; but failing to find the mouth of the Mississippi, he landed in Texas. Here he encountered great hardships, and was at length murdered by some of his own followers.

"*His capacity for large designs,*" says Sparks, "*and for procuring the resources to carry them forward, has few parallels amongst the most eminent discoverers.*"

Leisler, (*lice-ler*), **Jacob**, (16---1691), an adventurer and revolutionist, born at Frankfort-on-the-Main, Germany, emigrated to America in 1660, and took up his residence in Albany. In 1689, he became the leader of a mob which seized the fort and public funds of New York, "*for the preservation,*" as he said, "*of the Protestant religion.*" Sloughter having been soon after appointed Governor of the colony, Leisler was arrested and executed, (1691).

Marquette, (*mar-ket'*), **Father James**, (1637-1675), was born at Laon, France, of an ancient and noble family. His mother, Rose de La Salle, was a near relative of the Ven. La Salle, the founder of the Christian Brothers; and to her early training he owed much of that profound piety which distinguished him in after-life, especially his generous and unwavering devotion to the Mother of God. In his seventeenth year, he entered the Society of Jesus. Twelve years later, he sailed for Canada as a missionary. As soon as he had mastered the Indian languages, he began his course westward. He first founded the mission of Sault (*so*) St. Marie. Here, twenty years before, the cross had been planted by Father Jogues, but it had since fallen. The next year, (1669), he took the place of Allouez among the Ottawas and Hurons. His stay here was short. He followed the Hurons to Mackinaw, and there built the chapel of St. Ignatius. In 1673, he made with Joliet his celebrated *exploration of the Mississippi* (p. 105), and two years afterwards founded a mission at Kaskaskia. Here his earthly labors ended. Conscious that death was nigh, he attempted to return to Mackinaw; but, unable to proceed, expired on the shores of the small river which now bears his name. (See *Shea's Discovery and Exploration of the Mississippi Valley*.)

Penn, William, (1644–1718), the founder and legislator of Pennsylvania, was born in London. In his youth he became a Quaker, on which account he was banished from the ancestral home. He, however, continued to preach in public, and to write in defence of the doctrines which he had embraced. In consequence of this he was three times imprisoned, and once brought to trial. Many "*Friends*" had emigrated to America, and two had become proprietors of New Jersey. Penn acted as umpire between them in a dispute which arose, and thus his special attention was drawn to this country. He now looked with longing eyes across the Atlantic, for a home beyond the reach of persecution. On the death of his father, to whom he had been reconciled, he became heir to an immense fortune; and in payment of a debt of £16,000 due from the crown, he accepted the territory of Pennsylvania. Towards the close of 1682, Penn laid out the city of Philadelphia, and caused the boundaries of the streets to be marked on the trunks of the chestnut, walnut, spruce, pine, and other forest trees that covered the land. Mementoes of this fact still linger in the names of many streets in that city. In 1684, he returned to England, where he spent the ensuing fifteen years. As his friendship for James II. was well known, he fell into disfavor with William of Orange, who in 1692 deprived him of his authority as governor. Two years afterwards, however, he was reinstated in his rights. In 1699, he returned to America, and granted to the colony a new charter. Having undergone many pecuniary and other trials, he died in England. Penn was tolerant in matters of religion, humane in his dealings with the Indians, and benevolent in all his relations with his fellow-men.

Phipps, Sir William, (1650–1695), was born at a rude border settlement on the Kennebec. Until eighteen years of age, he was employed in keeping sheep. He then apprenticed himself to a ship carpenter, and a few years later removed to Boston, where he learned to read and write. Anxious to better his fortunes, he went to England, to procure means to recover a Spanish treasure-ship which had been wrecked near the Bahamas. A frigate was given him, but his search proved unsuccessful. On a second attempt, however, he recovered treasure to the amount of £300,000, a considerable portion of which fell to his share. He was then knighted and appointed high sheriff of New England. In 1690, he captured Port Royal, but failed in an attempt against Quebec. Two years afterwards, the king made him governor of Massachusetts, a post for which he was totally unfit. In 1694, he was summoned to England to answer certain charges brought against him, and there he suddenly died. He co-operated with

Cotton Mather, the Puritan pastor of the North Church of Boston, in the witchcraft delusion; but his last act as governor was to issue a general pardon to all convicted or accused of that offence.

Smith, Captain John, (1579–1631), the founder of Virginia, was born in Lincolnshire, England. He early showed a great inclination for daring adventure. About the year 1600, he enlisted in the Austrian army and performed many bold exploits against the Turks. He was taken prisoner, reduced to slavery, killed his master, and escaped to Russia. Having returned to England, he accompanied a party of emigrants to Virginia and soon became the leading man in that colony. (*See Virginia.*) The latter part of his life was spent in England.

Stuyvesant, (*sti-ves-ant*) **Peter,** (1602–1682), the last Dutch governor of the New Netherlands, was born in Holland. He served in the war in the West Indies, lost a leg in battle, and in 1645 was appointed governor or director-general of New Netherland. Here he conciliated the Indians, who had been provoked to hostilities by his predecessor, Kieft, and restored order in every department. His administration was rigorous and rather arbitrary. In 1664, New Amsterdam was attacked by an English fleet, to which Stuyvesant unwillingly surrendered. The ensuing year, he went to report to his superiors in Holland, but soon returned and spent the remainder of his days on his farm or "*bowerie,*" then outside the limits of New York city. Peter Stuyvesant forms a conspicuous character in Irving's humorous work, entitled, " *The History of New York, by Diedrich Knickerbocker.*"

Urban VIII, Pope, (*Maffeo Barberini*), (1568–1644), was born at Florence. He was distinguished for his learning and liberal patronage of science and art. By him the college of the "*Propaganda*" was founded.

Wheelwright, John, (1594–1679), a Puritan divine, who emigrated to this country from England in 1636. He had been the classmate and friend of Oliver Cromwell, and he was the brother-in-law of Mrs. Hutchinson, whose religious views he shared. In 1638, he formed, on the banks of the Piscataqua, a settlement which he called Exeter. He lied in Salisbury, N. H.

White, Father Andrew, (1579–1656), *the "Apostle of Maryland,"* was born in London. Denied by the laws of his native land the privilege of an education there, he made his studies at Douay. Having been ordained priest about the age of twenty-five, he returned to England to labor for the conversion of his countrymen. He was soon discovered and thrown into prison, and, with forty-six other Catholic priests, sentenced to perpetual banishment, (1606). The next year he entered the Society of Jesus. His novitiate was spent at Louvain. Twenty-five years afterwards, Lord Baltimore having applied to the Superior of the Jesuits for missionaries for his new colony, Fathers White and Altham, with two lay brothers, were selected for the mission. On the 25th of March he offered up the Holy Sacrifice for the first time on the shores of the Chesapeake; and during the ensuing years he labored with the ardent zeal of an apostle in this new field. Though fifty-six years of age, he patiently undertook the study of the Indian language; and so successful was he that he compiled in that tongue a grammar, a dictionary, and a catechism, tne last of which alone is extant. He and his companions were requested to sit in the first colonial Assembly; but as they earnestly requested to be excused from all part in secular concerns, their request was granted. Father White was soon joined by other members of his order, and the missions were thus rendered very successful. Clayborne endeavored to destroy their influence among the natives, but the Fathers remained undaunted at their posts. In 1640, Father White had the happiness of baptizing *Chilacomon*, or *King Charles*, the chief of the Piscataquays. Later, he conferred the same Sacrament on the chief of the Potomacs and the queen of Patuxent. In 1644, during the insurrection under Clayborne, Father White and his companions were seized, and in chains sent back to England, to be prosecuted as "*priests and Jesuits*." During his imprisonment in London, though borne down by old age, he never relaxed his austerities. The keeper, greatly surprised, said to him, "*If you continue this fasting and austerity, you will not be able to stand up under the gallows at Tyburne!*" The holy man replied: "*My fastings give me strength to bear all kinds of sufferings for the love of Jesus Christ.*" He was at length released, but he never again beheld the shores of America. His last years were spent in apostolic labor in his own country. History gives us few characters purer or more beautiful than that of Father Andrew White.

Williams, Roger, (1606–1683), the founder of Rhode Island, was born in Wales. He was educated at Oxford, and was ordained a minister of the Church of England. Becoming a dissenter, he emigrated to Massachusetts, (1631), and preached for a short time at Salem; but he was at length banished from the colony on account of his doctrines, (1635). He then removed to Rhode Island, where he founded the city of Providence; also the first Baptist Church in that city. He was for several years president of the colony, and lived in great peace with the Indians, over whom he acquired considerable influence. He was buried in the family cemetery, near the spot on which he landed.

CHRONOLOGICAL REVIEW.

SEVENTEENTH CENTURY.

1604.—First settlement in New England, made on Boone Island, Maine, by De Monts and Champlain. Champlain explored the coast of Maine, and entered the Penobscot River.

1605.—De Monts and Champlain explored the Maryland coast. Port Royal, Nova Scotia settled.

1607.—Virginia (I.) settled at Jamestown.

1608.—Quebec founded.

1609.—Champlain discovered Lake Champlain. The Hudson River discovered by Henry Hudson.

1610.—The "Starving Time" in Virginia.

1612.—A Jesuit mission founded on Mt. Desert Island, Maine.

1613.—New York (II.) settled by the Dutch at New Amsterdam. Rolfe and Pocahontas married.

1615.—The Franciscans in Canada. Champlain discovered Lake Ontario. The culture of tobacco commenced in Virginia.

1619.—The first Colonial Assembly.

1620.—Massachusetts (III.) settled at Plymouth. Slavery introduced at Jamestown, Virginia.

1622.—An Indian massacre in Virginia. New Hampshire granted to Gorges and Mason.

1623.—New Hampshire (IV.) settled at Dover and Portsmouth.

1625.—The Jesuits in Canada.

1633.—Connecticut (V.) settled by emigrants from Massachusetts.

1634.—Maryland (VI.) settled at St. Mary's, on the Potomac.

1635.—Clayborne's Rebellion. Roger Williams banished from Massachusetts. Champlain died.

1636.—Rhode Island (VII.) settled at Providence.

1637.—The Pequod War.

1638.—Delaware (VIII.) settled by the Swedes and Finns.

1640.—Montreal founded.

1643.—The Swedes and the Finns in Pennsylvania.

1646.—Father Jogues martyred. Father Druillettes commenced his mission among the Abnaki Indians. Father De Noué frozen.

1648.—Father Daniel martyred.

CHRONOLOGICAL REVIEW. 147

1649.—Fathers Brebœuf and Lallemant martyred. The Toleration Act passed in Maryland.
1650.—North Carolina (IX.) settled by emigrants from Virginia.
1653.—Onondaga salt-springs discovered by Father Le Moyne.
1654.—Penal laws against Catholics in Maryland.
1655.—Missions among the Onondagas. Civil War in Maryland. New Sweden conquered by the Dutch.
1660.—The Navigation Act passed.
1663.—Albemarle Colony (North Carolina) formed.
1664.—New York taken by the Dutch. New Jersey (X.) settled at Elizabethtown.
1665.—Father Allouez discovered the southern shore of Lake Superior.
1668.—Missions established among the Iroquois. Father Marquette founded the mission of Sault Saint Mary.
1669.—Green Bay founded by Father Allouez.
1670.—South Carolina (XI.) settled on Ashley River. Michigan settled at Detroit.
1673.—Father Marquette discovered and explored the Upper Mississippi.
1675.—King Philip's War. Death of Father Marquette.
1676.—Bacon's Rebellion.
1680.—Charleston, South Carolina, settled.
1682.—Pennsylvania (XII.) settled by the Quakers under Penn.
1683.—Philadelphia founded. Governor Dongan in New York. Kaskaskia (*the Village of the Immaculate Conception*), Ill., founded by Father Gravier.
1684.—La Salle passed from the Upper Mississippi to the Gulf of Mexico.
1685.—La Salle attempted a settlement in Texas. Arkansas Post, Ark., settled.
1686.—Andros governor of New England. First Catholic Chapel in Philadelphia.
1689.—King William's War. Catholicity proscribed in New York.
1690.—Indiana settled at Vincennes. Massacre of Lachine. Schenectady burned. Acadia reduced. Unsuccessful attack on Quebec.
1692.—Salem witchcraft delusion.
1695.—Archdale governor of the Carolinas.
1699.—Louisiana settled at Iberville.

CONTEMPORARY CHRONOLOGY.

1603.—James I. king of England.
1605.—The Gunpowder Plot.
1608.—Galileo constructed the telescope.
1610.—Louis XIII. king of France. *The Order of the Visitation* founded by St. Francis de Sales.
1616.—Shakespeare died.
1617.—*The Congregation of the Mission* founded by St. Vincent de Paul. St. Rose of Lima died.
1618.—The Thirty Years' War began.
1633.—*The Sisters of Charity* founded by St. Vincent de Paul.
1640.—Portugal revolted from Spain and gained her independence.
1642.—The Civil War in England began.
1643.—Louis XIV. king of France.
1649.—Execution of Charles I. Cromwell head of the Commonwealth.
1665.—The London Plague; 100,000 persons died.
1674.—John Sobieski king of Poland.
1685.—James II. king of England.
1688.—The Revolution in England. William of Orange ascended the throne.
1689.—Peter the Great czar of Russia.
1690.—Battle of the Boyne.
1697.—Treaty of Ryswick.

CONTEMPORARY POPES.

Clement VIII. (1592-1605); Leo XI. (1605-1605); Paul V. (1605-1621); Gregory XV. (1621-1623); Urban VIII. (1623-1644); Innocent X (1644-1655); Alexander VII. (1655-1667); Clement IX. (1667-1669); Clement X. (1670-1676); Innocent XI. (1676-1689); Alexander VIII. (1689-1691); Innocent XII. (1691-1700).

GEOGRAPHICAL TABLE NO. 3.

OF PLACES MENTIONED IN THE PRECEDING SECTION.

(1.) **Ashley,** a small river in South Carolina, which unites with Cooper River, at Charleston, to form Charleston harbor.

(2.) **Bermuda,** or **The Bermudas,** a group of islands in the North Atlantic Ocean, belonging to Great Britain.

(3.) **Buzzard's Bay,** a large indentation on the south coast of Massachusetts.

(4.) **Cape Cod,** projects from the southeast coast of Massachusetts, and curving inwards like a man's arm bent at the elbow and wrist, encloses Cape Cod Bay.

(5.) **Champlain, Lake,** a beautiful sheet of water, about 130 miles long, between the states of New York and Vermont.

(6.) **Charleston,** the largest city in South Carolina, on a tongue of land between the Ashley and Cooper Rivers.

(7.) **Cuttyhunk Island,** the most southwestern of the Elizabeth Islands, on Buzzard's Bay, Mass.

(8.) **Elizabethtown,** formerly the capital and principal town of New Jersey, is situated about five miles southwest of Newark.

(9.) **Green Bay,** a large arm on the west side of Lake Michigan.

(10.) **Jamestown** was situated on the west bank of the James River, in Virginia, about fifty miles from Richmond.

(11.) **Kingston,** a post village of Washington County, R. I., 27 miles southwest of Providence.

(12.) **Kewcenaw Point,** a peninsula in the north part of Michigan, well watered and generally very fertile.

(13.) **Lachine,** (*la'sheen*), a post-village of Canada East, on the island, and 9 miles south of Montreal.

(14.) **La Prairie,** (*la-pra'-ree*), a post-village of Canada East, on the south shore of the River St. Lawrence.

(15.) **Mackinaw,** a village of Michigan, situated on an island of the same name, in Lake Huron.

(16.) **Madagascar,** a great island in the Indian Ocean, generally considered as appertaining to Africa.

(17.) **Mohawk River,** a river of New York, which enters the Hudson about three miles above Troy. The chief towns on its banks are Rome, Utica, Little Falls, and Schenectady.

(18.) **Narragansett Bay,** a large body of water extending north from the Atlantic into Rhode Island, between Point Judith on the west and Seconnet Rocks on the east.

(19.) **Narrows, The,** a strait separating Long Island from Staten Island, and connecting New York Bay with New York Harbor. On either side, strong fortifications have been erected for its defence.

(20.) **Onondaga,** (*on-on-daw'-ga*), a county in the central part of New York State. It contains Cross, Onondaga, and Otisco Lakes, also a part of Skaneateles Lake, and is drained by Seneca River, Chittenango, Onondaga and Oneida Creeks, and other smaller streams.

(21.) **Potomac,** a large river forming the boundary between Virginia and Maryland. It passes through several ridges of mountains, and the scenery along its banks, especially at Harper's Ferry where it bursts through the Blue Ridge, is in the highest degree beautiful and picturesque.

(22.) **Providence,** one of the capitals of the State of Rhode Island, is situated on the northwest arm of Narragansett Bay (or Providence River), thirty-five miles from the ocean. The river divides the city into two nearly equal parts, which are connected by bridges.

(23.) **Ryswick,** (*ris-wik*), a village of Holland, 2 miles S. E. of the Hague. The peace concluded here, in 1697, between France on the one part, and Germany, England, Spain, and Holland on the other, is commemorated by a pyramidal monument.

(24.) **Salem,** a city in Essex County, Massachusetts. Next to Plymouth, it is the oldest town in New England. The place of execution of those condemned for supposed witchcraft, is a beautiful eminence overlooking the city, and is now known as *Gallow's Hill*.

(25.) **Sault** (*so*) **St. Mary,** a village of Michigan, on St. Mary's River, or Strait, 400 miles northwest of Detroit.

(26.) **Schenectady,** (*sken-ek'-ta-de*), a thriving city of New York, on the right bank of the Mohawk River, 16 miles N. E. of Albany.

(27.) **Starved Rock,** a perpendicular mass of limestone and sandstone, 150 feet high, on Illinois River, 8 miles below Ottawa. It received its name from a band of Illinois Indians, who, having taken refuge here, were hemmed in by the Pottowatomies, and who all died of thirst rather than of starvation.

(28.) **Vincennes,** the oldest town in Indiana, is situated on the left bank of the Wabash River, one hundred miles southwest of Indianapolis.

SECTION IV.

A.D. 1700 to A.D. 1800.

STUDY NO. 1.

THE AMERICAN COLONIES DURING THE FIRST HALF OF THE 18TH CENTURY.

1. Penal Laws in New York.—The year 1700 was disgraced in New York by the passage of a law against Catholic priests. It was decreed that any Catholic priest remaining in, or coming into, the province after November 1, 1700, should be "*deemed and accounted an incendiary and disturber of the public peace and safety, and an enemy to the true Christian religion, and should be adjudged to suffer perpetual imprisonment.*" In case of escape and capture, the penalty was death. Any person who gave shelter to a Catholic clergyman, was liable to a fine of $1000 and to three days torture in the pillory.

THE PILLORY.

2. In 1701, another law was enacted depriving Catholics of the right of voting or of holding office. In 1702, Queen Anne granted liberty of conscience to all in the province, Catholics excepted. The natural result of this unjust legislation was to prevent Catholics from settling in New York. These laws were not repealed until after the Revolution.

3. Queen Anne's War.—In 1702, war being declared by England against France and Spain, hostilities consequently ensued between their respective colonies in the New World. As the contest principally concerned the succession to the Spanish throne, it was termed in Europe the *War of the Spanish Succession.* Here it was called *Queen Anne's War.**

4. The English colonies, now entirely surrounded by the French and Spaniards, were filled with alarm. New York through the influence of Schuyler, obtained a neutrality with Canada; but New England had to contend with the French, and the Carolinas with the Spaniards.

5. Hostilities at the South.—As soon as war was proclaimed, Governor Moore of South Carolina made a descent on St. Augustine. He took the town; but while assailing the fort, two Spanish men-of-war entered the harbor, and Moore deeming discretion the better part of valor, beat a hasty retreat. The next year, he more successfully attacked the missions on the Appalachicola.[1] The Indian towns were destroyed and several of the missionaries killed, hundreds of converts sharing their fate, or worse still, being hurried off as slaves to the West Indies.

---

* The exiled king, James II, died in France (September, 1701). Louis, who had protected him, now acknowledged his son, James Francis Edward (who is known in history as *the Pretender*) to be the lawful king of England. This act was displeasing to the English, as the crown had been settled upon Anne, James's second and Protestant daughter. Louis also offended the English by placing his grandson, Philip of Anjou, on the Spanish throne, thus increasing French influence among the dynasties of Europe. William was preparing for war, when he suddenly died. He was succeeded by Anne; and the causes already mentioned, with others of less importance, impelled her to declare war against France.

6. The greatest blow was struck in 1704, when St. Marks, the centre of the Apalachee mission, was taken and destroyed by a body of English and Indians. Three Franciscans who directed the mission went out to sue for mercy; but they were seized and put to death with all the horrors of Indian cruelty. Eight hundred of the mission Indians were killed on the spot, and fourteen hundred taken captive by Governor Moore. Some of these he employed in cultivating his fields; the others he sold for his own pecuniary profit. A thorn was thus planted in the breasts of the surrounding Indians, which rankled for years and finally urged them into fierce retaliation.

7. Hostilities at the North.—A party of New England colonists attacked and plundered a French and Indian settlement on the Penobscot,[2] thus rousing all the eastern Indians to war. The Canadians retaliated, and after several minor attacks, a party of French and Indians fell on Deerfield, killed nearly fifty of the inhabitants, and hurried off one hundred as prisoners.* (March, 1704.)

8. Acadia Reduced.—The New Englanders under Church were now sent against the French on the Penobscot, but no important blow was struck. This was followed, in 1707, by an expedition against Port Royal, which, though unsuccessful, ravaged the farms of the French settlers. In 1710, the expedition being renewed, Port Royal was taken and its name changed to Annapolis, (*city of Anne*), in honor

---

* Among the captives, were the minister, Mr. Williams, and his family. Mrs. Williams, being too weak to travel, was tomahawked the second day. Her husband and children were taken to Canada; but after a captivity of nearly two years, they were ransomed and returned home. His youngest daughter, meanwhile, had been adopted by the Indians, and they refused to part with her. She grew up to womanhood, became a devout Catholic, and married a young Mohawk brave. Years afterwards, she visited her relations at Deerfield, but no entreaties could induce her to forsake her Indian home.

of the English queen. By this conquest, Acadia, under the name of Nova Scotia, became a British Province.

9. Two expeditions against Canada were now planned by the British;* one, organized in England, to proceed against Quebec; the other, in the colonies, to attack Montreal. The former proved a failure, a large fleet under the command of Admiral Walker, being wrecked on the St. Lawrence, and nearly a thousand persons perishing. (1711.) When the news of this disaster became known, the second expedition was abandoned. Providence itself seemed to favor the Canadians.

10. The Tuscaroras.—In 1711, the Tuscarora Indians, mindful of the wrongs of their race, suddenly fell upon the whites in North Carolina and massacred many. They were afterwards conquered by a force from South Carolina, and soon migrated to New York where they joined the Iroquois, thus forming the *sixth* nation of that Confederacy.

11. Peace.—The peace of Utrecht, (*you-trekt*)³ put an end to Queen Anne's War, and by it Nova Scotia was ceded to England, (1713).

12. The English and the Abnaki.—During Queen Anne's War, New England, which had just passed an act condemning Catholic missionaries to imprisonment for life, endeavored to persuade the Abnaki Indians to remain neutral. Having failed in this, the English determined to retaliate upon the Indians, and especially upon their venerable missionary, Father Rasle. Twice the New Englanders attacked Norridgewalk, now Indian Old Point,⁴ the Abnaki

---

* When the news of these preparations reached the governor at Montreal, everything was put in readiness for defence. Indian allies were secured, the fortifications were strengthened, and so enthusiastic were the inhabitants that even women worked on the forts.

settlement. The first time, (1705), they burnt the church and village; the second, (1722), they pillaged the church and his little cabin, carrying off everything, even his papers, inkstand, and his now celebrated Abnaki dictionary,* the result of years of patient toil.

13. Death of Father Rasle.—In 1724, during the absence of many of the Abnaki warriors at the hunting season, a party of English, and pagan Mohawks bore down upon the Christian village. The aged priest rushed from his little chapel to aid his people; a yell of exultation and a volley of bullets followed, and Father Rasle lay dead at the foot of the mission cross. Seven chiefs shared his fate. Having mangled the body of the saintly man who had spent a lifetime in the wilderness, the English profaned the tabernacle, burnt the church, and withdrew.

14. The Natchez Massacre.—The French at Fort Rosalie [5] having attempted to wrest from the Natchez Indians † their ancient capital, were cruelly massacred by the latter. Two hundred persons, including two missionaries (a Jesuit and a Franciscan), perished. Shortly afterwards, the Natchez were completely destroyed as a nation, by a French force from New Orleans, (1729).

At the Fort Rosalie massacre, the Indians spared the children. Many of these the whites purchased from the savages and committed to the care of the Ursulines, who had just founded a house at New Orleans. These bereaved little ones thus formed the nucleus of the first orphan asylum in that city.

* This dictionary is still preserved with the greatest care at Harvard College, and is regarded as a precious monument of philological research.

† These Indians were by far the most civilized to be found in the valley of the Mississippi. Their peculiar language, their worship, their division into nobles and plebeians, their funeral rites, have given rise to many singular conjectures with regard to their origin.

15. The Mississippi Scheme.—From 1713 to 1732, Louisiana was under the control of a company which had obtained from the French Government large colonial grants, as well as a monopoly of the foreign trade. On these as a basis of credit, they issued a large amount of paper money. The whole scheme, which was managed by an unscrupulous Scotch lawyer named John Law, then resident in Paris, completely fascinated the French people. Mines were to be opened in Louisiana, and the shareholders to become fabulously rich in a short space of time. The shares had risen to forty, fifty, and even sixty times their original value, when suddenly (May, 1720), the bubble burst. Law's bank failed, and those who had been millionaires one day, were penniless the next.

16. Georgia Settled.—In 1733, Georgia, the last of the *Thirteen Original States*, was founded by James Oglethorpe, as a refuge for oppressed debtors from England. Under four large pine trees, on the west bank of the Savannah River where the city of that name now stands, he first pitched his tent, and for a year this was his only dwelling. He was accompanied by about thirty-five families, among whom were some Piedmontese silk-weavers, one of the projects of the colony being the manufacture of silk.

SEAL OF GEORGIA.

<small>This industry was continued in Georgia till the Revolution. Oglethorpe took to England the first silk produced, and of it a robe was fashioned for the queen.</small>

17. The colony was called Georgia, in honor of the English king, and its charter granted lands and religious tolera-

GEORGIA SETTLED. 157

tion to all settlers except Roman Catholics. Jews were accordingly sent out by merchants of that faith from London; German Protestants from Salzburg founded Ebenezer; and Scotch Highlanders settled New Inverness.

In 1636, John Wesley, the founder of the Methodist Church, arrived at Savannah; but his reception was not favorable. On his return to England the next year, he himself wrote: "*I, who went to America to convert others, had never been myself converted.*" Soon after this, George Whitfield, the founder of the Calvinistic Methodists, visited the colony; and from this period dates the system of *revivals* and *camp-meetings*.

18. The Spanish War. (1739.)—This grew out of difficulties between France and Spain. It lasted about five years, and then merged into *King George's War*.

GENERAL OGLETHORPE, AGED 102.
(From an Old Print.)

In 1740, Oglethorpe made an unsuccessful attack on St. Augustine. Two years later, the Spaniards retaliated, and appeared in strong force before Frederica, on St. Simon's Island. By a stratagem,* Oglethorpe drove them from the coast.

19. Georgia a Royal Province.—The colonists sent over from England were, for the most part, idle, thriftless, and discontented, and the laws established by the trustees were unwise. The charter was, therefore, surren-

* By means of a letter written to a deserter, as if he had been a spy, Oglethorpe led the enemy to believe that a British fleet was near at hand, and thus frightened the Spaniards away.

dered to the crown (1752), and Georgia became a *Royal Province*. It was never thickly settled, and was the youngest and weakest of the *thirteen original colonies* when the Revolution broke out.

20. The Negro Plot.—Several houses in New York having been rather mysteriously burned, the negro slaves were accused of a conspiracy to set fire to the city and massacre the people. The accusation was never proved; nevertheless, four white persons were hanged, eleven negroes burned at the stake, eighteen hanged, and fifty transported to the West Indies. A letter from Oglethorpe having led to the idea that a Catholic priest was the guilty party, a poor schoolmaster, suspected of being one, was tried, condemned, and executed, (1741).

On the site of the present City Hall, three negroes were burnt at the stake at one time.

21. King George's War,[*] (1744-1748).—War having again broken out between England and France, the flame was soon kindled in the New World. The only event of importance was the capture of Louisburg, on Cape Breton Island, by a combined force of English and colonial troops. Peace was made, in 1748, by the treaty of Aix-la-Chapelle (*akes-la-sha-pél*). Louisburg was then restored to the French.

---

[*] So called, because King George II., then on the English throne, had espoused the cause of the Empress of Austria, the celebrated *Maria Theresa*, who fought for the Austrian crown against the Elector of Bavaria. The King of France took the opposite side, and this led to the war. In Europe it was called *The War of the Austrian Succession*.

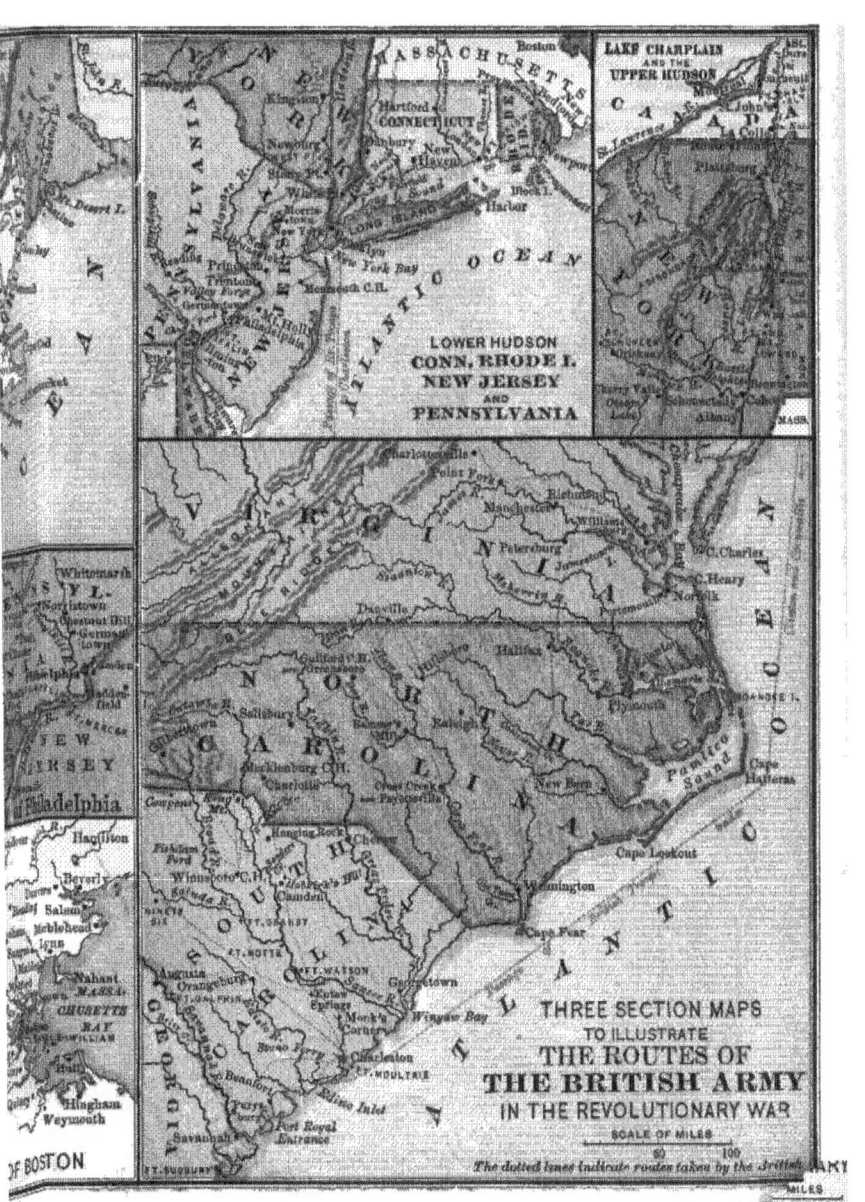

STUDY NO. 2.

FRENCH AND INDIAN WAR.

1. French and English Claims.—France and England both claimed the region west of the Alleghany Mountains, along the Ohio River. The former claim was based on discovery, exploration, and actual occupancy, the French having more than sixty posts guarding the long line of their possessions; the latter depended on royal charters and Indian deeds. At length, a grant of 500,000 acres on the Ohio, made by the English crown for the purpose of planting settlers beyond the Alleghanies, brought matters to a crisis.

2. The English soon had surveyors at work on the lands, but not before the French had established forts at Le Bœuf [*leh-buf*] and Venango, in the northwest of Pennsylvania. Dinwiddie, the Governor of Virginia, determined to send a remonstrance to the French commander, and to request his withdrawal from the Ohio Valley.

3. Washington's First Appearance in History.—For this mission, Governor Dinwiddie selected a young Virginian surveyor of great promise, who held the rank of major in the army. *His name was George Washington.* The very day he received his credentials, the young envoy set out on his perilous journey through the wilderness, from Williamsburg to Lake Erie. At Fort Le Bœuf he was cordially received by St. Pierre [*sang-pe-āre*], the French commander, who, soldierlike, referred him to the Governor of

Canada for explanations, at the same time offering to transmit Dinwiddie's letter. France was evidently determined to hold the territory explored by Marquette and La Salle, for the shore in front of the fort was even then lined with canoes ready for an intended expedition down the river.

4. Washington's Return.—The young officer's return was beset with danger. The streams were swollen. The snow was falling, and freezing as it fell. The horses

AN INCIDENT OF WASHINGTON'S RETURN.

gave out, and he was obliged to proceed on foot. With only one companion, and with his compass for guide, he quitted the usual path and struck out boldly through the forest. Here a treacherous Indian fired at him, but having missed his aim, was captured, and would have been put to death but

FRENCH AND INDIAN WAR. 161

for the interference of Washington. The travelers* at length reached home and delivered St. Pierre's reply.

5. French and Indian War.—A great struggle now commenced, which lasted from 1754 to 1763. A fort had already been begun by the English, at the junction of the Alleghany and Monongahela Rivers, on the present site of Pittsburgh. Dinwiddie now sent a force under Colonel Fry, (Washington being second in command), to protect the works. Before this could be done, the French took possession of the place, and having completed the fort, called it Fort du Quesne † (*du-kane*).

6. Fort Necessity.—Washington hastening forward, met and defeated the French at *Great Meadows*. He now threw up a stockade, which he aptly called *Fort Necessity*. Here Colonel Fry died, and Washington became chief commander. Being attacked by a superior body of French, he was compelled to surrender, though with the honorable privilege of returning to Virginia.

7. The Five Objective Points of the War.— Five points were persistently attacked by the English, and as obstinately defended by the French, namely: (1), *Acadia and Louisburg*, which had control of the fisheries, and threatened New England; (2), *Fort du Quesne* [*kane*], the key to the region west of the Alleghanies; (3), *Crown Point and Ticonderoga*, which controlled the route to Canada by way of Lakes George and Champlain, and offered a safe starting-point for French expeditions against New York and New England; (4), *Niagara*, which protected the great fur trade

---

* Attempting to cross the Alleghany on a rude raft, they were caught in the trembling ice. Washington thrust out his pole to check the speed, but was jerked into the foaming water. Swimming to an island, he barely saved his life. Fortunately, in the morning the river was frozen over, and he escaped on the ice.

† In honor of Du Quesne, the Governor of Canada.

of the upper lakes and the West; (5), *Quebec*, which being the strongest fortification in Canada, gave control of the St. Lawrence.

8. Acadia.—Scarcely had the war commenced, when an attack was made by the English on Acadia, (1754). The French forts at the head of the Bay of Fundy were easily taken, and the entire region of the Penobscot fell into the hands of the English. Their victory was disgraced by an act of cruelty almost without parallel in history. Acadia contained many French settlers who, at the close of the war twenty years before, had been promised freedom in religious matters, and exemption from bearing arms against the French. They were a simple, rural, God-fearing people, living in quiet happiness upon their well-cultivated farms. A beautiful picture of their peaceful life is given by Longfellow:

" There, in the midst of its farms, reposed the Acadian village.
Strongly built were the houses, with frames of oak and of chestnut,
Such as the peasants of Normandy built in the reign of the Henries.
Thatched were the roofs, with dormer windows, and gables projecting
Over the basement below protected and shaded the doorway.
There, in the tranquil evenings of summer, when brightly the sunset
Lighted the village street and gilded the vanes on the chimneys,
Matrons and maidens sat in snow-white caps and in kirtles
Scarlet and blue and green, with distaffs spinning the golden
Flax for the gossiping looms, whose noisy shuttles within doors
Mingled their sound with the whir of the wheels and the song of the
    maidens.
Solemnly down the street came the parish priest, and the children
Paused in their play to kiss the hand he extended to bless them.
*   *   *   *   *   *   *   *   Anon from the belfry
Softly the Angelus sounded, and over the roofs of the village
Columns of pale blue smoke, like clouds of incense ascending,
Rose from a hundred hearths, the homes of peace and contentment.
Thus dwelt together in love these simple Acadian farmers.
Dwelt in the love of God and of man."

FRENCH AND INDIAN WAR. 163

THE EXPULSION OF THE ACADIANS.

9. When their sky seemed serenest, the Acadians were suddenly seized, to the number of *seven thousand*, deprived of their lands, flocks, and other property, and at the point of the bayonet hurried on board an English fleet,* (Sept. 17, 1755). They were then landed penniless at various points along the coast from Maine to Louisiana. No regard was paid to family ties; parents were separated from children, wives from husbands, sisters from brothers. Thus, in misery and exile, this once happy people lingered out a sorrowful and weary existence. Long years afterwards, the colonial newspapers contained advertisements from the

---

* "Back from the cold beach, about a mile, stood the Church of Our Lady of Acadie. There they gathered for the last time, while Father Reynal offered the Holy Mysteries for them. Then they marched slowly out, weeping, telling their beads, chanting the Litanies of the Blessed Virgin, singing hymns to her Eternal Son and her. All the way from the chapel to the shore, the mournful procession passed through the kneeling ranks of their wild, weeping mothers and wives, of their sisters and little children; and when the men had passed, these rose and followed to the ships. And so, driven aboard, they passed away over the strange seas."—*MacLeod.*

scattered members of families seeking reunion with their kindred. The story of two of these exiles has been beautifully interwoven in Longfellow's "*Evangeline.*"

Such of the children as reached Louisiana formed the second inheritance of orphans which fell to the Ursulines at the South.

WASHINGTON AT BRADDOCK'S DEFEAT.

10. **Braddock's Defeat.** — The next year, (1755), another expedition was sent against Fort Du Quesne. It was commanded by General Braddock, who had just arrived with reinforcements from England, Washington acting as aide-de-

camp. The general was a regular British officer, proud and conceited; hence, though ignorant of Indian warfare, he treated with contempt the prudent suggestions of Washington. In consequence, when within a few miles of Fort du Quesne, his army was surprised by a small French and Indian force, and routed with great slaughter, Braddock himself being among the slain. The remnant of the army was saved only by the courage and coolness of Washington.

11. During this battle, Washington's life was remarkably preserved. Two horses were shot under him, and four bullets passed through his coat, yet he remained unharmed. Many years afterwards, an old Indian chief came "a long way" to see the Virginia officer at whom during the Monongahela fight, he had fifteen times fired a rifle, as often failing to reach his aim.

12. Battle of Lake George.—About the time of Braddock's ill-fated expedition, William Johnson was sent with another force against *Crown Point*. He encountered the French under General Dieskau [*de-es-ko*], near the head of Lake George. The English were victorious, and in honor of the king, they changed the name of the lake, (*Holy Sacrament*, given it by Father Jogues more than a century before,) to that which it now bears. The expedition against Crown Point was abandoned, and Johnson having built *Fort William Henry* near the battle-ground, disbanded his troops.

13. Capture of Fort William Henry. — Two years after, (1757), Montcalm [*mont-kahm*], the new French Governor of Canada, besieged and captured *Fort William Henry*. The English garrison was promised a safe escort to Fort Edward; but scarcely had the English left the fort, when they were attacked by the Indians. In vain did the

French officers peril their lives to save their captives. "*Kill me,*" cried Montcalm, "*but spare the English who are under my protection.*" The Indian fury was not to be appeased, and the march of the prisoners to Fort Edward became a flight for life.

14. William Pitt.—In the summer of 1757, a great change took place. William Pitt, afterwards Lord Chatham, the warm friend of the colonies, was made a member of the British Cabinet, and placed at the head of colonial affairs. Vigorous measures were at once adopted, and an army of English and colonial troops was raised that

WILLIAM PITT.

numbered as many as the whole male French population of Canada.

15. Campaign of 1758.—In June of this year, Louisburg was retaken from the French, with six thousand prisoners and a large amount of ammunition.

In July, the English met with a disaster at Fort Ticonderoga. General Abercrombie, at the head of 15,000 troops, made a fierce attack on the fort, but was driven back with great loss. Lord Howe, a gallant and much beloved young English officer, was slain in the first skirmish. The disgrace of this defeat was in some degree retrieved by Colonel Bradstreet, who, with three thousand of Abercrombie's troops, captured Fort Frontenac, (now Kingston).

In November, Fort du Quesne was taken, mainly by the exertions of Washington who led the advance. As the English flag floated over the ruined ramparts, this gateway of the *west* was named PITTSBURGH, in honor of the great British statesman.

16. Capture of Quebec.—The campaign of 1759 was the final one of the war. The genius of Pitt had planned three expeditions against Canada. Forts Ticonderoga, Crown Point and Niagara, feebly defended by the French, were soon taken, and the decisive blow was aimed at Quebec.

17. In June, General Wolfe with 8000 men and a powerful fleet, sailed up the St. Lawrence to Quebec. The citadel, far above the reach of his cannon, and the craggy bluff bristling with guns, for a long time resisted every effort. His sharp eyes at length discovered a narrow path winding among the rocks to the top, and he determined to lead his army up this steep ascent, to the plains back of the city.

18. At night the troops sailed silently down the stream*

* Wolfe was a great admirer of the poet Gray. As his boat was moving down the river, he softly repeated the stanzas of "The Elegy," which he had just received from England. Like a mournful prophecy, above the gentle rippling of the waters, floated the strangely significant words from the lips of the doomed hero:

"The boast of heraldry, the pomp of power,
And all that beauty, all that wealth e'er gave,
Await, alike, the inevitable hour ;
The paths of glory lead but to the grave."

"*Gentlemen*," said Wolfe, as he closed the recital, "*I would rather be the author of that poem than to have the glory of beating the French to-morrow.*"

to a spot known as Wolfe's Cove, and in the darkness they scaled the precipice. The morning light revealed to the French the whole British force drawn up in battle array on the *Plains of Abraham*. The engagement which now took place (Sept. 13) turned in favor of the English, and decided the fate of France in America.

19. Last Hours of the two Generals.—Although twice wounded, Wolfe was still pushing forward, when a third ball struck him and he was carried to the rear. "*They run! They run!*" exclaimed the officer upon whom he leaned. "*Who run?*" he faintly gasped. "*The French,*" was the reply. "*God be praised!*" said he, "*I die happy.*"

20. Montcalm, the French commander, was also mortally wounded. When told by the surgeon that he could survive but a few hours, "*So much the better,*" he replied; "*I shall not live to see the surrender of Quebec.*" He dictated a letter to the English commander, imploring his care and protection for the French who had been wounded or taken prisoners, gave advice to his officers, and then begged to be left "*alone with God,*" that he might prepare for eternity. Having received the last Sacraments, he lingered until the next morning, when he calmly expired.

21. Peace.—The Treaty of Paris (1763) put an end to the French and Indian War. By this treaty, Spain ceded Florida to England, and France gave up all her territory east of the Mississippi, except two small islands south of Newfoundland, which were retained as fishing stations. New Orleans, and all the country she owned west of the Mississippi, France ceded to Spain.

22. Pontiac's War.—The Indians in the valley of the great lakes, who owed so much to the French, beheld with regret the decline of French power; hence when British garrisons took possession of the western forts, great discontent was roused. Finally, a number of tribes, under Pontiac, a celebrated Ottawa chief, united in a general war. In a short time, most of the posts west of Niagara were surprised and taken by the savages. The border settlements of Pennsylvania and Virginia were laid waste, and hundreds of families driven from their homes or massacred. A furious war seemed inevitable, when, through the mediation of the French officers in Illinois, the Indians were induced to stop hostilities. Pontiac left Detroit, which he had besieged for some months, and fled to the hunting-grounds of the Illinois, where he was stabbed by a Peorian Indian.

PRINCIPAL BATTLES OF THE FRENCH AND INDIAN WAR.

Date of Battle.	Location.	Commanders.		Successful Party.
		English.	French.	
1754	Great Meadows	Washington	Jumonville	English.
	Fort Necessity	Washington	Villiers	French.
	In Nova Scotia	Moncton / Winslow		English.
1755	Near Fort du Quesne	Braddock		French.
	Near Lake George	Williams	Dieskau	French.
	Near Fort Edward	Johnson	Dieskau	English.
1756	Oswego	Mercer	Montcalm	French.
1757	Fort William Henry	Monroe	Montcalm	French.
1758	Louisburg	Amherst		English.
1759	Ticonderoga	Abercrombie	Montcalm	French.
	Fort Frontenac	Bradstreet		English.
	Fort Niagara	Prideaux		English.
	Quebec	Wolfe	Montcalm	English.

STUDY NO. 3.

CAUSES OF THE AMERICAN REVOLUTION AND ITS FIRST BATTLES.

1. The Remote Causes of the Revolution lay in the very nature of things. The country was isolated; the inhabitants had fled from persecution at home and looked upon freedom as their birthright; and the colonial governments were, in general, anti-monarchical. To provoke such a people by any injustice was to loosen the ties which bound them to the mother country.

2. How England Treated the Colonies.—The English government was determined to keep the colonies dependent. The laws were all framed to favor the English manufacturer and merchant at the expense of the colonist. The Navigation Acts compelled the American farmer to send his products across the ocean to England, and to buy his goods in British markets. American manufactures were prohibited. Iron works were denounced as "common nuisances." Even the exportation of hats from one colony to another was prohibited, and no hatter was allowed to have more than two apprentices at one time. The importation of sugar, rum, and molasses, was burdened with exorbitant duties; and the Carolinians were forbidden to cut down the pine-trees of their vast forests, in order to convert the wood into staves, or the juice into turpentine and tar, for commercial purposes.

CAUSES OF AMERICAN REVOLUTION.

3. Attempt to Tax the Colonies.—George III. had now become king of England. Pitt was dismissed, and the new monarch determined to tax the colonies in order to fill the English treasury depleted by the expenses of the late war.

The first measure was to enforce the odious Navigation Laws, by means of *Writs of Assistance*. These were warrants authorizing the king's officers to enter any house or store, to search for smuggled goods.

The second measure was the famous *Stamp Act*, (1765) which ordered that stamps bought of the British government, should be put on all legal documents, newspapers, pamphlets, etc.

The assembly of Virginia was the first to make public opposition to this law. Patrick Henry, then a brilliant young lawyer, introduced a resolution denying the right of Parliament to tax America. He boldly asserted that the king had played the tyrant; and, alluding to the fate of other tyrants, exclaimed, *"Cæsar had his Brutus, Charles I. his Cromwell, and George III."*—here pausing till the cry of *"Treason! Treason!"* from several parts of the house had ended, he deliberately added—*"may profit by their examples. If this be treason, make the most of it."*

The third measure was the sending of troops to enforce the new regulations. The *"Mutiny Act,"* as it was called, ordered that the colonies should provide these soldiers with quarters and necessary supplies.

4. Effects of these Measures.—The colonies declared that, as they were not represented in Parliament, these acts were in violation of their rights, and that "TAXATION WITHOUT REPRESENTATION IS TYRANNY." The laws were felt to be unjust, and were resisted in every possible way. The houses of British officials were mobbed. Prominent loyalists were hung in effigy. Stamps were seized, and the agents forced to resign. People

PATRICK HENRY ADDRESSING THE VIRGINIA ASSEMBLY.

agreed not to use any article of British manufacture. Associations called the "Sons of Liberty," were formed to resist the Stamp Act. Delegates from nine of the colonies met at New York and framed a Declaration of Rights, and a petition to the king and Parliament. The 1st of November, appointed for the law to go into effect, was observed as a day of mourning. Bells were tolled, flags raised at half-mast, and business was suspended. Samuel and John Adams, Patrick Henry, and James Otis, aroused the people over the whole land by their stirring and patriotic speeches.

5. The Mutiny Act, especially, excited the deepest indignation. To be taxed was bad enough, but to shelter and feed their oppressors was unendurable. The New York assembly, having refused to comply, was forbidden to pass any legislative acts. The Massachusetts assembly sent a circular to the other colonies urging a union for redress of grievances. Parliament, in the name of the king, ordered the assembly to rescind this action, but it almost unanimously refused. Meanwhile the assemblies of nearly all the colonies had declared that Parliament had no right to tax them without their consent.

6. **Repeal of Stamp Act.**—Alarmed by these demonstrations, the English government repealed the Stamp Act,* (1766), but still declared its right to tax the colonies. Soon new taxes were imposed on tea, glass, paper, etc., and a Board of Trade was established at Boston, to act independently of the colonial assemblies.

7. **The Boston Massacre.**—Boston being considered the hot-bed of the rebellion, General Gage was sent thither with two regiments of troops. They entered on a quiet Sunday morning, and marched as through a conquered

---

* This repeal was carried through Parliament by the strenuous efforts of Pitt, Burke, Barre and other members of the opposition, who befriended the colonies in the heartiest way. The eloquent speech of Barre on the Stamp Act has long been familiar to every school-boy. In the House of Commons, Phipps exclaimed, "*My heart will bleed for every drop of American blood that shall be shed whilst their grievances are unredressed.*"

174   EXCELSIOR HISTORY.

city, with drums beating and flags flying. Quarters having been refused, they took possession of the State House. The Common was soon crowded with tents. Cannon were planted, sentries posted, and citizens challenged. Frequent quarrels now took place between the people and the soldiers. One day (March 5, 1770) a crowd of men and boys insulted the city guard. A fight ensued and two citizens were wounded and three killed.

   8. Boston Tea Party, (Dec. 16, 1773).—The British government, alarmed by the turn events had taken, rescinded

BOSTON TEA PARTY.

the other taxes; but to maintain the principle, left that on tea, making an arrangement whereby, with the tax included, tea was cheaper in America than in England. This subterfuge exasperated the patriots. They were fighting for a great principle, not a paltry tax. At a crowded

CAUSES OF AMERICAN REVOLUTION. 175

meeting held in Faneuil Hall, it was decided that the tea should never be brought ashore. Accordingly, a party of men, disguised as Indians, boarded the vessels, and emptied three hundred and forty-two chests of tea into the water.

FANEUIL HALL—"THE CRADLE OF LIBERTY."

9. Action of England.—The British government at once adopted retaliatory measures. General Gage was appointed governor of Massachusetts. The port of Boston was closed by act of Parliament. Business was, of course, stopped in that city, and distress ensued. The Virginia assembly having expressed sympathy with Massachusetts, was dissolved by the governor.

10. Action of the Colonies.—Nine years had elapsed since the passage of the Stamp Act. The desire for liberty was finding new voices continually. The people, inflamed by so many instances of aggression, were now ready to act promptly. Party lines were drawn. Those opposed to royalty were termed *Whigs*, and those supporting it, *Tories*. Everywhere were repeated the thrilling words of Patrick Henry, " *Give me liberty or give me death!*" Companies of soldiers, termed "*Minute men*," were formed. The idea of a continental union became popular. Gage, being alarmed, fortified Boston Neck, and seized powder wherever he could find it. A spark only was needed to kindle the slumbering hatred into the flames of war.

11. The First Continental Congress (Sept. 5, 1774) was held in Philadelphia. It consisted of men of influence who represented every colony except Georgia. As yet, however, few members had any idea of independence The Congress voted that obedience was not due to any of the recent acts of Parliament, and sustained Massachusetts in her resistance. It issued a protest against the keeping of standing armies in the colonies without the consent of the people, and agreed to hold no intercourse with Great Britain.

12. The Quebec Act, (1774).—Parliament, in order to prevent the Canadians, who were nearly all Catholics, from joining the colonies, passed a law known as *the Quebec Act*. This granted certain political privileges as well as liberty of conscience, throughout Canada and the French communities at the west. Thus, "*the nation that would not legally recognize the existence of a Catholic in Ireland, now, from political considerations, recognized on the St. Lawrence the free exercise of the religion of the Church of Rome.*" This concession aroused the bitterest feeling on both sides of the Atlantic. The city of London petitioned the king not to sign the Act. The Continental Congress of this year, in its address to the people of Great Britain, protested against it; and in New York and New England, still greater hostility to the measure was shown. Had the English colonies manifested a more kindly spirit towards their Canadian neighbors, the aid of the latter would probably not have been withheld in the desperate struggle which ensued.

13. Battle of Lexington, (April 19, 1775).—General Gage having learned that the people were gathering military stores at Concord, sent eight hundred men under Lieut.-Col. Smith and Major Pitcairn to destroy them. The patriots of Boston, however, were on the alert, and hurried out messengers * to alarm the country. When *the red-coats*, as the British soldiers were called, reached Lexington,[20] they found the minute-men gathering on the village green. A skirmish ensued, in which seven Americans were killed.

The British now pushed on and destroyed the stores but alarmed by the gathering militia, they soon retreated.

PAUL REVERE'S RIDE.

The whole region then flew to arms, and every boy old enough to use a rifle hurried to avenge the death of his countrymen. From behind trees, fences, buildings, and rocks, so galling a fire was poured, that but for reinforcements from Boston,[10] none of the British would have reached the city alive. As it was, they lost nearly three hundred men.

14. Effects of the Battle.—The news that American blood had been spilled spread quickly through the country,

---

* The most famous of these were Paul Revere and Wm. Dawes. The former caused two lanterns to be hung in Christ Church steeple as a signal to the patriots in Charleston, and then hurried off with his companion to alarm the country. Compare with this correct version of the story the one given by Longfellow in his famous poem, "Paul Revere's Ride."

178   EXCELSIOR HISTORY.

and patriots rushed in from all sides. Putnam left his cattle yoked in the field, mounted his fastest horse, and hurried to Boston. Soon twenty thousand men were making intrenchments to shut up the British in the city. Congresses were organized in all the colonies. Committees of safety were ap-

ETHAN ALLEN AT TICONDEROGA.

pointed to call out the troops and provide for any emergency. The power of the royal governors was broken from Massachusetts to Georgia.

15. Fort Ticonderoga[33] was surprised (May 10) by a company of "Green Mountain Boys" under Ethan Allen and Benedict Arnold. As Allen rushed into the sally-port at day-break, a sentinel snapped his gun at him and fled. Making his way to the commander's quarters, Allen ordered him to surrender. "*By whose authority?*" exclaimed the frightened officer who had just been aroused from his sleep.

BATTLE OF BUNKER HILL.

"*In the name of the Great Jehovah and the Continental Congress!*" shouted Allen. No resistance was attempted. Crown Point [15] was soon after as easily taken.

16. Battle of Bunker Hill, (June 17). The patriotic leader before Boston, Gen. Ward, having learned that the British were about to fortify Bunker Hill, deter-

CHARGE AT BUNKER HILL.

mined to anticipate them. A body of men under Colonel Prescott accordingly marched toward Charlestown. Breed's Hill was now chosen as a more commanding location. It was bright moonlight, and they were so near Boston that the sentinel's "*All's well,*" was distinctly heard. Yet so quietly did they work that there was no alarm. At daylight, the British officers were startled by seeing the redoubt which had been constructed. Resolved to drive the Americans from their position, Howe crossed the river with three thousand men.

17. In the afternoon the battle began. The British, in two assaults, were severely repulsed by the Americans. The latter, however, had now used up all their ammunition, and on the third assault, the Battle of Bunker Hill was a British victory.

18. Though defeated, the effect upon the Americans of this first regular battle was that of a victory. Their untrained farmer soldiers had nobly coped with British veterans. All felt encouraged, and the determination to fight for liberty was intensified.

19. Washington Commander-in-chief.—The second Continental Congress met at Philadelphia, on the very day Ticonderoga was captured. It voted to raise twenty thousand men, appointed *General Washington Commander-in-chief of the army*, and prepared a petition to the king, which he refused to receive.

20. Expedition against Canada.—Late in the same summer, General Montgomery, leading an army by way of Lake Champlain, captured St. John's and Montreal, and then appeared before Quebec. Here he was joined by Colonel Benedict Arnold with a crowd of half-clad, half-famished men, who had ascended the Kennebec and then struck across the wilderness. Their united force was less than a thousand effective men.

21. Attack upon Quebec.—Having besieged the city for three weeks, it was at last decided to hazard an assault. In the midst of a terrible snow-storm, they led their forces to the attack. Montgomery advancing along the river, lifting with his own hands the huge blocks of ice, and struggling through the drifts, cheered on his men. As they rushed forward, a rude blockhouse appeared through the blinding snow. Charging upon it, Montgomery fell at the first fire, and his followers, disheartened, fled. Arnold, in the meantime, approached the opposite side of the city. While bravely fighting, he was severely wounded and borne to the rear. Morgan, his successor, was forced to surrender. The remnant of the army, crouching behind mounds of snow and ice, maintained a blockade of the city until spring. At the approach of British reinforcements, the Americans were glad to escape, leaving all Canada in the hands of England.

22. Aid from the Abnaki.—Early in 1775, Washington asked and obtained aid from the Catholic Indians of Maine. Deputies of all the tribes from Gaspé to the Penobscot met at Watertown and agreed to stand by the colonists. Orono, the noble and virtuous chief of the Penobscots, bore a commission in our army, and his clansmen fought by his side. Devotedly Catholic, each of the tribes petitioned for a priest. Puritan Massachusetts promised to endeavor to obtain French missionaries for them.

23. "Strange revolution in the minds of men!" says John Gilmary Shea, "the very body which, less than a century before, had made it felony for a Catholic priest to visit the Abnakis, which had offered rewards for the heads of the missionaries of that tribe, which had exulted in slaying one at the altar, now regretted that it could not give these Christian Indians a missionary of the same faith and nation."

24. Commissioners to Canada.—The tardy justice of England had kindled the loyalty of the Canadians. The colonists, however, still hoped that the co-operation of Canada might be secured, and accordingly appointed an embassy consisting of Benjamin Franklin, Samuel Chase, Charles Carroll (of Carrolton), and Rev. John Carroll, to make an alliance, if possible, against Great Britain. But the anti-Catholic conduct of some members of the committee and the recently-expressed hostility of the colonists to the *Quebec Act*, prevented the provincials from securing aid from the Canadians.

Had Congress recognized at the very first, the folly of perpetuating religious bigotry, and welcomed the Canadians with them to a common birthright of liberty, there is no doubt that an alliance might have been perfected and the English been driven from the continent. They saw, when too late, their mistake.

25. Evacuation of Boston, (March 17, 1776).—Washington having resolved to force General Gage to fight or flee, sent a force by night to fortify Dorchester Heights. In the morning, the English were once more astonished by seeing intrenchments which overlooked the city. General Howe, who was then in command, remembering the lesson of Bunker Hill, finally decided to leave, and accordingly set sail for Halifax with his army, fleet, and many loyalists. The next day, Washington entered Boston amid great rejoicing. For eleven months, the inhabitants had endured the horrors of a siege and the insolence of the enemy.*

EVACUATION OF BOSTON.

* The boys of Boston were wont to amuse themselves in winter, by building snow-houses, and by skating on a pond in the Common. The soldiers having disturbed them in their sports, complaints were made to the inferior officers, who only ridiculed their petition. At last a number of the largest boys waited on General Gage. "*What!*" said Gage, "*have your fathers sent you here to exhibit the rebellion they have been teaching you?*" "*Nobody sent us,*" answered the leader, with flashing eye,

26. Attack on Fort Moultrie, (June 28).—Early in the summer, a British fleet appeared off Charleston Harbor, and opened fire on Fort Moultrie.* Meanwhile, General Clinton, who commanded the British land troops, tried to attack the fort in the rear, but the fire of the southern riflemen was too severe. The fleet was at last so badly shattered that it withdrew and sailed for New York.

27. Declaration of Independence, (July 4, 1776).—During the session of Congress this summer, Richard Henry Lee, of Virginia, moved that "*The United Colonies are, and ought to be, free and independent states.*" This resolution was passed by a majority of one colony, and a committee appointed to draw up a DECLARATION OF INDEPENDENCE.† At two o'clock on the fourth of July, its report was adopted.‡

"*we have never injured your troops, but they have trampled down our mow-hills and broken the ice of our skating-pond. We complained, and they called us young rebels, and told us to help ourselves if we could. We told the captain, and he laughed at us. Yesterday our works were destroyed for the third time, and we will bear it no longer.*" The British commander could not restrain his admiration. "*The very children,*" said he, "*draw in a love of liberty with the air they breathe. Go, my brave boys, and be assured, if my troops trouble you again, they shall be punished.*"

* This fort was built of palmetto logs, which are so soft that balls sink into them without splitting the wood. Here floated the first republican flag in the South. In the early part of the action the staff was struck by a ball, and the flag fell outside the fort. Sergeant Jasper leaped over the breastwork, caught up the flag, and springing back, tied it to a sponge-staff (an instrument for cleaning cannon after a discharge), and hoisted it again to its place. The next day Governor Rutledge offered him a sword and a lieutenant's commission. He refused, saying, "*I am not fit for the company of officers; I am only a sergeant.*"

† Thomas Jefferson, John Adams, Benjamin Franklin, Roger Sherman, and Robert R. Livingston composed this committee.

‡ During the day, the streets of Philadelphia were crowded with people anxious to learn the decision. In the steeple of the old State House was a bell

LIBERTY BELL.

28. The declaration was signed by fifty-four delegates from the various states. As John Hancock, the president, wrote his name in a bold clear hand, he exclaimed: "*There! John Bull can read that without spectacles, and may now double his reward of five hundred pounds for my head. That is my defiance.*" Turning to the rest, he added: "*Gentlemen, we must be unanimous; we must all hang together.*" "*Yes,*" replied Franklin, "*or we shall all hang separately.*"

29. As Charles Carroll affixed his signature, one of the members alluding to his great wealth, remarked: "*There go millions!*" "*No,*" said another, "*There are several Charles Carrolls; he cannot be identified.*" Mr. Carroll hearing the conversation, immediately added to his name the words "*of Carrollton,*" exclaiming as he did so: "*They cannot mistake me now!*"

on which, by a happy coincidence, was inscribed, "*Proclaim liberty throughout all the land unto all the inhabitants thereof!*" In the morning, when Congress assembled, the bell-ringer went to his post, having placed his boy below to announce when the Declaration was adopted, that his bell might be the first to peal forth the glad tidings. Long he waited, while the deliberations went on. Impatiently the old man shook his head and repeated, "*They will never do it! They will never do it!*" Suddenly he heard his boy clapping his hands and shouting, "*Ring! Ring!*" Grasping the iron tongue, he swung it to and fro, proclaiming the glad news of liberty to all the land. The crowded streets caught up the sound. Every steeple re-echoed it. All that night, by shouts, and illuminations, and booming of cannon, the people declared their joy.

"How they shouted! What rejoicing!
How the old bell shook the air,
Till the clang of freedom ruffled
The calm, gliding Delaware!
How the bonfires and the torches
Illumed the night's repose,
And from the flames, like Phœnix,
Fair Liberty arose!

"That old bell now is silent,
And hushed its iron tongue,
But the spirit it awakened
Still lives,—forever young,
And while we greet the sunlight,
On the fourth of each July,
We'll ne'er forget the bellman,
Who, twixt the earth and sky,
Rang out OUR INDEPENDENCE;
Which, please God, *shall never die!*"

STUDY NO. 4.

CAMPAIGNS IN NEW YORK, NEW JERSEY, AND PENNSYLVANIA, (1776—1777).

1. Preparations.—General Howe with his army soon set sail from Halifax for New York. Thither also came Admiral Howe, his brother, with reinforcements from England, and Clinton from the defeat at Fort Moultrie. Washington, divining Howe's plans, gathered all his forces at New York to protect that city.

2. Battle of Long Island, (Aug. 27).—The British army, 30,000 strong, landed on the southwest shore of Long Island. General Putnam, with about nine thousand men, held a fort at Brooklyn and some defences on a range of hills south of the city. The English advanced in three divisions. Two of these attacked the Americans in front, while General Clinton, by a circuitous route, gained their rear. The patriots were fighting gallantly, when, to their dismay, they heard firing behind them. They attempted to escape, but out of five thousand engaged in this battle, nearly two thousand were killed, wounded, or captured.*

3. Had Howe attacked the fort at Brooklyn immediately, the Americans would have been destroyed. Fortunately, he delayed for the fleet to arrive. For two days the patriots lay

---

* Those who were taken captive were confined in crowded prisons. Nothing could exceed the sufferings of these poor victims. Many died in the Sugar House, but by far the saddest scenes occurred on the prison-ships. These were old hulks anchored in the waters around New York. Almost eleven thousand bodies were carried out from these loathsome places of confinement during the war and buried in the sand of the beach. In 1808 their remains were reinterred, and now rest in a vault on Hudson avenue, Brooklyn.

helpless, awaiting the assault. On the second night after the battle, there was a dense fog on the Brooklyn side, while in New York the weather was clear. At midnight, the Americans moved silently down to the shore and crossed the river.* In the morn-

THE RETREAT FROM LONG ISLAND.

ing, when the sun had scattered the fog, Howe was chagrined to find that his prey had escaped.

* The Americans embarked near the present Fulton Ferry. A woman sent her negro servant to the British, to inform them of the movements of the Americans. He was captured by the *Hessians*, who were Germans from Hesse Cassel, hired to fight by the British government. These, not being able to understand English, detained him until the morning, when his message was too late.

CAMPAIGN IN NEW JERSEY. 187

4. Washington's Retreat.—The British, crossing to New York,* moved to attack Washington, who had taken post on *Harlem Heights*. Finding the American position too strong, Howe sailed up the Sound, in order to gain the rear. Washington then withdrew to *White Plains*.[86] Here Howe came up and defeated a part of his army. Washington next retired into a fortified camp at *North Castle*. Howe, not daring to attack him, returned to New York and sent the Hessians to take *Fort Washington*, which they captured after a fierce resistance.

5. Flight Through New Jersey, (Nov.-Dec.).— Washington, apprehending that the British intended to march next against Philadelphia, had already crossed into New Jersey. Thither Cornwallis quickly followed with 6000 men, in hot chase of the patriot army. For three weeks he pursued the flying Americans, now reduced to three thousand. Many of Washington's men had no shoes, and left their blood-stained foot-prints on the frozen ground. Oftentimes the van of the pursuing army was in sight of the American rear-guard. At last Washington reached the Delaware, and all the boats having been secured, crossed into Pennsylvania.† Howe resolved to wait until the river should freeze over, and

---

* Washington desiring to gain some knowledge of Howe's movements, sent Captain Nathan Hale to visit the camps on Long Island. He passed the lines safely, but on his way back was recognized by a tory relative, who arrested him. He was taken to Howe's headquarters, tried, and executed as a spy. During his imprisonment, he was forbidden all religious instruction, and even his farewell letters to his mother and sister were destroyed. The brutality of his enemies did not, however, crush his noble spirit, for his last words were, "*I only regret that I have but one life to give to my country.*"

† During this retreat, Washington repeatedly sent orders to General Lee, who had been left at North Castle with a portion of the army, to join him at once. Lee hesitated, and at last moved very slowly. Five days after this, while quartered in a small tavern at Baskingridge, remote from his troops, he was taken prisoner by English cavalry. His capture was thought a great misfortune to the Americans, who considered him the best officer in the army. Events have since shown him to have been a traitor.

then capture Philadelphia. In the meantime he quartered his troops along the river, in the neighboring villages.

6. Battle of Trenton.[24]—In this time of gloom, when his army consisted of only a handful of ragged fugitives, and the enemy's camp was thronged with persons anxious to take the oath of allegiance to George III., Washington stood firm. Suddenly he struck a daring blow. On Christmas night, in a driving storm of sleet and amid drifting ice, he crossed the Delaware, fell upon the Hessians at Trenton, in the midst of their festivities,* captured one thousand prisoners, slew their leader, and escaped back safely to camp, with the loss of only four men—two killed and two frozen to death.

7. The effect of this brilliant feat was to kindle anew the fires of patriotism. Troops whose time of enlistment was expiring agreed to remain, and new recruits were received. Howe was alarmed, and ordered Cornwallis to attack the exultant Americans at once.

8. Battle of Princeton,[25] (Jan. 3, 1777).—Washington soon crossed the Delaware again, and took post at Trenton. Cornwallis came up with the British forces toward night, and his first onset being repulsed, decided to wait till morning. Washington's situation was critical. Before him was a powerful army, and behind a river full of floating ice. That night, leaving his camp-fires burning to deceive the enemy, he swept, by country roads, around the

---

* Hunt, a trader with friends and foes, had invited Rall, the Hessian commander, to a Christmas supper. Amusements were kept up all night long. A messenger came in haste, at early dawn, with a note to the colonel. It was sent by a tory to give warning of the approach of the American forces. The negro servant refused admittance to the bearer. Knowing its importance, he bade the negro to take the note directly to the officer. The servant obeyed, but the colonel thrust it unopened into his pocket. Soon the roll of drums was heard, and before the pleasure-loving officer could reach his quarters, the Americans were in pursuit of his flying soldiers.

British, fell upon the troops near Princeton, routed them,* took three hundred prisoners, and by rapid marches reached Morristown Heights in safety. Cornwallis heard the firing and hurried to the rescue, but he was too late.

9. Burgoyne's Invasion.—In June, 1777, General Burgoyne marched south from Canada, with an army of ten thousand British and Indians. Forts Crown Point,[15] Ticonderoga,[33] and Edward successively fell into his hands. General Schuyler, with the small force at his command, could only obstruct his path through the wilderness, by felling trees across the road, and breaking down bridges. The loss of so many strongholds caused general alarm. Lincoln, with the Massachusetts troops; Arnold, noted for his headlong valor; and Morgan, with his famous riflemen, were sent to check Burgoyne's advance. Militiamen gathered from the neighboring States, and an army was rapidly collected and drilled. So much dissatisfaction, however, arose with Schuyler that he was superseded by Gates, just as he was ready to reap the results of his well-laid schemes. With noble-minded patriotism, he made known to Gates all his plans, and generously assisted him in their execution. The army was now stationed at Bemis Heights, where fortifications were thrown up under the direction of Kosciusko [*kos-se-us'-ko*].

10. Burgoyne's Difficulties. — Meanwhile two

---

* Just before the moment of victory, Washington was in imminent peril of his life. A large British force unexpectedly coming up, the American militia hesitated to advance. Washington dashing to the front within thirty paces of the enemy, reined in his horse just as both lines fired a volley. His aid-de-camp, Colonel Fitzgerald, a warm-hearted Irishman, aware of the danger of his beloved general, drew his hat over his eyes, that he might not see him die. A shout of victory immediately ensued, the smoke cleared away, and there stood Washington as calm and unmoved as if on parade. Fitzgerald, who was celebrated as one of the finest horsemen of the American army, spurring his steed, dashed forward to the side of the general, exclaiming: " *Thank God, your Excellency is safe!* " then, unable to support the sudden transition from despair to joy, he wept like a child. Washington grasped his hand with warmth, and only said: "*Away, my dear Colonel, and bring up the troops. The day is ours!*"

events had occurred which materially deranged the plans of Burgoyne.

1. *St. Leger's Expedition.*—St. Leger had been sent to take Fort Schuyler (now Rome), and thence to ravage the Mohawk valley and join Burgoyne's army at Albany. General Arnold was dispatched by General Schuyler to relieve this fort. Arnold accomplished his mission by a stratagem. A half-witted tory

THE ALARM AT FORT SCHUYLER.

boy who had been taken prisoner, was promised his freedom, if he would spread the report among St. Leger's troops that a large body of Americans was close at hand. The boy, having cut holes in his clothes, ran breathless into the camp of the besiegers, showing the bullet holes and describing his narrow escape from the enemy. When asked their number, he mysteriously pointed upward to the leaves on the trees.

CAMPAIGN IN NEW YORK. 191

The Indians and British were so frightened that they fled precipitately, leaving their tents and artillery behind them.

2. Battle of Bennington.[9]—Burgoyne sent a detachment under Colonel Baum to seize the supplies the Americans had collected at Bennington, Vt. General Stark with the militia met him there. As Stark saw the British lines forming for the attack, he exclaimed, *"There are the red-coats; we must beat them to-day, or Molly Stark is a widow."* His patriotism and bravery so inspired his raw troops that they defeated the British regulars and took about six hundred prisoners.*

11. Two Battles of Saratoga,[10] (Sept. 19 and Oct. 7).—Disappointed in his expectation of supplies from both these directions, Burgoyne moved south and attacked Gates' army at *Bemis Heights* near *Saratoga*. An obstinate struggle ensued, without advantage to either side. For two weeks afterward, both armies lay in camp, each watching a favorable moment for attack. At last Burgoyne's supplies became so low that he was compelled to take action, and accordingly moved out to attack the Americans.

12. Benedict Arnold, who had been unjustly deprived of his command, rushed into the thickest of the fight. He had no authority to fight, much less to direct; but, dashing to the head of his old troops, he ordered a charge on the British line. Urging on the fight, leading every onset, delivering his orders in person where the bullets flew thickest, he was at last wounded in the same leg that was injured at Quebec. But he had already won a victory while Gates was staying in his tent.

---

* One old man had five sons in the patriot army at Bennington. A neighbor, just from the field, told him that one had been unfortunate. *"Has he proved a coward or a traitor?"* asked the father. *"Worse than that,"* was the answer; *"he has fallen, but while bravely fighting."* *"Ah,"* said the father, *"then I am satisfied."*

13. Effects of these Battles.—Surrender of Burgoyne.
— Burgoyne now fell back to Saratoga.[30] Hemmed in on all sides, there was no hope of escape. Provisions were low and water was scarce, as no one, except the women, dared to go to the river for it. Under these circumstances he had no choice but to surrender, and his entire army, nearly six thousand strong, laid down their arms.

At the news of this victory, the hopes of the American people rose to the highest pitch of confidence.

14. Battle of Brandywine,[11] (Sept. 11, 1777).—
Having wintered at New York, Howe, in the spring, sent out several marauding expeditions.* Washington was then in New Jersey watching his movements; and Howe, later in the summer, made every effort to force the American army to give battle. As Washington was too wary † for him, the British general suddenly embarked 18,000 men on his brother's fleet, and set sail. Washington hurried south to meet him. The patriot army numbered only eleven thousand men, but when Washington learned that the British had arrived in the Chesapeake, he resolved to hazard a battle for the defence of Philadelphia. The Americans accordingly took position at *Chad's Ford*, on the Brandywine. Here they were attacked in front, while Cornwallis stole around in the rear,

---

* One of these, under Howe himself, ascended the Hudson to Peekskill and burned the military stores at that point. Another, commanded by the notorious Tryon, destroyed the town of Danbury, Conn., the men plundering and destroying everything *en route*. A third, commanded by Gen. Clinton, went up the Hudson after Howe had gone to Philadelphia. It was expected that this expedition would move against Albany, and so create a diversion in favor of Burgoyne, then hard pressed at Saratoga. Clinton easily eluded Gen. Putnam, commanding the American forces on the lower Hudson, and captured Forts Clinton (named after Gov. Clinton of New York) and Montgomery, but, when the way was clear before him, lingered, leaving Burgoyne to his fate.

† Washington, at this time, merited the surname of the *American Fabius*, from the resemblance of his policy to that of the celebrated Roman general, who, contending with Hannibal, avoided engagements, and harassed him by continual delay.

as Clinton had done in the battle of Long Island. Sullivan, Sterling, La Fayette, Wayne, and Count Pulaski, in vain performed prodigies of valor. The patriots were routed, Philadelphia was taken, and the British army went into quarters there and at Germantown.

15. Battle of Germantown,[19] (Oct. 4).—Washington would not let the enemies of his country rest in peace. A few weeks after they had settled down for the winter, he made a night march, and at sunrise fell upon their troops at *Germantown*. At first the attack was successful, but a few companies of British desperately defending a stone house caused delay. The co-operation of the different divisions was prevented by a dense fog, which also hid the confusion of the enemy, so that the Americans retreated just at the moment of victory.

16. Capture of Forts on the Delaware.—Although the British had possession of Philadelphia, the Americans still held *Forts Mifflin* and *Mercer* on the banks of the Delaware, and thus prevented the English fleet from ascending to that city. The gallant defenders of these posts held them against assault and bombardment, and it was not until late in the fall that they were compelled to leave, by the approach of Cornwallis with greatly superior forces.

17. Washington at Valley Forge.[20]—The American army passed the next winter at Valley Forge. It was the gloomiest season of the war. The continental paper money was so depreciated in value that an officer's pay would not keep him in clothes. Many of the officers having spent their entire fortune in the war, were now compelled to resign in order to earn a living. The men were encamped in cold, comfortless huts. Barefooted, they left their tracks in blood, on the frozen ground. Few had blankets; straw could not be

IN CAMP AT VALLEY FORGE.

obtained, and they were compelled to sleep, half-clothed as they were, on the bare earth. The sick had no change of clothing, no suitable food, and no medicines. Amid this terrible suffering the fires of patriotism burned brightly. Washington felt that his cause was just, and inspired all around him with his sublime confidence.*

* During this winter Washington was quartered at the house of Isaac Potts. One day, while Potts was on his way up the creek he heard a voice of prayer. Softly following its direction, he soon discovered the General upon his knees, his cheeks wet with tears. Narrating the incident to his wife, he added with much emotion, "*Under such a commander our independence is certain.*"

STUDY NO. 5.

ALLIANCE WITH FRANCE. CAMPAIGN AT THE SOUTH.

1. We now enter on a new period of the war. It is distinguished chiefly for two facts; first, that France now entered into an alliance with the Americans; and second, that after this, the war was carried on principally in the South.

2. French Help.—From the beginning of the Revolution, the patriots had hoped to obtain aid from France, nor were they disappointed. Early in 1776, Silas Deane was sent to Paris to urge an alliance. After the Declaration of Independence, he was joined by Benjamin Franklin and Arthur Lee. Though France sympathized with the Americans, she could give them no open aid without incurring the hostility of Great Britain. Secretly, however, she furnished them with money, arms, provisions and clothing. Louis XVI. permitted French officers to leave their country to aid the American cause, and encouraged commerce with the colonies, by exempting from duty all vessels bearing supplies to the United States.

3. La Fayette.—Among the most distinguished French officers who gave themselves to our cause, was the young Marquis of La Fayette. Contrary to the entreaties of his friends, when American affairs looked gloomiest, he fitted out a vessel at his own expense, and with eleven officers, among whom was the German veteran, Baron de

MARQUIS DE LA FAYETTE.

BARON DE KALB.

Kalb, sailed for the New World, (1777). His departure created a great sensation in France and England, and was hailed with intense joy by the Americans.* On his arrival in the United States,† he was almost immediately appointed to the rank of major-general in the army. A few days after, began his acquaintance with Washington, which soon ripened into intimate friendship.

* "The sensation produced by his appearance in this country," says Ticknor, "was, of course, much greater than that produced in Europe by his departure. It still stands forth as one of the most prominent and important circumstances in our revolutionary contest; and, as has often been said by one who bore no small part in its trials and success, none but those who were then alive can believe what an impulse it gave to the hopes of a population almost disheartened by a long series of disasters."

† Congress expressed its high sense of the value of his example and of his personal worth by the following resolution : " Whereas the Marquis de La Fayette, out of his great zeal to the cause of liberty in which the United States are engaged, has left his family and connections, and at his own expense has come over to offer his services to the United States, without pension or particular allowance, and is anxious to risk his life in our cause: *Resolved, that his services be accepted, and that, in consideration of his zeal, illustrious family and connections, he have the rank and commission of major-general in the army of the United States.*"

ALLIANCE WITH FRANCE.

4. Kosciusko and Pulaski.—Among the other foreign patriots who crossed the sea to fight the battle of our freedom, were two noble Poles, Kosciusko (*kos-se-us-ko*) and Pulaski. When *Kosciusko* presented himself before Washington with letters of introduction from Franklin, "*What can you do?*" inquired the general. "*Try me!*" was the laconic reply. Washington was much pleased with him and made him his aid. He became a colonel in the engineer corps, and afterwards planned the works at West Point.

KOSCIUSKO.

Pulaski had already honorably distinguished himself in the struggles of his native country. Here he organized the "*American Legion*," which did excellent service and won great renown.

5. French Alliance.—Franklin, meanwhile, had gained considerable influence at the French court; Marie Antoinette was our hearty friend; and when the news of Burgoyne's surrender reached Europe, Louis XVI. was induced to acknowledge the independence of the United States, and to make a treaty of alliance with the young Republic, (Feb. 6, 1778).

PULASKI.

6. Great was the rejoicing of the Americans over this event; and by it a bond was knit between France and this country which is felt to the present time. To Washington, in his camp at Valley Forge,[36] it brought renewed hope and courage. The 6th of May was set apart for a military fête. There was a solemn thanksgiving by the chaplains, at the head of each brigade, followed by a grand parade and a national discharge of thirteen guns amid the shouts of the whole army: "*Long live the king of France!*" "*Long live the friendly European Powers!*" "*Huzza for the American States!*"

7. English Proposals.—At this juncture, England sent commissioners with liberal proposals, which, before the war commenced, would have been accepted; but that day was now past. Next bribery was tried. Among those approached was General Reed of Pennsylvania. He was offered ten thousand guineas and distinguished honors, if he would exert his influence to effect a reconciliation. "*I am not worth purchasing,*" said the honest patriot, "*but such as I am, the king of Great Britain is not rich enough to buy me.*"

8. Results of the Alliance.—France now openly took part in the war; and in April, 1778, a French fleet under D'Estaing (*des-tang*) sailed for America. The effect of this was electric. The British authorities at once ordered their army and fleet from Philadelphia to New York. Washington followed from Valley Forge.

9. Battle of Monmouth,[28] (June 28, 1778).—The retreating army was overtaken near Monmouth, New Jersey, where an action took place. Gen. Charles Lee held the advance; but, instead of attacking the enemy as he had been directed, he ordered a retreat. Washington riding up at this moment of peril, bitterly rebuked Lee, by his personal presence rallied the men, and sent them back against the enemy.

The fight lasted all that long sultry day.* In the darkness of night, Clinton stole away with his men to New York.

10. Attack on Newport.[20]—Upon the arrival of the French fleet off the American coast, D'Estaing arranged with Gen. Sullivan to aid in an attack upon Newport, R. I.

MOLLY PITCHER AT THE BATTLE OF MONMOUTH. (*See note.*)

Soon after the French entered Narragansett Bay, (July 29), Howe appeared off the harbor with the English fleet, and D'Estaing went out to meet him. A terrible storm now came on, which so shattered both fleets that they were

---

* In the midst, an artilleryman was shot at his post. His wife, Mary Pitcher, while bringing water to her husband from a spring, saw him fall, and heard the commander order the piece to be removed from the field. Instantly dropping the pail, she hastened to the cannon, seized the rammer, and with great skill and courage performed her husband's duty. The soldiers gave her the nickname of *Major Molly.* On the day after the battle, she was presented to Washington, and Congress afterwards voted her a sergeant's commission with half-pay through life.

compelled to put back for repairs. General Sullivan thereupon retreated, just in time to escape Clinton, who came up from New York with reinforcements.

11. Change of the Theatre of War.—In the fall, D'Estaing sailed to attack the British possessions in the West Indies; and the English fleet followed to aid in their defence. This move had an important effect upon the war. The British deprived of the assistance of the navy, despaired of success at the north, and turned their attention to the less populous south. Thenceforth the principal battles of the war were fought in that region.

12. The Massacre of Wyoming.[20]—In July, 1778, a band of Indians and Englishmen disguised as Indians, burst into the beautiful valley of Wyoming, laid waste the settlements, and slew the inhabitants, men, women and children. They even cut out the tongues of the horses and cows, and left the poor beasts to die.

13. Conquest of Georgia.—December 23, 1778, the British fleet appeared off Savannah, troops landed, and after a brief engagement at *Brewton's Hill*, captured the city. Soon after, Gen. Prevost led the British forces from Florida northward through the wilderness, and, taking command of the English, by his vigorous efforts, conquered the entire state. The royal governor was reinstated in office, and everything was restored as it was before the war.

14. French-American Attack on Savannah.[x]—In the fall of 1779, D'Estaing, with the French fleet of twenty ships-of-the-line, appeared off the coast of Georgia, and he at once planned with Lincoln for a combined attack upon Savannah. After a severe bombardment, an unsuccessful assault was made, in which a thousand lives were lost.

Count Pulaski was mortally wounded. The simple-hearted Sergeant Jasper died grasping the banner presented to his regiment at Fort Moultrie. D'Estaing, dreading the approaching winter storms, then returned to the Indies.

15. Capture of Charleston, (May 12, 1780).—Georgia being subdued, the war was now carried into South Carolina. Charleston was attacked by land and sea, and General Lincoln, having endured a siege of forty days and a terrible bombardment, was forced to surrender. The British at once sent out expeditions in every direction, and the whole State was soon overrun.

16. Partisan Corps.—The Carolinas were full of tories. Many of them joined the British army; others organized companies which mercilessly robbed and murdered their whig neighbors. On the other hand, there were *patriot bands* which rendezvoused (*ron-da-vood*) in swamps, and sallied out as occasion offered. These partisan corps kept the country in continued terror. Marion,* Sumter, Pickens, and Lee, were noted patriot leaders, and their bands were often strong enough to cut off British detachments, and even successfully attack small garrisons. The issue of the struggle at the south was largely decided by the bravery of these citizen soldiers.

17. Battle of Camden,[12] (Aug. 16, 1780).—General Gates, "*the conqueror of Burgoyne,*" now taking command of the troops at the South, marched to meet the enemy under Cornwallis, near Camden. Singularly, both generals

---

* A British officer sent to negotiate concerning an exchange of prisoners, dined with Marion. The dinner consisted of roasted potatoes. Surprised at this meagre diet, he made some inquiries, when he found that this was their customary fare, and also that the patriot general served without pay. This devotion to the cause of liberty so affected the officer that he resigned his commission, thinking it folly to fight such men.

had appointed the same time to make a night attack. While marching for this purpose, the advance guards of the two armies unexpectedly encountered each other in the woods. At dawn, Cornwallis ordered a charge. The militia, taken by surprise, fled at the first fire. De Kalb, with the continental regulars, consisting of Maryland an

A RENDEZVOUS OF MARION AND HIS MEN.

Delaware regiments, stood firm, but at last fell, pierced with eleven wounds. His brave comrades fought desperately over his body until they were overwhelmed by numbers. The army was so scattered that it could not be collected.

18. Battle of Cowpens,[14] (January 17, 1781).—
General Greene, who was appointed to succeed General Gates, found the army to consist of only two thousand half-clothed, half-starved men. A part of his force, under Morgan, was attacked at *Cowpens* by the British under Tarleton; but the Americans proved victorious. Tarleton himself narrowly escaped capture at the hands of Colonel Wm. Washington, by whom he was wounded while retreating from the field. Cornwallis, hearing of the disaster at *Cowpens*, set out in hot haste, eager to punish the victors and recapture the prisoners. Morgan started for Virginia, and crossed the Catawba[19] just before Cornwallis came in sight. Night came on, and with it rain, which raised the river so high as to keep the impatient Cornwallis waiting for three days.

19. This defeat was a source of great mortification to Tarleton. He was occasionally reminded of it in a very disagreeable manner. At one time, after having indulged in much braggart talk about his own gallantry, he remarked to a whig lady: *"I should like to see your far-famed hero Colonel Washington."* *"Your wish, Colonel, might have been fairly gratified,"* was the prompt reply, *"had you ventured to look behind you after the battle of Cowpens."* A still more pointed retort was given him by another lady, to whom he observed, *"I have been told that Colonel Washington is so ignorant a fellow that he can hardly write his own name."* *"Ah, Colonel,"* she replied, *"but no one knows better than yourself that he can make his mark."*

20. Greene's Retreat.—General Greene now joined Morgan, and conducted the retreat. At the Yadkin,[40] just as the Americans had reached the other side, it began to rain. When Cornwallis came up, the river was so swollen that he could not cross. He, however, marched up the stream, effected a passage, and was soon in full pursuit again. Now came a race, on parallel roads, thirty miles per day, for the fords of the Dan. Greene reached them first, and Cornwallis gave up the chase. This signal deliverance of

MRS. STEELE AND GENERAL GREENE.

Greene's exhausted army awoke a feeling of gratitude in every American heart.*

* One night during this famous retreat, Greene alighted at the Salisbury inn, after a hard day's ride through mud and rain. The army physician, who had charge of the sick and wounded prisoners, met him at the door and inquired after his wellbeing. "*Fatigued, hungry, cold, and penniless*," was the heavy-hearted reply. The patriotic landlady, Mrs. Elizabeth Steele, overheard the words. Lighting a cheerful fire, she spread a warm supper before him, and then quietly producing two bags of specie, her hoarded treasure, "*Take these*," she said ; "*you will want them, and I can do without them.*" It is hard to decide which was the happier, the noble-hearted giver or the relieved receiver. Cheered and comforted, Greene renewed his journey with a lightened heart.

Another story illustrative of the patriotism of the Southern women is told of Mrs. Motte. The British had taken possession of her house, fortified and garrisoned it. On Colonel Lee's advance this patriotic woman furnished him a bow and arrows, by means of which fire was thrown upon the shingled roof. Her mansion was soon in flames. The occupants, to save their lives, surrendered.

21. Close of the War at the South, (1781).—
Having rested his men, Green again took the field, harassing
the enemy by a fierce partisan war-
fare. At *Guilford (ghil'-ford)
Court-House* (March 15) he haz-
arded a battle. The militia fled
again at the first fire, but the continental regulars fought as in the
time of De Kalb. The Americans
at last retired, but the British had
bought their victory so dearly
that Cornwallis also retreated.
Greene again pursuing, Cornwallis shut himself up in Wilmington.
Thereupon Greene turned his

PICKENS.

course to South Carolina, and with the aid of Marion, Sumter, Lee, and Pickens, nearly delivered this State and Georgia
from the English.

22. In the battle of *Eutaw
Springs* [17] (Sept. 8), the forces of the
enemy were so crippled that they
retired toward Charleston. Though
the partisan warfare still distracted
the country, this engagement closed
the long and fiercely fought contest
at the South.

MORGAN.

During the retreat, Manning, a noted soldier of Lee's legion, was in
hot pursuit of the flying British, when he suddenly found himself surrounded by the enemy, and not an American within forty rods. He did
not hesitate, but, seizing an officer by the collar, and wresting his sword
from him by main force, kept his body as a shield while, under a heavy
fire, he backed off from the dangerous neighborhood. The frightened
British officer, when thus summarily captured, began immediately to

enumerate his titles: "*I am Sir Henry Barry, deputy adjutant-general, captain of the fifty-second regiment, etc., etc.*" "*Enough!*" interrupted his captor, "*You are just the man I was looking for.*"

23. Cornwallis, meanwhile, had gone north into Virginia. Here the British were partially kept in check by Lafayette, who had been sent thither with a small force. Lafayette proved himself at this time, as he had done throughout the war, prudent, skillful, brave, and above all, generous to his men, whose wants he supplied from his own purse.

24. Spanish Aid.—About the time that France sent her first offering of money, Spain gave a similar amount, $200,000. She subsequently sent cargoes of supplies to us from Bilbao[9]; and from Madrid, she forwarded blankets for ten regiments and a gift of $150,000.

SUMTER.

25. The English having seized an American schooner on the Louisiana lakes, Count Bernardo de Galvez, the young Spanish governor of Louisiana, confiscated English vessels in reprisal. In 1780, he besieged the English at Baton Rouge and compelled them to surrender. Finally, he took Pensacola,[a] (1781), which blow crushed the British power on our southern frontier.

STUDY NO. 6.

EVENTS OF THE WAR AT THE NORTH THE FINAL CAMPAIGN (1778-1781).

1. The North-West Secured.—Congress having resolved to secure the West, Colonel George Clark, under authority from Virginia, after a long and toilsome march, surprised Kaskaskia and Cahokia (July, 1778). The French settlers immediately joined his standard, and by the mediation of Father Gibault [*gee-bo*], the pastor of Kaskaskia, Vincennes also acknowledged the United States. Clark, having secured the Illinois country, built a fort where Louisville now stands, and thus checked any Indian hostility in the West.

2. Father Gibault blessed the arms of the French volunteers in the American cause, administered in his own church the oath of allegiance to Congress, and enlisted the Christian Indians in favor of the Americans. "Next to Clark and Vigo," remarks Judge Law, "the United States are more indebted to Father Gibault for the accession of the States comprised in what was the original Northwestern Territory, than to any other man."

3. The Capture of Stony Point, (July 15, 1779,) by General Wayne, with only eight hundred men, was one of the most brilliant exploits of the war. The countersign, which, curiously enough, was "*The fort is ours,*" was obtained from a negro who was in the habit of selling strawberries at the fort. In the darkness of night he guided them to the causeway leading over the flooded marsh around the foot of the hill on which the fort was situated. The unsuspicious sentinel having received the countersign, was chatting with

THE COUNTERSIGN AT STONY POINT.

the negro, when he was suddenly seized and gagged. Wayne's men passed over the causeway, scaled the fort, and captured it at the point of the bayonet.

4. General Sullivan's Expedition.—The atrocities of the Indians had kept the inhabitants of the Wyoming and Mohawk valleys in continual terror. In the summer of 1779, General Sullivan led an expedition into the Genesee country. The savages were everywhere defeated, and forty of their villages were burned.

5. The Winter of 1779–'80 was the severest of the eighteenth century. New York Bay was so completely frozen over that the British troops, with heavy cannon, crossed to Staten Island. The sufferings of Washington's army in camp at Morristown, N. J., surpassed those even of Valley Forge. Congress had previously issued paper money to a large amount, and it had now become so depreciated in value that $40 in Continental bills were worth only $1 in coin. A pair of boots cost $600, and a soldier's pay for a month would hardly buy him a dinner. The British, too, had set in circulation so well-executed counterfeits that many persons refused to take the Continental currency. The patriot troops were often five or six days without bread, then as long without meat, and sometimes two or three days without food of any kind.

6. In this crisis, Robert Morris, a wealthy citizen of Philadelphia, sent three million rations to the army. Soldiers' relief associations were also organized by the women of that city. Those who had money gave it, and the poor contributed their work. Twenty-two hundred shirts were thus made, on each of which was inscribed the name of the lady who sewed it. About the same time, Franklin, at the court of France, obtained from Louis XVI. a gift of 6,000,000 livres.

7. Treason of Arnold (1780).—General Arnold, who had been distinguished for his bravery at Quebec and Saratoga, was now stationed at Philadelphia. Here he lived in great extravagance, and, by various acts of oppression, rendered himself so odious that on one occasion he was publicly mobbed. Charges having been preferred against him, he was convicted and sentenced to be reprimanded by the commander-in-chief. Washington performed the duty very gently; but Arnold, stung by the disgrace, resolved to gratify both his revenge and love of money, by betraying his country.

8. He accordingly secured from Washington the command of West Point, at that time the most important post in the United States. He then proposed to Clinton, with whom he had previously corresponded, to surrender it to the British. The offer was accepted, and Major André appointed to confer with him. André ascended the Hudson, and, on the night of September 21, went ashore from the English ship *Vulture* to meet the traitor. Morning dawned before they had completed their plans.

9. In the mean time, fire having been opened on the *Vulture*, she had dropped down the river. André, now left within the American lines, dressed himself in citizen's clothes and endeavored to make his way back by land to New York. He had reached Tarrytown in safety, when, at a sudden turn in the road, his horse's reins were seized, and three men * sprang before him. They searched him, and finding papers which seemed to prove him a spy, they carried him to the nearest American post. Arnold was at breakfast, when he received a note announcing André's capture. He called aside his wife and told her of his peril. Terrified by his words, she fainted. Kissing his boy, who lay asleep in the cradle, Arnold darted out of the house, mounted a horse, reached the river, jumped into his boat, and was rowed to the *Vulture*, which lay a few miles below. André was tried and hanged as a spy. Arnold received £6,315 and a colonelcy in the English army.

* The names of these men were Paulding, Van Wart, and Williams. André offered them his horse, watch, purse, and any sum they might name, if they would release him. The incorruptible patriots declared that they would not let him go for ten thousand guineas. Congress voted to each of them a silver medal and a pension for life.

NAVAL EXPLOITS. 211

10. Naval Exploits.—No American successes caused more annoyance to the British than those of the navy. In 1775, Washington fitted out several vessels to cruise along the New England coast as privateers; and in the same year Congress established a naval department. The first capture on the seas in the name of the United Colonies, (that of the British store-ships *Margaretta* and *Tapnaquish*), was made in Machias Bay, by five brothers named O'Brien, sons of Maurice O'Brien, then residing in Maine, (May 11, 1775). Soon swift sailing vessels, manned by bold seamen, infested every avenue of commerce. Within three years, they captured five hundred ships. They even cruised among the British Isles, and, entering harbors, seized and burned the ships lying at English wharves.

11. Among the first naval commissions issued by Congress, was that of *Captain John Barry*, surnamed "THE FATHER OF THE AMERICAN NAVY." In February 1776, he was appointed to the command of the "*Lexington*," and two months later, he encountered, and after a sharp engagement, captured "*The Edward*," a British sloop-of-war. This, the first naval victory by a commissioned officer of the United States, was hailed with intense joy throughout the country.

12. *Paul Jones* was a still more famous naval hero. While cruising off the north-east coast of England with a squadron of five vessels, he met the *Serapis* and the *Countess of Scarborough* convoying a fleet of merchantmen. At half-past seven in the evening (Sept. 23, 1779), he laid his own vessel, the *Bon Homme Richard*, [*bo-nom-re-shar*], alongside the *Serapis*, and a desperate struggle ensued. In the midst of the engagement he lashed the ships together. The muzzles of the guns touched and the crews fought hand to hand. Three times both vessels were on fire. At ten o'clock the

Serapis surrendered. As Jones' vessel was already in a sinking condition, he transferred his crew to the captured frigate, and sailed for the Texel (Holland).

13. More French Aid.—Lafayette, at the end of the campaign of 1778, returned to France, in order to plead the patriot cause with his countrymen. He was received by Marie

THE BON HOMME RICHARD.

Antoinette with marked consideration, and the king promised that an army and fleet should be sent to the United

States. *"It is fortunate for the king,"* said Maurepas [*mo-re-pah*], the French minister, *"that Lafayette did not take it into his head to strip Versailles of its furniture to send to his dear America, as his Majesty would have been unable to refuse it."*

14. Early in the spring (May 11, 1780), Lafayette rejoined Washington at the headquarters of the army. He brought with him a commission from Louis XVI. appointing Washington lieutenant-general in the army of France and vice-admiral of its navy. This was intended to prevent difficulties respecting official etiquette, between the French and American commanders. In July, Rochambeau [*ro-sham-bo*] arrived at Newport with a squadron and 6000 men. The Americans gratefully welcomed

ROCHAMBEAU.

their allies, and immediately put them in possession of the forts on Rhode Island. In order to cement more firmly the union between the two nations, Washington ordered the distinctive colors of the national flags to be blended in the banners of his army.

15. The Final Campaign.—In the summer of the next year, (1781), Washington planned with Rochambeau for a joint attack upon New York city. The allied forces accordingly encamped at Dobb's Ferry. Clinton becoming alarmed, directed Cornwallis, who was now marauding in Virginia, to keep near the sea-coast, so as to be able to come to New York, if desired. Cornwallis, after having destroyed $15,000,000 worth of property, took post at Yorktown.

16. Siege of Yorktown.[40]—The arrival off the Chesapeake of Count de Grasse with a powerful French fleet, now proved of the highest importance to America. It was arranged to attack Cornwallis with the combined American and French forces. Washington, by a feint on New York, kept Clinton in the dark regarding his plans until he was far on his way South with the continental army.

17. On the 28th of September, the joint forces, twelve thousand strong, took up their position before Yorktown.[40] Batteries were opened upon the city, and the vessels in the harbor were fired by red-hot shells. Two redoubts were carried; one by the Americans, the other by the French. "*On that night, victory twined double garlands around the banners of France and America.*" Breaches having been made in the walls, Cornwallis saw no hope of escape, and capitulated, (Oct. 19, 1781).

18. The Surrender of Cornwallis.—The scene of the surrender was imposing. The allied forces were drawn up on opposite sides of the road for over a mile, the French on the left and the Americans on the right. Washington and Rochambeau, each with his staff, stood at the head of his army. The English, about seven thousand in number, marched between the lines, with slow step, shouldered arms, and cased colors. Every eye was turned to catch a sight of Cornwallis; but, vexed and annoyed, he feigned sickness, and sent his sword by the hand of General O'Hara.

THE FINAL CAMPAIGN. 215

SURRENDER OF CORNWALLIS AT YORKTOWN.

19. The Effect.—Both parties felt that this surrender virtually ended the war. Joy pervaded every patriot heart, and all the hardships of the past were forgotten in the thought that America was free. The news reached Philadelphia at two o'clock A. M. The people were awakened by the watchman's cry, "*Past two o'clock and Cornwallis is taken!*" Lights flashed through the houses, and soon the streets were thronged with crowds eager to learn the glad news. Some were speechless with delight. Many wept, and the old door-keeper of Congress died of joy. The names of Washington, Lafayette, and Rochambeau were echoed on every side, and Congress voted them the highest honors. In St. Joseph's Church, Philadelphia, a solemn Mass of thanksgiving was offered, at which the victorious generals attended.

All hope of subduing America was now abandoned by the people of England, and they loudly demanded the removal of the ministers who still counselled war.

When the news reached Lord North, the British minister, he received it, says an eye-witness, as he would "*a cannon-ball in his breast.*" He paced the room, tossing his arms, and crying: "*It is all over! It is all over!*"

20. Perilous Position of the Country.—Though the war was apparently ended, the condition of the United States continued threatening. The British held Savannah and Charleston for nearly a year, and New York for over two years, after the surrender at Yorktown. The English might resume the struggle at any time. Meanwhile the American army was in almost open rebellion, the soldiers being afraid they would be disbanded and sent home without pay. They petitioned Congress, but received no satisfaction, as the treasury was empty.

21. At this crisis, Washington, who was yet at his headquarters in Newburg, was invited to become king. The noble patriot, shocked at the proposal, spurned it with indignation. A paper having been circulated advising violent measures, Washington addressed a meeting of the officers, and besought them not to mar their fair record of patriotic service, by any rash proceedings. On this occasion, just before he commenced the reading of his memorable address, a touching incident took place. He removed his spectacles to wipe them, and turning to those around him, said, "*My eyes have grown dim in the service of my country, but I have never yet learned to doubt her justice.*" Washington finally secured a grant of five years' full pay to the officers, instead of half-pay for life, and the whole matter was happily adjusted.

22. A Treaty of Peace was finally signed at Paris, (Sept. 3, 1783). New York was evacuated by the British Nov. 25. Soon after, Washington entered the city, bade his officers an affecting farewell, and retired to Mount Vernon,[34] followed by the love and respect of an admiring and grateful people.

"*The annals of mankind*," says Archbishop Hughes, "*have never presented, in the order of merely human moral grandeur, a moment or a spectacle more sublime than this.*"

REVIEW OF THE PRINCIPAL BATTLES OF THE REVOLUTION.

Date.	Location.	Commanders. American.	Commanders. British.	Army Successful.
1775...	Lexington	Parker	Smith and Pitcairn	American.
	Ticonderoga	Allen	De Laplace	American.
	Bunker Hill	Prescott	Howe and Clinton	British.
	Quebec	Montgomery	Clinton	British.
1776...	Fort Moultrie	Moultrie	Clinton and Sir Peter Parker	American.
	Long Island	Putnam	Howe and Clinton	British.
	White Plains	McDougall	Howe	British.
	Fort Washington	Magaw	Howe	British.
	Trenton	Washington	Rahl	American.
	Princeton	Washington	Mawhood	American.
1777...	Ticonderoga	St. Clair	Burgoyne	British.
	Fort Schuyler	Arnold	St. Leger	American.
	Bennington	Stark	Baum	American.
	Brandywine	Washington	Howe	British.
	Stillwater	Gates	Burgoyne	American.
	Fort Mercer	Col. Greene	Donop	American.
1778...	Monmouth	Washington	Clinton	American.
	Wyoming	Zeb. Butler	John Butler	British.
	Rhode Island	Sullivan	Pigot	American.
	Savannah	Robt. Howe	Campbell	British.
	Sunbury	Lane	Prevost	British.
1779...	Stony Point	Wayne	Johnson	American.
	Paulus Hook	Lee	Sutherland	American.
	Savannah	Lincoln	Prevost	British.
1780...	Monk's Corner	Huger	Tarleton	British.
	Charleston	Lincoln	Clinton	British.
	King's Mountain	Campbell	Ferguson	American.
	Cowpens	Morgan	Tarleton	American.
	Guilford C. H.	Greene	Cornwallis	British.
1781...	Fort Griswold	Ledyard	Arnold	British.
	Eutaw Springs	Greene	Stewart	Indecisive.
	Yorktown	Washington, De Grasse, Rochambeau	Cornwallis	American.

STUDY NO. 7.

THE CONSTITUTION ACCEPTED.—ADMINISTRATIONS OF WASHINGTON AND ADAMS.

1. The Articles of Confederation, under which the Congress of the United States acted at this time, gave little strength to the government. Congress could recommend, but not enforce legislation. It could *suggest* to the different States the sum of money needed to carry on the government, but could not *collect* the taxes itself. "*We are*," said Washington, "*one nation to-day and thirteen to-morrow.*" Each State made its own regulations concerning trade; local prejudices were aroused; and, in some cases, feeling ran so high as to threaten civil war. Many of the best men of the nation felt that there must be a stronger central government.

2. Constitutional Convention.—A convention was accordingly called at Philadelphia, for the purpose of revising the Articles of Confederation. Washington was chosen president. It was soon found necessary to form an entirely fresh bond of union. A New Constitution was therefore adopted, Sept. 17, 1787.

Among the prominent delegates were Roger Sherman and Oliver Ellsworth of Connecticut, Alexander Hamilton of New York, Benjamin Franklin and Robert Morris of Pennsylvania, Daniel Carroll and James McHenry of Maryland, Rutledge and the Pinckneys of South Carolina, and Edmund Randolph and James Madison of Virginia.

3. Bitter Opposition was at once aroused against the New Constitution. The people were divided into two

THE CONSTITUTION ACCEPTED. 219

parties,—the *Federalists* and the *anti-Federalists*. The former favored the Constitution and sought to increase the powers of the national government, and thus strengthen the

INAUGURATION OF WASHINGTON.

Union at home and abroad. The latter wished the authority to rest with the States, opposed the Constitution, were jealous of Congress, and feared too much national power, lest a monarchy might be established. The nation was agitated by the most earnest and thoughtful, as well as the most virulent speeches on both sides. Within a year, however, the Constitution was ratified by nine States, the number necessary to make it binding.

4. Washington First President of the United States.—The first Presidential election under the Constitution was held in 1788. By it, GEORGE WASHINGTON was chosen President and John Adams Vice-President. The inauguration took place in Federal Hall, New York, (April 30, 1789). Robert Livingston, Chancellor of the State of New York, administered the oath in the presence of a large concourse of people, who shouted at its conclusion: *"Long live Washington, President of the United States!"* He was already looked upon as, in truth, the *"Father of his Country."*

5. Washington's Administration, (1789–1797), is memorable for

    (1.) THE ORGANIZATION OF THE GOVERNMENT;

    (2.) THE RESTORATION OF THE PUBLIC FINANCES;

    (3.) THE WHISKY REBELLION, (1794);

    (4.) THE REDUCTION OF THE INDIANS NORTH OF THE OHIO, (1794);

    (5.) TREATIES WITH ALGIERS, ENGLAND, AND SPAIN, (1795);

    (6.) THE ADMISSION INTO THE UNION OF VERMONT, (1791), KENTUCKY, (1792), AND TENNESSEE. (1796).

6. Washington's Cabinet.—Washington, on taking the Presidential chair, called to his Cabinet* some of the ablest men the country had produced. *Thomas Jefferson* was chosen Secretary of State; *Alexander Hamilton*, Secretary of the Treasury; *General Knox*, Secretary of War; and *Edmund Randolph*, Attorney General.

---

* Three executive departments were now established: *The Department of Foreign Affairs*, (now *the Department of State*), *the Department of War*, and the *Department of the Treasury*. The heads of these departments were called *Secretaries*, and with the *Attorney-General* formed the President's *Cabinet*.

ADMINISTRATION OF WASHINGTON. 221

7. Difficulties beset the new government on every hand. The treasury was empty, and the United States had no credit. The Indians were hostile. Pirates from the

JEFFERSON.   KNOX.   RANDOLPH.   HAMILTON.   WASHINGTON.
WASHINGTON AND HIS CABINET.

Barbary States⁶ attacked our ships, and American citizens were languishing in Algerine dungeons. Spain refused us the navigation of the Mississippi. England had not yet condescended to send a minister to our government, and had made no treaty of commerce with us.

8. The Finances.—Through the judicious management of Hamilton, the public finances were soon placed in a good condition, and the credit of the country established.

9. Whisky Rebellion, (1794).—To provide funds taxes had been levied on imported goods and the distillation of spirits. To this, great opposition was made. In Western Pennsylvania, the people resolved that no tax should be paid on whisky. The rioters were so numerous and so thoroughly organized, that fifteen thousand of the militia were ordered out to subdue them. Finding the government in earnest, the malcontents laid down their arms.

10. Indian Wars.—Two armies sent against the Indians of the northwest were defeated. At last General Wayne,—"*Mad Anthony*,"—was put in command. Little Turtle, the Indian chief, now advised peace, declaring that the Americans had "*a leader who never slept;*" but his counsel was rejected. A desperate battle was fought on the Maumee, (Aug. 20, 1794). Wayne routed the Indians, chased them for a great distance, laid waste their towns for fifty miles, and finally compelled them to make a treaty giving up what is now Ohio and part of Indiana.

11. England.—Hardly had the Revolution closed, when the English complained that debts could not be collected in America. On the other hand, the Americans charged that the British armies had carried off their negroes; that posts were still held on the frontier; and that our seamen were *impressed, i. e.,* forced to serve in the British navy. Chief Justice Jay was sent as envoy extraordinary to England. He negotiated *a treaty,* which was ratified by the Senate (1795) only after the most violent opposition, as it was thought to be derogatory to this country, insulting to France, and an abandonment of all our claims against Great Britain.

12. Spain and Algiers.[2]—The same year *a treaty* was made with *Spain,* securing to the United States the free navigation of the Mississippi, and fixing the boundary of Florida, still held by that nation. Just before this, *a treaty* had been concluded with *Algiers*, by which our captives were released, and the commerce of the Mediterranean was opened to American vessels.

13. States Admitted.—In 1789 and 1790, North Carolina and Rhode Island, which had at first refused to ratify the Constitution, joined their sister States in the Union. *Vermont*, the first new State, was admitted in 1791, *Kentucky* in 1792, and *Tennessee* in 1796.

14. France.—The French Revolution was now at its height; and as the Americans warmly sympathized with France, when war broke out between that country and England, Washington had great difficulty in preserving neutrality. He saw that the true American policy was to keep free from all European alliances. Genet, the French minister, relying on the popular feeling, went so far as to fit out privateers in the ports of the United States, to prey on British commerce. At length, at Washington's request, Genet was recalled; but, as we shall see, the difficulty did not end.

15. Political Parties.—During the discussion of these various questions, two parties had arisen. Jefferson became the great leader of the Republican (afterward Democratic) party, which opposed the United States Bank, the English treaty, and the assumption of the State debts. Hamilton was the principal leader of the Federalist party, which supported the administration.*

---

* The federalists favored the granting of power to the general government, which they thought should be made strong. The republicans, fearing lest the republic should become a monarchy and the President a king, opposed this idea and advocated State rights. In this election, the republicans were accused of being friends of France, and the federalists of being attached to Great Britain and its institutions. The republicans declared themselves to be the only true friends of the people, and stigmatized all others as aristocrats and monarchists.

16. Retirement of Washington.—In September, 1796, Washington having definitely declined to serve a *third term*, presented to his fellow-citizens his celebrated "*Farewell Address.*" It crowned in a fitting manner, an illustrious life; while its sentiments of patriotism and its sagacious political maxims, remain as a legacy to future generations. He warned his countrymen against disunion, and besought

MOUNT VERNON.

them "*indignantly to frown upon the first dawnings of an attempt to alienate any portion of our country from the rest.*" Above all, he recommended religion and morality as indispensably necessary to political prosperity. "*In vain,*" says he, "*would that man claim the tribute of patriotism, who would labor to subvert these great pillars of human happi-*

ness, these firmest props of the duties of men and citizens." Washington was present at the inauguration of the second President, John Adams, (March 4, 1797), and then withdrew to Mount Vernon, to spend the remainder of his days in retirement.

17. Adams' Administration, (1797–1801), is memorable for
  (1.) THE ALIEN AND SEDITION LAWS;
  (2.) A THREATENED WAR WITH FRANCE, (1798–'99);
  (3.) THE DEATH OF WASHINGTON, (1799).

18. Alien and Sedition Laws.—Owing to the violent denunciations of the government by the friends and emissaries of France, the *Alien and Sedition Laws* were now passed. Under the former, the President could expel from the country any foreigner whose conduct or principles he might consider dangerous to the United States; under the latter, any one libelling Congress, the President, or the government, could be fined or imprisoned. This measure excited the bitterest feeling.

19. War with France.—French affairs early assumed a serious aspect. Our flag was insulted, our vessels were captured, and our envoys were refused audience by the French Directory, unless a bribe should be paid. The news of this insult aroused the nation, and the friends of France were silenced. Orders were given to raise an army, and Washington was appointed commander-in-chief. Everywhere was repeated the motto, "*Millions for defence, but not a cent for tribute.*" Hostilities had already commenced on the sea, when Napoleon became the First Consul of France, and the impending war was happily arrested.

20. Political Parties.—An intense party feeling prevailed during this entire administration. The unpopularity of the alien and sedition laws, especially, reduced the vote for Adams, the federal candidate for re-election; and the republican nominee, Thomas Jefferson of Virginia, became the next President.

21. Death of Washington.—In the *last month* of the *last year* of the 18th century, the entire nation was plunged into grief by the death of Washington, which occurred at Mount Vernon, (Dec. 14, 1799). Everywhere, in city and hamlet, there were manifestations of the public sorrow by solemn services, by the adjournment of all public bodies, and by glowing eulogies on the character and services of the deceased. His remains were deposited in a family vault on the banks of the Potomac, where they still lie entombed.

STUDY NO. 8.

OCCUPATIONS, MANNERS, EDUCATION, Etc.

1. Occupations, etc.—Up till the time of the Revolution, *agriculture* was the chief pursuit. The implements were rude, but the fertile soil yielded abundant harvests. Wheat, corn, and potatoes were the staple productions at the North; tobacco, rice, and cotton at the South. The flour of the Mount Vernon estate was packed under the eye of

EARLY AMERICAN PLOW.

Washington himself; and we are told that barrels of flour bearing his brand passed in the West India market without inspection.

2. *Manufactures* and *commerce* had already received considerable attention; but owing to the selfishness of English policy, little progress could be made.

3. The *fisheries* gave employment to many; and the daring fishermen of New England even pushed their whaling crafts far into the icy regions of the north. As cities were still near to the wilderness, the gun and the fishing-rod were to be found in every house.

In the south, the chase was still a favorite diversion. Washington was exceedingly fond of it; and the names of his fox-hounds,—Vulcan, Singer, Music, etc.,—are carefully registered in his household books.

4. Household Comforts.—Although the majority of houses were still humbly and sparingly furnished, yet comforts had greatly increased during the growing prosperity of the colonies; and a few really elegant homes were found in

THE WOOLEN SPINNING-WHEEL.

every city of importance. Crimson leather furnished a dignified upholstery to the straight, high-backed, mahogany chairs and sofas; while heavy damask curtains steadied the glitter from ponderous andirons and brass clock. Carpets had begun to supersede the curved and figured white sand. They were used, however, to cover only a portion of the floor in the centre of the apartment; and the unaccustomed visitor oftentimes showed signs of genuine distress at being obliged to walk on them, endeavoring, by stealing closely along the wall, to avoid soiling the beautiful thing upon the floor.

5. In every household, especially in New England, *the spinning-wheel*, whether the small one worked by the foot for spinning linen thread, or the large, which was turned by the hand for woolen yarn, was an honored article. Mrs. Washington, it is said, kept running sixteen spinning-wheels.

6. The lighting of the houses was accomplished by means of candles. An Argand lamp, in which was burned whale oil, was a rare luxury. Towards the close of the century, Thomas Jefferson brought the first one from abroad.

Stoves and Franklins were somewhat used, but the open fireplace still had the preference.

7. Dress.—In the eighteenth century, the dress of the colonial gentry, especially in the cities, began to lose its simplicity. Knee-breeches of broadcloth and plush, with velvet surtouts and camlet cloaks, were much worn by the men;* while wide laced ruffles falling over the hand, a gold or a silver snuff-box, and a gold-headed cane were deemed indispensable to gentility. The ladies were arrayed in gay silks and velvets, with cambric caps,† and aprons of lawn or taffeta. In the country, however, homespun garments were still worn.

Wigs went out of style about twenty years before the Revolution, and about the same time *boots* came into vogue.

---

* The early part of the century was particularly characterized by the use of high colors in dress, as may be inferred from the following advertisement (1724) concerning a runaway barber. "*He wore a light wig, a grey kersey jacket lined with blue, a light pair of drugget breeches, black roll-up stockings, square-toed shoes, a red leathern apron, and white vest with yellow buttons and red linings.*"

† The fashionable caps were the "*Queen's Nightcap*," the style always worn by Mrs. Washington, and the "*cushion head-dress*," made of gauze, stiffened out in cylindrical form with white spire wire, and having a border called a "*balcony*."

8. Travelling.—The usual mode of travel was on foot or horseback, or between important places, in public wagons, sometimes without springs. In 1772, the first stage-coach was put on the route between Boston and Providence, the trip occupying two days. When, in 1776, the journey from New York to Philadelphia was made by a new line of vehicles, in the unprecedented period of two days, the new conveyances were termed "*flying machines.*"

THE OLD STAGE-COACH.

9. Washington's Receptions.—Every Tuesday afternoon, Washington gave formal receptions, at which considerable ceremony was required. On entering, the visitor saw the tall, manly figure of Washington, clad in black silk velvet, with white or pearl-colored vest, yellow gloves, and silver knee and shoe buckles. He always stood in front of the fire-place, with members of his cabinet, or other eminent men, around him. The visitor was conducted to the President, and his name distinctly announced. Washington received him with a dignified bow, avoiding to shake hands, even with his best friends. As visitors came, they formed a circle round the room. At a quarter past three, the door being closed, the President began on the right, and spoke to each person, calling him by name, and exchanging a few words. Having finished the circuit, he resumed his first position, and the visitors approaching him in succession, bowed and retired. Within an hour the ceremony was over. Washington's deportment was uniformly grave. His presence, it is said, inspired a feeling of awe and veneration.

10. Inventions and Discoveries.—In 1752, Benjamin Franklin, by means of an experiment with a kite, made the brilliant discovery of the identity of lightning with the electric fluid.

In 1791, a hunter wandering on the bleak Mauch Chunk [*mawk chunk*] Mountain in Pennsylvania, discovered the celebrated coal-beds of that region.

11. In 1792, Eli Whitney of Massachusetts invented the cotton-gin, a machine for cleaning cotton. It had been easy enough to raise the plant, but very difficult to separate the seed from the fibre, which was called "*ginning*" it. Previous to Whitney's invention, the operation was performed by hand, and it took a day to gin a pound. Since then, the cultivation of cotton has been a prominent feature in the agricultural history of this country, and its results have revolutionized the commerce of the world.

12. Education.—Among the institutions of learning founded during this century were Yale, Princeton, King's (now Columbia), and Georgetown Colleges; also the Sulpitian Seminary, Baltimore.

13. Literature.—American literature was as yet in its infancy. Among the most noted prose writers of the period, the following may be mentioned:

Benjamin Franklin, (1706-1790), whose principal works are his *Autobiography*, his political and philosophical *Essays*, and his *Letters and Papers on Electricity;* *

---

* Some of his lesser pieces, such as "*The Whistle*" and "*The Grindstone*," have found their way into many school readers. Many of his sayings, under the title of "*Poor Richard's Maxims*," are also familiar; such as, "*One to-day is worth two to-morrows*," "*Constant dropping wears away stones*," "*A small leak will sink a great ship*."

Jeremy Belknap, (1744-1798), one of the founders of the Massachusetts Historical Society, chiefly noted for his *History of New Hampshire;*

Alexander Hamilton, (1757-1804), one of the authors of "*The Federalist,*" a profound and lucid treatise on politics;

Thomas Jefferson, (1743-1826), the author of the "*Declaration of Independence;*"

Alexander Wilson, (1766-1813), the founder of American ornithology, whose work on *The Birds of the United States* is not only the earliest, but, in some respects, the best that has been written.

14. Among the poets:

Philip Freneau, (1752-1832), the author of many political and miscellaneous poems;

Francis Hopkinson, (1737-1791), the author of a once celebrated humorous poem, entitled, "*The Battle of the Kegs;*"

Joseph Hopkinson, son of the preceding, whose fame rests upon the popular national ballad, "*Hail Columbia.*"

15. The first permanent newspaper, "*The Boston Weekly News Letter,*" was commenced in 1704, and the first sheet was taken damp from the press to exhibit as a curiosity. In 1750, there were only seven weekly newspapers. The first daily, "*The Federal Orrery,*" was issued in 1792.

STUDY NO. 9.

CATHOLICITY AND THE REVOLUTION.

1. Patriotic Spirit among Catholics. — Although in the *thirteen original colonies* Catholics had been unjustly legislated against; although here, as in England, they had been proscribed, loaded with heavy taxes, and deprived of civil rights,—still, when the tocsin of freedom was sounded, they buried the remembrance of their wrongs, and with one accord, espoused the cause of liberty and popular rights. They could not but revere the great principles of liberty cherished by an Edward and an Alfred, and which Catholic Englishmen, led on by their Archbishop, had forced the tyrant John to promulgate in the Magna Charta (*kartah*). Hence we find that the Church gave none but patriots to our country in her days of trial.

2. A Kindlier Feeling. — With the Revolution dawned a new era for Catholicity in the Colonies. "Men began to be ashamed of bigotry when George III. personated it." The necessity for a perfect union among all the colonies became evident; and the Convention of 1774 entreated all classes *to put away religious disputes and animosities which could only withhold them from uniting in the defence of their common rights and liberties.* The French alliance also was not without its effect in this regard. With a Catholic ally, the government could not well denounce Catholicity.

3. During the Revolution. — The conduct of Catholics during the war made a deep impression. Such men as Charles, Daniel, and Rev. John Carroll; Paca, Fitzsimon, Moylan, Burke, Barry, O'Brien; the French noblemen, De Lafayette, De Rochambeau, De Montmorenci, De Lausun, De Grasse, De Chartelleaux (*shar-tel-o*); the noble Poles, Kosciusko and Pulaski; and the Indian chief, Orono,— all Catholics,—distinguished themselves in the legislature, the council-hall, the army or the navy. Washington's "*Life Guard,*" a choice body of men, was composed largely of Catholics. The friends of the young Republic were Catholic France, Ireland, and Spain.*

4. Washington's Words. — In his reply to the Address of the Roman Catholics after the Revolution, Washington expressed himself as follows:

"*I hope ever to see America among the foremost nations in examples of justice and liberality; and I presume that your fellow-citizens will not forget the patriotic part which you took in the accomplishment of their Revolution, and the establishment of their government, or the important assistance they received from a nation, in which the Roman Catholic Faith is professed.*" . . . . . "*May the members of your Society in America, animated alone by the pure spirit of Christianity, and still conducting themselves as the faithful subjects of our free Government, enjoy every temporal and spiritual felicity.*"

G. WASHINGTON.

---

* In 1771, Dr. Franklin who visited Dublin, writes: "Being desirous of seeing the principal patriots there, I staid till the opening of Parliament. *I found them disposed to be friends to America.*"

In 1775, the Continental Congress in an address to "*The Irish people,*" spoke thus: "*We acknowledge with pleasure and with gratitude that your nation has produced patriots who have nobly distinguished themselves in the cause of humanity and America.*"

Of France, the immortal Washington writes thus: "In the midst of a war, the nature and difficulties of which are peculiar and uncommon, *I cannot flatter myself in any way to recompense the sacrifices France has made. To call her brave were to pronounce but common praise. Wonderful nation! ages to come will read with astonishment the history of your brilliant exploits.*"

5. Our First Bishop.—Immediately after the "*Peace of Paris*," the reigning Pontiff, Pius VI., through Dr. Franklin, applied to Congress for some such arrangement as would enable him, without interfering with the laws of the young Republic,* to appoint a Bishop for the United States. On learning that the American government claimed no control whatever in matters purely spiritual, His Holiness, in 1784, appointed Rev. John Carroll, Prefect Apostolic, and 1789, Bishop of Baltimore. The new prelate's diocese included the whole United States; his priests numbered but thirty or forty, and his flock about fifty thousand.

BISHOP CARROLL.

6. Bishop Carroll's first care was to provide for the education of youth. He had already begun the erection of Georgetown College; and, in 1791, it was opened under the care of the Jesuits. The same year he invited the Sulpitians to commence a Theological Seminary in Baltimore. About the same time (1790), a Carmelite Convent was established

---

* The Episcopalians at this time also desired to have a Bishop; but the Archbishop of Canterbury refused to proceed in the matter, unless the candidate would take the oath of allegiance to the English king, and acknowledge the royal supremacy. In consequence of this, the American Episcopalians received their first Bishop from Scotland. Subsequently, the English Parliament passed an Act, by which American Bishops might be ordained by English prelates.

at Port Tobacco, Maryland; and in 1799, the first Convent of the Visitation in this country, was founded at Georgetown.

7. Spiritual Help from France.—The French Revolution, such a misfortune to the land in which it originated, proved a blessing to America. Between the years 1791 and 1799, twenty-three French priests sought refuge on our shores. Among them were the *Abbés Benedict J. Flaget, John Cheverus, John Dubois, John B. David, Louis Dubourg, Ambrose Maréchal*, all of whom subsequently became bishops.

8. The arrival of these apostolic men enabled Bishop Carroll partly to supply the wants of his vast diocese. "*The Catholic Church of the United States*," says Archbishop Spaulding, "*is deeply indebted to the zeal of the exiled French clergy. Though trained up amid all the refinements of polished France, they could yet submit without a murmur to all the hardships and privations of a mission on the frontiers of civilization, or in the very heart of the wilderness.*"

9. The Indians.—Bishop Carroll was deeply interested in the spiritual welfare of the Indians. Had it been in his power, he would have revived the Indian missions on a scale equal to those of the seventeenth and eighteenth centuries. Soon after his consecration, the Abnaki of Maine, the descendants of Father Rale's devoted flock, hearing that the sovereign Pontiff had appointed a Father over the American Church, sent a solemn deputation to Bishop Carroll to ask for a priest (1781).

10. As proof of their sincerity, the deputies bore with them Father Rale's crucifix, which from the time of his death had been sacredly treasured among the Abnaki. Bishop

INDIAN DEPUTATION.

Carroll, deeply moved by their earnest faith, embraced the crucifix, returned it to them according to the Indian custom, and promised to send them the desired "Black Gown." Since that time, they have rarely been without a missionary; and to this day they remain true to the faith.

11. New York.—During the last year of the war, the Catholics of New York assembled above a carpenter's shop in Barclay street. The first priest who officiated for them, was the venerable Father Farmer, S. J., of Philadelphia; but Father Whelan, a Franciscan, who had been a chaplain in the French fleet, was the first to assemble a permanent congregation in that city (1783).

12. Pennsylvania.—Before the close of the Revolution, churches, or mission stations, had been established at Philadelphia, Lancaster, Conewago, and other places; and the venerable Father Farmer, S. J., was already an old missionary in that field.* At midnight Christmas, 1799, Mass was celebrated for the first time in the wilds of Western Pennsylvania, by the Prince-priest, Demetrius Gallitzin, surnamed the "Apostle of the Alleghanies."

13. The West.—Here Catholicity had already gained a foothold, as the French posts in the Mississippi Valley had been regularly attended by chaplains. Moreover, some of the old Jesuit stations were still in existence; though, for many years, the only priest in the territory of Indiana and Illinois was the Rev. Father Gibault (*gee-bo*).

14. Missions in California.—Meanwhile Catholicity had been planting the cross on the Pacific coast. A few days before the Declaration of Independence, the mission, afterwards the city of San Francisco, was founded by the Spanish Franciscans, under Father Serra. Between the years 1768 and 1822, twenty-one missions were founded along the Pacific coast by the Franciscans. The most noted of these posts were San Diego, Monterey, San Francisco, Los Angelos, and Santa Barbara. At their most flourishing period, the missions numbered 75,000 converted Indians.

15. Old Prejudices.—Although the Constitution of the United States professed to grant full freedom of conscience, still, in some of the original-States, Catholicity had for many years to struggle against old enactments and old prejudices. These, however, are gradually dying out.

> "*Truth crushed to earth shall rise again,*
> *The Eternal years of God are hers;*
> *But Error, wounded, writhes with pain*
> *And dies among his worshippers.*"

---

* St. Joseph's Church, Philadelphia, was erected by Father Greaton, S. J., 1733, and St. Mary's, by Father Farmer, in 1763.

BIOGRAPHICAL SKETCHES

OF DISTINGUISHED PERSONAGES MENTIONED IN THE PRECEDING SECTION.

Adams, John, (1735-1826), an American lawyer and statesman who came into prominence at Boston, during the early stages of the Revolution. He was a member of the first and the second Congress, and nominated Washington as commander-in-chief. *Jefferson wrote* the Declaration of Independence, but *Adams secured its adoption* in a three-days debate. He was a tireless worker, and had the reputation of having the clearest head and firmest heart of any man in Congress. In his position as President, he lost the reputation he had gained as Congressman. His enemies accused him of being a bad judge of men, of clinging to old unpopular notions, and of having little control over his temper. They also ridiculed his egotism, which they declared to be inordinate. He lived, however, to see the prejudice against his administration give place to a juster estimate of his great worth and exalted integrity. As a delegate to the Constitutional Convention, he was honored as one of the fathers of the republic. Adams and Jefferson were firm friends during the Revolution, but political strife afterwards alienated them. On their return to private life they became reconciled. They died on the same day,—the fiftieth anniversary of American independence. Adams' last words were, "*Thomas Jefferson still survives.*" Jefferson was, however, already lying dead in his Virginia home.

Allen, Ethan, (1742-1789), a famous leader of the "*Green Mountain Boys,*" and brigadier-general in the Revolutionary army, was born in Connecticut, but was educated in Vermont. He was noted for his early and active efforts in behalf of liberty. In 1775, soon after the battle of Lexington, he captured Ticonderoga and Crown Point. During the same year, in an attempt to conquer Montreal, he was taken prisoner and sent to England in irons. After a long captivity, being released, he returned to his home. Generous and frank, a strong and vigorous writer, loyal to his country, and true to his friends, he did much for Vermont, and to no one is that State more indebted for its independence.

One of his daughters having become a Catholic, joined the community of Hospital Nuns at Montreal, and there died a saintly death.

The edifying spectacle of her last moments was the cause of the conversion of the Protestant physician who attended her.

Arnold, Benedict, (1740-1801), best known in history as "*the Traitor,*" was born in Connecticut. During the early part of the Revolution, he won great renown. In the capture of Ticonderoga, the attack on Quebec, and in a naval action on Lake Champlain, (Oct. 11, 1776), he manifested unusual skill. At the battle of Saratoga he was brave, but rash, exhibiting "the frenzy of a madman rather than the wisdom of a general." After his escape to the British, he led a marauding expedition into Virginia, and another into Connecticut. The former ravaged the country without mercy; the latter captured Fort Griswold, and massacred the garrison after they had surrendered. On the restoration of peace, he went to England, where he lived and died in obscurity, shunned and despised by all. On one occasion, a member of Parliament, rising to address the House, noticed Arnold in the gallery. Pointing to the traitor, he exclaimed: "*Mr. Speaker, I shall not proceed while that man is in the House!*"

Barry, Commodore John, (1745-1803) the "*Father of the American Navy,*" was born in Wexford County, Ireland, and early entered on a seafaring life. At the age of sixteen, he emigrated to America, which henceforth became his adopted country; and from this period, he made regular voyages between Philadelphia and the British ports. The intervals between his voyages he devoted to the culture of his mind, by which means he acquired an excellent practical education. He rose rapidly in his profession, and at the age of twenty-five, he became Captain of the "*Black Prince,*" one of the best packets then running between London and Philadelphia.

When the Revolution broke out, he gave himself, with all the enthusiasm of his nature, to the American cause, and Congress appointed him to superintend the equipment of the new fleet just then purchased. About the same time, he was named Captain of the "*Lexington;*" while Paul Jones, afterwards so celebrated, entered as first lieutenant on the "*Alfred.*" The *Lexington*, soon after, (April 17,) encountered and captured "*The Edward,*" a British vessel. This being the first naval victory of the Revolution, caused intense joy throughout the country.

In 1776, Captain Barry was transferred to the "*Effingham*" of twenty-eight guns. About this time, Lord Howe offered him 15,000 guineas and a commission in the English navy, if he would join the royal standard. The bribe Barry indignantly rejected, adding: "*Not the value, nor the command of the whole British fleet, could tempt me from the American cause!*"

Captain Barry continued to distinguish himself throughout the

Revolution. In his famous frigate, the "Alliance," he made many captures, especially those of the British sloop-of-war "*Atlanta*," and her consort, the brig "*Trespassy*" (May, 1781). In the spring of 1782, returning from Havana with supplies, he encountered a British squadron. Being hailed and questioned by the commander, he gave the characteristic reply: "*The United States Ship Alliance, Saucy Jack Barry, half Irishman, half Yankee! Who are you?*"

On the establishment of the present navy in 1794, he was named Senior Officer, with the rank of Commodore. Under him were trained Dale, Decatur, Ross, Stewart, and Murray. Barry was, throughout life, a devout practical Catholic. Dying childless, he made the Catholic Orphan Asylum of Philadelphia his chief heir. In person, he was tall, commanding, and graceful; in manners, simple, courteous, and dignified; in character, frank, generous, and conscientious.

Carroll of Carrolton, Charles, (1737-1832), an eminent Revolutionary patriot, was born at Annapolis, Maryland. He commenced his studies with the Jesuits in his native State, and continued them in Europe, at St. Omer's, and other colleges. In 1764, he returned to Maryland, a profound scholar and polished gentleman. As soon as the Revolution broke out, he became at once a champion leader of the patriot party. In 1775, he was sent with Franklin, Chase, and his cousin, Rev. John Carroll, on the Canadian embassy; and in 1776, was chosen to represent his native State in the Continental Congress. He was one of the signers of the "Declaration," and outlived all the others. "*The good and great then made pilgrimages to his dwelling, to behold with their own eyes the venerable political patriot of America.*"

Having continued his political career until 1801, he then retired into private life. He was ever a devout Catholic. At his family residence, he had erected an elegant chapel; and it was a touching sight to behold this illustrious and venerable patriot, even at the advanced age of eighty, serving the priest during Mass with unaffected simplicity and devotion. His character is well shown in these words of his later days: "*I have lived to my ninety-sixth year; I have enjoyed continued health; I have been blessed with great wealth, prosperity, and most of the good things which the world can bestow,—public approbation, esteem, applause;—but what I now look back on with the greatest satisfaction to myself, is that I have practised the duties of my Religion.*"

Carroll, Most Rev. John, Archbishop of Baltimore, (1735-1815), was born in Maryland. As is often the case with great and good men, the virtuous training of his accomplished and pious mother largely influenced his character and career. He commenced his education with the Jesuits in Maryland; and at the age of fourteen was sent to St. Omer's College, France, where he finished his collegiate course. Here he was distinguished for his brilliant talents, close application to study, and sincere piety. In 1753, he entered the Society of Jesus, and seven years later was elevated to the priesthood. In 1773, the Society being suppressed, he proceeded to England, and was there appointed chaplain to Lord Arundel. On the breaking out of the American Revolution, Father Carroll hastened to his native land, and for a time took up his residence with his venerable mother, to whose declining years he was anxious to minister. Meanwhile he devoted himself to missionary labor in the surrounding country. In 1776, by special invitation of Congress, he formed one of the committee sent to secure the aid of the Canadians. During their association on this embassy, a sincere friendship sprang up between Father Carroll and ·Dr. Franklin, which was cherished through life. On his return he again devoted himself to his duties in the sacred ministry, which he continued uninterruptedly during the entire Revolutionary War. In 1784, Father Carroll was appointed by the reigning Pontiff, Pius VI., Prefect Apostolic of the United States. In 1789, he was made Bishop, and in 1808, Archbishop. He governed his immense diocese with great prudence and ability; and before his death, he had the consolation of beholding a rich harvest as the reward of his labors, in the establishment of four suffragan sees, the erection of numerous churches, the increase of the clergy, the establishment of religious orders and collegiate and ecclesiastical institutions, and the general progress of the Faith throughout the country. Archbishop Carroll was below the medium height, yet his bearing was dignified and majestic. He was distinguished for his sincere patriotism, varied learning, amiable disposition, and saintly life.

Franklin, Benjamin, (1706-1790), a Revolutionary patriot and distinguished philosopher, was born in Boston, Mass. His father was a soap and candle maker, and being very poor and having a family of seventeen children, he could afford the youthful Benjamin but little opportunity to gratify his desire for knowledge. By abstaining from meat for two years, the boy managed to buy a few books, which he diligently studied. At seventeen years of age, he landed in Philadelphia with a silver dollar and a shilling in copper. As, with his extra shirts and stockings stuffed in his pockets, he walked along the streets, eating the roll of bread which served for his breakfast, his future wife stood at her father's door and watched his awkward appearance, little dreaming of his brilliant future, or of its interest to her. He soon obtained employment as a printer, but being induced by false representations to go to England, he found himself almost penniless in a strange land. With his usual industry he went to work, and soon made friends and a good living. Having returned to Philadelphia, he established a newspaper; and in 1732, he commenced to publish "*Poor Richard's Almanac*," which for twenty years was quite as popular in Europe as it was in America. Its common-sense proverbs and useful hints are household words to this day. Retiring from business with a fine fortune, he devoted himself chiefly to science. His discoveries in electricity are world-renowned. Franklin was an unflinching patriot. While in England he defended the cause of liberty with great zeal and ability. He helped to draft the Declaration of Independence, and was one of its signers. Having been appointed ambassador to France, he first invested all his ready money, $15,000, in the continental loan, a practical proof of his patriotism, since its repayment was extremely improbable. His influence at the French court was unbounded. He was much admired for his dignity, genius, wit, and charming conversation. He became to the American cause in the old world, what Washington was to it in the new. On his return he was elected president of Pennsylvania for three successive years, and in his eighty-second year he was a member of the Constitutional Convention. After his death, which occurred in Philadelphia, twenty thousand persons assembled to do honor to his memory. His services to science and liberty are epitomized in the following famous line by Turgot : "*Eripuit cælo fulmen, sceptrum que tyrannis.*" "*He snatched the thunderbolt from heaven and the sceptre from tyrants.*"

Gallitzin, Prince Demetrius, (1770-1840), the Apostle of Western Pennsylvania, long known as "*Father Smith,*" was a Russian Prince. Having, by his entrance into the Catholic Church, forfeited the position which was his birthright at home, he determined to travel. On reaching the United States, in 1792, the spiritual destitution of that country touched his heart, and awakened in his soul a desire to enter the priesthood. Having prepared himself at the Sulpitian Seminary, Baltimore, he was ordained in 1795. For four years he labored on various missions, and in 1799, commenced the grand work of his life, the establishment of the Catholic colony of Loretto, amid the wilds of Western Pennsylvania. For forty-one years he toiled among his flock, so that where, on his arrival, he found twelve Catholics, he left at his death twelve thousand. The field of his missionary labor is now occupied by the Diocese of Pittsburg. Though of a delicate constitution, and nearly always in feeble health, he underwent, especially during his long missionary journeys, the greatest hardships and privations. Nevertheless, he bore all with heroic patience and even joy, like the Apostles, *counting it gain to suffer for Christ.*

Grasse, Count de, (1723-1788), a French naval officer, our ally during the Revolution, was born at Vallette. His great abilities and zeal in our behalf gained him universal confidence ; and the co-operative measures concerted by Washington, Rochambeau and himself, brought about the defeat of Cornwallis, and virtually concluded the war. Congress tendered him a vote of thanks, and also presented to him four pieces of cannon, taken from the British at Yorktown, "*in testimony of the inestimable services rendered by him on that day.*"

Hamilton, Alexander, (1757-1804), an illustrious general, orator and statesman, was born in one of the West India Islands. At the age of nineteen he was appointed to the command of a company of artillery. His conduct at the battles of Long Island, White Plains, Trenton, etc., gained Washington's notice, and he was chosen aide-de-camp. Henceforth he was that great commander's most intimate friend and adviser. With Madison and Jay, he wrote "*The Federalist*," a series of essays which powerfully contributed to the ratification of the Constitution by the people. His financial policy, when Secretary of the Treasury, established the credit of the rising nation. Having retired from political life, he devoted himself to the law, but was unfortunately involved in a quarrel with Aaron Burr, and he died in a duel.

Henry, Patrick, (1736-1799), an orator and patriot whose memory is inseparably linked with the early triumphs of liberty, was a native of Virginia. Though a young man at the beginning of the struggle, his impassioned eloquence gave him a tremendous influence. Among the greatest triumphs of his eloquence was a speech in the Virginia Convention (March, 1775). He insisted on the necessity of fighting for independence, and closed with the words: "*Give me liberty, or give me death.*" He was repeatedly elected Governor of Virginia. Always in the advance of his compeers, he headed every movement that looked toward liberty and independence. He was opposed to the Constitution, however, and refused any position under the new government. His sturdy republicanism held out to the last against those who, in his opinion, aped the manners of a monarchy.

Jefferson, Thomas, (1743-1826), an eminent statesman and the third President of the United States, was born in Virginia. "*Of all the public men who have figured in the United States,*" says Parton, "*he was incomparably the best scholar and the most variously accomplished man.*" He was a bold horseman, a skilful hunter, an elegant penman, a fine violinist, a brilliant talker, a superior classical scholar, and a proficient in the modern languages. On account of his talents he was styled "*The Sage of Monticello.*" That immortal document, the Declaration of Independence, was, with the exception of a few words, entirely his work. He was an ardent supporter of the doctrine of State rights, and led the opposition to the federalists. After he became President, however, he found the difficulty of administering the government upon that theory. "*The executive authority had to be stretched until it* cracked, to cover the purchase of Louisiana ;" and he became convinced, on other occasions, that the federal government, to use his own expression, must "show its teeth." Like Washington, he was of aristocratic birth, but his principles were intensely democratic. He hated ceremonies and titles; even "Mr." was distasteful to him. These traits were the more remarkable in one of his superior birth and education, and peculiarly endeared him to the common people. Coming into power on a wave of popularity, he studiously sought to retain this favor. There were no more brilliant levees or courtly ceremonies, as in the days of Washington and Adams. On his inauguration day, he rode down to Congress unattended, and, leaping from his horse, hitched it himself, and went into the chamber dressed in plain clothes to read his fifteen-minutes inaugural. Some of the sentences of that short but memorable address have passed into proverbs. The last seventeen years of his life were passed at Monticello, near the place of his birth. He died on the fiftieth anniversary of American Independence.

Jones, John Paul, (1747-1792), a famous naval officer, was born in Scotland. He emigrated to Virginia, entered the colonial naval service in 1775, and in June 1777 took command of the *Ranger*, a vessel of eighteen guns. Later, he was transferred to the *Bon Homme Richard*, and in September, 1779, he attacked the *Serapis*, an English frigate, which surrendered after a long battle. For this victory, Congress voted Captain Jones a gold medal. After the Revolution, he entered the Russian service with the rank of rear-admiral; but having quarreled with one of the Russian admirals, he was soon removed from the command. He died in Paris.

Kosciusko, Thaddeus, (1750-1817), an illustrious Polish patriot and general of noble family, was born in Lithuania. He embarked for America in 1776, and soon received a commission as an officer of engineers. He planned the encampment and post of the American army at Bemis' Heights, from which, after two well-fought actions, Burgoyne found it impossible to dislodge the patriots. Later, he was the principal engineer in executing the works at West Point, and became one of the adjutants of Washington, under whom he served with distinction. Finally he was made brigadier-general, and was honored with the public thanks of Congress. At the close of the Revolution, he returned to Poland and took a prominent part in the struggles of 1792 and 1794. He was wounded and taken prisoner by the Russians, and kept in confinement until the death of the Empress Catharine, when he was liberated by the Emperor Paul. The czar, on releasing his prisoner, returned to him his sword. "*I have no need of a sword*," said Kosciusko, mournfully, "*I have no country to defend.*" Henceforth, his life was passed in retirement. At his death, his remains were removed by the Emperor Alexander to the Cathedral Church of Cracow, where they repose near those of Sobieski. At West Point, within the works which he erected, the cadets have raised a monument to his memory.

Lafayette, Marquis de, (1757-1834), a celebrated French nobleman, statesman and patriot, and a distinguished general in the American Revolution. In 1777, having heard the Declaration of Independence, he favored its principles, and notwithstanding the opposition of friends, he fitted out a frigate at his own expense, and sailed for this country. He fought as a volunteer at the battles of Brandywine and Monmouth, and commanded Washington's vanguard at the surrender of Cornwallis. On the restoration of peace, he returned to France, and there espoused the cause of the French Revolution; but as a commander of the National Guard, he protected the royal family as long as he could. He was finally outlawed for endeavoring to conduct the king out of Paris (Aug. 1792). Having fled into Austria, he was taken prisoner and confined at Olmutz for five years. Through the influence of Napoleon, he was then liberated; and from this time until 1814 he remained in private life. In 1824, he visited America, and his progress through the country was one continued ovation. He died in Paris.

Lee, Richard Henry, (1732-1794), a remarkable Virginia statesman and a signer of the Declaration of Independence.

Lee, Henry, (1756-1818), a famous general in the patriot army, often called "*Light-horse Harry.*" He performed many daring exploits. In 1779, he was selected by Congress to pronounce a eulogy on Washington, whom he declared to be "*first in war, first in peace, and first in the hearts of his countrymen.*"

Marion, Francis, (1732-1795), a distinguished partisan general, known as "*The Bayard of the South.*" The history of the Revolution in the Carolinas abounds in legends of his daring, skill, and vigilance. He baffled or defeated every effort of the British to capture him, and kept alive the spirit of patriotism through all the dark years of British occupation.

Morris, Robert, (1734-1806), a statesman and financier. It has been said that we owe as much to his monetary skill as to the diplomacy of Franklin or the valor of Washington. He repeatedly saved the army from ruin; and when funds were wanted to outfit the expedition against Yorktown, he supplied the amount ($1,400,000) by his own notes. It is sad to think that this noble patriot, who had so often rescued the republic, in his old age lost his fortune and was confined in prison for debt.

BIOGRAPHICAL SKETCHES. 247

Moylan, General Stephen, (1748-1811), was a native of Cork, Ireland, and brother to the Roman Catholic Bishop of that diocese. Having emigrated to this country, he threw himself heart and soul into the American struggle for liberty. He soon won the confidence of Washington, by whom he was made aid-de-camp and commissary general. Later, he was appointed to the command of a division of cavalry, and in almost every action of the war we hear of "*Moylan's Dragoons.*" At the close of the war, he ranked a full brigadier-general. He died in Philadelphia, and was interred in the cemetery of St. Mary's Church.

Pitt, Wm., Earl of Chatham, (1708-1778), an English orator and statesman. His rare disinterestedness, his contempt of all that was mean or low, and his wonderful talents made him the favorite of the people. He opposed the ministers who advocated schemes of colonial taxation, and remained the staunch friend of America during the Revolutionary struggle. A proposition having been made in Parliament to grant the independence of the United States, Lord Chatham was brought in to protest against this "dismemberment of the British Empire." While speaking, he fell in an apoplectic fit and soon after died.

Pulaski, Count Casimer, (1747-1779), was a Polish patriot who, having lost his father and brothers in the hopeless defence of his own country, and being himself outlawed, came to fight for the freedom of America. At first he served as a volunteer, and gained distinction at the battle of Brandywine. During the second year, he commanded an independent corps of cavalry, lancers, and light infantry, called "*Pulaski's Legion,*" with which he did effectual service. He was killed at the siege of Savannah. The corner-stone of a monument raised to his memory in that city, was laid by Lafayette, while visiting that city during his triumphal progress through the United States.

Putnam, Israel, (1718-1790), a patriot general of rare gifts, was born at Salem, Massachusetts. As soon as the news of the battle of Lexington reached him, he left his oxen yoked in the field, and buckling on his sword, started for the camp at Boston. At the battle of Bunker Hill, he was conspicuous for his bravery; and in 1777, he was appointed to the command of the army of the Highlands above New York City. The most famous incident of his career happened while Tryon was making a marauding tour near Horse Neck. Putnam hastily gathered a few militia and annoyed the British as long as possible, when giving orders to his men to hide in an adjacent swamp, he spurred his spirited horse over a precipice, and descended a zigzag path, where the British dragoons did not dare to follow.

Sullivan, John, (1740-1795), an American general of the Revolution, was born in Maine. He acted under Putnam at Long Island, and by a combat of two hours in the woods, contributed to the preservation of the American army; commanded the right wing at Trenton and Brandywine; and defeated the Indians and tories, near Elmira, New York, (Aug. 1779). He then resigned his commission on account of ill health. Afterwards, he was thrice elected President of New Hampshire.

Sumter, Thomas, (1734-1832), a Southern partisan leader, known as the "*Carolinian Game-cock,*" and whom Cornwallis characterized as his "*greatest plague.*"

Washington, General George, (1732-1799), the first President of the United States, deservedly styled the "*Father of his Country,*" was born in Westmoreland County, Virginia. At eleven years of age, he was left fatherless; and his education was henceforth directed by his mother, a woman of singularly fine character. Through her careful training, he acquired habits of self-command, truthfulness, industry, frugality, and love of the true and good, which clung to him through life. Little did she dream of the greatness of her boy's destiny, as he stood at her knee, and listened to her counsel; but when, long years afterwards, a conqueror and hero, he laid his head upon her aged shoulder and wept his farewell before he started to take his place at the head of the republic he had saved, she more than reaped the fruit of her labors. He had a decided taste for mathematics; and he passed rapidly from simple arithmetic into geometry, trigonometry, and surveying.

He first appears in history when sent by Governor Dinwiddie with a remonstrance to the French commander at Fort Le Bœuf. Having distinguished himself in the French and Indian War, he retired for some time into private life. On the breaking out of the Revolution, he was chosen commander-in-chief of the American army, and from that moment he directed all his energies to the accomplishment of one object, the independence of his country. When at length the treaty of peace had been signed, he retired once more into private life, but only to be called forth again to receive the highest gift in the power of the people. Having served two terms, he declined a re-election, and again sought repose in the retirement of Mount Vernon. At his death, Europe and America vied in tributes to his memory. He left no children, and it has been beautifully said: "*Providence left him childless, that his country might call him Father!*"

CHRONOLOGICAL REVIEW.

EIGHTEENTH CENTURY.

1700.—An Act against priests passed in New York.
1702.—Queen Anne's War begun. Delaware secured a separate legislative assembly.
1703.—The English from South Carolina destroyed the Indian missions in Florida.
1710.—Port Royal, N. S., captured by English, and named Annapolis.
1713.—Queen Anne's War closed by treaty of Utrecht.
1718.—New Orleans founded by the French.
1724.—Death of Father Rasle.
1733.—Georgia (XIII,) settled by Oglethorpe at Savannah.
1739.—The Spanish War began.
1741.—"Negro Plot" in New York.
1744.—King George's War began.
1745.—Louisburg captured by English, (June 17).
1748.—King George's War ended by treaty of Aix la Chapelle.
1753.—Washington sent by Dinwiddie to St. Pierre, (Oct. 31).
1754.—Battle at *Great Meadows; Fort Necessity* captured. The French driven from Acadia, (1755).
1755.—Braddock defeated in battle of *Monongahela*, (July 9). The British defeated Dieskau at *Lake George*, (Sept. 8).
1756.—War first formally declared between English and French, (May 17). French under Montcalm captured *Fort Oswego*, (Aug. 14).
1757.—*Fort William Henry* surrendered to Montcalm, (Aug. 9).
1758.—Abercrombie repulsed at *Fort Ticonderoga*, (July 8) *Louisburg* taken by Amherst and Wolfe, (July 26). *Fort Frontenac* captured by colonists, (Aug. 27). *Fort du Quesne* taken by English, Nov. 25).
1759.—*Ticonderoga* and *Crown Point* abandoned by the French. *Niagara* taken by Johnson, and *Quebec* by Wolfe. Battle of the *Plains of Abraham*. Death of Montcalm and Wolfe.
1760.—*Montreal* taken by the English, (Sept. 8). Pontiac's War.
1763.—The Peace of Paris.
1765.—The Stamp Act passed, (March 8).
1766.—The Stamp Act repealed, (March 18).

1767.—Tax on tea, etc., (June 29).

1768.—British troops arrived at Boston, (Sept. 27). Upper California visited by Spanish Franciscans.

1770.—The Boston Massacre, (March 5). All duties, except on tea, repealed, (April 12).

1773.—Tea thrown overboard in Boston Harbor, (Dec. 16).

1774.—"Boston Port Bill" passed, (March 31). FIRST CONTINENTAL CONGRESS MET AT PHILADELPHIA, (Sept. 5).

1775.—Battle of *Lexington*, (April 19). *Ticonderoga* taken by Allen and Arnold, (May 10). *Crown Point* taken, (May 12). *Washington elected commander-in-chief*, (June 15). Battle of *Bunker Hill*, (June 17). Washington took command of troops before Boston, (July 2). Montreal surrendered to Montgomery, (Nov 13). Battle of *Quebec*,—Montgomery killed, (Dec. 31).

1776.—Boston evacuated by the British, (March 17). Embassy from U. S. to Canada, (April). Attack on *Fort Moultrie*, (June 28). DECLARATION OF INDEPENDENCE, (July 4). Battle of *Long Island*, (Aug. 27). Battle of *White Plains*, (Oct. 28). *Fort Washington* taken, (Nov. 16). Washington's retreat through New Jersey, (Nov. and Dec.). Battle of *Trenton*, (Dec. 26).

1777.—Battle of *Princeton*, (Jan. 3). Arrival of Lafayette, (April 25). Battle of *Bennington*, (Aug. 16). Battle of *Brandywine*, (Sept. 11). First battle of *Saratoga*, (Sept. 19). *Philadelphia* captured by the British, (Sept. 25). Battle of *Germantown*, (Oct. 4). Second battle of Saratoga, (Oct. 7). SURRENDER OF BURGOYNE, (Oct. 17). Washington encamped at Valley Forge.

1778.—American independence acknowledged by France, (Feb. 6). British evacuate Philadelphia, (June 18). Battle of *Monmouth*, (June 28). Massacre of *Wyoming*, (July 3). French fleet arrived in Narragansett Bay, (July 29). British capture *Savannah*, Ga., (Dec. 29).

1779.—*Stony Point* captured by General Wayne (July 15). Sullivan defeated tories and Indians near Elmira, N. Y., (Aug. 29). Paul Jones' victory, (Sept. 23). Savannah besieged by Americans and French (Sept. and Oct.). D'Estaing and Lincoln repulsed at Savannah; death of Pulaski (Oct. 9).

1780.—Charleston surrendered to British, (May 12). Second French fleet arrived at Newport, (July 10). Battle of *Hanging Rock*, S. C., (Aug. 6). Battle of *Camden*, (Aug. 16). Treason of Arnold, (Sept. 22). Execution of André (Oct. 2). Battle of *King's Mountain*, (Oct. 7).

1781.—Richmond burned by Arnold, (Jan. 5). Battle of *Cowpens*, (Jan. 17). Greene's celebrated retreat, (Jan. and Feb.). Battle of *Guilford Court-House*, (March 15). Battle of *Eutaw Springs*, (Sept. 8). Battle of Yorktown, SURRENDER OF CORNWALLIS, (Oct. 19).

1783.—Savannah evacuated by the British, (July 11). Treaty of

CHRONOLOGICAL REVIEW. 251

Peace signed at Paris, (Sept. 3). New York evacuated by British, (Nov. 25). Washington resigned his commission, (Dec. 23).

1784.—Rev. John Carroll made Prefect Apostolic in the U. S.

1786.—St. Peter's Church erected in New York.

1787.—Shay's Rebellion ; the Constitution adopted, (Sept. 17).

1789.—**George Washington** (I.) first PRESIDENT, (April 30). Georgetown College founded. **Dr. Carroll** appointed first BISHOP in the U. S.

1790.—The city of Washington laid out by General Washington The Carmelites settled in Maryland.

1791.—*Vermont* admitted to the Union. St. Mary's Seminary, Baltimore, founded.

1792.—*Kentucky* admitted to the Union, (June 1).

1793.—First priest (Father Badin) ordained in the United States. Difficulties with Genet.

1794.—Indians defeated by Wayne. Whisky insurrection.

1795.—Jay's treaty ratified, (June 24). Prince Gallitzin ordained.

1796.—*Tennessee* admitted to the Union.

1797.—**John Adams** (II.) President of the United States.

1799.—Sulpitian College founded at Baltimore. First Mass offered in Western Pennsylvania. Washington died at Mount Vernon, (Dec. 14).

CONTEMPORARY CHRONOLOGY.

1702.—Death of King William III.
1714.—Accession of George I.
1715.—Death of Louis XIV. of France.
1727.—Accession of George II.
1740.—Austrian War of Succession. Frederick the Great.
1756.—Beginning of *Seven Years' War*.
1757.—Beginning of the British Empire in India.
1760.—Accession of George III.
1772.—First Division of Poland.
1789.—Beginning of French Revolution.
1793.—Execution of Louis XVI. and Marie Antoinette.
1798.—Napoleon Bonaparte in Egypt.

CONTEMPORARY POPES.

Clement XI., (1700-1721); Innocent XIII., (1721-1724); Benedict XIII., (1724-1730); Clement XII., (1730-1740); Benedict XIV., (1740-1758); Clement XIII., (1758-1769); Clement XIV., (1769-1774); Pius VI., (1775-1799).

GEOGRAPHICAL TABLE NO. 4,

OF PLACES MENTIONED IN THE PRECEDING SECTION.

(1.) **Aix-la-Chapelle** (*akes-la-sha-pel*), a frontier city of Rhenish Prussia, 40 miles southwest of Cologne. Two celebrated treaties of peace were concluded here : (1) between France and Spain, by which France secured possession of Flanders (1688); and (2) that which terminated the war of the Austrian Succession.

(2.) **Algiers,** a city of northern Africa, capital of Algeria.

(3.) **Alleghany River,** The, rises in the northern part of Pennsylvania, flows in a generally southerly direction 400 miles, when it unites with the Monongahela River to form the Ohio.

(4.) **Altamaha,** a river of Georgia, formed by the union of the Oconee and Ogeechee Rivers.

(5.) **Appalachicola,** a river of Florida, formed by the union of the Chattahoochee and Flint, which unite at the southwest extremity of Georgia.

(6.) **Barbary States,** The, are situated on the southern coast of the Mediterranean. They include *Tripoli, Tunis, Algeria,* and *Morocco.* The name is derived from the Berbers,—the ancient inhabitants.

(7.) **Baton Rouge,** the former capital of Louisiana, situated on the east bank of the Mississippi, 129 miles above New Orleans.

(8.) **Bennington,** a town in the southeastern part of Vermont, 87 miles east of Albany.

(9.) **Bilbao,** a city in the north of Spain, enclosed by lofty mountains.

(10.) **Boston,** the capital of Massachusetts.

(11.) **Brandywine Creek** rises in Chester County, Pennsylvania, flows southeast, and empties into Christiana Creek, Wilmington, Delaware.

(12.) **Camden,** a town of South Carolina, on the Wateree River, 142 miles northwest of Charleston.

(13.) **Catawba,** a river of North and South Carolina. In the latter State it is called the Wateree, and unites with the Congaree to form the Santee.

(14.) **Cowpens.** This was a place in the northern part of South

Carolina, so called because of an enclosure used by neighboring farmers, for herding cattle.

(15.) **Crown Point,** a town of New York, on the west shore of Lake Champlain.

(16.) **Deerfield,** a village of Massachusetts at the junction of the Deerfield and Connecticut Rivers.

(17.) **Eutaw Springs,** a small branch of the Santee River, South Carolina.

(18.) **Genesee,** a river of western New York, which flows in a northerly direction, and empties into Lake Ontario. It gives its name to a very fertile and beautiful portion of the State, once famous as the home of the *Five Nations*.

(19.) **Germantown,** now a part of Philadelphia.

(20.) **Lexington,** a town of Massachusetts, 7 miles east of Concord.

(21.) **Louisburg,** once an important seaport of Cape Breton. Its fortifications were very extensive, and are said to have cost $6,000,000. The English, on taking possession in 1763, demolished these works at an expense of $50,000. The town is now in ruins.

(22.) **Miami,** a river of Ohio, which empties into the Ohio River about 20 miles below Cincinnati.

(23.) **Monmouth,** a central county of New Jersey, drained by the Neversink, Shrewsbury, Shark and Tom's Rivers. The battle took place at Freehold.

(24.) **Mount Vernon** is situated on the Potomac River, 8 miles below Alexandria.

(25.) **New Orleans,** the capital of Louisiana, is situated on the Mississippi River, about 100 miles from its mouth.

(26.) **Newport,** a city of Rhode Island, famed as a fashionable watering-place.

(27.) **Ogdensburg,** a city of northern New York, situated on the St. Lawrence River.

(28.) **Pensacola,** a city on the west coast of Florida, situated on the bay of the same name.

(29.) **Princeton,** a town of New Jersey, 11 miles northeast of Trenton.

(30.) **Saratoga,** a famous watering-place, 38 miles north of Albany.

(31.) **Savannah,** the largest city of Georgia. It contains a monument to General Greene, and one to Count Pulaski.

(32.) **Stillwater,** a village of Saratoga County, New York, 24 miles above Albany.

(33.) **Ticonderoga,** a village of New York, situated at the outlet of Lake George. Two or three miles below this village, are the ruins of the old Fort Ticonderoga, on the west shore of Lake Champlain.

(34.) **Trenton,** the capital of New Jersey, situated on the left bank of the Delaware River, 30 miles northeast of Philadelphia.

(35.) **Utrecht,** a city of Holland, 33 miles southeast of Amsterdam.

(36.) **Valley Forge,** a village of Pennsylvania, situated on the Schuylkill River, 6 miles from Norristown.

(37.) **West Point,** the site of the United States Military Academy, is situated on the right bank of the Hudson, 52 miles north of the city of New York. The natural strength of the place led to its selection for a fortress during the Revolution; and a heavy chain was stretched across the river (which is here very narrow) to prevent the passage of the enemy's ships.

(38.) **White Plains,** a post village of Westchester County, New York, 26 miles northeast of New York City.

(39.) **Wyoming Valley,** a beautiful and fertile tract on the Susquehanna River, in Luzerne County, Pennsylvania.

(40.) **Yadkin,** a large river which, rising in North Carolina, flows first in a northerly and then in a southeasterly direction, and entering South Carolina, takes the name of *Great Pedee.*

(41.) **Yorktown,** a town of Virginia situated on the right bank of the York River, 11 miles from its mouth.

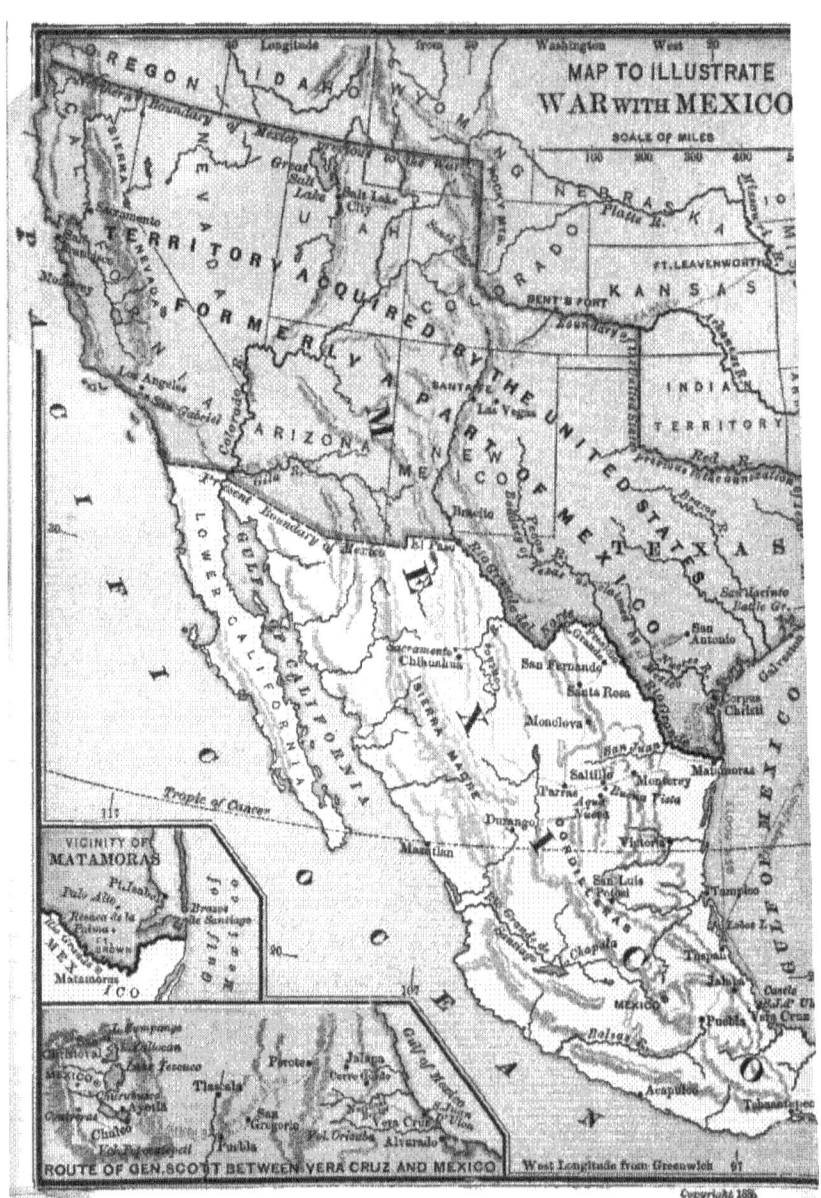

SECTION V.

A.D. 1800 to A.D. 1893.

STUDY NO. 1.

ADMINISTRATIONS OF JEFFERSON AND MADISON.—WAR OF 1812.

1. Washington, the Capital.—In the summer of 1800 the seat of government was removed from Philadelphia to Washington.[68] A single packet-sloop carried all the office furniture of the several departments, besides the "*seven large boxes and four or five smaller ones,*" which contained the archives of the government. In the same year, a *Free School* was established, in connection with St. Peter's Church, New York City.

2. Thomas Jefferson's Administration, (1801—1809), was chiefly noted for

(1.) THE ADMISSION OF OHIO (1802).

THOMAS JEFFERSON.

(2.) THE PURCHASE OF LOUISIANA (1803).
(3.) DEATH OF HAMILTON (1804).
(4.) A WAR WITH TRIPOLI (1801–1805).
(5.) DIFFICULTIES WITH GREAT BRITAIN.

3. Ohio.—Ohio, the seventeenth State, was admitted to the Union November 29, 1804. It was called from the river of that name, signifying the "*beautiful river.*" The first explorations were made by the French, under La Salle, about 1680, and the first permanent settlement was at Marietta, in 1788. It was the first State carved out of the great *Northwest Territory.**

4. Louisiana.—*Louisiana* then embraced a vast region chiefly west of the Mississippi, reaching northward to the British Possessions, and westward to the Rocky Mountains. It was purchased from France for the sum of $15,000,000.

When the purchase had been concluded, Napoleon remarked: "*This accession of territory strengthens forever the power of the United States; and I have just given to England a maritime rival that will, sooner or later, humble her pride.*"

5. Death of Hamilton.—*Aaron Burr*, the Vice-President under Jefferson, was Alexander Hamilton's bitter rival, both in law and in politics, and at last challenged him to a duel. Hamilton accepted, and the affair took place at Weehawken, N. J. (July 11, 1804). Hamilton fell at the first fire, on the very spot where his eldest son had been killed shortly before, in the same manner. His death produced the most profound sensation. The virtuous were filled with horror, and echoed the sentiments of a senator who exclaimed: "*God grant that it may be the last, as it is the first time that a man, presiding in the American Senate, is indicted for murder!*"

---

* This territory was created in 1787, and included all the public land north of the Ohio. It embraced the present States of Michigan, Ohio, Indiana, Illinois, Wisconsin, and part of Minnesota. It was a part of New France before the French authority ceased in 1763. The British held possession for twenty years, and then the country was ceded to the United States.

ADMINISTRATION OF JEFFERSON. 257

Trial of Burr for Treason.—Burr afterward went west and organized an expedition with the avowed object of forming a settlement in northern Mexico. Being suspected, however, of a design to break up the Union and found a separate confederacy beyond the Alleghanies, he was arrested and tried (1807) on a charge of treason. Although acquitted for want of proof, he yet remained an outcast.

6. War with Tripoli.—The Barbary States had for many years, sent out cruisers which captured vessels of all Christian nations, and held their crews as slaves until ransomed. The United States, like the European nations, was accustomed to pay annual tribute to these pirates to secure exemption from their attacks. The Bashaw of Tripoli at last became so haughty that he declared war (1801) against the United States. Jefferson sent a fleet which blockaded* the port and bombarded the city of Tripoli, until the frightened Bashaw was glad to make peace.

7. Difficulty with England.—During this time England and France were engaged in a desperate struggle. England tried to prevent trade with France, and, in turn, Napoleon forbade all commerce with England. As the United States were neutral, they did most of the carrying trade of Europe, and our vessels thus became the prey of both the hostile nations. Besides, England claimed the right of stopping American vessels on the high seas, to search for seamen claimed to be of English birth, and to press them into the British navy. The feeling in the United States was intensified, when the British frigate *Leopard* fired into

---

* During this blockade a valiant exploit was performed by Lieutenant Decatur. The frigate Philadelphia had unfortunately grounded and fallen into the enemy's hands. Having concealed his men below, Decatur entered the harbor with a small vessel, which he warped alongside the Philadelphia, in the character of a ship in distress. As the two vessels struck, the pirates first suspected his design. Instantly he leaped aboard with his men, swept the affrighted crew into the sea, set the ship on fire, and amid a tremendous cannonade from the batteries, escaped without the loss of a man.

the American frigate *Chesapeake*, off the coast of Virginia. The latter vessel, being wholly unprepared for battle, soon struck her colors. Four of the crew, three being Americans by birth, were taken, on the pretence that they were deserters. Jefferson immediately ordered all British vessels of war to quit the waters of the United States. Though England disavowed the act, no reparation was made.

8. Embargo Act.—An embargo was then laid by Congress on American vessels, forbidding them to leave port; but this was so injurious to our foreign trade that it was removed. The *Embargo Act* * followed, forbidding commerce with England or France.

9. Political Parties.—While the country was in this feverish state, Jefferson's second term expired. James Madison, the republican candidate, who was closely in sympathy with his views, was elected as his successor by a large majority. The republicans were generally in favor of a war with England. The federalists, however, were a strong minority, and throughout this administration warmly opposed the war policy of the republicans.

10. Madison's Administration (1809–1817) was chiefly noted for

(1.) CONTESTS WITH THE INDIANS (1811).

(2.) SECOND WAR WITH GREAT BRITAIN (1812–15).

(3). THE ADMISSION INTO THE UNION OF LOUISIANA (1812) AND INDIANA (1816).

11. Battle of Tippecanoe (1811).—British emissaries had been busy arousing the Indians of the north-west to war. Tecumseh, a chief of the Shawnees, formed a strong confederacy against the Americans, and Indian outrages along

---

* The opponents of this Act spelling the name backward nicknamed it The " *O Grab Me* " Act.

the border became frequent. General Harrison, Governor of Indiana Territory, was sent against Tecumseh with a strong force. The Americans were attacked in the night, near the Tippecanoe; but they routed the Indians with great slaughter, and all the tribes sued for peace.

12. War against England.—This Indian difficulty aroused intense feeling against Great Britain. Meanwhile the British government went so far as to send war-vessels into our waters, and to seize many of our ships as prizes. One day, in May, 1811, the American frigate *President* having hailed the British sloop-of-war *Little Belt*, received a cannon-shot in reply. The fire was returned, and the sloop soon disabled; a civil answer was then returned. This state of things could not be tolerated; and as the British government refused to relinquish its offensive course, war was finally declared against Great Britain (June 19, 1812).

13. Surrender of Detroit by Hull (August 16).—As in the previous wars, it was determined to invade Canada. General William Hull, Governor of Michigan Territory, accordingly crossed over from Detroit and encamped on Canadian soil. He was preparing to march against Fort Malden (*maŭl-den*), when he learned that the British and Indians were gathering to attack him, whereupon he ignominiously retreated to Detroit. Here he was pursued by a force of British under General Brock, and Indians under Tecumseh. The Americans had the advantage in numbers and position, and awaited impatiently, in line of battle, the order to fire. At this moment Hull seemed to lose all presence of mind, and, in an agony of fear, raised the white flag. Without stipulating even for the honors of war, he surrendered not only Detroit, with its garrison and stores, but the whole of Michigan.

14. Battle of Queenstown Heights (October 13).—Late in summer, another attempt was made to invade Canada. General Van Rensselaer (*ren'-se-ler*) sent a small body of men across the Niagara River, to attack the British at Queenstown Heights. The English were driven from their position, and General Brock was killed. General

Van Rensselaer now returned to the American shore to bring over the rest of the army; but the militia had lost their courage, and denying the constitutional right of their commander to take them out of the State, refused to embark. Meantime their comrades on the Canadian shore, thus basely abandoned, were, after a desperate struggle, compelled to surrender.

15. Constitution and Guerriere (August 9).— The fight off the coast of Massachusetts, between the Amer-

"OLD IRONSIDES."

ican frigate Constitution (popularly called *Old Ironsides*) and the Guerriere (*găre-e-ăre*) is memorable in our naval history. The latter vessel opened fire first. Captain Isaac Hull (a nephew of General Hull) refused to answer until he had brought his ship into the exact position he desired, when he poured broadside after broadside into his antagonist, sweeping the deck, shattering the hull, and cutting the masts and rigging to pieces. Within half an hour the Guerriere became unmanageable and the captain surrendered. The ship was so badly injured that it could not be brought into port; while the *Old Ironsides*, in a few hours, was ready for another fight.

16. Frolic and Wasp (October 13).—The next noted achievement was the defeat of the English brig *Frolic*

CAPTURE OF THE FROLIC.

by the sloop-of-war *Wasp*, off the coast of North Carolina. When the former was boarded by her captors, her colors were still flying, there being no one to haul them down. The man at the helm was the only sailor left on deck unharmed.

17. Other victories followed. Privateers scoured every sea, inflicting untold injury on British commerce. During the year over three hundred prizes were captured. So many naval triumphs inspired the people with confidence, and made it easy to obtain volunteers for the army. They also helped, no doubt, to bring about by a large majority the re election of Madison.

STUDY NO. 2.

MADISON (Continued).—WAR WITH ENGLAND (Continued).

1. Plan of the Campaign of 1813.—Three armies were raised this year: (1) the *Army of the Centre,* under General Dearborn, on the Niagara River; (2) the *Army of the North,* under General Hampton, along Lake Champlain; and (3) the *Army of the West,* under General Harrison, of Tippecanoe fame. All three were ultimately to invade Canada. Proctor was the British general, and Tecumseh had command of his Indian allies.

2. The Armies of the Centre and the North did little. General Dearborn attacked York (now Toronto), General Pike gallantly leading the assault. Unfortunately, in the moment of success the magazine blew up, killing Pike, and making sad havoc among his men. General Wilkinson, Dearborn's successor, was directed to descend the St. Lawrence in boats, and join General Hampton in an attack on Montreal. At *Chrysler's Field* he repulsed the British, but owing to a disagreement with General Hampton he returned. General Hampton went north as far as *St. John's,* where he was defeated by the British. He then made the best of his way back to Plattsburg, where, in the winter, he was joined by General Winchester's men. Thus ingloriously ended the campaign of these two armies.

3. Army of the West.—A detachment of General Harrison's men was captured at Frenchtown, on the River Raisin, by Proctor, who then besieged Harrison himself at *Fort Meigs* (*megz*). Repulsed here, Proctor stormed *Fort Stephenson,* which was defended by a small garrison under Major Croghan, a young man of twenty-one. Beaten again, he returned to Malden.

4. The Chesapeake and Shannon (*June 1*).—Captain Lawrence, of the *Hornet*, having captured the British brig *Peacock*, on his return was placed in command of the *Chesapeake*, the ill-starred frigate which struck her flag to the *Leopard* off the coast of Virginia. While refitting his vessel at Boston, a challenge was sent to fight the *Shannon*, then lying off the harbor. Lawrence, although part of his crew were discharged, and the unpaid remainder were almost mutinous, consulted only his own heroic spirit, and at once put to sea. The action was brief. A hand-grenade having burst in the *Chesapeake's* arm-chest, the enemy took advantage of the confusion, and boarded her. A scene of carnage ensued. Lawrence, mortally wounded, was carried below. As he left the deck he exclaimed, "*Don't give up the ship!*" But the feeble crew were soon overpowered, and the colors hauled down.

5. Perry's Victory (*Sept. 10*).— When Captain Perry, then only twenty-seven years old, was assigned the command of the flotilla on Lake Erie, the British were undisputed masters of the lake, while his fleet was to be made, in part, out of the trees in the forest. By indefatigable exertion he had got nine vessels, carrying fifty-four guns, ready for action, when the British fleet of six vessels and sixty-three guns bore down upon his little squadron. Perry's flag-ship, the *Lawrence*,[*] engaged two of the heaviest vessels of the enemy, and fought them, till but eight of his men were left. He helped these to fire the last gun, and then leaped into a boat and bore his flag to the *Niagara*. He had to pass within pistol-shot of the British, who turned their guns directly upon him; but though he was a fair mark for every shot, he escaped without injury. Breaking through the enemy's line and firing right and left, within fifteen minutes

---

[*] From its mast-head floated a blue pennant, bearing the words of the dying Lawrence, "*Don't give up the ship!*"

after he mounted the deck of the Niagara the victory was won. Perry then sent his famous despatch to General Harrison, "*We have met the enemy, and they are ours; two ships, two brigs, one schooner, and a sloop.*" This victory filled the Americans with joy, and on it virtually hung the issue of the war.

PERRY LEAVING THE LAWRENCE.

6. Battle of the Thames (October).—Proctor and Tecumseh were at Malden with their motley array of British and Indians, waiting to lay waste the frontier. Harrison, at Sandusky Bay, was nearly ready to invade Canada, and at the news of this victory pushed across the lake. Landing at

Malden, which he found deserted, he hotly pursued the flying enemy, and overtook them on the River Thames (*temz*). Having drawn up his troops, he ordered Colonel Johnson, with his Kentucky horsemen, to charge the English in front. Dashing through the forest, they broke the enemy's line, and forming in their rear prepared to pour in a deadly fire. The British surrendered, but Proctor escaped by the swiftness of his horse. Johnson pushed forward to attack the Indians. In the heat of the action, a bullet, said to have been fired by Johnson himself, struck Tecumseh. With his death the savages lost all hope, and fled in confusion.

7. War with the Creeks.—Tecumseh had been (1811) among the Alabama Indians, and had aroused them to take up arms against the Americans. They accordingly formed a league (1813), and fell upon *Fort Mimms*, massacring the garrison and the defenceless women and children. Volunteers flocked in from all sides to avenge this horrid deed. Under General Jackson, they drove the Indians from one place to another, until they took refuge on the *Horseshoe Bend*, where they fortified themselves for the last battle* (March 27, 1814). The soldiers, with fixed bayonets, scaled their breastwork. Six hundred of the Indians were killed, and the remainder were glad to sue for peace.

8. Ravages on the Atlantic Coast.—Early in the spring of this year, the British commenced to devastate the southern coast. New England was spared because of a

---

* An event occurred on Jackson's march which illustrates his iron will. For a long time his soldiers suffered extremely from famine. At last they mutinied. General Jackson rode before the ranks. His left arm, shattered by a ball, was disabled, but in his right he held a musket. Sternly ordering the men back to their place, he declared he would shoot the first who advanced. No one stirred, and at last all returned to duty.

belief that the northern States were unfriendly to the war, and that they would yet return to their allegiance to Great Britain. Admiral Cockburn, especially, disgraced the British navy by conduct worse than that of Cornwallis in the Revolution. Along the Virginia and Carolina coast, he burned bridges, farm-houses, and villages; robbed the inhabitants of their crops, stock, and slaves; plundered churches, and murdered the sick in their beds.

COLONEL MILLER AT LUNDY'S LANE.

9. **The Campaign of 1814** was prosecuted by the British more vigorously, as the Peace of Paris released the fleet and army that had been so long employed against Napoleon. Fourteen thousand veterans, who had served under Wellington, were sent to Canada.

10. **Battle of Lundy's Lane** (July 25).—The American army, under General Brown, now crossed the

Niagara River once more, and for the last time invaded Canada. Fort Erie having been taken, General Winfield Scott leading the advance, attacked the British at *Chippewa* (July 5), and gained a brilliant victory. A second engagement was fought at *Lundy's Lane,* opposite Niagara Falls. Here, within sound of that mighty cataract, occurred one of the bloodiest battles of the war. General Scott had only one thousand men, but he maintained the unequal contest until dark. A battery located on a height was the key to the British position. Calling Colonel Miller to his side, the commander asked him if he could take it. "*I'll try, sir,*" was the fearless reply. Heading his regiment, Miller steadily marched up the height and secured the coveted position. Three times the British rallied for its re-capture, but as many times were hurled back, and at midnight they retired from the field.

11. Battle of Lake Champlain (September 11) All but fifteen hundred of the troops at Plattsburg had gone to reinforce General Brown. Prevost, the commander of the British army in Canada, learning this fact, took twelve thousand veteran soldiers who had served under Wellington, and marched against that place. As he advanced to the attack, the British fleet on Lake Champlain assailed the American squadron under Commodore McDonough. The attacking squadron was nearly annihilated. The little army in Plattsburg by their vigorous defence prevented Prevost from crossing the Saranac River. When he found that his ships were lost, he fled precipitately.

12. Ravages on the Atlantic Coast.—The British blockade extended this year to the north; and commerce was so completely destroyed that the lamps in the light-houses were extinguished, as being of use only to the

English. Several towns in Main were captured. Stonington, Conn., was bombarded. Cockburn, too, continued his depredations along the Chesapeake. General Ross marched to Washington, burned the capitol (August 24) and other public buildings, libraries and records, together with private

BRITISH SOLDIERS BURNING BOOKS IN THE LIBRARY OF CONGRESS.

dwellings and storehouses. He then sailed around by sea to attack Baltimore. The troops, which had disembarked (September 12) below the city, were to move upon it by land,* while the fleet was to bombard Fort McHenry from the river. They met, however, with a determined resistance; and as the fleet had made no impression on the fort, the army retired to their ships.

13. **The Star Spangled Banner.**—During the bombardment, Francis S. Key, who had gone to the British fleet with a flag of truce to

---

* While the British troops were marching toward Baltimore, General Ross rode forward with a part of his staff, to reconnoitre. Two mechanics, who were in a tree watching their advance, fired upon them, and Ross fell mortally wounded. The two patriots were instantly shot.

procure the release of a friend, and who was not permitted to return lest he might carry back valuable information, watched the flag of his country waving above Fort McHenry. The British commander had boasted to Key that the place could hold out only a few hours; but the next morning the flag was still waving defiantly and triumphantly in the face of the foe. The incident inspired Key to write the words of a song which will be sung as long as the flag is known:

> "Oh, say, can you see, by the dawn's early light,
> What so proudly we hailed at the twilight's last gleaming?
> Whose broad stripes and bright stars, through the perilous fight,
> O'er the ramparts we watched were so gallantly streaming?
> And the rocket's red glare, the bombs bursting in air,
> Gave proof through the night that our flag was still there.
> Oh, say, does that star-spangled banner yet wave
> O'er the land of the free and the home of the brave?"

14. The Hartford Convention.—The greatest excitement was produced by these events. Every seaport was fortified; militia were organized; and citizens of all ranks labored in throwing up defences. Bitter reproaches were cast upon the administration because of its mode of conducting the war. Delegates from New England States met at Hartford (December 15) to discuss this subject. The meeting was branded with odium by the friends of the administration, and to be called a *Hartford Convention Federalist* was long a term of reproach.

15. Peace, as afterward appeared, had been made before the convention adjourned, a treaty having been signed at Ghent,[40] December 24. Before the news reached this country, a terrible battle had been fought in the South.

16. Battle of New Orleans (January 8, 1815).— A powerful British fleet and a force of twelve thousand men, under General Pakenham, undertook the capture of New Orleans. General Jackson, anticipating this movement, had thrown up intrenchments* several miles below the city. The British advanced steadily, in solid columns, heedless of the artillery fire which swept their ranks, until they came within range of the Kentucky and Tennessee riflemen, when they wavered. Their officers rallied them again and again. General Pakenham fell into the arms of the same officer who had caught General Ross as he fell at Baltimore. Neither discipline nor bravery could prevail. General Lambert, who succeeded to the command, drew off his men in the night, hopelessly defeated, after a loss of over two thousand; while the American loss was but seven killed and six wounded.

17. The Results of the War of 1812-14 were, in general, favorable to the United States. It is true that the treaty left the question of *impressment* unsettled; yet it was tacitly understood that England would not again attempt to enforce her claims. We had gained the respect of European nations, mainly because our navy had dared to meet on the open sea, and often successfully, the greatest maritime power of the world. The impossibility of any foreign power gaining permanent foothold on our territory was proved. The fruitless invasion of Canada by the militia, compared with the brave defence of their own territory by the same men, showed that the strength of the United States consisted in defensive warfare. Extensive manufactories were established to supply the place of the English goods cut off by the blockade. The immediate evils of the war were apparent: trade ruined, commerce gone, no specie to be seen, and a general depression. Yet the wonderful resources of the

---

* Jackson at first made his intrenchments in part of cotton bales, but a red-hot cannon-ball having fired the cotton and scattered the burning fragments among the barrels of gunpowder, it was found necessary to remove the cotton entirely. The only defence of the Americans in this battle was a bank of earth, five feet high, and a ditch in front.

country were shown by the rapidity with which it entered upon a new career of prosperity. The national debt of $127,000,000 was paid from the ordinary revenue within twenty years.

18. The Algerines had taken advantage of the war with England to renew their depredations on American commerce. In May, 1815, Decatur was sent with a squadron to protect our rights in the Mediterranean. Proceeding to Algiers, Tunis, and Tripoli, he obtained the liberation of American prisoners, and full indemnity for all losses. The United States was the first nation to effectually resist the demands of the Barbary pirates for tribute.

19. Political Parties.—When Madison's term of office expired, the federalist party had been broken up by its opposition to the war. *James Monroe*, the Presidential candidate of the republican party, was almost unanimously elected. He was generally beloved, and all parties united in his support. This period is therefore remarkable, and is characterized as the *Era of Good Feeling*.

PRINCIPAL BATTLES OF THE WAR OF 1812.

Date.	Location.	Commanders.		Victor.
		American.	British.	
1812...	Detroit (surrendered)..	Hull............	Brock...........	British.
	Queenstown Heights..	Van Rensselaer..	Brock......	British.
	Frenchtown.............	Allen..............	....	American.
	River Raisin (massacre)	Winchester	Proctor	British.
	York...................	Pike...............	Sheaffe.....	American.
1813...	Fort Stephenson.....	Croghan..	Proctor	American
	Stonington............	....	Hardy........ ..	American.
	Fort Mimms..........	Beasley..........	....	Indians.
	Thames................	Harrison.........	Proctor	American.
	Chrysler's Field.......	Boyd	Morrison.........	British.
	Horseshoe Bend.......	Jackson	....	American.
	Chippewa.............	Brown............	Riall	American.
	Lundy's Lane.........	Brown............	Drummond	American.
1814...	Fort Erie (besieged)..	Gaines	Drummond.......	American.
	Fort Mackinaw.......	Croghan..........	....	British.
	Plattsburg.............	McComb..........	Prevost..........	American.
	North Point..........	Strycker..........	Rose.............	American.
1815.....	New Orleans..........	Jackson.....	Pakenham.......	American.

STUDY NO. 3.

MONROE.—J. Q. ADAMS.—JACKSON.

1. James Monroe's Administration, (1817-1825), was noted for

(1.) THE MISSOURI COMPROMISE BILL, (1820).

(2.) THE ACCESSION OF FLORIDA, (1820).

(3.) THE PROMULGATION OF THE MONROE DOCTRINE, (1823).

(4.) THE ADMISSION INTO THE UNION OF FIVE NEW STATES; MISSISSIPPI (1817), ILLINOIS (1818), ALABAMA (1819), MAINE (1820), AND MISSOURI (1821).

2. The Slavery Question and the Missouri Compromise.—The slavery question had now become one of vast importance in the political history of this country. At first, slaves were owned in the northern as well as the southern States. But at the North, slave labor was unprofitable, and it had gradually died out; while at the South it was a success, and had steadily increased. Hence when the admission of Missouri as a State was proposed, a violent discussion arose whether it should be free or slave. Finally it was admitted as a slave State (1821), with the *compromise* advocated by Henry Clay, that *slavery should be prohibited in all other territories west of the Mississippi and north of parallel 36° 30'*, the southern boundary of Missouri.

3. Accession of Florida.—Florida was purchased of Spain by a treaty proposed February 22, 1819, though not signed by the King of Spain until October 20, 1820, while the United States did not obtain full possession before July 17, 1821. (These facts account for the different dates assigned to this purchase in the various histories.) The treaty with Spain which secured Florida, also relinquished all Spanish authority over the region west of the Rocky Mountains, claimed by the United States as belonging to the Louisiana purchase, but not previously acknowledged by Spain.

4. The Monroe Doctrine.—In 1823, President Monroe in his annual message declared that the American continents "*are henceforth not to be considered as subjects for future colonization by any European power, and that any attempt on the part of Europeans to gain dominion in America would be deemed by the United States an unfriendly act.*" This is known as the *Monroe Doctrine.*

5. Lafayette's Visit to this country (1824), as "*the nation's guest,*" was a joyous event. He traveled through each of the twenty-four States, and was everywhere welcomed with delight. His visit to the tomb of Washington was full of affectionate remembrance. He was carried home in a national vessel, *the Brandywine,* so named in honor of the battle in which Lafayette first drew his sword in behalf of the colonies.

6. Political Parties.—Divisions now became apparent in the great party which had twice so triumphantly elected Monroe as President. The whig party, as it came to be called in Jackson's time, was forming in opposition to the republican,—thenceforth known as the democratic party.* The whigs were in favor of a protective tariff, and

---

* John Quincy Adams and Henry Clay were the champions of the whigs; Andrew Jackson and John C. Calhoun of the democrats. In 1834, the democrats began to be called *Locofocos,* because, at a meeting in Tammany Hall, the lights having been extinguished, were relit with locofoco matches, which several, expecting such an event, had carried in their pockets.

a general system of internal improvements;* the democrats opposed these important measures. No one of the four candidates having obtained a majority of votes, the election went to the House of Representatives, and *John Quincy Adams*, son of John Adams, was chosen.

7. John Quincy Adams' Administration, (1825–1829), was noted for

(1.) NATIONAL PEACE AND PROSPERITY.

(2.) THE COMPLETION OF THE FIRST RAILROAD IN THE UNITED STATES AND THE OPENING OF THE ERIE CANAL.

8. An Era of General Prosperity was inaugurated by the "era of good feeling" which characterized Monroe's election. After the ravages of war, all parties gave themselves up to the development of the resources of the country and the progress of its varied industries. There were great financial difficulties, the legacy of the war; but both Monroe's and Adams' administrations were periods of national prosperity.

JOHN QUINCY ADAMS.

9. The Erie Canal.—An Irishman named Christopher Colles is entitled to the credit of having made the first suggestion of this great undertaking. He came to New York before the Revolution, and in 1785 issued a pamphlet called "*Proposals for the Speedy Settlement*

---

* A protective tariff is a duty imposed on imported goods for the purpose of encouraging their manufacture at home. By internal improvements are meant the improving of the navigation of rivers, the building of bridges and railroads, the dredging of harbors, etc.

of the Western Frontier of New York." It contained a plan for the canal, but it was considered utterly impracticable. In 1810, De Witt Clinton advocated the measure in the senate of New York, and it afterwards found strong supporters. Work was not commenced upon it until the 4th of July, 1817, when Governor Clinton, in the presence of many thousands of citizens and amid great demonstrations of joy, threw the first spadeful of earth. Even then the people were incredulous. It was a common remark, *"If I can live until Clinton's ditch is done, I shall be content."*

On the 26th of October, 1825, the whole canal was formally opened by a magnificent celebration. The governor, State officers, and invited guests took passage from Buffalo for New York, in a gorgeously decorated boat, accompanied by a numerous fleet. One of the ceremonies near Sandy Hook was the emptying of a keg of Lake Erie water into the Atlantic, thus typifying the union of the waters of the Lake with those of the Ocean.

10. **The First Railroad in the United States.**—The year 1827 witnessed the building of the first railroad in the United States at Quincy, Massachusetts. It was operated by horse-power, and

THE FIRST RAILROAD.

was three miles in length, extending from the granite quarries to the Neponset River. The next year, the Delaware and Hudson Canal Company constructed a road from their coal mines to Honesdale, a locomotive being imported from England. This was the first steam-engine used in the United States.

11. **Secret Societies.**—Under the administration of the elder Adams, secret societies had been formed in connection with the Jacobins and other clubs in France. On their dissolution they were succeeded by the Freemasons. In

1826, the horrible murder of William Morgan, of Batavia, N. Y., who had threatened to reveal their secrets, caused intense excitement, and resulted in the formation of an anti-Masonic party.

12. The Tariff.—The debt of the United States was fast diminishing, and there was a surplus of $5,000,000 in the treasury. A protective tariff, known as the *"American System,"* now reached its height. It was popular at the east, but distasteful to the south.* Adams was a candidate for re-election; but Andrew Jackson, the hero of New Orleans, and the democratic nominee, was chosen. The principle of a protective tariff was thus rejected by the people.

ANDREW JACKSON.

13. Andrew Jackson's Administration, (1829-1837), was characterized by great vigor and resolution. It was noted for

(1.) THE NULLIFICATION ORDINANCE AND CLAY'S COMPROMISE BILL, (1832).

(2.) TROUBLES CONCERNING THE UNITED STATES BANK, (1833).

(3.) THE BLACK HAWK WAR, (1832).

* The southern States, devoted to agricultural pursuits, desired to have foreign goods brought to them as cheaply as possible; while the eastern States, engaged in manufactures, wished to have foreign competition shut off by heavy duties.

MONROE AND JACKSON.   277

(4.) THE FLORIDA OR SEMINOLE WAR, (1835).

(5.) THE ADMISSION INTO THE UNION OF ARKANSAS (1836) AND MICHIGAN (1837).

14. Immediately on his accession, Jackson surrounded himself by his political friends, thus establishing the now popular principle of "*rotation in office.*" *

15. Nullification and Compromise, (1832).—South Carolina passed a nullification ordinance, declaring the tariff law of 1828 "null and void," and that the State

HENRY CLAY ADDRESSING THE SENATE.

would secede from the Union if force should be employed to collect any revenue at Charleston. President Jackson acting

---

* "During the first year of his administration, there were nearly seven hundred removals from office, not including subordinate clerks. During the forty years preceding, there had been but sixty-four."

with his accustomed promptness, at once issued a proclamation announcing his determination to execute the laws, and ordered troops, under General Scott, to Charleston. In the meantime, Henry Clay's celebrated "*Tariff Compromise Bill*" was adopted by the Senate. This measure offering a gradual reduction of the tariff, it was accepted by both sides, and quiet restored. Clay being told that his action would injure his prospects for the Presidency, nobly replied: "*I would rather be right than be President.*"

16. Bank of the United States.—During his first term, Jackson vetoed a bill renewing the charter of the United States Bank at Philadelphia. After his re-election by an overwhelming majority, considering his policy sustained by the people, he ordered the public money to be removed from its vaults (1833). The bank thereupon contracted its loans, money became scarce, and people being unable to pay their debts, great commercial distress ensued. This measure excited the most violent clamor; but Jackson was sustained by the democratic majority in the House of Representatives.

Speculations.—When the public money which had been withdrawn from the Bank of the United States (1833) was deposited in the local banks, it became easy for any one to borrow money. Speculation extended to every branch of trade, but especially to western lands. New cities were laid out in the wilderness, and fabulous prices were charged for building-lots, which existed only on paper. Scarcely a man could be found who had not his pet project for realizing a fortune. The bitter fruits of these hot-house schemes were gathered in Van Buren's time.

17. The Black Hawk War [*] broke out in the

---

[*] In this war, Abraham Lincoln (afterwards President) served as captain of the volunteers, and Jefferson Davis as second lieutenant of the regulars.

Northwest Territory during 1832. The Sacs and Foxes had, some time before, sold their lands to the United States; but when the settlers came to take possession, the Indians refused to leave. After some skirmishes they were driven off, and their leader, the famous *Black Hawk*, was captured.

18. The Cherokees.—One of Jackson's plans was to remove all Indians beyond the Mississippi; but the removal of the Cherokees and Seminoles of the South was not effected without much trouble. The Cherokees had been guaranteed the quiet possession of their lands, with promises of future admission into the Union. The neighboring States having infringed on their rights, the Indians appealed to the President; but he declining to defend them, they were forced to leave their villages, and retire to the wilderness.

19. The Seminole War.—The cession of Florida to the English by the treaty of 1763, proved the death-blow of the Catholic missions. The poor Indians being deprived of their villages, and forced to resume the nomadic life from which Christianity had reclaimed them, took the name of Seminoles (*wanderers*), gradually lost the Faith, and became the scourge of the whites. In 1832, a few unauthorized chiefs, at the request of the United States government, agreed to migrate; but the tribe, with their king, Micanopy, refused to depart.

20. In 1835, the celebrated Seminole chief, Osceola, a half-breed of great talent and bravery, paid a visit to Fort King. While there, his wife was seized and carried off as a slave. Osceola, enraged at this and other injuries, declared war; whereupon he was seized by the government agent, and put in irons. Dissembling his wrath, Osceola consented to the treaty; but no sooner was he released, than he plotted a general massacre of the whites.

21. General Thompson was shot and scalped while sitting at dinner, under the very guns of Fort King. The same day, Major Dade, with over one hundred men, was waylaid near the Wahoo Swamp. All but four were killed, and these finally died of their wounds. After several battles the Indians retreated to the Everglades of southern Florida, in whose tangled swamps they hoped to find a safe retreat. Expeditions that failed to find the enemy, and murders and surprises by an invisible foe, disheartened the army, and discouraged the country. Osceola was the soul of the resistance. To every overture for peace, he replied: "*Here I hunted when a boy; here my father lies buried; here I wish to die!*"

22. In October, 1837, while holding a conference with General Jesup in a magnolia grove, under a flag of truce, Osceola was treacherously seized and taken to Fort Moultrie. Here he died the next year. Jesup was severely censured for this violation of the sanctity of a flag.

Two months later (Dec. 25), the Seminoles were defeated in a sanguinary battle at Okechobee, by Colonel Zachary Taylor; but they were not fully subdued till 1842. This war, brought on by the injustice of the whites towards their Indian brethren, cost the United States multitudes of valuable lives, and millions of treasure.

23. Political Parties.—The democratic candidate, *Martin Van Buren*, was chosen President; and as no Vice-President had been elected by the people, the Senate selected Col. R. H. Johnson, the hero of the Thames. The people, by the choice of Van Buren, supported the policy of Jackson—no United States Bank, and no Protective Tariff.

STUDY NO. 4.

VAN BUREN.—HARRISON.—TYLER.—POLK

1. Martin Van Buren's Administration (1837-41) was chiefly noted for
(1.) THE FINANCIAL CRISIS OF 1837.
(2.) THE CANADIAN REBELLION (1837-38).
(3.) DIFFICULTIES CONCERNING THE N. E. BOUNDARY.

2. Crisis of 1837.—The financial storm which had been gathering through the preceding administration, now burst with terrible fury. The banks contracted their circulation.* Business men could not pay their debts, and failures were every-day occurrences. Those in New York city alone, during March and April, exceeded $100,000,000. Eight of the States in part or wholly failed, and even the United States government became unable to meet its engagements.

3. The "Patriot War," (1837-1838).—The Canadian rebellion, at this time, against England, stirred the sympathies of the American people. Meetings were held, volunteers offered, and arms

---

* The direct causes of this were (1) the specie circular, which was issued by Jackson in 1836, just at the close of his last term, directing that payments for public lands should be made in gold and silver. The gold and silver were, consequently, soon gathered into the United States treasury. (2) The surplus public money, amounting to about $28,000,000 (about $9,000,000 of the $37,000,000 ordered to be distributed being finally withheld on account of the financial crisis), which, distributed among the States, had served to produce the most extravagant speculation. (3) During the season of high prices and speculation, when fortunes were easily made, there had been heavy importations of European goods, which had to be paid for in gold and silver. Thus the country was drained of its specie. (4) A terrible fire in the city of New York on the night of Dec. 16, 1835, which had burned 600 valuable stores, and property to the amount of $18,000,000.

contributed. Thereupon the President issued a proclamation refusing the protection of the United States government to any who should aid the Canadians, and sent General Scott to the frontier to preserve the peace.

4. The Northeast Boundary between Maine and New Brunswick had never been settled. The people of that region threatened to take up arms to support their respective claims, and for some time there was peril of a war with England. During Tyler's administration, (1842), the difficulty was adjusted by what is known as the *Ashburton Treaty*, which was negotiated between the United States and Great Britain, Daniel Webster and Lord Ashburton acting as commissioners.

5. Political Parties.—The financial difficulties caused a change in political feeling, and for the time weakened the confidence of the people in the wisdom of the democratic policy. Van Buren failed of a re-election, and *General Harrison*, the *hero of Tippecanoe*, the whig nominee, was chosen President.

6. Death of President Harrison, (1841).—General Harrison had scarcely entered upon the duties of his office and selected his cabinet, when he died. *John Tyler*, the Vice-President, in accordance with the Constitution of the United States, became President.

7. John Tyler's Administration, (1841-1845), was noted for

(1.) THE DORR REBELLION, (1842).
(2.) THE ANTI-RENT DIFFICULTIES, (1844).
(3.) TROUBLES WITH THE MORMONS, (1844).
(4.) THE ANNEXATION OF TEXAS, (1845).

8. Disappointment of the Whigs.—Tyler was elected as a whig; but he did not carry out the favorite measures of his party. Immediately on coming into power, the whigs in Congress passed a bill to establish a United States Bank; but it was vetoed by Tyler, to the great disap-

TYLER'S ADMINISTRATION.

pointment of the men who had elected him. Every member of President Tyler's Cabinet, except Daniel Webster, hereupon immediately resigned.

9. The Dorr Rebellion, (1842), in Rhode Island, grew out of efforts to secure a more liberal State constitution. The people were divided into two parties, each of which elected State officers. Thomas W.

JOHN TYLER.

Dorr, who was chosen by the suffrage party, made an attack upon the State arsenal, but was driven off by the United States troops. He was afterwards arrested, tried for treason, and sentenced to imprisonment for life.*

10. Anti-Rent Difficulties, (1844).—The tenants on some of the old "patroon" estates in New York refused to pay their rent. Though very light, it was considered illegal, and therefore resisted. The "Anti-renters," as they were called, assumed the disguise of Indians, tarred and feathered those tenants who paid their rents, and even killed officers who served warrants upon them. The disturbances were suppressed by military force.

* The old charter granted to the Rhode Island colony by Charles II., was still in force. It limited the right of suffrage to owners of a freehold worth $134, or renting for $7 per year, and their eldest sons. It also fixed the number of deputies to the Assembly from the different towns. In 1840, it appeared that Providence, with a population of over 23,000, had four representatives, while Newport, with only 8,000 inhabitants, had six representatives. The injustice of this was apparent, and a new and liberal constitution having been adopted by the people almost unanimously, went into effect in 1843. Dorr was finally released, under a proclamation of general amnesty to all engaged in this rebellion. and, in 1851, was restored to all his civil rights and privileges.

11. The Mormons.—About the year 1830, a man named Joseph Smith, living in western New York, pretended to have received from Heaven revelations written in mystic characters on plates of brass. These he translated, according to his own account, by means of two transparent stones found with the plates. He now founded a new religion, in which his followers were allowed to have as many wives as they chose. As his character became known, he was for some years driven from place to place; but in 1840, he and his followers founded the city of Nauvoo, Ill. Having by their moral corruption incurred the enmity of the people about them, their leader, Joseph Smith, was taken from the custody of the authorities, to whom he had entrusted himself, and killed. A mob bombarded the city for three days, and finally (Sept., 1845) drove out the inhabitants, who fled to Iowa. After the death of Smith and the expulsion from Nauvoo, a company under the leadership of Brigham Young crossed the Rocky Mountains, and settled near Great Salt Lake, in Utah.

12. Annexation of Texas.—The Texans, under General Houston, having won their independence from Mexico, applied for admission into the Union. Their petition was at first rejected by Congress; but, being endorsed by the people in the fall elections, it was accepted before the close of Tyler's administration.

13. Political Parties.—The democrats, who favored the admission of Texas, nominated *James K. Polk*, who, after a close contest, was elected President. The whigs, who opposed its admission, had nominated Henry Clay.

14. James K. Polk's Administration, (1845–1849), was noted for

(1.) THE WAR WITH MEXICO (1845–1848).

(2.) THE DISCOVERY OF GOLD IN CALIFORNIA (1848).

(3.) THE ADMISSION INTO THE UNION OF FLORIDA (1845), TEXAS (1845), IOWA (1846), WISCONSIN (1848).

15. Taylor's Campaign in Mexico (1846–1847). —As had been feared, the annexation of Texas occasioned a war with Mexico, that government not having recognized the independence of the revolted province. General Taylor having been ordered with his troops into the disputed territory, advanced to the Rio Grande and built Fort Brown (now Brownsville). Having, on two successive days, defeated the Mexicans in the battles of Palo Alto (*pah'-lo ahl'-to*), (May 8th), and Resaca de la Palma (*ray-sah'-kah-day-lah-pahl-mah*), (May 9th), he advanced to the strongly fortified city of Monterey (*mon-ta-ray'*), and compelled it to capitulate (Sept. 24th).

CAPTURE OF MEXICAN BATTERY.

16. During the battle of Resaca de la Palma, the Mexican guns were splendidly served, and the success of the Americans depended upon their capture. Taylor accordingly rode forward to his dragoons, and shouted to their leader, "*Captain May, you must take that battery!*" "*I will do it, sir*," was the gallant reply. Placing himself at the head of his command, May dashed forward through a fire that cost him half his men, leaped over the cannon, sabred the gunners, and captured their commander, General La Vega, as he was in the act of firing a gun.

17. Battle of Buena Vista (*bwä-nah vees'-tah*) (Feb. 23, 1847).—The flower of Taylor's troops was now withdrawn by General Scott in order to invade Mexico with a powerful army from the east. Santa Anna, the Mexican general, having learned this fact, determined to fall upon Taylor's diminished force. To meet this formidable attack, the little American army took post at *Buena Vista*, a narrow mountain pass with hills on one side and a ravine on the other. Here they were attacked by twenty thousand of the best troops of Mexico. The battle, which raged from two o'clock in the morning till dark, terminated in favor of the Americans, and secured to them the frontier of the Rio Grande. They were thus left free to direct their whole force against Vera Cruz.

18. Conquest of New Mexico and California. —While these stirring events were transpiring, General Kearney (*kår-ne*), who had been directed to take the Spanish provinces of New Mexico and California, had set out from Fort Leavenworth (June, 1846), and by a march of one thousand miles had reached Santa Fe.*

---

* Colonel Doniphan, with one thousand men, the main body of General Kearney's command, marched over one thousand miles through a hostile country, from Santa Fé to Saltillo, having fought two battles and conquered the province and city of Chihuahua (*che-wåh-wah*). His men's term of service having expired, he marched them back to New Orleans and discharged them. The men had been enlisted, marched three thousand miles, and disbanded, all in a year.

This war was remarkable also for another wonderful march, that of Gen. Wool from San Antonio, Texas. He set out (Sept. 20) with 3000 raw troops, whom he disciplined while marching over desert regions and through mountain gorges, and joined Taylor in time for the battle of Buena Vista. Unfurling here the United States flag, he continued his march toward California. On his way, however, he was informed by *Kit Carson*, the noted hunter, that he was too late. The winter before, Captain John C. Fremont, with a company of sixty men, had been engaged in surveying a new route to Oregon. Having learned that the Mexican commandant intended to expel the American settlers, he went to their rescue, although he was not aware that war had broken out between the United States and Mexico. With greatly inferior numbers, he was victor over the Mexicans in every conflict. By the help of Commodores Sloat and Stockton, and also General Kearney, who came in time to aid in the last battle, the entire country was conquered.

SCOTT'S CAMPAIGN IN MEXICO. 287

19. Scott's Campaign in Mexico.—*Capture of Vera Cruz.*⁶⁶—*Battle of Cerro Gordo.*—Gen. Winfield Scott, who had become commander-in-chief of the American forces in Mexico, was ordered to proceed against the city of Mexico. Having landed at *Vera Cruz*, he compelled this strongly fortified city to surrender (Mar. 29, 1847), and then marched into the interior. At the mountain pass of *Cerro Gordo*, he again defeated the Mexicans, who fled in such haste that Santa Anna himself only escaped on his wheel mule, leaving behind him his wooden leg.

20. Battles before Mexico.—Capture of the City.—Scott was delayed some months at Puebla (*pwĕb-lah*) where, reinforcements having been received, the march was resumed (August 7). In three days the army reached the crest of the Cordilleras, where the magnificent valley of Mexico lay stretched before them. The capital was defended by 30,000 Mexicans, and intrenched in a series of works in the vicinity of the city. Having defeated the enemy in the intrenched camp of Contreras (*kon-tray'-ras*), at Churubusco (*choo-roo-boos'-ko*), in the stone building called Molino del Rey (*mo-le'-no del-ray*), and at the castle of Chapultepec (*chah-pool-ta-pek*), General Scott and his army entered the city of Mexico in triumph (Sept. 14), and soon the *stars and stripes* waved proudly over the palace of the Montezumas.

During this war, several young officers distinguished themselves, who fifteen years later, on a broader field, attracted the attention of the world. Among them were *Grant, McClellan, Lee, Beauregard, Hill, Jackson, Hooker, Longstreet, Buell, Johnston, Lyon, Anderson, Kearney, Reynolds, French, Sherman, Thomas, Ewell, Sumner,* and *Davis.* Of those officers especially mentioned by Scott in his despatches, fourteen became generals in the Confederate service, and sixteen in that of the Federals.

Foremost among the defenders of Chapultepec, were the students of the military school. Amid the storm of the assault, these gallant lads were seen fighting heroically to drive back the invader from the scene of their study and their sports.

21. **The Treaty of** Guadaloupé Hidalgo (*guad-a-loop'-ay he-dahl'-go*) concluded Feb. 2, 1848, ended the war. By it the United States gained the vast territory reaching south to the Gila (*ghée-lah*), and west to the Pacific. In return, Mexico received a compensation of $15,000,000.

22. **The Discovery of Gold in California** occurred in the same month with the Treaty of Peace. A workman digging a mill-race in the Sacramento valley (February, 1848) found shining particles of gold. A further search proved that the soil for miles around was full of the precious metal. The news flew in every direction. Emigration began from all parts of America, and even from Europe and Asia. In eighteen months one hundred thousand had gone from the United States alone to this El Dorado, where a fortune was to be picked up in a few days.

Thousands made their way across the desert, amid privations which strewed the route with skeletons. The bay of San Francisco was soon surrounded by an extemporized city of shanties and booths. All ordinary employments were laid aside. Ships were deserted by their crews, who ran to the mines sometimes, it is said, headed by their officers. Soon streets were laid out, houses erected, and from this Babel grew up, as if by magic, a beautiful city.⁶⁹ For a time, lawlessness reigned supreme. But, driven by the necessity of events, the most respectable citizens took the law into their own hands, organized vigilance committees, and administered a rude but prompt justice, which soon reduced the disorderly elements to submission.

23. **Irish Immigration.**—During the Mexican War (1846), the sympathies of the Americans were roused by the news of a terrible famine in Ireland. Considerable amounts were collected and sent to the aid of the sufferers, and a ves-

sel of the United States navy carried over a cargo of provisions. The tide of Irish immigration, which had been steadily on the increase for more than a decade of years, now made rapid progress. Between the years 1847 and 1866, the number of Irish exiles who landed at New York alone, amounted to 3,659,000.

On this subject read Thébaud's "IRISH RACE," Chap. XV.

24. Political Parties.—Three parties now divided the suffrages of the people. The whigs nominated General Taylor for President ; the democrats Lewis Cass ; and the free-soilers, who were opposed to the extension of slavery, Martin Van Buren. The personal popularity of *General Taylor*, on account of his many sterling qualities, and his brilliant victories in the Mexican war, made him the favorite candidate, and he was elected.

PRINCIPAL BATTLES OF THE MEXICAN WAR.

Date.	Location.	Commander. American.	Commander. Mexican.	Victors.
1846...	Fort Brown	Brown	Ampudia	Americans.
	Palo Alto	Taylor	Arista	"
	Resaca de la Palma	Taylor	Arista	"
	Monterey	Taylor	Ampudia	"
	Buena Vista	Taylor	Santa Anna	"
	Vera Cruz (siege)	Scott		"
	Cerro Gordo	Scott	Santa Anna	"
1847...	Contreras	P. F. Smith	Valencia	"
	Churubusco	Worth	Santa Anna	"
	El Molino del Rey	Worth	Santa Anna	"
	Chapultepec	Scott	Santa Anna	"
	City of Mexico (surren.)	Scott	Santa Anna	"

STUDY NO. 5.

TAYLOR.—FILLMORE.—PIERCE.—BUCHANAN.

ZACHARY TAYLOR.

1. Death of President Taylor (July 9, 1850). General Taylor, like General Harrison, died soon after his elevation to the Presidency. He had been in office sixteen months. *Millard Fillmore*, the Vice-President, succeeded him.

2. Millard Fillmore's Administration (1850–1853) was noted for

(1.) THE OMNIBUS BILL (1850).

(2.) THE ADMISSION OF CALIFORNIA INTO THE UNION (1850).

3. The Slavery Question continued to be prominent during this administration, and gave rise to a bitter sectional controversy. When California applied for admission as a free State, an angry debate arose in Congress, which for a time threatened the disruption of the Union.

Henry Clay, the "*Great Pacificator*," came forward at this crisis, and, with his wonderful eloquence, urged the necessity of mutual compromise and forbearance. Daniel Webster warmly seconded this effort at conciliation.

4. The Compromise of 1850.—The *Omnibus Bill*, Clay's measure, was thereupon adopted as the best solution of the problem. It proposed (1) that California should come in as a free State; (2) that the Territories of Utah and New Mexico should be formed without any provision concerning slavery; (3) that Texas should be paid $10,000,000 to give up its claims on the Territory of New Mexico; (4) that the slave trade should be prohibited in the District of Columbia, and (5) that a *Fugitive Slave Law* should be enacted providing for the return to their owners of slaves escaping to a free State.

5. Invasion of Cuba.—During this year (1850), about six hundred adventurers, "fillibusters," undertook to effect the annexation of Cuba to the United States. The attempt failed, and a second trial the ensuing year ended in the execution, at Havana, of Lopez, the leader of the band.

6. Kossuth.—Near the close of 1851, Louis Kossuth, a Hungarian exile, arrived upon our shores. He was received with honors such as had been paid to no foreigner since the time of Lafayette. The people everywhere welcomed him as the exponent of European democracy, and thronged to hear his impassioned appeals in behalf of his native land. He secured about $100,000, with which he returned to Europe; but events not favoring a political revolution, he made himself comfortable, it is said, with our generous contributions.

7. Political Parties.—The democratic and whig parties both declared that they stood by the Omnibus Bill, while the free-soil party was outspoken against it. *Franklin Pierce*, the Presidential nominee of the democratic party, was elected by a large majority of votes over General Scott, the whig candidate.

8. Franklin Pierce's Administration—(1853-1857) was noted for

(1.) THE REPEAL OF THE MISSOURI COMPROMISE BILL (1854).

(2.) CIVIL WAR IN KANSAS.

(3.) THE KNOW-NOTHING MOVEMENT.

(4.) THE GADSDEN PURCHASE.

(5.) TREATY WITH JAPAN (1854).

9. Kansas-Nebraska Bill (1853).—The Compromise Bill of 1850 produced only a lull in the slavery excitement. The agitation burst out anew when Stephen A. Douglas brought forward his famous bill organizing the Territories of Kansas and Nebraska, and advocating the doctrine of "*squatter sovereignty;*" *i. e.*, the right of the inhabitants of each Territory to decide for themselves whether the State should come into the Union free or slave. This bill being a virtual repudiation of the Missouri Compromise, excited the most intense feeling. It, however, became a law (May, 1854).

10. Civil War in Kansas.—The struggle was now taken from Congress to Kansas. A bitter contest arose between the pro-slavery and anti-slavery men—the former anxious to secure the State for slavery; the latter, for freedom. Each party sent bodies of armed emigrants to the Territory. Civil war ensued, houses were attacked and pillaged; men were murdered in cold blood, and for several years Kansas was a scene of lawless violence.

11. The Know Nothing Movement about this time greatly agitated the country. A violent prejudice was aroused against foreigners, especially Catholics, and a secret organization called the "Know Nothing" or American party was formed for the avowed purpose of opposing the Roman Catholic Church. Archbishop Bedini, the Papal Nuncio who visited this country by direction of the Holy See, was repeatedly mobbed, and his life threatened. Catholic churches were destroyed at Newark, N. J.; at Bath, Me.; and at Manchester and Dorchester, N. H. At Ellsworth,[21] Me., Father Bapst, a venerable Jesuit, was inhumanly tarred and feathered by a brutal mob. In Louisville, Ky., there was a fearful riot, in which many Catholics were killed, (1855). The Know Nothings carried several of the State elections, at the expense of arousing the sectarian hate of all classes of society. It speaks well, however, for the good sense of the American people, that the Know Nothings secured in the ensuing Presidential election only a single State, after which the entire movement soon faded out of existence.

12. Gadsden Purchase.—Owing to the inaccuracy of the map used in the treaty between the United States and Mexico, a dispute arose with regard to the boundary line. General Gadsden negotiated a settlement whereby $10,000,000 were paid to Mexico, and additional territory, known as the "*Gadsden purchase*," was secured to the United States.

13. Japan.—An expedition to Japan (1854), under Commodore Perry, brother to the "*Hero of Lake Erie*," excited great attention. He negotiated a treaty securing great commercial advantages to the United States over any other country.

14. Political Parties.—The compromises of 1820 and 1850 having now been abolished, the slave question became the turning point of the election. New party lines being drawn to meet this issue, the whig party ceased to exist. The republican party, absorbing all opposed to the extension of slavery, nominated John C. Fremont, who received the vote of eleven States. The democratic party, retaining its organization, nominated *James Buchanan*, who was elected President.

15. James Buchanan's Administration (1857-1861) was noted for

JAMES BUCHANAN.

(1.) THE AGITATION OF THE SLAVERY QUESTION.

(2.) THE SECESSION OF THE SOUTH (1860).

(3.) THE ADMISSION INTO THE UNION OF MINNESOTA (1858), OREGON (1859), KANSAS (1861).

16. The Fugitive Slave Law had intensified the existing angry feeling, and the subject of slavery absorbed all others. The provision which commanded citizens to aid in the arrest of fugitives was especially obnoxious to the North. Disturbances arose whenever attempts were made to restore runaways to their masters. Several of the northern States passed "Personal Liberty" bills, securing to fugitive slaves, when arrested, the right of trial by jury.

17. Dred Scott* Decision, (1857).—The Supreme Court of the United States, through Chief-Justice Taney, now declared that slave-owners might take their slaves into any State in the Union without forfeiting authority over them. At the North, this was considered as removing the last barrier to the extension of slavery, and as changing it from a local to a national institution. At the South, it was deemed only a right guaranteed them by the Constitution, whereby they should be protected in the possession of their property in every State.

Taney was bitterly assailed for having used the expression: "the negro has no rights which white men. are bound to respect." The Chief-Justice did not state this as his view, but as the prevailing sentiment at the time of the Declaration of Independence. He was not an advocate of slavery; for in early life he had himself given freedom to all the slaves he had inherited from his father.

18. John Brown, a man who had brooded over the exciting scenes through which he had passed in Kansas, until he thought himself called upon to take the law into his own hands, seized upon the United States Arsenal at Harper's Ferry (1859), and proclaimed freedom to all slaves in the vicinity. His feeble band was soon overpowered by United States troops, and Brown himself hanged as a traitor. Though it was soon known that in his wild design he had never asked counsel of any one, yet at the time the Southern feeling was aroused to frenzy, his act being looked upon as significant of the sentiments of the North.

19. Political Parties.—The fall elections again turned on the

---

* Scott and his wife were slaves belonging to a surgeon in the United States army. They were taken into Illinois and resided there and at Fort Snelling, in territory from which, by the ordinance of 1787, slavery was forever prohibited. Afterward they were carried into Missouri, where they and their children were held as slaves. They claimed freedom on the ground that, by the act of their master, they had been taken into free territory. The decision of the court against their claims created an intense excitement throughout the country.

question of slavery. The democratic party divided, and made two nominations for President: Stephen A. Douglas, who favored squatter sovereignty, and John C. Breckinridge, who claimed that slavery could be carried into any territory. The republican party nominated Abraham Lincoln, who held that while slavery must be protected where it was, it ought not to be carried into any free territory.* *Lincoln* was elected.

20. Secession of the South.—Throughout the fall campaign, the Southern leaders had threatened to secede if Mr. Lincoln were elected.† They now declared it to be

ABRAHAM LINCOLN.

time to leave a government which had fallen into the hands of their avowed enemies. Since the time of Calhoun, they had been firm believers in the doctrine of State rights, which taught that a State could leave the Union whenever it pleased. In December (1860) South Carolina led off, and soon Mississippi, Florida, Alabama, Georgia, Louisiana, and Texas passed ordinances of secession.

21. In February (1861) delegates from these States met at Montgomery, Ala., and formed a government called the

---

* The "Union" party put up John Bell, of Tennessee. Their motto was, "The Union, the Constitution, and the Enforcement of the Laws."

† This was not a sudden movement on their part. The sectional difference between the North and the South had its source in the difference of climate, which greatly modified the character and habits of the people; also, while the agricultural pursuits and staple products of the South made slave labor profitable, the mechanical pursuits and the more varied products of the North made it unprofitable. These antagonisms, settled first by the *Missouri Compromise of 1820*, re-opened by the *tariff of 1828*, bursting forth in the *nullification of 1832*, pacified by *Clay's compromise tariff*, increased through the *annexation of Texas* and the consequent war

"*Confederate States of America.*" Jefferson Davis, of Mississippi, was chosen President, and Alexander H. Stephens, of Georgia, Vice-President. United States forts, arsenals, mints, custom-houses, and ships were seized by the States in which they were situated. President Buchanan did nothing to prevent the catastrophe. General Scott urged action, but John B. Floyd, the Secretary of War, a zealous secessionist, protested, and nothing was done. Moreover, the regular army was small, and the troops widely scattered. The navy had been sent to distant ports. The Cabinet largely sympathized with the secessionists. Numerous unsuccessful efforts were made to effect a compromise. It was the general expectation, however, that there would be no war; and the cry, "*No coercion,*" was

JEFFERSON DAVIS.

with Mexico, irritated by the *Wilmot proviso*, lulled for a time by the *compromise of 1850*, awakened anew by the "*squatter sovereignty*" policy of 1858, roused to fury by the *agitation in Kansas*, spread broadcast by the *Dred Scott decision*, the attempted execution of the *Fugitive Slave Law* and the *John Brown raid*, had now reached a point where war was the only remedy. The election of Lincoln was the pivot on which the result turned. The cause ran back through thirty years of controversy to the difference in climate, in occupation, and in habit of life and thought. Strange to say, each section misunderstood the other. The Southern people believed the North to be so engrossed in money-making and so enfeebled by luxury that it could send to the field only mercenary soldiers, who would easily be beaten by the patriotic Southerners. They said, "*Cotton is King;*" and believed that England and France were so dependent upon them for that staple, that their republic would be recognized and defended by those European powers. On the other hand, the Northern people did not believe that the South would dare to fight for slavery, when it had 4,000,000 slaves exposed to the chances of war. They thought it to be all bluster, and hence paid little heed to the threat of secession or of war. Both sides sadly learned their mistake, only too late.

general. In fact, on the very day that the delegates met in Montgomery (Feb. 4) a Peace Conference, representing twenty-one States, assembled in Washington. But Congress rejected the terms of settlement which were suggested by that body. So affairs steadily drifted on toward war.

22. Fort Sumter.—All eyes were now turned on Fort Sumter. Here Major Anderson kept the United States flag flying in Charleston harbor. He had been stationed in Fort Moultrie; but fearing an attack, he had crossed over (December 26) to Fort Sumter, a much stronger position. The South Carolinians, looking upon this as a hostile act, took possession of the remaining forts, commenced erecting batteries, and prepared to reduce Fort Sumter. Major Anderson was compelled by his instructions to remain a quiet spectator of these preparations. The *Star of the West*, an unarmed steamer, bearing troops and supplies to the fort, was fired upon and driven back. The Southern leaders declared that any attempt to relieve Fort Sumter would be a declaration of war. The government seemed paralyzed with fear. All waited for the new President.

FORT SUMTER.

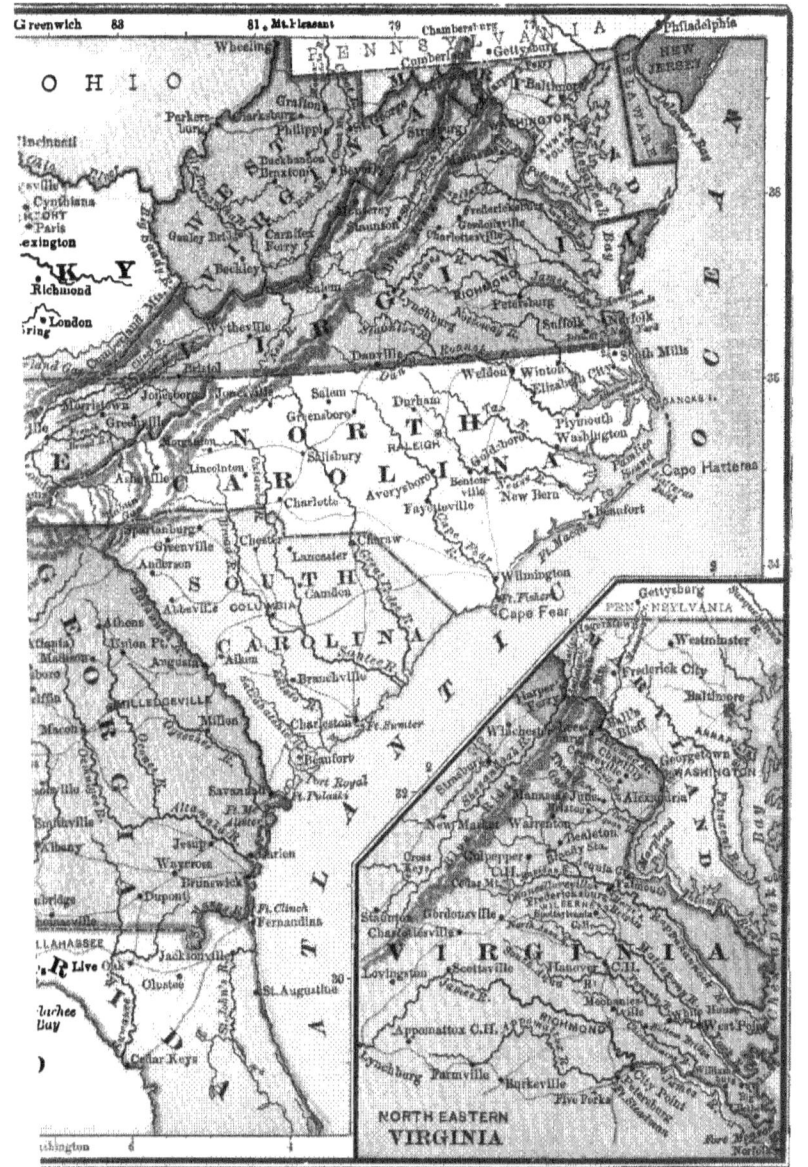

NORTH EASTERN VIRGINIA

STUDY NO. 6.

LINCOLN.—FIRST YEAR OF THE CIVIL WAR.

1. Abraham Lincoln's Administration, (1861–'65), is memorable for
  (1.) THE GREAT CIVIL WAR.
  (2.) THE ADMISSION INTO THE UNION OF WEST VIRGINIA (1863) AND NEVADA (1864).

2. Inauguration. — Rumors of a plan to assassinate Lincoln impelled him to come to Washington in disguise. He was there inaugurated, March 4, 1861, surrounded by troops under the command of General Scott.

3. Capture of Fort Sumter,[35] (April 14, 1861).— Finding that supplies were to be sent to Fort Sumter, General Pierre G. T. Beauregard [*bō-re-gard*], who had command of the Confederate troops at Charleston, called upon Major Anderson to surrender. Upon his refusal, fire was opened from all the Confederate forts and batteries. This "*strange contest between seventy men and seven thousand,*" lasted for thirty-four hours, no one being hurt on either side. The barracks having been set on fire by the shells, the garrison worn out, suffocated, and half-blinded, was forced to capitulate. They were allowed to retire with the honors of war, saluting their flag before hauling it down.

4. The Effect of this event was electrical. All hesitation vanished, and people at once took sides *for* or *against* the Union. Lincoln issued a requisition for seventy-five thousand troops. It was responded to by *three hundred thousand* volunteers. The American flag, the symbol of Revolutionary glory and of national unity, was everywhere unfurled, and the best men of the nation were eager to enlist.

5. At the South, the military enthusiasm was equally ardent, and Virginia, Arkansas, North Carolina, and Tennessee, which had before hesitated, now joined the Confederacy. It soon became evident that Virginia would be the battlefield of the war. The Confederate capital was removed to Richmond; Virginia troops seized the United States armory at Harper's Ferry[42] and the Navy Yard at Norfolk;[53] and Lieutenant-Colonel Robert E. Lee, the son of "*Light-horse Harry,*" was put in charge of the forces of his native State. Troops from the extreme South were rapidly pushed into Virginia, and threatened Washington.

GENERAL ROBERT E. LEE.

6. A regiment of Massachusetts militia hurrying to the defence of the national capital, was attacked in the streets of Baltimore,⁶ and several men were killed. Thus the first blood shed in the Civil War was on April 19, the anniversary of Lexington and Concord.

7. Operations in the East.—*Arlington Heights* and *Alexandria** were seized (May 24) by the national troops. This protected Washington from any immediate danger of attack. *Fortress Monroe*³⁴ was now garrisoned by a heavy force under General B. F. Butler.† An expedition made soon after against *Big Bethel*⁹ was singularly mismanaged. The troops fired into each other by mistake on the route. After a gallant attack upon the Confederate defences, they were repulsed with loss.

8. *Western Virginia* adhered to the Union, and was ultimately formed into a separate State. The Confederates, however, occupied it in force. The Federals, under General George B. McClellan, afterward commander of the Potomac army, defeated them at *Philippi*,⁵⁴ *Rich Mountain*, and *Carrick's Ford*, thus wresting the entire State from their control. Shortly afterward, a Confederate force advanced into that region; but, at *Carnifex Ferry*, it was met by General Rosecrans [*rōz'-krants*], and compelled to retreat. General Robert E. Lee, McClellan's future antagonist on the Potomac, having been repulsed at *Cheat Mountain*, (September 14) now came to the rescue. Nothing decisive, however, was effected, and the Confederate government recalled their forces.

9. Battle of Bull Run,¹¹ (July 21).—The Northern people, seeing so many regiments pushed forward to Washington, were impatient for an advance; and the cry, "*On to*

---

* Alexandria was occupied by Colonel Elmer E. Ellsworth and his Zouaves. After the capture, the Colonel seeing the Confederate flag still flying from the roof of a hotel, went up and tore the banner down. As he descended, he was shot by the landlord, Jackson, who in turn fell at the hands of private Brownell.

† At Hampton, whence the Confederates under General Magruder were driven, some negroes were captured who said they had been employed by the Confederates in building fortifications. Butler declared them "*contraband of war.*" This gave rise to the popular term. "*Contrabands.*"

302   EXCELSIOR HISTORY.

STONEWALL JACKSON AT BULL RUN.

Richmond!" became too strong to be resisted. General Irvin McDowell, in command of the Army of the Potomac, moved to attack the main body of the Confederates at Bull Run. After a sharp conflict, the Confederates were driven from the field. They were rallied, however, by General T. J. Jackson and others on a plateau in the rear. General Bee, as he rallied his men, shouted, "*There's Jackson standing like a stone wall!*" From that time the Southern general was known as "*Stonewall Jackson.*" While the Federal troops were struggling to drive them from this new position, at the crisis of the battle, seventeen hundred men, under Kirby Smith, rushing across the fields from Manassas Station,* struck the Union forces and poured in a cross-fire.

---
* These troops composed a part of General Johnston's command at Winchester. General Patterson, with twenty thousand men, had been left to watch him, and prevent his joining Beauregard. Johnston was too shrewd for his antagonist, and, slipping out of his hands, reached Bull Run in time to decide the battle.

FIRST YEAR OF THE WAR. 303

The right flank of the Union army was thrown into great disorder, and the troops fled panic-stricken to Washington.

10. The Effect of this defeat was momentous. At first the Northern people were chagrined and disheartened. Then came a renewed determination. They now saw the real character of the war, and no longer dreamed that the South could be subdued by a mere display of military force. Congress voted $500,000,000 and five hundred thousand men. General McClellan,* upon whom all eyes were turned, on account of his brilliant campaign in Western Virginia, was appointed to the command of the Army of the Potomac.

GENERAL GEORGE B. McCLELLAN.

11. During the remainder of the year 1861, the only military operation in *the East* was the battle of *Ball's Bluff*,[3] in which the Union forces were defeated.

---

* Soon after, General Scott, weighed down by age, retired from active service, and General McClellan became General-in-Chief of all the armies of the United States.

12. Operations in the West.—The Confederates made great efforts to secure Missouri, and sent up troops from Texas and Arkansas into that State. The two most important actions in the *Missouri Campaign of 1861* were the engagement at *Carthage*,[12] (July 5), and the battle of *Wilson's Creek*, (Aug. 10), in both of which the Union troops were forced to retreat.

Later in the fall, General Grant, who here first came into notice, made an unsuccessful attack upon a Confederate force at *Belmont*.[7]

13. Naval Operations.—Early in the war, Davis issued a proclamation offering to commission privateers. In reply, Lincoln declared a blockade of the Southern ports. At that time there was but one efficient vessel on the Northern coast, and only forty-two ships in the United States navy; but, at the close of the year, there were two hundred and sixty-four.

14. Two Joint Naval and Military Expeditions were made during the year. The first captured the forts at *Hatteras Inlet*, N. C. The second, under Commodore Dupont and General Thomas W. Sherman, took the forts at Port Royal[59] Entrance, S. C., and Tybee island, at the mouth of the Savannah. Port Royal now became the great depot for the Union fleet.

15. Foreign Relations.—*The Trent Affair.*—England and France had acknowledged the Confederate States as *belligerents*, thus placing them on the same footing with the United States. The Southern people having, therefore, great hopes of foreign aid, appointed Messrs. Mason and Slidell commissioners to those countries. Having run the blockade, they took passage at Havana on the British steamer *Trent*. Captain Wilkes, of the United States steamer *San Jacinto*, followed the *Trent*, took off the Confederate envoys, and brought them back to the United States. This produced intense excitement in England. The United States government, however, promptly disavowed the act, and returned the prisoners.

16. In order to counteract the influence of the Confederate commissioners, the United States government sent to Europe, as unofficial envoys, Archbishop Hughes, and Mr. Thurlow Weed, of New York. The former, especially, rendered the cause of the Union most effective service.

17. Summary of the First Year of the War.—The Confederates had captured the large arsenals at Harper's Ferry and Norfolk. They had been successful in the two great battles of the year, *Bull Run*[11] and *Wilson's Creek;* also in the minor engagements at *Big Bethel,*[9] *Carthage,*[12] *Lexington, Belmont,*[7] and *Ball's Bluff.*[5] The Federals had saved *Fort Pickens** and *Fortress Monroe,*[34] and had captured the forts at *Hatteras Inlet* and *Port Royal.*[59] They had gained the victories of *Philippi,*[56] *Rich Mountain, Booneville,*[10] *Carrick's Ford, Cheat Mountain, Carnifex Ferry,* and *Dranesville*. They had saved to the Union, Missouri, Maryland, and West Virginia.

Most important of all, however, the Federal military movements had placed the whole South in a state of siege,—the armies on the North and West by land, and the navy on the East by sea, maintaining a vigilant blockade.

---

* This fort was situated near Pensacola. Lieutenant Slemmer, seeing that an attack was about to be made upon him, transferred his men from Fort McRae, an untenable position, to Fort Pickens, an almost impregnable fortification, which he held until reinforcements arrived.

STUDY NO. 7.

LINCOLN (Continued).—SECOND YEAR OF THE WAR (1862).

1. The Situation.—The national army now numbered 500,000; the Confederate, about 350,000. During the first year, there had been random fighting; the war henceforth assumed a general plan. The year's campaign on the part of the North had three main objects·

(1.) THE OPENING OF THE MISSISSIPPI;
(2.) THE BLOCKADE OF THE SOUTHERN PORTS;
(3.) THE CAPTURE OF RICHMOND.[60]

2. Operations at the West.—The Confederates held a line of defence, with strongly fortified posts at *Columbus, Fort Henry, Fort Donelson, Bowling Green, Mill Spring,* and *Cumberland Gap.* It was determined to pierce this line near the centre, along the Tennessee River. This would compel the evacuation of Columbus, which was deemed impregnable, and open the way to Nashville.[51]

3. Capture of Forts Henry[28] and Donelson.[29]—Accordingly, General Grant with his army, and Commodore Foote with his gunboats, moved from Cairo (*ka'-ro*) upon Fort Henry, which was reduced in about an hour (Feb. 6). The garrison having escaped to Fort Donelson, the

Union forces followed thither, and, after an assault of three days, captured the fort* (Feb. 16).

During four nights of most inclement winter weather, amid snow and sleet, with no tents, shelter, fire, and many with no blankets, these hardy western troops maintained their position. The piteous wail of the wounded resounded through the bleak nights, and death came to many of them who froze as they lay on the icy ground.

4. Effect of these Victories.—As was expected, Columbus and Bowling Green were evacuated, while General Buell at once occupied Nashville. The Confederates fell back to Corinth,[19] the great railroad centre for Mississippi and Tennessee, where their forces were gradually collected under the command of Generals Albert Sidney Johnston and Beauregard. The Union army ascended the Tennessee to Pittsburg Landing.[57] Grant was placed in command, and General Buell ordered to reinforce him.

The next movement was to secure the Memphis and Charleston railroad, thus cutting off Memphis and obtaining another section of the Mississippi River.

5. Battle of Shiloh[64] (April 6, 7). The Confederates having determined to rout Grant's army before the arrival of Buell,—suddenly, at daybreak, Sunday morning, April 6, fell upon the Union camps. At first the Confederates were successful, and drove the Union forces down to the river's brink. Before night came on, however, their general had been killed, and fresh troops had reinforced the Union army. The next morning, after a brisk fight, the Confederates retreated to Corinth.

---

* When General Buckner, commander of the fort, wrote to General Grant, offering capitulation, Grant replied that no terms would be accepted except an "*unconditional surrender*," and that he "proposed to move immediately upon their works." These expressions have been much quoted, and U. S. Grant has been said to signify "*Unconditional Surrender Grant.*"

6. Capture of Corinth[19] (May 30). General Halleck now assumed command, and by slow stages followed the Confederates. Beauregard, finding himself outnumbered, evacuated Corinth, and Halleck took possession.

7. Capture of Island No. 10.—The Confederates, on retreating from Columbus, after the fall of Fort Donelson, fell back to *Island No 10.** Here they were bombarded by Commodore Foote for three weeks, with little effect. General Pope, crossing the Mississippi in the midst of a fearful storm, took the batteries on the opposite bank, and prepared to attack the fortifications in the rear. The garrison, seven thousand strong, surrendered (April 7) the very day of the conflict at Shiloh.

Fort Pillow[22] was abandoned by the Confederates on the 4th of June; and, two days afterwards, the Union forces took possession of *Memphis.*[43]

Kentucky, and all Western Tennessee were now lost to the Confederacy.

8. The War in Missouri.—In February, General Curtis pushed General Price out of Missouri into Arkansas; and, in a desperate battle, totally defeated General Van Dorn at *Pea Ridge*[34] (March 7, 8). During the rest of the war, no important battles were fought in this State.

9. Battles of Iu'ka, Corinth, and Murfreesboro.—In the autumn, the Union forces under General Rosecrans defeated the Confederates in the battles of *Iuka* and *Corinth;*[19] under Buell, forced them to retreat from *Perrysville;* and again, under Rosecrans and Sheridan,

* The islands in the Mississippi are numbered in order, from the mouth of the Ohio to New Orleans.

maintained at *Murfreesboro*[50] a three days' battle, which resulted in a Union victory (Jan. 3, 1863).

10. First Vicksburg[67] **Expedition.**—While Rosecrans was repelling this advance of the Confederates, an expedition against *Vicksburg* had been planned by Grant. He was to move along the Mississippi Central Railroad; while Sherman was to descend the river from Memphis, with the gunboats under Porter. In the meantime, however, by a brilliant cavalry dash, Van Dorn destroyed Grant's depot of supplies at *Holly Springs*.[44] This spoiled the whole plan. Sherman, ignorant of what had happened, pushed on, landed on the Yazoo River, and made an attack at *Chickasaw Bayou* (*bi-o*), north of Vicksburg, but suffered a bloody repulse.

11. Capture of New Orleans (April 25).—The effort to open the Mississippi was not confined to the north. Early in the spring, Captain Farragut, with a fleet of forty-four vessels, carrying eight thousand troops under General Butler, advanced towards New Orleans.* The fleet passed up the Mississippi to Forts Jackson[29] and St. Philip, which defended the passage to the city. These forts having been bombarded with little effect for three days, Farragut then determined to dart past them with his gunboats. Having run a fearful gauntlet of shot, shell, and the flames of fire-rafts, he encountered the Confederate fleet of thirteen armed steamers, including the steam-battery Louisiana and the iron-plated ram Manassas. A desperate struggle ensued, during which twelve of the

---

* To conceal the vessels, they were dressed out with leafy branches, which, except by close observation, rendered them undistinguishable from the green woods. The direction had been accurately calculated, so that the gunners did not need to see the points toward which they were to aim. So severe was the bombardment that "windows at the Balize, thirty miles distant, were broken. Fish, stunned by the explosion, lay floating on the surface of the water."

Confederate flotilla were destroyed (April 24). The city of New Orleans surrendered the next day.

Captain Farragut afterward ascended the river, took possession of Baton Rouge and Natchez, and, running the batteries at Vicksburg, joined the Union fleet above.

12. Movements on the Atlantic Coast.—*Burnside's Expedition against Roanoke Island* * was an important step toward the enforcement of the blockade. The Confederate forts were captured, and the fleet destroyed. *Newbern,* an important seaport,—*Elizabeth City,* and, finally, *Fort Macon,*[30] at the entrance to *Beaufort* [*bu'-fort*] harbor, were taken. Thus all the coast of North Carolina, with its intricate network of water communication, fell into the Union hands.

13. *Florida and Georgia Expeditions.*—Port Royal, after its capture in the autumn of 1861, became the base of operations against Florida and Georgia. *Fernandina, Fort Clinch, Jacksonville, Darien,* and *St. Augustine* were taken. Fort Pulaski,[33] also, was reduced after a severe bombardment, and thus the port of Savannah was closed. At the end of the year, every city of the Atlantic sea-coast, except Savannah and Charleston, was held by the Federal armies.

14. The Merrimac and the Monitor.—About noon, March 8, the iron-clad *Merrimac,*† convoyed by a fleet of small vessels, steamed from Norfolk into Hampton Roads.[41] Steering directly for the sloop-of-war *Cumberland,* whose terrific broadsides glanced harmlessly, "*like so many peas,*"

---

* Roanoke Island, the scene of Raleigh's colonization scheme, was the key to all the rear defences of Norfolk. " *It unlocked two sounds, eight rivers, four canals, and two railroads.*"

† When the navy-yard at Norfolk was given up, the steam-frigate *Merrimac* was scuttled. The Confederates afterward raised it, razeed the deck, and fitted the ship with an iron prow, and a sloping iron roof. Thus prepared, the *Merrimac* looked not unlike a green house sunk in the water to the eaves.

MONITOR AND MERRIMAC.

from the *Merrimac's* iron roof, she struck that ship squarely with her iron beak, making a hole large enough for a man to enter. The *Cumberland*, with all on board, went down.*

Warned by the fate of the *Cumberland*, the captain of the frigate *Congress* ran his vessel ashore; but the *Merrimac*, taking a position astern, fired shells into the vessel till the helpless crew were forced to surrender. At sunset, the *Merrimac* returned to *Norfolk*,[33] awaiting, the next day, an easy victory over the rest of the Union fleet.

15. That night the *Monitor* † arrived in harbor. Though of but nine hundred tons burden, she prepared to meet her adversary of five thousand. Early in the morning the *Merrimac* appeared, moving toward the steam-frigate *Minnesota*. Suddenly the *Monitor* hurled at the monster two one hun-

---

* As the *Cumberland* sank, her crew continued to work their guns until the vessel plunged beneath the sea. Her flag was never struck, but floated above the water from the mast-head after she had gone down.

† This "*Yankee cheese-box*," as it was nicknamed at the time, was the invention of Captain Er'icsson. It was a hull, with the deck a few inches above the water, and in the centre a curious round tower made to revolve slowly by steam-power, thus turning in any direction the two guns it contained. The upper part of the hull, which was exposed to the enemy's fire, projected several feet beyond the lower part, and was covered with thick iron plates.

dred and sixty-eight pound balls. Startled by the appearance of this unexpected and queer-looking antagonist, the *Merrimac* poured in a broadside, such as the night before had destroyed the *Congress*, but the balls rattled harmlessly off the *Monitor's* turret, or broke and fell in pieces on the deck. Then began the battle of the iron ships. It was the first of the kind in the world. Often in actual contact, they exchanged their heaviest volleys. Five times the *Merrimac* tried to run down the *Monitor;* but her huge beak only grated over the iron deck, while the *Monitor* glided out unharmed. Despairing of doing anything with her doughty antagonist, the *Merrimac* now steamed back to Norfolk.*

16. The Effect of this contest can hardly be overestimated. Had the *Merrimac* triumphed, aided by other iron vessels then being prepared by the Confederacy, she might have destroyed the rest of the Union fleet in Hampton roads;[41] reduced Fortress Monroe;[34] prevented the Peninsular campaign, (see the next paragraph); steamed up the Potomac and terrified the capital; sailed along the coast and broken up the blockade; swept through the shipping at New York; opened the way for foreign supplies; made an egress for cotton; and perhaps secured the acknowledgment of the Confederacy by European nations. On this battle, hinged the fate of the war.

17. Operations in the East.—McClellan's Peninsular Campaign.—*Richmond*[60] was the objective point. In April, General McClellan who commanded the Army of the Potomac, began to move up the Virginia Peninsula towards Yorktown.

---

* The fate of these two historic vessels was strangely mean and unworthy. The *Merrimac* was blown up on the evacuation of Norfolk a few months after, and the *Monitor* foundered at sea.

18. Siege of Yorktown.—At this place, General Magruder, with only about five thousand men, by his masterly skill maintained so bold a front along a line thirteen miles in length, that McClellan was brought to a stop. Instead of breaking through at some weak point, he set his

BUILDING A CORDUROY ROAD THROUGH A SWAMP.

magnificent army down in the swamps to begin a regular siege. Heavy guns were ordered from Washington, miles of corduroy roads were built, and the open fields were filled with ditches and intrenchments. As McClellan was ready to open fire, Magruder, having delayed the Union army a month, quietly evacuated the place and proceeded to Richmond.

19. Williamsburg.[71]—McClellan having taken possession of Yorktown, then pushed after the retreating army, and overtook the rear at *Williamsburg*. Here an action took place, with some success for the Union army; but the Confederates made good their retreat.

20. **Fair Oaks.**[23]—McClellan hereupon advanced to the Chickahominy, and placed his army partly on one side of the river and partly on the other. On the last day of May, the Southern commander attacked that part of the Union army on the south side of the river. The result was the indecisive battle of *Fair Oaks*.

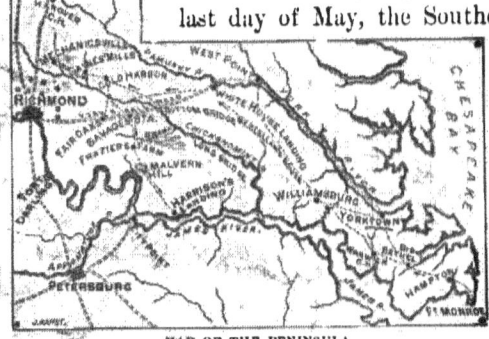

MAP OF THE PENINSULA.

Conspicuous for his bravery in this engagement was General Kearney, who had lost an arm at the gates of Mexico. Taking his bridle in his teeth, and his sword in his left hand, he led his men in the most dashing charges.

21. **Stonewall Jackson in the Shenandoah.**[23]—While the Army of the Potomac was lying waiting, the Confederate commander sent Stonewall Jackson on a raid northward. He fell upon the Union forces under Fremont, Banks, and McDowell, and compelled them to retreat. Then eluding the Union forces who returned to attack him, he rapidly retreated, burning the bridges as he passed, and thus made good his escape from the Shenandoah Valley.

The effect of this adroit movement was evident. With 15,000 men, Jackson had occupied the attention of three major-generals and 60,000 men, prevented McDowell's junction, alarmed Washington, and saved Richmond.

LINCOLN'S ADMINISTRATION. 315

22. The Seven Days' Battles.—McClellan now endeavored to change his base of operations to the James River.* This brought on a series of destructive battles (*Savages Station, Glendale,* and *Malvern Hill*), which lasted through *seven days* (June 25 to July 1), and left the Union army in a weakened condition. In the last battle, Lee's army met a repulse. This enabled McClellan to withdraw to *Harrison's Landing,* on the James River.

The Effect of this campaign was triumphant for the Confederate cause. The Union retreat had been conducted with skill, the troops had shown great bravery and steadiness, the repulse at *Malvern* was decided, and Lee had lost probably twenty thousand men; yet the siege of Richmond had been raised, ten thousand prisoners captured, immense stores taken or destroyed, and the Union army was now cooped up on James River, under the protection of the gunboats. The discouragement at the North was as great as after the battle of Bull Run. Lincoln called for a levy of three hundred thousand troops.

23. Lee's Invasion of the North.—*Battles of Cedar Grove and Bull Run.*—Flushed with success, Lee now marched towards Washington; but he was confronted by the Union forces under General Banks and Pope. These he defeated in the battle of *Cedar Mountain,*[14] (Aug. 9), and in the second battle of *Bull Run,*[11] (Aug. 29). Lee then crossed the Potomac into Maryland, and captured *Harper's Ferry* and *Frederick City.*

24. Death of General Kearney.—A sharp conflict occurred at *Chantilly,* Sept. 1st, in the midst of a furious thunder-storm. General Phil. Kearney dashing forward in advance, met a Confederate soldier, of whom he made an inquiry. Seeing his mistake, he wheeled, the soldier fired, and this gallant officer fell mortally wounded.

25. Antietam.[2]—McClellan having meanwhile been recalled from the James, assumed command of the army in

* The distance from Fair Oaks to James River is seventeen miles. Along the single road traversing the swamp, five thousand wagons, the heavy siege guns, and two thousand five hundred beef cattle, making in all a train forty miles long, were to be passed. During this famous retreat, the army fought by day, to give time for the passage of the baggage trains, and fell back at night to a new position,

Maryland. He now set out in pursuit of Lee, whom he met and defeated in the great battle of *Antietam*,² [*an-te'-tam*], (Sept. 17). Lee retreated across the Potomac; but McClellan

DEATH OF GENERAL KEARNEY.

made no pursuit, and in October was ordered to deliver up his command to General Burnside.

* A messenger bearing the despatch arrived at McClellan's tent in Rectortown, during a heavy snow-storm, at midnight (Nov. 7). The General read the letter, and handing it over to his successor, said indifferently : *"Well, Burnside, you are to command!"*

The latter was reluctant to accept the responsibility, declaring that he was unfit to handle so large a body of men ; and he, at last, yielded only to positive orders.

26. Fredericksburg.[36]—Burnside crossed the Rappahannock, (Dec. 11, 12), and fought the sanguinary

LINCOLN'S ADMINISTRATION. 317

battle of *Fredericksburg*,[36] in which he was defeated with immense loss. At his own request, he was now superseded in the command by General Hooker.

During the battle of Fredericksburg, the Confederates, intrenched behind a long stone wall, easily repulsed the assaults of the Union troops. In this action, Meagher's Irish Brigade especially distinguished itself. The *London Times*' correspondent, who watched the battle from the heights, speaking of their desperate valor, says: "*Never at Fontenoy, Albuera, or Waterloo was more undoubted courage displayed by the sons of Erin, than during those six frantic dashes which they directed against the almost impregnable position of their foe.*"

27. Summary of the Second Year of the War. —The Confederates had gained the victories of Jackson in the Shenandoah;[63] of Lee in the Peninsular campaign and those against Pope; Bragg's great raid in Kentucky; and the battles of *Chickasaw Bluff* and *Fredericksburg*.[36]

The Federals had taken *Forts Henry*,[26] *Donelson*,[26] *Pulaski*,[33] *Macon*,[50] *Jackson*,[29] *St. Philip*, and *Island No. 10;* had opened the Mississippi to *Vicksburg*,[67] occupied *New Orleans, Roanoke Island, Newbern*,[42] *Yorktown, Norfolk*,[58] and *Memphis;* had gained the battles of *Pea Ridge*,[54] *Williamsburg*,[71] *Fair Oaks*,[23] *South Mountain, Antietam*,[3] *Iuka, Corinth*,[19] and *Murfreesboro*.[50]

STUDY NO. 8.

THIRD YEAR OF THE WAR (1863).

1. On New Year's Day, the **Emancipation Proclamation,** declaring freedom to all the slaves in the seceded States, was issued.

LEE AND JACKSON PLANNING THE BATTLE OF CHANCELLORSVILLE.

2. Operations in the East.—*Battle of Chancellorsville.*[15]—About the end of April, General Hooker, who, as we have seen, succeeded Burnside in the command of the Army of the Potomac, moved to attack Lee. The latter, divining Hooker's intention, rapidly swung his army into position. On the eve of May 1st, "*seated upon some cracker-boxes, under a pine-tree*," with his famous lieutenant, Stonewall Jackson, Lee planned his mode of attack. The result was the great battle of *Chancellorsville*,[15] a terrible defeat to the Union forces.

In this battle the South was called to mourn the death of Stonewall Jackson, whose magical name was worth to their cause more than an army. In the evening after this successful onslaught upon the flank of the Union line, while Jackson was riding back to camp, he was killed by his own men, who mistook his escort for Federal cavalry.

3. Lee's Second Invasion of the North.—Battle of Gettysburg.[39]

Encouraged by success, Lee now determined to carry the war into the Northern States, and dictate terms of peace in Philadelphia or New York. With the finest army the South had ever sent forth carefully equipped and confident of success, he rapidly moved down the Shenandoah, crossed the Potomac, and advanced up the Cumberland Valley.

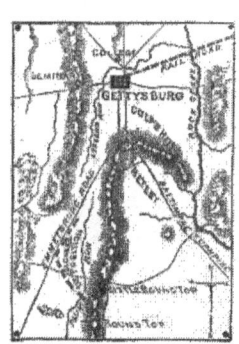
VICINITY OF GETTYSBURG.

The Federals, now under the command of General Meade, hastened forward to meet the invaders, and the two mighty armies encountered each other, July 1, 1863, in the tremendous battle of GETTYSBURG,[39] the greatest of the war. For three days the conflict raged, and at their close Lee was compelled to retreat. Meade slowly followed, and took up a position back of the Rapidan.

The battle of Gettysburg put an end to the idea of Northern invasion.

4. Operations in the West. — *Siege of Vicksburg.*⁶⁷—Early in the year, Grant, in pursuance of a bold and skilful plan, marched down the west side of the Mississippi, while the gunboats, running the batteries, passed below the city and ferried the army across. On his way to Vicksburg, Grant five times met and defeated the Confederates under Pemberton, and at length forced him within the works of that city. The siege which now commenced lasted six weeks.

RUNNING THE BATTERIES AT VICKSBURG.

THIRD YEAR OF THE WAR.

Mines and countermines were dug. Not one of the garrison could show his head above the fortifications without being picked off by the watchful riflemen. A hat, held at an open port-hole, was pierced in two minutes with fifteen balls. Shells reached all parts of the city. The inhabitants burrowed in caves to escape the iron storm which rained upon them. The garrison, worn out by forty-seven days' labor in the trenches, surrendered on the 4th of July.

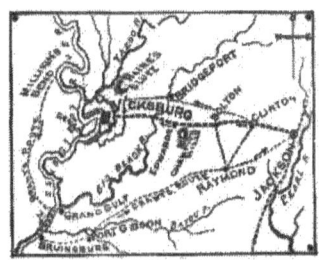

VICINITY OF VICKSBURG.

Port Hudson,[58] which had been besieged by General Banks for many weeks, also surrendered. The Mississippi was now open to the Gulf, and the Confederacy was cut in twain.

5. The capture of *Vicksburg* took place at the same time as the decisive battle of *Gettysburg*. This, therefore, may be considered the supreme moment of the war. Henceforth the doom of the Confederacy was sealed. Yet the issue did not then seem so clear as it now does to the historian.

6. Rosecrans' Campaigns.—Battles of *Chickamauga*,[17] (Sept. 19, 20), and *on Chattanooga*,[16] (Nov. 24, 25).

Rosecrans, after the battle of Murfreesboro, made no formal movement until June. He then marched against General Bragg, and the two armies met on the Chickamauga. The Union army was defeated; but General Thomas *

---

* He was thenceforth styled the "*Rock of Chickamauga.*" He was in command of men as brave as himself. Col. George, of the Second Minnesota, being asked "*How long can you hold this pass?*" replied, "*Until the regiment is mustered out of service.*"

fought so stubbornly that it was able to retire and fortify itself in Chattanooga.[16] Bragg occupied the hills commanding the city, and cutting off all communication, threatened the Union army with starvation.*

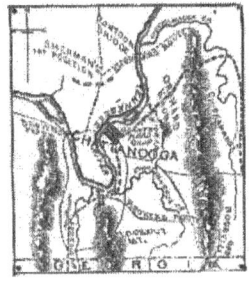
CHATTANOOGA AND VICINITY.

7. Sherman now came with troops from Vicksburg, and Hooker brought a corps from Virginia. Grant, meanwhile, being put in command of the Western armies, hastened to Chattanooga. Affairs thus began to wear a different aspect. Communications were re-established; Thomas made a dash and seized *Orchard Knob*, (Nov. 23), and the next day, Hooker charged the fortifications on *Lookout Mountain*,[46] (Nov. 24).

8. His troops had been ordered to stop on the high ground; but, carried away by the ardor of the attack, they swept over the crest, driving the enemy before them. Through the mist that filled the valley, the anxious watchers below caught only glimpses of this so-called "*battle above the clouds*." The next morning Hooker advanced on the south of Missionary Ridge.† Sherman during the whole time had been pounding away on the northern flank. Grant, from his position on Orchard Knob, perceiving that the Confederate line in front of him was being weakened to repel these attacks on the flanks, launched Thomas's corps on its centre. The Confederates were defeated and forced to flee southward.

* Fearful that Thomas might surrender before reinforcements could reach him, Grant telegraphed him to defend his post. The characteristic reply was: "*I will stay till I starve.*"

† This name was given to the Ridge because it was formerly the site of a Catholic school for the Indians.

9. The War in Tennessee.—While Rosecrans was moving on Chattanooga, Burnside, having been relieved of the command of the Army of the Potomac, was sent into East Tennessee, where he met with great success. In the meantime the Confederate President Davis, having visited Bragg, and thinking Chattanooga sure to be captured, sent Longstreet with his corps to the defence of Tennessee. His men were in a deplorable state,—hungry, ragged, and tentless; but under this indefatigable leader, they shut up Burnside's force in Knoxville[45] (September 17). Meanwhile, Grant, in the moment of his splendid triumph at Chattanooga, ordered Sherman's torn, bleeding, barefoot troops over terrible roads one hundred miles to Burnside's relief. Longstreet, in order to anticipate the arrival of these reinforcements, made a desperate assault upon Burnside (November 29), but was repulsed. As Sherman's advance guard reached Knoxville (December 4), Longstreet's troops filed out of their works in retreat.

10. Attack on Charleston (April 7).—Such was the confidence felt in the ability of the iron-clads to resist cannon-balls, that Admiral Dupont determined to run the fortifications at the entrance to Charleston, and force his way up to the city. The attempt was a disastrous failure. General Gilmore now took charge of the Union troops, and, landing on Morris Island, by regular siege approaches and a terrible bombardment captured Fort Wagner and reduced Fort Sumter to a shapeless mass of rubbish. A short time after, a party of sailors from the Union fleet essayed to capture it by night; but its garrison, starting up from the ruins, drove them back with great loss.

11. Draft Riots.—The Federal Government passed a conscription law, March 3d, enrolling all able-bodied citizens between twenty and forty-five years, and in May, the President ordered a draft of three hundred thousand men. The project was exceedingly unpopular, and was bitterly denounced on every hand. In July, a riot broke out in New York City, and for four days the populace ruled. Veterans from the army of the Potomac then arrived upon the scene, and law and order were soon restored. Meanwhile, many murders had been committed, and about $2,000,000 worth of property had been destroyed. Riots also occurred in Boston, Jersey City, and other places.

12. Indian Massacres.—In the midst of this civil strife, the Sioux (*soo*) Indians became dissatisfied with the Indian traders, and the non-payment of the money due them. Bands of warriors under *Little Crow* and other chiefs perpetrated horrible massacres in Minnesota, Iowa, and Dakota. Over seven hundred whites were slain, and many thousands driven from their homes. Colonel Sibley, after a month's pursuit of the savages, routed them, and took five hundred prisoners, thirty-nine of whom were hanged on one scaffold, at Mankato, Minn., December 26.

13. Summary of the Third Year of the War.—The Confederates had gained the great battles of *Chickamauga* and *Chancellorsville*,[15] seized *Galveston*,[35] and successfully resisted every attack on *Charleston*.

The Federals had gained the battles before *Vicksburg*, and at *Chattanooga*[16] and *Gettysburg*.[59] They had captured the garrisons of *Vicksburg*[67] and *Port Hudson*.[58] The Mississippi was patrolled by gunboats, and the supplies from the West were entirely cut off from the Confederate army. Arkansas, East Tennessee, large portions of Louisiana, Mississippi, and Texas, as far as the Rio Grande, had been won for the Union.

STUDY NO. 9.

LINCOLN (Continued). — FOURTH YEAR OF THE WAR (1864).

1. The Situation.—General Grant was now Lieutenant-General in command of all the forces of the United States. Up to this time, the different armies had acted independently; but they were henceforth to move in concert, and thus prevent the Confederate forces from aiding one another. The strength of the South lay in the armies of Lee in Virginia, and Joseph E. Johnston in Georgia. Grant was to attack the former, and Sherman the latter.

2. The Overland Campaign.—On the 4th of May, Grant crossed the Rapidan. The next day he encountered Lee, in a terrible contest, known as the battle of the *Wilderness*,[70]

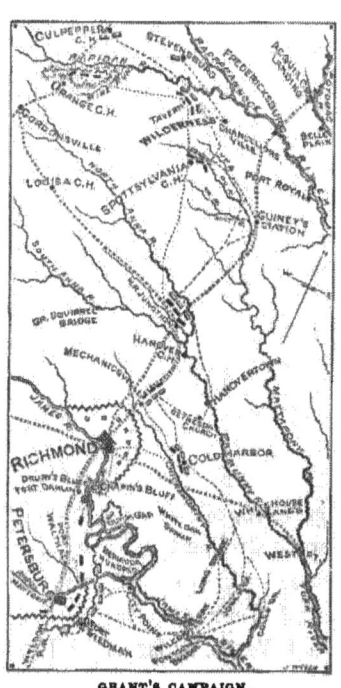

GRANT'S CAMPAIGN.

which lasted for two days. This, as well as the battles of *Spottsylvania*,[85] *North Anna*, and *Cold Harbor*,[18] which followed, had no decisive result.

After the battle of Spottsylvania, Grant sent a despatch to the War Department, in which he said: "*I propose to fight it out on this line, if it take all summer.*" It took all summer and all winter too.

3. Siege of Petersburg and Richmond.—Grant now crossed the James River, and being here joined by Butler from *Fortress Munroe*,[34] he prepared to attack Petersburg[55] and Richmond.[60] The siege of these two cities lasted until the ensuing spring; but although a number of actions and several important battles took place, there was no decisive combat.

4. *The Mine Explosion.*—An operation from which much was expected, was the mine explosion. From a hidden ravine in front of Petersburg, a mine had been dug underneath a strong Confederate fort. Just at dawn, the blast of 8000 pounds of powder was fired. The Federal artillery opened along the whole line, and soon an assaulting column rushed forward. But the men stopped in the crater produced by the explosion, while the Confederates turned the artillery in their other works commanding this position, and poured a destructive fire upon the Union troops crowded within the demolished fort. To retreat was only less dangerous than to stay, yet many of the soldiers jumped out of this slaughter-pen and ran headlong back to the Federal lines. Those who remained were killed or captured.

5. Siege of Washington.—Lee now threatened Washington by the Shenandoah Valley, hoping thus to draw off Grant from the siege of Richmond. General Early, with twenty thousand men, accordingly hurried northward along this oft-traveled route. Defeating General Wallace at *Monocacy River*, he appeared before Fort Stevens, one of the defences of Washington (July 10). Had he moved by forced marches, he might have captured the city; but he stopped a day. Reinforcements having now arrived, he was compelled to retreat; and, laden with booty, he rapidly recrossed the Potomac. Not being pursued, he returned and sent a party of cavalry into Pennsylvania. They entered Chambersburg, and, failing to obtain a tribute of $500,000, which they demanded, they set fire to the village, and escaped safely back into the Shenandoah Valley.

SHERIDAN AT CEDAR CREEK.

6. Sheridan's Campaign.—General Sheridan was thereupon put in command of all the troops in this region. He defeated Early at *Winchester*[2] (Sept. 19) and *Fisher's Hill*, and, to use his own expression, sent that general "*whirling up the Shenandoah Valley.*" * Sheridan believing the valley to be now freed from Confederates in arms, departed for Washington. Early, however, being quickly reinforced, under cover of a dense fog, surprised the Union army at Cedar Creek[13] (Oct. 19), and put it to flight. When the battle commenced, *Sheridan* was at Winchester, 13 miles distant.

As the sound of conflict fell upon his ear, he put spurs to his powerful black steed, and never drew rein until he reached the scene of combat. On his arrival, finding that the Confederates had become scattered in plundering the captured camp, he ordered an instant attack. As his steed thundered over the magnificent stone road which traverses the Shenandoah Valley, he waved his hat, and shouted to his men; "*Face the other way, boys; face the other way! We are going back!*" In an instant the disordered troops turned, a severe struggle ensued, and very soon Early's army was defeated with great slaughter. This short, but brilliant campaign put an end to hostilities in the Shenandoah.

At that time, it is said that the wags in the vicinity were accustomed to label cannon designed for the Valley; "*General Sheridan, care of Jubal Early.*"

7. Sherman's Campaign.

—While the army of the Potomac was crossing the Rapidan (May 4), Grant, seated on a log by the wayside, penciled a telegram to Sherman to start on his march to Atlanta.[4] Accordingly, on May 6, Sherman, with 100,000 men, moved upon Johnston, who, with 50,000, was stationed at Dalton, Ga.

Both armies were led by profound strategists. Sherman

---

* To prevent any further raids upon Washington from this direction, Sheridan devastated the Valley so thoroughly, that it was said: "*If a crow wants to fly down the Shenandoah, he must carry his provisions with him.*"

GRANT'S TELEGRAM.

would drive Johnston into a stronghold, and then with consummate skill outflank him, when Johnston with equal skill would retreat to a new post, and prepare to meet his opponent again. At *Dalton, Resaca, Dallas,*[20] and *Lost*[47] and *Kenesaw Mountains* bloody battles were fought. Finally, Johnston retired to the intrenchments of Atlanta (July 10).

8. **Capture of Atlanta.**—Davis, dissatisfied with this Fabian policy, now put Gen. Hood in command. This general fiercely attacked the Union army three times, but was repulsed with great slaughter. Sherman, thereupon reënacting his favorite flank movement, filled his wagons with fifteen days rations, dexterously shifted his whole army on Hood's line of supplies, and thus compelled the evacuation of the city (Sept. 2).*

* During this campaign, Sherman's supplies had all been brought up by a single line of railroad from Nashville, a distance of three hundred miles, and exposed

9. Hood's Invasion of Tennessee.—Sherman now longed to sweep through the Atlantic States; but this was impossible as long as Hood's army was in front. With unconcealed joy, therefore, he learned that Hood was to invade Tennessee. Relieved of this anxiety, Sherman at once prepared for his celebrated "*March to the Sea.*"

Thus two campaigns were carried on at the same time, Hood's campaign against Thomas, and Sherman's "*March.*"

10. Battle of Nashville (December 15, 16).—Hood crossed the Tennessee, and after severe fighting, shut up General Thomas within the fortifications at Nashville. For two weeks little was done. When Thomas was fully ready, he suddenly sallied out on Hood, and in a terrible two days battle drove the Confederate forces out of their intrenchments into headlong flight.

11. Sherman's March to the Sea.—While Hood was making his disastrous campaign against Thomas, Sherman broke loose from his communications with Nashville, burned the city of Atlanta,[4] and started with 60,000 men for the Atlantic coast.

The army moved in four columns, with a cloud of cavalry under Kilpatrick, and skirmishers in front to disguise its route. The wings destroyed the Georgia Central and Augusta Railroads, and the troops foraged on the country as they passed. In five weeks they marched three hundred miles, reached the sea, stormed Fort McAllister,[31] and captured Savannah,[*] (Dec. 21).

throughout to the attacks of the enemy. Yet so carefully was it garrisoned, and so rapidly were bridges built and breaks repaired, that the damages were often mended before the news of the accident had reached camp. Sherman said that the whistle of the locomotive was frequently heard on the camp-ground, before the echoes of the skirmish fire had died away.

[*] Sherman sent the news of its capture with 25,000 bales of cotton and 150 cannon to President Lincoln, as a *Christmas present* to the nation.

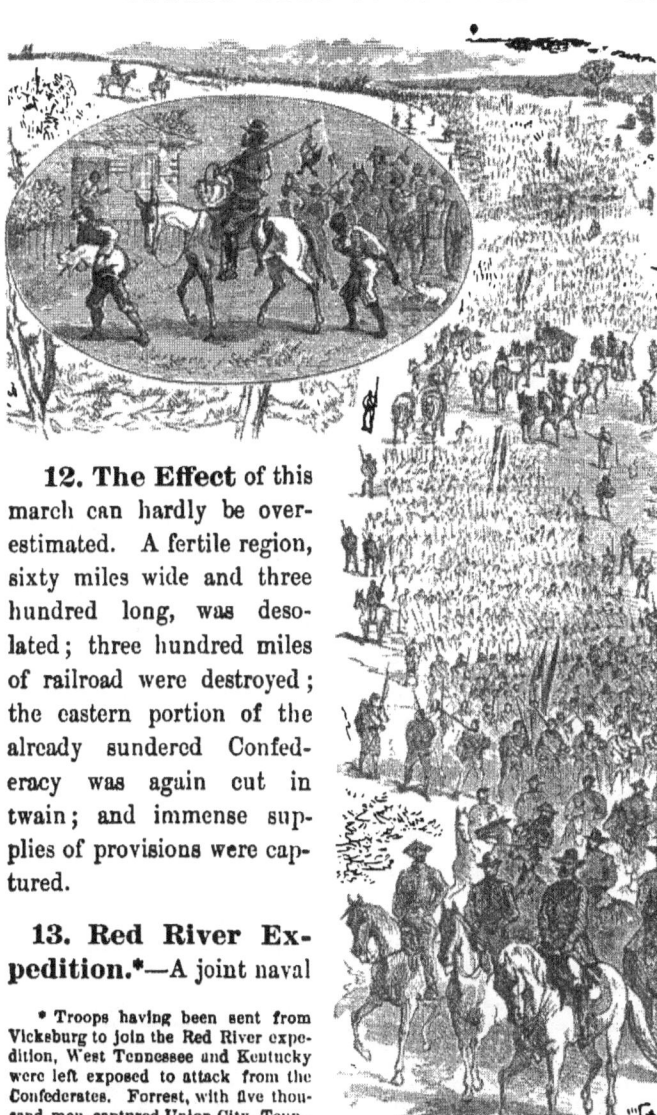

12. The Effect of this march can hardly be overestimated. A fertile region, sixty miles wide and three hundred long, was desolated; three hundred miles of railroad were destroyed; the eastern portion of the already sundered Confederacy was again cut in twain; and immense supplies of provisions were captured.

13. Red River Expedition.*—A joint naval

---

* Troops having been sent from Vicksburg to join the Red River expedition, West Tennessee and Kentucky were left exposed to attack from the Confederates. Forrest, with five thousand men, captured Union City, Tenn., with its garrison of about five hun-

and land expedition, under the command of General Banks, was sent up the Red River in the hope of destroying the Confederate authority in that region and in Texas. *Fort de Russy*²⁸ was taken (March 14), whence Banks moved on toward Shreveport. The line of march became extended a distance of nearly thirty miles along a single road. At *Sabine Cross Roads*⁶¹ (April 8) the Confederate forces, under General Dick Taylor, attacked the advance, and a *miniature Bull Run retreat* ensued. The Union troops, however, rallied at *Pleasant Hill*, and the next day, reinforcements coming up from the rear, they were able to repulse the Confederates. The army thereupon returned to New Orleans,* and Banks was relieved of the command.

14. Naval Operations.—*The Expedition against Mobile*,⁴⁹ (Aug. 5), was under the command of Admiral Farragut. That he might oversee the battle more distinctly, he took his position in the maintop of his flag-ship,—*the Hartford*. The vessels, lashed together in pairs for mutual assistance, in an hour fought their way past the Confederate forts, and engaged the iron-clad fleet beyond. After a desperate resistance, the great iron ram *Tennessee* was taken, and the

---

dred troops, occupied Hickman, and advanced rapidly upon Paducah, Ky. This, protected by the gunboats, maintained so stout a defence, that Forrest retired. Moving south, he next fell upon Fort Pillow (April 12). His men crept along under shelter of a ravine until very near, and then charged upon the intrenchments. Rushing into the fort, they raised the cry "*No quarter!*" "The Confederate officers," says Pollard, "lost control of their men, who were maddened by the sight of negro troops opposing them." An indiscriminate slaughter followed.

* Porter, who commanded the gunboats in the Red River, hearing of Banks's retreat, attempted to return with his fleet; but the river fell so rapidly that this became impossible. It was feared that it would be necessary to blow up the vessels to prevent their falling into the enemy's hands, when, by the happy suggestion of Colonel Bailey, formerly a Wisconsin lumberman, they were saved. He constructed a series of wing-dams below the rapids, and when the water rose, the boats were safely floated over. This skilful expedient was almost the only relieving feature of the campaign, which was believed to have been undertaken simply as a gigantic cotton speculation, in behalf of certain parties, who seemed to be more intent on gathering that staple, than on conserving the interests of the Union cause.

FOURTH YEAR OF THE WAR. 333

FARRAGUT LASHED TO THE RIGGING.

other vessels were either captured or put to flight. The forts were soon after reduced, and the harbor was closed against blockade runners. The city was not captured until the next year, after a gallant defence by Gen. Maury.

15. *The Expedition against Fort Fisher,*[n] which defended the harbor of Wilmington, N. C., was commanded by Commodore Porter. In consisted of seventy vessels and a land force under General Butler. After a fierce bombardment (December 24, 25), Butler decided that the fort could not be taken by assault, and the army returned to Fortress Monroe. Commodore Porter, dissatisfied with the result, lay off the place, and asked for a second trial, and the troops were sent back under General Terry. Protected by a terrible fire from the fleet, a column of sailors and one of soldiers worked their way, by a series of trenches, within two hundred yards of the fort. At the word, the former leaped forward on one side, and the latter on another. The sailors were repulsed, but the soldiers burst into the fort. The hand-to-hand fight within lasted for hours. Late at night, the garrison, hemmed in on all sides, surrendered (January 15, 1865). The fort had been defended with so much skill and courage, that its capture was justly regarded as one of the most brilliant exploits of the war.

16. **The Blockade** was now so effective that the prices of all imported goods in the Confederate States became fabulous.* Led by the enormous profits of a successful voyage, foreign merchants were constantly seeking to run the gauntlet. Their swift steamers, making no smoke, long, narrow, low, and of a mud color, occasionally escaped the vigilance of the Federal squadron. During the war, it is said, over fifteen hundred blockade runners were taken or destroyed.

17. **Confederate Cruisers** had practically driven the American commerce from the ocean. They were not properly privateers, for they were built in England and manned by British sailors, and were only officered and commissioned by the Confederate government. They sailed to and fro upon the track of American ships, plundering and burning, or else bonding them for heavy sums.

18. **The Alabama.**—The *Alabama* was the most noted of these Anglo-Confederate steamers. She is said to have destroyed sixty-five American vessels and their cargoes, valued at $10,000,000. Against the urgent remonstrances

---

* Coffee was sold at $50 and salt at $1 per pound in Confederate currency; ordinary calico brought from $30 to $35 per yard; Balmoral boots for ladies were $250 a pair, and French gloves from $125 to $175; Irish linen ranged from $50 to $100 per yard, etc. Dried sage, willow, and currant leaves were substituted for tea. A Southern writer, as early as November, 1862, said: "Pins are now so rare that we pick them up with avidity in the streets."

of the United States Minister at the Court of England, she was allowed to sail, although her mission was well known. An English captain took the ship to the Azores, where other English vessels brought her arms, ammunition, and the Confederate Captain Semmes with an additional crew. After capturing over sixty vessels, Semmes sailed to Cherbourg, France. While there, he sent out a challenge to the national ship-of-war *Kearsarge* (keer'-sarj). This was accepted, and a battle took place off that harbor. After a desperate conflict, the Confederate vessel ran up the white flag and soon sank. Captain Winslow of the *Kearsarge* rescued a part of the crew, and, at his request, the rest were picked up by the *Deerhound*, an English yacht. The latter, however, steamed off to the British coast with those she had saved, among whom was Captain Semmes.

THE ALABAMA.

The unlawful conduct of Great Britain in this affair, led to difficulties with that country which were not settled till 1872. Then England paid the United States $15,500,000, in satisfaction of the Alabama Claims.

19. Political Affairs.—Lincoln Re-elected.—At the North, there was much dissatisfaction with the conduct of the war. The debt had become about $2,000,000,000. In July of this year, paper money reached its greatest depreciation, and it required two dollars and ninety cents in greenbacks to buy one dollar in gold. Yet, in the midst of these discouragements, Abraham Lincoln was renominated by the republican party. George B. McClellan was the democratic candidate. He stood firmly for the prosecution of the war, and the maintenance of the Union, but was not in full sympathy with the policy of the administration. He carried only three States. *Lincoln* had a popular majority of over four hundred thousand.

20. Summary of the Fourth Year of the War.—The Confederates had gained the battles of *Olustee, Sabine Cross Roads,* the *Wilderness, Bermuda Hundred,*[6] *Spottsylvania, New Market, Cold Harbor,* and *Monocacy;* had defeated the expeditions into Florida and the Red River country, the two attacks upon Petersburg, and one against Fort Fisher, and yet held Grant at bay before Richmond. They had, however, lost ground on every side. Of the States east of the Mississippi, only North and South Carolina were fully retained. Mississippi, Alabama, Tennessee, Virginia, Georgia and Florida were overrun by the Union armies.

The Federals had gained the battles of *Pleasant Hill, Resaca, Dallas,*[20] *Kenesaw, Atlanta,*[4] *Winchester,*[72] *Fisher's Hill, Cedar Creek*[18] and *Nashville.*[51] They had captured *Fort de Russy,*[25] the forts in Mobile harbor, and *Fort McAllister,*[31] and had taken Atlanta and Savannah. Sherman had swept across Georgia; Sheridan had devastated the Shenandoah, driving its defenders before him; Thomas had annihilated Hood's army; Grant held Lee firmly grasped at Richmond, and the navy swept the entire coast.

STUDY NO. 10.

THE LAST YEAR (1865) OF THE WAR.— JOHNSON.

1. Sherman's March through the Carolinas.
Early in February, General Sherman, having taken but a month's rest at Savannah, put his troops (60,000 strong) in motion northward. Describing the difficulties which now beset him, the General wrote: "*We began a march which, for perils, labor, and results, will compare with any ever made by an organized army. The floods of the Savannah,*

SHERMAN.

the swamps of the Combahee and the Edisto, the high hills and rocks of the Santee, the flat quagmires of the Pedee and Cape Fear Rivers, were all passed in midwinter with its floods and rains, in the face of an accumulating enemy."

2. Columbia* was captured (February 17); and Charleston,† thus threatened in the rear, was evacuated the

---

* The cotton stored in the city was scattered throughout the streets and destroyed by fire. The flames quickly spread to the houses adjoining. All efforts to subdue the conflagration were unsuccessful, and a large portion of the city was destroyed.

† General Hardee, on leaving. set fire to every shed and warehouse in which cot-

next day. In this emergency, Johnston was again called to the command of the Confederate forces. He gathered their scattered armies, and vigorously opposed Sherman's advance. After fierce engagements at *Averysboro* and *Bentonville* (March 15, 18), he was driven back, and Raleigh was captured (April 13).

3. Operations of Sheridan, Wilson, and Stoneman.

SHERIDAN.

— Meanwhile, *Sheridan* with 10,000 troopers swept down through the Shenandoah, captured most of the remnants of *Early's* force, cut the railroads north of Richmond, and took his place in the Union lines before Petersburg (March 26).

Wilson, with 13,000 horsemen, rode at large through Alabama and Georgia, capturing towns and destroying railroads.

Stoneman, with 5,000 cavalry from Tennessee, poured through the passes of the Alleghanies, and waited in North Carolina for the issue in Virginia.

4. Attack on Fort Steadman.—Notwithstanding

ton was stored. The flames spread to a quantity of powder in the depot, which exploded with fearful destruction. Two hundred lives were lost. In spite of the efforts of the Union troops, a vast amount of private property was involved in the general devastation. The ravages which the war had made were well illustrated by the appearance of this city after its evacuation. An eye-witness says : "No pen, no pencil, no tongue can do justice to the scene ; no imagination can conceive the utter wreck, the universal ruin, the stupendous desolation. Ruin, ruin, ruin, above and below, on the right hand and on the left—ruin, ruin, ruin, everywhere and always, staring at us from every paneless window, looking out at us from every shell-torn wall, glaring at us from every battered door, pillar, and veranda, crouching beneath our feet on every sidewalk. Not Pompeii, nor Herculaneum, nor Tadmor, nor the Nile has ruins so saddening, so plaintively eloquent."

that Lee's position was fast becoming desperate, he would not give up hope. On the contrary, he planned an attack on the Union lines. This was made (March 25) on Fort Steadman; but it proved a failure.

5. Grant's Operations.—The Final Campaign.—Grant opened the final campaign by sending a force under Generals Sheridan and Warren to attack the right flank of the Confederates. Concealing the movements of his infantry by a thick screen of cavalry, Sheridan threw a heavy force behind the Confederate position at *Five Forks*.[24] The garrison was overwhelmed, and five thousand were taken prisoners (April 1).

6. Capture of Petersburg and Richmond, (April 2, 3).—The next day an attack was made along the whole line of works in front of Petersburg. By noon, the Confederate line of intrenchments, before which the Army of the Potomac had lain so long (see p. 330) was broken. That night Petersburg and Richmond were evacuated, and the next morning the Union troops took possession of the *Confederate Capital*.

Before night, order had been restored in the streets, and every one was safe under the National protection; yet sad indeed were the hearts of those who lay down by the side of the blackened walls, amid the quiet of a great desolation, their hearts aching the while with "*a dull sense that the work of years had been ruined, and that all they possessed had been swept away.*"

7. Lee's Surrender.—Lee, with the wreck of that proud army with which he had dealt the Union forces so many crushing blows, hurried west, seeking some avenue of escape. Grant pursued with untiring energy, throwing every man, horse, and gun into the chase.

The Confederates were reduced to such straits, that often

they had only the young shoots of trees to eat. Many dropped their guns from pure exhaustion. If they sought a moment's repose, they were awakened by the clatter of the

LEE AND GRANT SIGNING THE TERMS OF SURRENDER.

pursuing cavalry. Lee, like a hunted fox, turned hither and thither; but, at last, Sheridan planted himself squarely across the front. Lee ordered a charge, and the half-starved troops, with a rallying of their old courage, dashed forward, when suddenly, the Federal cavalry moving aside, revealed dense bodies of infantry in battle line. It was the last charge of the Army of Northern Virginia. A white flag appeared on the Confederate front. The battle was stayed.

General Grant had already sent in a note demanding the

surrender of the army, and Lee now accepted the terms. The two generals accordingly met in one of the largest of the five houses in Appomattox.⁸ Having simply greeted each other, they proceeded at once to business. Seated at a plain table, they drew up the papers of the surrender; then having exchanged bows, they parted. On April 9th, 8,000 men,—the remains of the Army of Virginia,—laid down their arms near *Appomattox Court-House*, and then turned homeward, no longer Confederate soldiers, but American citizens.

8. The Effect.—This surrender was soon followed by that of the other Confederate Generals, Johnston, Dick Taylor, and Kirby Smith; and the sad civil war which had so long desolated the country, was at an end. Jefferson Davis fled southward, hoping to escape, but was overtaken near Irwinsville, Georgia, (May 11), and sent a prisoner to Fortress Monroe.

9. Losses of the War.—The sacrifices made during the Civil War were as great as those made in the Revolution; while the armies and the battles were on a far larger scale. There were few families North or South that did not lose some member during the long contest.

In the Union armies, probably three hundred thousand men were killed in battle, or died of wounds or disease; while doubtless two hundred thousand were crippled for life. If the Confederate armies suffered as heavily, the country thus lost one million able-bodied men.

10. The Union Debt (Jan. 1, 1866), was nearly $2,750,000,000, at one time, the daily expenses having reached the sum of $3,500,000. The Confederate war debts were never paid, as that government was overthrown.

11. Female Patriotism.—On both sides, the devotedness of the women at home, equalled that of the soldiers on the field. The Southern women devoted themselves to the struggle with all the ardor of the Southern race, and bore with heroism the greatest privations. Their fortitude held good to the last; and when Lee surrendered, hundreds of delicate ladies were living on half-rations, that they might share with his famishing men their few remaining comforts.

12. Charity and Piety.—Throughout the terrible struggle, humanity and charity had also their triumphs. The Sanitary and Christian Commissions devised and provided every possible comfort for the sick and wounded, as also decent burial for the dead. *Sanitary Fairs* were held in the principal towns and cities, and voluntary contributions flowed in. The Sanitary Commission alone, thus became the almoner of nearly $25,000,000. All over the country, women went to work to prepare lint and bandages for the wounded, and hospital garments for the sick and maimed. Hundreds who had been nurtured in the lap of ease, hastened to hospitals in camps and towns, to perform the duties of nurses, and to minister in every way to the sick and dying.

13. The Sisters of Charity and of Mercy, in particular, gave themselves to the holy work with that devoted self-sacrifice which belongs to their vocation. "What our noble Sisters did around those beds of agony to alleviate human suffering," says Bishop Spaulding, "has not been written. Their deeds belong to God's history, and when the final reckoning is made, they perhaps may weigh more than victories won, or battles lost. In the hospitals of Louisville, alone, they baptized over six hundred men, who, when the world was fading from sight, sought the light of Heaven!"

14. Hundreds of Chaplains, many of them Catholic priests, followed the varying fortunes of the army, to administer the last consolations of religion to the dying. Their devotedness, as well as that of the Sisterhoods just mentioned, did much to soften the bitterness of anti-Catholic prejudice; and now, we doubt if there be an American soldier worthy of the title, whose heart is not filled with grateful reverence at the name or the thought of a Sister of Charity.

PRINCIPAL BATTLES OF THE CIVIL WAR.

Date.	Location.	Commander.		Victors.	Loss.	
		Union.	Confederate.		Union	Conf
1861.						
Apr. 14	Fort Sumter	Anderson	Beauregard	Conf.		
June 10	Big Bethel	Butler	Magruder	Conf.	100	8
July 6	Carthage	Sigel	Price	Indec.	43	190
" 10	Rich Mountain	Rosecrans	Pegram	Union		725
" 21	Bull Run	McDowell	Beauregard	Conf.	3051	1897
Aug. 10	Wilson's Creek	Lyon	McCulloch	Conf.	1236	1095
" 26–30	Hatteras Expedit'n	Butler	Barron	Union		700
Sept. 20	Lexington	Mulligan	Price	Conf.	160	100
Oct. 21	Ball's Bluff	Baker	Evans	Conf.	1000	155
Oct. 29 to Nov. 7	Port Royal Exped'n	T. W. Sherman	Drayton	Union		
Nov. 7	Belmont	Grant	Polk	Indec.	400	800
1862.						
Jan. 19	Mill Spring	Thomas	Crittenden	Union	246	343
Feb. 7–9	Roanoke Island	Burnside	Wise	Union	260	2500
" 16	Fort Donelson	Grant	Floyd	Union	2000	12000
Mar. 7–8	Pea Ridge	Curtis	Van Dorn	Union	1351	1300
Apr. 6–7	Shiloh	Grant	Johnston	Union	13375	10699
" 7	Island No. 10	Pope	Makall	Union		6976
May 5	Williamsburg	McClellan	Johnston	Union	2228	1300
" 25	Winchester	Banks	Jackson	Conf.	904	397
" 27	Hanover Court H'se	McClellan	Johnston	Union	397	930
May 31 to June 1	Fair Oaks or Seven Pines	McClellan	Johnston	Union	5739	4282
June 8	Cross Keys	Fremont	Jackson	Indec.	664	829
June 26 to July 1	Seven Days' Battles	McClellan	Lee	Indec.	15249	19000
Aug. 5	Baton Rouge	Williams	Breckenridge	Union	300	400
" 9	Cedar Mountain	Banks	Jackson	Conf.	2000	1314
" 30	Bull Run (2d battle)	Pope	Lee	Conf.	18000	8400

PRINCIPAL BATTLES—Continued.

Date.	Location.	Commander. Union.	Commander. Confederate.	Victory.	Loss. Union	Loss. Conf.
1862.						
Sept. 14....	South Mountain....	McClellan......	Lee.........	Union	1568	2000
" 15 ...	Harper's Ferry.....	Miles...........	Jackson......	Conf.	11583	....
" 17....	Antietam	McClellan	Lee.........	Indec.	12649	13583
" 19–20..	Iuka	Rosecrans......	Price.........	Union	782	1438
Oct. 3.....	Corinth...........	Rosecrans.......	Van Dorn....	Union	2359	9271
" 8....	Perryville	Buell...........	Bragg..... ..	Indec.	4848	2500
Dec. 7.....	Prairie Grove	Blunt...........	Hindman	Union	1148	1317
" 13...	Fredericksburg....	Burnside........	Lee	Conf.	12000	6000
" 20...	Holly Springs.....	Murphy........	Van Dorn....	Conf.	1900	30
" 27–29..	Chickasaw Bayou..	Sherman........	Pemberton...	Conf.	2000	207
" 31 to						
1863.	Stone River........	Rosecrans.....	Bragg........	Union	8778	10000
Jan. 2...						
" 11....	Arkansas Post	McClernand....	Churchill....	Union	977	4640
May 1....	Port Gibson.......	McClernand....	Bowen.......	Union	848	580
" 1–4...	Chancellorsville...	Hooker.........	Lee...........	Indec.	17197	13000
" 12....	Raymond	McPherson.....	Gregg........	Union	442	823
" 14....	Jackson..........	McPherson.....	Walker	Union	265	845
" 16....	Champion Hill....	Grant..........	Pemberton...	Union	2457	4400
" 17....	Big Black.........	Grant	Pemberton...	Union	276	1500
June 27....	Hanover Junction.	McClellan......	Johnston.....	Union	399	930
July 1–4...	Gettysburg........	Meade.........	Lee...........	Union	23186	36000
" 4....	Vicksb'rg (sur'nd'r)	Grant...........	Pemberton...	Union	4236	27000
" 4.....	Helena............	Prentiss........	Holmes.......	Union	250	1635
" 9....	Port Hudson......	Banks...........	Gardiner.....	Union	3000	7208
" 16....	Jackson...........	Sherman........	Johnston.....	Union	500	600
" 10–18 .	Fort Wagner......	Gillmore........	Keitt.........	Conf.	1700	670
Sept. 19–20.	Chickamauga Creek	Rosecrans......	Bragg.........	Conf.	16351	18000
Nov. 16 ...	Campbell's Station.	Burnside.......	Longstreet....	Indec.	300	800
Nov. 17 to Dec. 4.	Knoxville (besieg'd)	Burnside.......	Longstreet...	Union	1000	2500
Nov. 24 ...	Lookout Mountain.	Grant...........	Bragg........	Union	} 5616	8000
" 25...	Missionary Ridge..	Grant...	Bragg........	Union		
1864.						
Feb. 20.....	Olustee	Seymour........	Finegan.......	Conf.	2000	730
Apr. 8....	Sabine Cross Roads	Banks...........	Smith.........	Conf.	} 5000	5000
" 9....	Pleasant Hill	Banks...........	Smith.........	Union		
" 12....	Fort Pillow	Booth...........	Forrest.......	Conf.	550	80
May 5–6....	Wilderness........	Grant...........	Lee	Indec.	29410	8000
" 7–12..	Spottsylvania	Grant...........	Lee...........	Indec.	10931	....
June 1–3 ..	Cold Harbor.......	Grant...........	Lee...........	Conf.	13153	1600
" 21–22..	Weldon Railroad..	Birney..........	Hill..........	Conf.	4000	....
" 27....	Kenesaw Mountain	Sherman........	Johnston.....	Conf.	3000	442
July 20....	Peach Tree Creek	Sherman........	Hood	Indec.	1500	5000
" 22.....	Decatur...					
" 20–26..	Atlanta	Sherman........	Hood	Union	....	18000
June 15 to July 30..	Petersb'g (3 assa'lts)	Grant...........	Lee...........	Conf.	18989	....
Aug. 18–21..	Weldon Railroad...	Warren	Hill.........	Union	4543	1200
Sept. 2.....	Atlanta (captured)..	Sherman........	Hood	Union	....	....
" 19....	Winchester	Sheridan........	Early	Union	3000	8000
" 22....	Fisher's Hill	Sheridan........	Early	Union	....	1100
Oct. 6......	Allatoona Pass....	Corse	French.......	Union	707	642
" 19....	Cedar Creek.......	Sheridan........	Early	Union	3000	3250

PRINCIPAL BATTLES—Concluded.

Date.	Location.	Commander. Union.	Commander. Confederate.	Victor.	Loss. Union	Loss. Conf
1864.						
Oct. 27.....	Hatcher's Run.....	Grant..........	Lee	Conf.	1600	1500
Nov. 30....	Franklin...........	Schofield........	Hood	Union	2300	5500
Dec. 14.....	Fort McAllister....	Hazen............	....	Union	90	240
1865.						
Jan. 16...	Fort Fisher (capt'd)	Terry..........	Whiting.....	Union	646	2068
Feb. 5.....	Hatcher's Run.....	Grant............	Lee	Conf.	2000	1000
Mar 16.....	Averysborough...	Sherman........	Hardee........	Union	554	550
" 13.....	Bentonville	Sherman........	Johnston.....	Union	1643	1892
Mar. 31 to Apr. 1....	Five Forks.........	Sheridan........	Lee...........	Union	1000	6000
Apr. 2.....	Petersburg (evac'd).	Grant...........	Lee...........	Union	....	....
" 8–12....	Mobile............	Canby..........	Taylor........	Union	885	....
" 9.....	Appomattox C. H..	Grant...........	Lee...........	Union	....	27000
" 26.....	Smithfield..........	Sherman........	Johnston.....	Union	....	35000

15. Assassination of Lincoln.—In the midst of the universal rejoicings over the advent of peace, on the evening of April 14, the intelligence was flashed over the country that Lincoln had been assassinated. While seated with his wife and friends in his box at Ford's Theatre, he was shot by John Wilkes Booth, who insanely imagined he was ridding his country of a tyrant. About the unconscious body of the President gathered the most prominent men of the nation, who mourned and watched, waiting in vain for some sign of consciousness, until the next morning, when he expired. The body was borne to Springfield over the very route he had pursued when coming to Washington as President-elect. The procession may be said to have extended the entire distance. The churches, principal buildings, and even the engines and cars were draped in black; and almost every citizen wore the badge of mourning.

16. The Death of Lincoln produced no disorder. Within three hours afterwards, the Vice-President, Andrew Johnson, quietly assumed the duties of the Presidency.

17. Johnson's Administration (1865-1869) is noted for

(1.) THE RECONSTRUCTION OF THE STATES.

(2.) THE ADOPTION OF THE THIRTEENTH (1865) AND FOURTEENTH (1868) AMENDMENTS.

(3.) THE FREEDMEN'S BUREAU, CIVIL RIGHTS, AND TENURE-OF-OFFICE BILLS (1867).

(4.) THE IMPEACHMENT AND ACQUITTAL OF THE PRESIDENT.

(5.) TROUBLES WITH THE INDIANS.

(6.) THE PURCHASE OF ALASKA.

(7.) A TREATY WITH CHINA.

RECONCILIATION.

18. Reconstruction of the States.—In May, 1865, President Johnson issued a *Proclamation of Amnesty and Pardon* to all who had been engaged in Secession, except certain specified classes. He claimed that the Seceded States, as soon as they had complied with certain conditions, should be fully restored to their position in the Republic. They were required to rescind their ordinances of Secession, to declare void the Confederate war debt, and to vote for an Amendment to the Constitution abolishing Slavery.

19. Reconstruction Policy of Congress.—On the assembling of Congress, decided grounds were taken against the policy of the President. It was claimed that Congress alone had power to prescribe the conditions for the re-admission of the seceded States, and his proclamation and orders were treated as of no value. The *Freedmen's Bureau,* the *Civil Rights,* and the *Tenure-of-Office* bills were passed over the President's veto.

The Freedmen's Bureau Bill provided for the establishment of a department of the National government for the care and protection of the freedmen, *i. e.,* the emancipated slaves, and also of the destitute whites at the South.

The Civil Rights Bill guaranteed to the negroes the rights of citizenship.

The Tenure-of-Office Bill made the consent of the Senate necessary for the removal by the President of any person from a civil office.

20. The Seceded States Admitted.—Tennessee promptly ratified the *Fourteenth Amendment,* and was restored to her former position in the Union. The other ten States having refused to do this, Congress passed the *Reconstruction Act* (March 2, 1867) over the President's veto. This act prescribed the conditions under which those States not then represented in Congress should be reconstructed, and made them subject to military authority until such conditions had been fulfilled. After a bitter and protracted struggle, governments were established in Arkansas, Alabama, Florida, Georgia, Louisiana, North and South Carolina, and their representatives* admitted (June 24, 1868)

---

* As a requisite for holding office, Congress demanded that every candidate should swear that he had not participated in the secession movement. Few Southerners being able to take this "*iron-clad oath,*" as it was termed, most of the representatives were Northern men who had gone South after the war, and were, therefore, called "*carpet-baggers.*"

to Congress over the President's veto. These States had been unrepresented during a period of seven years.

21. The Thirteenth Amendment abolishing slavery having been ratified by the States, was declared duly adopted as a part of the Constitution of the United States (December 18, 1865).

22. The Fourteenth Amendment guaranteeing equal civil rights to all regardless of race or color, and basing representation in each State on the number of voters, was adopted July 28, 1868.

23. Impeachment of the President.—The constantly-increasing hostility between the President and Congress came to an issue, when the former attempted to remove Edwin M. Stanton, Secretary of War. This act being considered a violation of the *Tenure-of-Office Bill*, the impeachment of the President was at last ordered (February 24, 1868). After a long and tedious trial, he was acquitted. The Constitution requires a two-thirds vote to convict on impeachment; and in Johnson's case, one vote was lacking.

24. The Indian War along the Southwest having, in 1865 and 1866, increased to such dimensions as to demand active measures for its suppression, General Sheridan was ordered thither. Black Kettle and a large body of his warriors being surprised and slain by a charge of Custer's cavalry in the battle of the Wacheta (*wah-che'-tah*), hostilities ceased (1868).

25. The French in Mexico.—While the United States were absorbed in the Civil War, Napoleon III., emperor of France, took advantage of the opportunity to secure a foothold in America. By the assistance of the French army, the *imperialists* of Mexico defeated the *liberals*, and tendered the crown to Maximilian, Archduke of Austria. The United States government protested against the measure, but was,

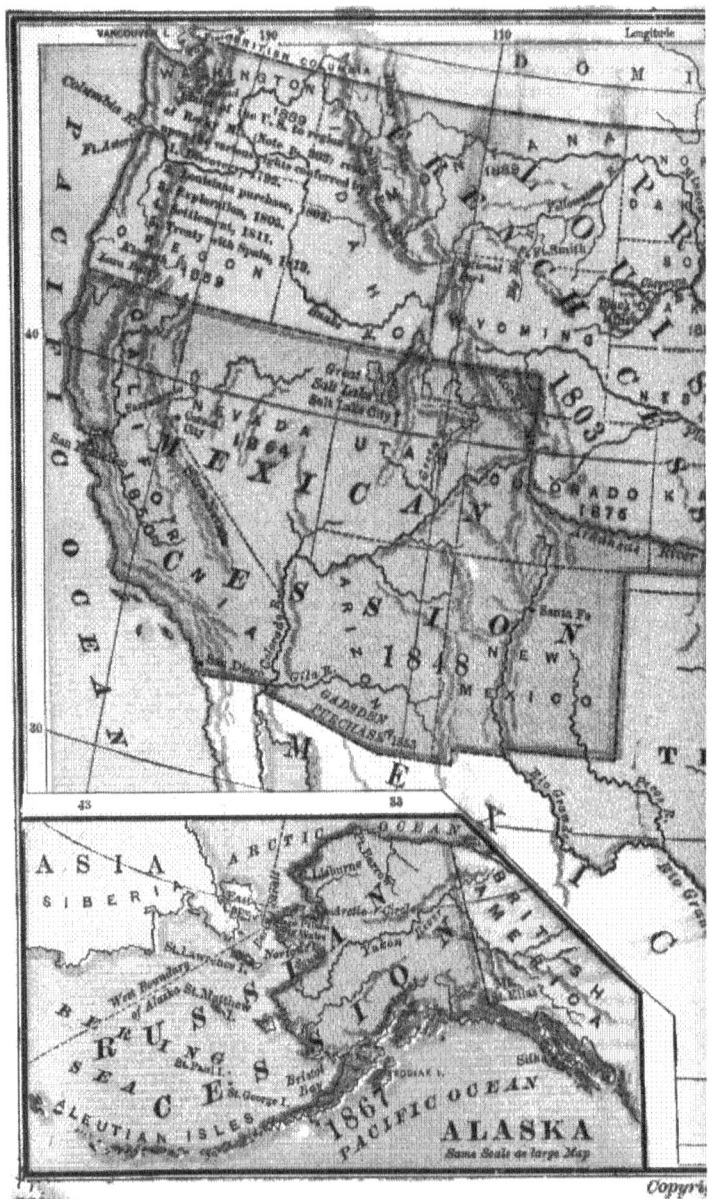

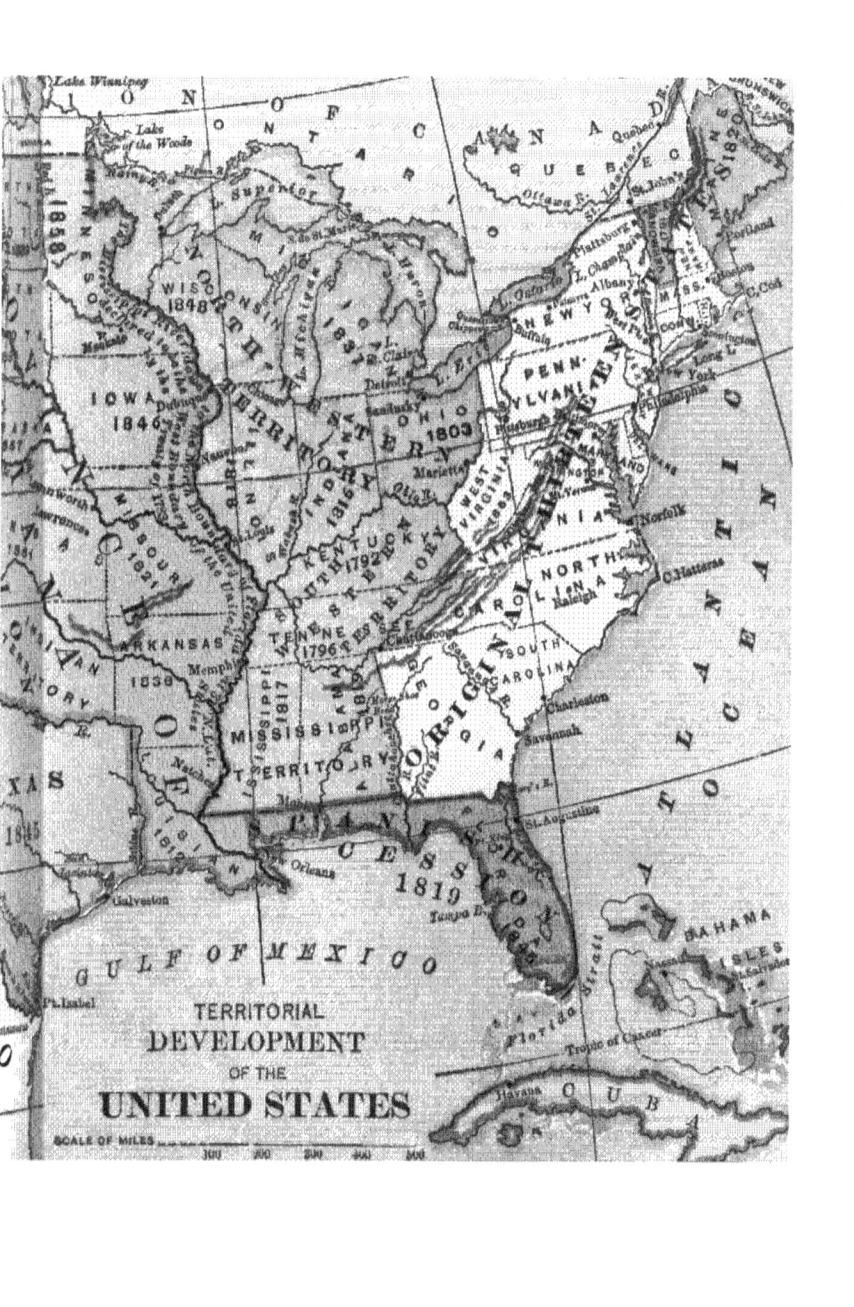

at that time, unable to enforce the "*Monroe doctrine.*" When the American people had been relieved from the pressure of civil strife, they turned their attention to Mexico, and demanded that the French troops should be withdrawn from this Continent. Maximilian, deprived of foreign aid, was defeated, and, falling into the hands of the Mexican liberals, was shot June 19, 1867. His young wife, Carlotta, overwhelmed by grief and misfortune, became a hopeless lunatic. Thus ended the dream of French dominion on this continent.

26. Purchase of Alaska[1] (October, 1867).—Through the diplomacy of William H. Seward, Secretary of State, Alaska was purchased of Russia for $7,200,000 in gold. It contains about 500,000 square miles, but is principally valuable for its harbors, furs, and fisheries.

27. Fenian Excitement.—The Fenians, a secret society organized for the purpose of delivering Ireland from British rule, crossed the Canadian frontier at Buffalo, N. Y., and at St. Albans, Vt., in large numbers. President Johnson issued a proclamation declaring the movement a violation of our neutrality, and sent thither General Meade to execute the laws. After some skirmishing with British troops, the expedition returned.

28. Treaty with China (1868).—An embassy from the Chinese Empire, under charge of Anson Burlingame (formerly the American Minister to China), visited the United States. It was an event of much importance, and the first of its kind in the history of that exclusive nation. A treaty was perfected guaranteeing liberty of conscience to Americans in China, also valuable commercial privileges.

29. Political Parties.—The republican party nominated *Ulysses S. Grant* of Illinois, for President, and Schuyler Colfax of Indiana, for Vice-President. The democratic party nominated *Horatio Seymour*, of New York, and General Frank P. Blair, of Missouri. Virginia, Mississippi, and Texas were not allowed to vote. As the other Southern States had been "*reconstructed,*" had granted negro suffrage, and enforced a strict registry law, they were permitted to participate in the election. *Grant* and *Colfax* were elected.

STUDY NO. 11.

GRANT.—HAYES.

1. Grant's Administration (1869-1877) is noted for

GENERAL ULYSSES S. GRANT.

(1.) THE ADOPTION OF THE FIFTEENTH AMENDMENT, (1870).

(2.) THE TREATY OF WASHINGTON, (1871).

(3.) THE CELEBRATION OF THE CENTENNIAL OF AMERICAN INDEPENDENCE, (1876).

(4.) WAR WITH THE SIOUX [*soo*], (1877).

2. The Fifteenth Amendment, guaranteeing the right of suffrage to all, irrespective of "*race, color, or previous condition of servitude,*" having been ratified by the requisite number of States, was formally announced as a part of the Constitution, by Hamilton Fish, Secretary of State, March 30, 1870.

3. Prosperity of the Country. — The nation rapidly recovered from the effects of war. The price of gold fell to 110, and the national debt was reduced $204,000,000 during the first two years of this administration. A general amnesty to all connected with the Civil War was proclaimed, and the bitter feelings engendered by fraternal strife fast melted away. The South, devastated and scourged by the march of contending armies, gradually became accustomed to the novel conditions of free labor, and began to rebuild her railroads, cultivate her fields, and repair the ravages of war. The census of 1870 showed that the population of the United States was over thirty-eight millions, an increase of about seven millions, while the manufacturing establishments of the country had nearly, if not quite, doubled in number and value during the preceding decade.

4. **Fires.**—(1.) A great fire broke out in Chicago, Sunday night, October 8, 1871. For two days it raged with tremendous violence, devastating 3,000 acres. 25,000 buildings were burned, $200,000,000 worth of property was destroyed, and 100,000 persons were rendered homeless. Contributions for the sufferers were taken in nearly all parts of the world, and over $7,500,000 were raised. (2.) During the same fall, wide-spread conflagrations raged in the forests of Wisconsin, Minnesota, and Michigan. Entire villages were consumed. In Wisconsin alone, 1,500 people perished. (3.) An extensive fire occurred in Boston, November 9, 1872. It swept over sixty acres in the centre of the wholesale trade of that city, and destroyed $70,000,000 worth of property.

5. **Treaty of Washington.**—The refusal of the English government to pay the damages to American commerce caused by the *Alabama* and other Confederate cruisers, produced bitter feeling, and even threatened war. A *High Commission*, composed of distinguished statesmen and jurists from both countries, accordingly met in Washington, and arranged the basis of a treaty between the United States and Great Britain, settling this and other causes of dispute. According to its provisions, the claim for losses was submitted to a board of *arbitrators*. This body having convened at Geneva, Switzerland, awarded the United States $15,500,000

HON. HAMILTON FISH, JUSTICE NELSON, EARL GREY, PROF. BERNARD,
GEN. SCHENCK, ATTY.-GEN. WILLIAMS, LORD TENTERDEN, SIR JOHN MACDONALD.

THE HIGH JOINT COMMISSION IN SESSION.

in gold, (1877). The difficulty with regard to the Northwestern boundary between the United States and British America was submitted to the Emperor of Germany, and was decided in favor of the United States. All danger of war was thus happily averted, and the great principle of the settlement of disputes by peaceful arbitration rather than by the sword was finally established.

6. Proposed Annexation of Santo Domingo.*

—This republic, comprising a large part of the island of

* The island of Santo Domingo is the "*New World's classic land.*" Here Columbus founded the first white colony on this side of the Atlantic, and transporting hither animals, trees, shrubs, vines, and grains, grafted, so to speak, the old world upon the new. Hither, also, flocked the bold, adventurous, ambitious Spanish multitude. Great cities sprung up, rivaling the majestic proportions of Moorish capitals. Magnificent enterprises were set on foot and prospered. Here Ponce de Leon renewed his ambition, and set forth afresh on an expedition to Porto Rico, and thence to Florida, in search of the Fountain of Youth (see p. 96). "*A century before Henry Hudson sailed up the noble river that perpetuates his name,—more than a century before the Puritans landed at Plymouth Rock,—the city of Santo Domingo was a rich and populous centre of industry and trade. Some of its massive and splendid palaces and churches still remain; among them, the great cathedral begun in 1514 and*

Hayti, applied for admission to the United States. A commission of eminent men, appointed by the President to visit the island and examine its condition, reported favorably. The measure, however, was rejected by Congress.

7. "The Virginius."—In 1868, Cuba attempted to throw off the Spanish yoke. Great sympathy for the patriots was felt in the United States, and repeated efforts were made to send them aid. In spite of the vigilance of the authorities, the *Virginius*, laden with men and supplies, escaped from port in the fall of this year. While still on the high seas, and flying the American flag, she was captured by the Spanish war steamer *Tornado*, and carried into Santiago. Many of her crew and passengers were summarily shot. The United States consul at that port in vain protested. President Grant interfered, and the *Virginius* was thereupon released, and suitable apologies were made for the insult offered to the United States flag.

8. Political Parties.—The liberal republican party, consisting of republicans opposed to the administration, nominated Horace Greeley of New York for the Presidential term commencing 1873. The democratic party endorsed this nomination. The republicans renominated *President Grant*, who was elected.

finished in 1540." But in 1795, when Santo Domingo was ceded to France, it was *"abandoned to such a degree that it was a mere wilderness, devoted to the grazing of cattle."* Yet, in spite of past tyranny, neglect, and the knowledge that they had been *"sold like a herd of cattle"* to a foreign master, the Dominicans were loyal to Spain, and when Napoleon I. took possession of Madrid in 1808, they indignantly rose in arms, overpowered the French garrisons, and made themselves masters of their own country. They then rehoisted the Spanish flag, and in 1814, by the Treaty of Paris, Santo Domingo was formally restored to that country. Meanwhile, the few years of interval had taught them some of the pleasures of liberty, and the seed then implanted grew rapidly. In 1821, they severed their connection with the mother country, but only to be absorbed by the more thriving and populous Hayti. In 1844, the Dominican Republic declared itself free and independent. Great Britain, France, Spain, Denmark, Holland, and Sardinia formally recognized it, and sent representatives to its capital. After seventeen years of struggle against European intrigue and Haytien aggression, it again lapsed into a Spanish dependency. Its story for the next four years is successively one of oppression, of revolt, of bloody wars, and of ultimate success. The Spanish fleet took final leave in 1865, and left the brave Dominicans to their well-earned freedom.

9. Grant's Second Term.—The Modoc Indians having refused to stay upon their reservation in Oregon, troops were sent against them. The savages thereupon retreated to their fastnesses in the Lava Beds. The peace commissioners, hoping to arrange the difficulty, held a conference with the chiefs. In the midst of the council, the Indians treacherously slew General Canby and Rev. Dr. Thomas, and wounded Mr. Meachem. The Modocs were then bombarded in their stronghold, and finally forced to surrender. Captain Jack and several of the leaders of the band were executed at Fort Klamath, October 3, 1873.

10. The Crédit Mobilier was a company organized for the purpose of building the Pacific Railroad. The undertaking proved a profitable one, and enormous dividends were paid. An investigation developed the startling fact that various high officers of the government had accepted presents of stock, the value of which necessarily depended largely upon their official action.

11. Railroad Panic.—In the autumn of 1873, Jay Cooke & Co., bankers of Philadelphia, having engaged too extensively in railroad schemes, failed. A financial crisis ensued, and hundreds of prominent firms all over the Union were involved in ruin. A settled stringency of the money market and stagnation of business followed.

12. Centennial Anniversaries.—The year 1875, being the hundredth anniversary of the first year of the Revolutionary War, was marked by various centennial observances.

April 19, the battles of Lexington and Concord were celebrated with patriotic pride. May 20, the citizens of Mecklenburg County, North Carolina, honored the memory of those who, at Charlotte, signed a Declaration of Independence only ten days after the capture of

Ticonderoga. June 17 witnessed, at Bunker Hill, an unprecedented gathering from all parts of the country, Northern and Southern soldiers vying in devotion to the flag of the Union.

13. The Centennial Exhibition.—To commemorate the signing of the Declaration of Independence, an exhibition of the arts and industries of all nations was held at Philadelphia, during the summer of 1876.

The beautiful grounds of Fairmount Park were the scene of this imposing display. The principal edifices were the *Main Exhibition Building*, the *Memorial Hall*, tue *Machinery Hall*, the *Horticultural* and *Agricultural Buildings*, and the *Woman's Pavilion*. The first-named covered an area of over 26 acres. In addition to these structures, there were more than 200 smaller buildings scattered over the extensive grounds. In these buildings, thirty-three nations besides our own exhibited the products of their industry, namely: *Argentine Republic, Austria, Hungary, Belgium, Brazil, Canada, Chili, China, Denmark, Egypt, France, Germany, Great Britain and Ireland, India and British Colonies, Hawaiian Islands, Italy, Japan, Luxembourg Grand Duchy, Liberia, Mexico, Netherlands, Norway, Orange Free State, Peru, Portugal, Russia, San Domingo, Spain and Spanish Colonies, Siam, Sweden, Switzerland, Tunis, Turkey, Venezuela.* The Exhibition opened May 10, and lasted 6 months. The average daily attendance was about 61,000 persons.

14. War with the Sioux, (1877). — The Black Hills, which occupy portions of Dakota and Wyoming Territories, had been set apart by the United States government as a *reservation* for the Sioux [*soo*] Indians. About the year 1873, rumors began to spread that *gold* was to be found there, and before the close of the year, prospecting miners appeared on the Indian domain. In 1874, a bill was introduced into Congress to extinguish the Indian title to a portion of the *Black Hill* region. These proceedings, together with the advent, in 1875, of surveyors and military forces, roused the ire of the Indians, and hostilities ensued. June 25,

1876, General Custer and his entire command of two hundred and fifty soldiers were slain. The Indians were commanded by an educated and skilful chief named "*Sitting Bull.*"

The war was continued through the summer and fall; but the Indians were at length defeated, and in the following spring *Sitting Bull* and his followers retired into the British possessions, (1877).

15. Political Parties. — The republican party nominated General Rutherford B. Hayes, of Ohio, for President, and Wm. A. Wheeler, of New York, for Vice-President. The democratic party chose Samuel J. Tilden, of New York, and Thomas A. Hendricks, of Indiana. The independent greenback party selected Peter Cooper, of New York, and Samuel F. Cary, of Ohio. The votes for the republican and the democratic candidates were so evenly divided, and such irregularities were charged against the elections in Oregon, South Carolina, Florida, and Louisiana, that both these parties claimed the victory. In order to settle the dispute, Congress agreed to refer the contested election-returns to a *Joint Electoral Commission*, composed of five senators, five representatives, and five judges of the Supreme Court. This body decided that 185 electoral votes had been cast for *Hayes* and *Wheeler*, and 184 for *Tilden* and *Hendricks*. The republican candidates were therefore declared to be elected.*

---

* The principal political questions which agitated the country during this campaign were (1) the Southern policy of the government, and (2) the civil service reform.

It was held on one side that negroes and republicans at the South were intimidated by force and prevented from voting, and that the presence of the United States troops was necessary to the preservation of the rights of the citizens, free discussion, a free ballot, and an enforcement of the laws. It was asserted, on the other side, that the use of the troops for such purposes was unconstitutional; that the intimidation was only imaginary, or could be readily controlled by the local authorities; and that the presence of the military provoked violence and was a constant insult and menace to the States.

President Jackson, as we have seen (p.   ), introduced into our politics the principle of "*rotation in office.*" This policy steadily gained favor, until Marcy's maxim "*To the victors belong the spoils,*" became the commonly-accepted view; and after every important election, the successful party was accustomed to fill even the menial offices of government with its favorites. Under such a system, the qualification of the applicant was of much less importance than the service he had done the party. Hayes promised to make "*no dismissal except for cause, and no promotion except for merit.*"

16. Hayes's Administration (1877–1881) is noted for
(1.) CONCILIATORY MEASURES TOWARDS THE SOUTH.
(2.) INDIAN TROUBLES (1877–1879).
(3.) THE FISHERY AWARD (1878).
(4.) TREATY WITH CHINA (1880).

17. United States Troops at the South Withdrawn.—President Hayes's Southern policy was one of conciliation. The troops which had hitherto sustained the republican State governments in South Carolina and Louisiana were withdrawn, and democratic officials at once took control of the local affairs.

18. War with the Nez Percé (*nay-pair say*) **Indians.**—In 1877, a war which, like others that had preceded it, originated in the injustice and cupidity of the whites, occurred between the United States and the *Nez Percé* (*Pierced Nose*) Indians of Idaho.

19. From time immemorial, these friendly red-men had inhabited the beautiful Wallowa Valley. After a while, whites began to settle on the Indian lands, and when they had become strong enough, they endeavored to dispossess the original inhabitants. Even the United States government took part in the work. From 1856 to 1868, various treaties were made with portions of the tribe to leave their lands, but Joseph the chief, who belonged to one of the most illustrious families of the tribe, refused to depart from the Valley.

Settlers still continued to encroach on the lands of the *non-treaty* Indians; and in 1873, Grant issued an order prohibiting it. In 1875, however, he promulgated another order revoking the first, and declaring that "*said described tract of country is hereby restored to the public domain.*"

Hostilities now ensued, with the usual events that mark the wars of our government with the Indians,—slaughter on both sides and the final defeat of the Indians. October 5, 1877, Joseph and his band surrendered to General Miles, at Eagle Creek, Montana Territory.

20. New Indian Troubles (1879).—The Ute Indians at the White River agency, dissatisfied by the encroachments of the miners and the non-payment of money promised by the government, took up arms. The U. S. troops were hurried thither, and peace was once more restored.

21. The conduct of the whites towards the Indians has, in general, been characterized by great injustice and cruelty. The latter, at the pleasure of the whites, have been dispossessed of their lands and driven to the far West. With the exception of the Catholic missionaries, who have devoted to them their labors and their lives, few seem to consider the rights or the welfare of the Indians as of any account.*

22. Treaty with China (1880).—Two treaties between China and the United States were signed at Pekin,—one in relation to commerce, and the other granting to our government the regulation of the Chinese immigration.

23. Political Parties.—The nominees for President and Vice-President were: republican, General James A. Garfield, of Ohio, and Chester A. Arthur, of New York; democratic, General Winfield S. Hancock, of Pennsylvania, and William H. English, of Indiana; greenback-labor, James B. Weaver, of Iowa, and Benjamin J. Chambers, of Texas.

After one of the most bitter and exciting contests, the republican candidates were elected by a small majority on the popular vote.

---

* This the United States government itself is forced to confess, as may be seen from the following extract from the first report of the Board of Indian Commissioners appointed by Grant:

"*It must be admitted that the actual treatment they (the Indians) have received, has been* UNJUST AND INIQUITOUS BEYOND THE POWER OF WORDS TO EXPRESS.

"*Taught by the Government that they had rights entitled to respect, when these rights have been assailed by the rapacity of the white man, the arm which should have been raised to protect them has ever been ready to sustain the aggressor.*

"*The history of the Government connections with the Indians is* A SHAMEFUL RECORD OF BROKEN TREATIES AND UNFULFILLED PROMISES."

STUDY NO. 12.
GARFIELD—ARTHUR—CLEVELAND—HARRISON.

1. The Inauguration of Garfield (1881-1885), the twentieth President, marked the hundredth year after the close of the Revolutionary War.

2. Star Route Frauds.—The new administration promptly set to work to reform abuses in the public service. A gigantic scheme of fraud, in connection with the letting of mail contracts in the West, was early discovered in the Post-Office Department, and was promptly exposed.

3. Assassination of President Garfield.—On the morning of July 2, the sorrowful tidings flashed over the country that the President, while standing in the railroad depot at Washington, had been shot by a man named Charles J. Guiteau. Party differences were at once hushed in the common sorrow, and the nation awaited in anxious suspense the result of the terrible deed. The illustrious sufferer expired Sept. 19th, the anniversary of the Battle of Chickamauga. On the last day of June (1882), Guiteau suffered on the scaffold the penalty of his crime.

On receiving official information of the death of President Garfield, Chester A. Arthur, the Vice-President, immediately took the oath, and assumed the duties of President.

4. Arthur's Administration (1881-1885) is noted for

(1.) The Civil Service Bill (1883).
(2.) The Organization of Alaska as a Territory (1884).

5. The Civil Service Bill aims to regulate, by means of examinations, the system of civil service appointments and promotions.

6. The most important political questions of this period were the Civil Service Reform and the Tariff.

7. Political Parties. — The democratic party nominated Grover Cleveland, of New Jersey, for President, and Thomas A. Hendricks, of Indiana, for Vice-President. The republican party selected James G. Blaine, of Maine, and John A. Logan, of Illinois. The people's party chose B. F. Butler, of Massachusetts, and A. M. West, of Mississippi. The national prohibition party nominated J. P. St. John, of Kansas, and William Daniel, of Maryland.

The democratic candidates were elected.

8. Cleveland's Administration (1885-1889) is noted for

GROVER CLEVELAND.

(1.) The Presidential Succession Law (1886).
(2.) Subjection of the Apache Indians.
(3.) The Agitation of the Tariff Question.

9. The Presidential Succession Law provides that if at any time there should be no President or Vice-President, the office of President should devolve upon a member of the Cabinet, the order of succession being as follows : The Secretaries of State, Treasury, and War, the Attorney-General, the Postmaster-General the Secretaries of the Navy and the Interior.

10. The Apaches.—For more than a year these Indians had eluded the pursuit of both United States and Mexican troops, but they were at last captured (July, 1886) by Captain Lawton, an officer under General Miles.

11. Political Parties.—The democrats who advocated a reduction of the duties on imports, renominated Grover Cleveland for President, with Allen G. Thurman, of Ohio, for Vice-President. The republican (protectionist) candidates were Benjamin Harrison, of Indiana, and Levi P. Morton, of New York. The prohibition party named Clinton B. Fisk, of New Jersey, and John A. Brooks, of Missouri. Besides these, there were five other tickets—namely, union labor, united labor, industrial reform, American, and equal rights. The republican candidates were elected.

12. Harrison's Administration (1889-1893).—President Harrison chose his Cabinet as follows :

James G. Blaine, of Maine, Secretary of State ; William Windom, of Minnesota, Secretary of the Treasury ; Redfield Proctor, of Vermont, Secretary of War; William H. H. Miller, of Indiana, Attorney-General ; John Wanamaker, of Pennsylvania, Postmaster-General.

13. The Washington Centennial.—On April 30, 1889, the centennial anniversary of Washington's inauguration occurred. It was celebrated by great national rejoicing. Business was suspended for three days, and in New York, naval, military, and civic parades took place.

At the Sub-Treasury Building on Wall Street, which occupies the site of Federal Hall, the scene of Washington's inauguration, commemorative exercises were held, at the close of which the benediction was given by His Grace Archbishop Corrigan, of New York, in the following words:

"The grace of Our Lord Jesus Christ and the charity of God, and the communication of the Holy Spirit be with you all; and may the blessing of God Almighty, Father, Son, and Holy Spirit, descend upon our beloved country and abide with it forever!"

BENJAMIN HARRISON.

14. The Tariff.—Very early in the history of our Government there were two opinions on this subject, and these differences continue to the present day. One party maintains that the American manufacturer should be protected, by imposing high duties on articles made abroad. The other argues that high protective duties are unjust to the American consumer.

15. In 1890, the McKinley Bill,—so called from the congressman who proposed it,—and favoring a high protective tariff, went into effect.

16. In October, 1892, the four-hundredth anniversary of the discovery of America was celebrated throughout the country.

17. The World's Columbian Exposition.

In May, 1893, the World's Columbian Exposition was opened at Chicago. The Exposition grounds are located on the lake front in the southern part of the city and embrace more than one square mile.

18. Political Parties.

—The tariff was still the important issue of the Presidential campaign of 1892. The Democrats once more nominated Grover Cleveland for President, with Adlai Stevenson of Illinois for Vice-President.

The People's Party nominated James B. Weaver of Iowa and James G. Field of Virginia. The candidates of the prohibition party were John Bidwell of Calfornia and James B. Cranfill of Texas. The democratic candidates were elected.

STUDY NO. 13.

ARTS, LITERATURE, ETC.

1. Increase of Population.—At the close of the 18th century, the total population in the United States and in all the National Territory, was about 4,000,000. Philadelphia, then the largest city in the Union, contained a population of about 45,000; New York, 33,000.

The census of 1890 gives to our country a population of more than 60,000,000; to New York City, more than 1,500,000.

2. Occupations.—Agriculture, commerce, manufacturing, and mining are now the leading occupations. In colonial times, the restrictive policy of Great Britain kept our commerce within very narrow bounds; but during the last century, it has had a wonderful growth.

3. Inventions.—The inventive genius of the Americans has passed into a proverb. Among the more important American inventions of the present century are the *reaper*, the *mower*, the *thresher*, the *electro-magnetic telegraph*, the *sewing-machine*, the *cylinder press*, the *phonograph*, the *telephone*, the *type-writer*, the *elevator*, and the *electric light*.

4. The Magnetic Telegraph was invented by Samuel F. B. Morse, of Massachusetts. Its conception first came into his mind in the autumn of 1832, as he was crossing the ocean. After he had undergone a long struggle to bring his discovery into notice, Congress finally appropriated $30,000 to make a trial of his invention. The first, or *experimental* line, between Washington and Baltimore, was completed

ARTS AND LITERATURE. 365

in 1844. The first message ever forwarded by a recording telegraph, "*What hath God wrought!*" was sent May 27, 1844. The first public message was the announcement of the nomination of James K. Polk for Presidency by a Democratic Convention then sitting in Baltimore. At present, there are about 180,000 miles of telegraph in operation in the United States.

5. The Atlantic Telegraph.—A very remarkable application of the electric telegraph is seen in the Atlantic Cable, which, through the untiring efforts of Cyrus W. Field of New York, was successfully laid in 1866. It connects Valentia Bay, Ireland, with Heart's Content,⁴⁸

THE GREAT EASTERN LAYING THE CABLE.

Newfoundland, and the two continents are thus brought into almost instant communication. By this wonderful invention, the affairs of one day in Europe, are known in the United States within a few hours.

6. The Sewing Machine was invented in 1845, by Elias Howe, of Massachusetts. Having at first met with little success in its sale in this country, he went to Europe. On his return, in 1849, he found a competitor in I. M. Singer, who had made some improvements in the machine, and was rapidly bringing it into notice. A lawsuit ensued, in which Howe's claim was allowed.

7. The Telephone and Phonograph were invented by Thomas A. Edison, of Michigan. By the former, persons can hold vocal communication through intervening miles; and by the latter, sounds of various kinds, even the intonations of the human voice and the harmonies of music, can be preserved, as it were, and reproduced long after the original agents have disappeared.

8. Steam-Vessels.—An American, Robert Fulton, was the first to apply the steamboat to practical uses, thus proving to the world the possibility of steam-navigation. Though others had conceived, he was the first to *realize* the idea. On Friday, Sept. 4, 1807, at 9 A. M., he launched upon the Hudson his little boat, the *Clermont*, (by some named "*Fulton's Folly*"); and on Saturday, at 9 P. M., it reached Albany. During a part of the way, the wondrous vessel, (smaller than the smallest ferry-boat of to-day), was gazed upon by crowds of admiring spectators, who gathered along the banks of the river.

THE CLERMONT.

9. Railroads.— Although it is to Stephenson, an *Englishman*, that we are indebted for the adaptation of the locomotive to iron roads, still America takes the lead in railroad construction. In 1830, there were in the United States 23 miles of railroad; in 1886, 127,000 miles. In 1869, the famous *Pacific* or *trans-continental* railroad was completed.

ARTS AND LITERATURE.

DRIVING THE LAST SPIKE.

This railroad is 1800 miles long, and it completes the union between the Atlantic and the Pacific. In one week the traveler can pass from Boston to San Francisco. This great highway has linked the West to the East by iron bands, has carried thousands of pioneers into the hitherto wild country along its route, developed fresh sources of industry and mines of wealth, and opened up the United States to the silks, teas, and spices of Asia. American ingenuity has solved the problem which foiled Columbus and the olden navigators, and has made for itself *a route to India.*

The last tie connecting the two lines was laid with much ceremony at Ogden, May 10, 1869. It was of polished laurel-wood bound with silver bands. Three spikes were used: a gold one, presented by California; a silver one, by Nevada; and a gold, silver, and iron one, by Arizona. The strokes of the hammer were telegraphed all over the Union.

10. Literature.—During the present century, our literature has made remarkable progress. American authors of considerable merit have arisen, and their works are read and appreciated on both sides of the Atlantic.

As prose writers, the following are the most noted:

Washington Irving (1783-1859) of New York, sometimes called "the American Goldsmith," the author of *Knickerbocker*, (a humorous history of New York), *The Sketch Book*, *The Life of Columbus*, and *The Life of Washington*.

Wm. H. Prescott (1796-1859) of Massachusetts, the author of *Ferdinand and Isabella*, *Conquest of Mexico*, *Conquest of Peru*, etc. Unfortunately, Prescott is often biased by religious prejudice, and thus the beauty of his works is marred.

Jared Sparks (1794-1866), the author of *The Life of Washington*, *Life of Franklin*, etc., and the editor of *American Biography*, in 25 volumes.

George Bancroft (1800-1891) of Massachusetts, whose principal and not altogether unobjectionable work is *The History of the United States*, in 6 volumes.

Francis Parkman (1823-   ), author of *The Pioneers of France in the New World*, *The Jesuits in N. America*, *La Salle*, *The Conspiracy of Pontiac*.

As writers of fiction, Fennimore Cooper (1789-1851), and Nathaniel Hawthorne (1804-1864), are most distinguished.

11. Among American Catholic prose writers of the present century, the most noted are

Right Rev. John England (1786-1842), Bishop of Charleston, whose writings, chiefly on controversial and historical subjects, are comprised in eight octavo volumes.

Most Rev. Francis P. Kenrick (1796-1863), third Bishop of Philadelphia and sixth Archbishop of Baltimore, noted for his *Dogmatic and Moral Theology* in seven volumes, which constitutes a complete course of sacred science suited to the wants of this country.

Most Rev. Martin J. Spaulding (1810-1872), first Bishop of Louisville and seventh Archbishop of Baltimore. He wrote *The Life of Bishop Flaget, Early Catholic Missions in Kentucky, History of the Protestant Reformation*, etc.; but his most popular work is *The Miscellanea*, a series of essays, reviews, etc.

Orestes A. Brownson (1803–1876) of Vermont, a singularly gifted man, remarkable as an essayist and reviewer. From 1844 (at which time he became a Catholic) until 1864, he supported, almost alone, his celebrated *Quarterly Review*. He wrote also, *The Convert, Liberalism and the Church*, etc.; but his best work is, probably, *The American Republic*.

Rt. Rev. Mgr. Preston (1824–1891), author of *Reason and Revelation, Christian Unity, Christ and the Church, The Ark of the Covenant, God and Reason, The Divine Paraclete, The Watch on Calvary*.

Rev. I. T. Hecker, C. S. P. (1819–1888), author of *Questions of the Soul, Aspirations of Nature, The Church and the Age*.

Rev. A. F. Hewitt, C. S. P. (1820), author of *Problems of the Age* and other works.

John Gilmary Shea (1824–1892), of New York, the author of *The History of the Catholic Missions among the Indian Tribes of the United States; Discovery and Exploration of the Mississippi; History of the Catholic Church in the United States;* an excellent translation of Charlevoix's *New France*, etc.

Rev. Aug. Thebaud, S. J. (1807–1886), the author of *The Irish Race, Gentilism, The Church and the Gentile World*.

Rt. Rev. Mgr. O'Reilly (1824–   ), author of *The Mirror of True Womanhood, True Men as We Need Them, Heroic Women of the Bible*.

Brother Azarias, of the Christian Schools (1847–   ), the author of *Development of English Literature, Philosophy of Literature*, also several essays on Literature, in the *American Catholic Quarterly*.

Among writers of fiction, the best-known names are George H. Miles, Mrs. Anna H. Dorsey, Mrs. Mary A. Sadlier, Christian Reid.

12. The most noted American poets are:

William Cullen Bryant, Henry Wadsworth Longfellow, John G. Whittier, James R. Lowell, Oliver W. Holmes, John G. Saxe, Bayard Taylor, Alice Carey.

Among our Catholic poets may be mentioned Rev. C. C. Pise, Rev. Abr. J. Ryan (the poet-priest of the South), Rev. Father Edmund (Hill), C. P., Maurice Egan, Mrs. Mary A. Ford (*Una*), and Eleanor Donnelly

STUDY NO. 14.

RELIGION.

1. Increase of Bishoprics.—Before his death, which occurred in 1815, Archbishop Carroll had the consolation of beholding Baltimore raised to the rank of an Archiepiscopal See, with the suffragan Bishoprics of Boston, New York, Philadelphia, and Bardstown (1808).

2. Growth of the Church.—Already had commenced that marvellous growth of the Church in the United States, which to-day engages the attention of the world. Churches and religious houses, Catholic institutions of piety, learning, and charity sprang up on every side; while the ranks of the faithful were recruited, not alone from the descendants of the early Catholic settlers, but also by the numerous European emigrants who flocked to our shores, and by the many (often illustrious) converts who found in the Ancient Fold, that peace of conscience they had elsewhere sought in vain.

3. Religious Orders.—The Augustinians were already located in Philadelphia (1790); the Sulpitians in Baltimore (1791); the Ursulines in New Orleans (1727); and the Carmelites in Maryland (1790).

In 1808, the Jesuits were restored in the United States; and that illustrious body then resumed those labors which form so glorious a portion of our country's annals. After this, in quick succession, St. Rose's Dominican Monastery was established in Kentucky (1805); a Convent of the Visitation was commenced at Georgetown (1808); and the

American branch of the Sisters of Charity was founded at Emmetsburg, Md., by the accomplished and saintly Mother Seton (1809).

Then followed the establishment of the Lazarists in Missouri (1816); the Ladies of the Sacred Heart in Missouri (1818); the Redemptorists in Baltimore (1832); the Sisters of St. Joseph in Illinois (1836); the Fathers of the Holy Cross in Indiana (1841); the Sisters of Mercy in Pennsylvania (1843); the Christian Brothers in Baltimore (1846). At the present day, there are in the United States about *thirty* different religious orders of men, and *fifty* of women.

4. Sanctity of the Confessional.—In 1813, Father Kohlman, of New York, was cited before the Court in that city to give evidence concerning matter known only through the Confessional. The Reverend gentleman refused; and after the case had been thoroughly argued, De Witt Clinton, the mayor, decided in favor of Father Kohlman. The principle of this decision was afterwards embodied in a statute.

5. First Provincial Council.—In 1829, the first Provincial Council met at Baltimore. It was the first *ever* held north of Mexico; the first in any English-speaking land since the rise of Protestantism (16th century), and the first in any country during the 19th century. There were present, one Archbishop, and five Bishops. Four prelates were absent on account of illness or other grave causes.

It is interesting to notice that on this occasion, in accordance with the views of the Holy Father, the Bishops formed an association for the publication of text-books free from objectionable matter, and suitable for Catholic youth.

6. The First Archbishop of New York.—In 1838, Rev. John Hughes, who had already distinguished himself as pastor of St. John's Church, Philadelphia, was made Coadjutor of Bishop Dubois, of New York, and on the death of the latter (1841), succeeded him in that See. From this time until his death (1864), this eminent prelate contin ued to exercise a marked influence not only over the Catholics of his own diocese, but even throughout the entire United States. In 1850, New York was made an Archiepiscopal See, and in 1858, the Archbishop laid the corner-stone of that magnificent Cathedral which is now the pride of this Continent.

ARCHBISHOP HUGHES.

7. **Anti-Catholic Feeling.**— Between the years 1834 and 1844, an anti-Catholic spirit gradually gained ground among certain parties bearing the name of "*Native Americans,*" and it at length resulted in riots. In Philadelphia, churches, schools, and the houses of Catholics were pillaged and burned, and New York was saved from similar scenes only by the prompt and decisive intervention of Bishop Hughes.

In 1852, this feeling again culminated, and New York, Boston, Brooklyn, Newark, St. Louis, and other cities were disgraced by mobs and riots. The authors of these shameful proceedings bore the name of "*Know Nothings.*"

8. **The Blessed Virgin the Patroness of the United States.**—In 1846, the Sixth Council of Baltimore

assembled. Twenty-three bishops took part in its deliberations; and their first act was solemnly to choose the *Blessed Virgin Mary, conceived without sin,* as the Patroness of the United States. This was eight years before the definition of the dogma of the Immaculate Conception (1854).

During this Council, the Bishops had the consolation of seeing two Catholic Chaplains, Fathers McElroy and Rey, appointed to accompany the American army then invading Mexico. The two Chaplains were brevetted as Captains to give them rank in the army. About the same time, the Archbishop of New York was invited to preach in the halls of Congress; and the President, with his ministry, joined the funeral cortege of the Archbishop of Baltimore. These kindly acts were in marked contrast to the proceedings of 1844.

9. The First Plenary Council of the Church in the United States (1852).—This assembly, convened in Baltimore by Archbishop Kenrick, was composed of six Archbishops and twenty-six Bishops. The prelates proposed the erection of several new dioceses, urged the importance of Catholic schools, and solemnly condemned secret societies, especially the Free Masons.

10. Civil War.—During the sad struggle which, from 1860 to 1865, desolated our country, Catholicity took no sides. Her priests and religious ministered alike to the spiritual and temporal welfare of the sick and dying of both armies; her earnest prayers and entreaties were constantly directed to the reconciliation of the warring brethren; and the reigning Pontiff, when addressed by the President of the seceding States, counseled peace, and even proffered his services to restore harmony.

In 1861, Archbishop Hughes, at the request of the Administration at Washington, undertook a journey to Europe, on business connected with the then unhappy state of the country. The spirit of his mission is well expressed in his own words: " I made known to the President that if I should come to Europe it would not be as a partisan of the North more than of the South; that I should represent the interests of the South as well as of the North; in short, the interests of the United States just as if they had not been distracted by the present civil war."

11. The Second Plenary Council of the Church in the United States (1866).—This august assembly, convened at Baltimore in 1866, was presided over by Archbishop Spaulding.

Seven Archbishops, thirty-nine Bishops, two mitred Abbots, and one hundred and twenty theologians, took part in its deliberations. In point of numbers, it was the largest assembly of Prelates since the Council of Trent.

Its objects were the securing of greater uniformity of discipline and the general well ordering of the affairs of the Church in America. After a session of two weeks, it was formally brought to a close, amid a scene of solemn grandeur that belongs only to our Faith.

12. At the great Ecumenical Council of the Vatican (1869), the United States was represented by forty-nine prelates, a glorious evidence of the progress of Catholicity in this country.

13. The Indian Missions.—The Catholic missions among the American Indians, which commenced with the very discovery of the continent and which have furnished so many beautiful pages in our history, still continue to supply material for record. Maine, New York, Michigan, Wisconsin, Arizona, New Mexico, and California, still have their Catholic Indians, the descendants of the converts of the early missionaries; but the course of our government has always been fatal to the red man, and on the removal of the

Indians to the far West, new fields of missionary labor opened in that region.

14. In 1835, the Council of Baltimore confided the Indian Missions to the Society of Jesus; and, soon after, the celebrated Father De Smet was sent to found a mission among the Pottowatomies. In a few years, he and his companions had founded missions among the Flatheads and other tribes of the Rocky Mountains.

Often might the traveler in those Western wilds come upon a scene such as Longfellow has described :
" Under a towering oak that stood in the midst of the village,
Knelt the Black-robe chief with his children. A crucifix fastened
High on the trunk of the tree, and overshadowed by grape-vines,
Looked with its agonized face on the multitude kneeling beneath it.
This was their rural chapel. Aloft through the intricate arches
Of its aerial roof, arose the chant of their Vespers,
Mingling its notes with the soft susurrus and sighs of the branches.
Silent, with heads uncovered, the travelers nearer approaching,
Knelt on the swarded floor, and joined in the evening devotions.
But when the service was done, and the Benediction had fallen
Forth from the hands of the priest, like seed from the hands of the sower,
Slowly the reverend man advanced to the strangers and bade them Welcome."

15. In 1870, President Grant formed a plan for dividing the Indians among the various religious denominations of the country. Not a single superintendency was given to Catholics; and of the *seventy-two* agencies, but *seven*[*] were confided to that Church, which has ever proved herself the friend and protector of the Indian. Thus the Catholics of New Mexico, whose forefathers had been converted by Catholic

---

[*] These seven agencies are those of *Tulalip* and *Colville*, in Washington Territory; *Grande Ronde* and *Umatilla*, in Oregon; *Flathead*, in Montana; and *Standing Rock* (or Grand River) and *Devil's Lake*, in Dakota.

missionaries long before a Protestant set foot on our soil, and the Catholic Kansas, Osages,* Chippewas, Yakamas, and others, were handed over to the Quakers and various Protestant denominations. Tribe after tribe has appealed to the government, but their petitions have been unheeded. What wonder that Indian wars constantly darken the pages of our history!

16. Later Administrations seem disposed to do something to better the condition of the Indians. What they will accomplish, yet remains to be seen.

17. The total number of Indians now living within the limits of the United States is estimated at 300,000. Of these 50,000 are located in Alaska.

Here, in 1887, the venerable Archbishop Seghers, who had laid down the archiepiscopal crozier of Oregon, to return to the poor Indians, was treacherously murdered, while endeavoring to found new missions.

In Montana and Idaho, the scene of the labors of Father de Smet, the Jesuits have seven flourishing missions and schools, the Ursuline Nuns and the Sisters of Charity having charge of the girls.

In Washington and Oregon, the Catholic Indians are attended by six priests, and are provided with schools.

---

* The Indian agent, Isaac Gibson, a *Quaker* or *Orthodox Friend*, in his report dated Oct. 1, 1870, thus speaks of the Catholic Osages:

"This class of Indians are richly endowed by nature, physically and morally. A finer-looking body of men, with more grace and dignity, or better intellectual development, could hardly be found on this globe. They were once the most numerous and warlike nation on this continent, with a domain extending from the Gulf to the Missouri River, and from the Mississippi to the Rocky Mountains; but they have been shorn of their territory, piece by piece, until at last they have not a settled and undisputed claim to a single foot of earth. It is strictly true, that one great cause of their decline has been *fidelity to their pledges*. More than sixty years ago, they pledged themselves by treaty to perpetual peace with the white man. That promise has been nobly kept.—kept in spite of great and continual provocation. White men have committed upon them almost every form of outrage and wrong, unchecked by the government and unpunished. Every aggressive movement of the whites tending to the absorption of their territory has ultimately been legalized."

In Dakota and Northern Minnesota, the Benedictines have eight mission stations, and schools for the Indians.

Northern Wisconsin and Michigan have many Catholic Indians cared for in twelve stations and schools, by Franciscan Fathers and Brothers, some secular priests and the Sisters of St. Joseph.

In New Mexico, the Catholic Indians live near their ancient churches, in twenty *pueblos* or towns. Owing to lack of means, there are few schools, and the Indians depend for their instruction entirely on their pastors. They are good agriculturalists, intelligent and industrious in their own way, thrifty, honest, and moral. Recently, the government has rendered assistance in the establishment of three day schools for the Indians of San Juan, St. Domingo, and Tsleta.

Arizona has about 14,000 Indians, most of whom since the departure of their Spanish missionaries, have relapsed into barbarism. The most noted of these tribes are the Apaches. They are among the fiercest, most nomadic, and least cultivated of the Indians. They roam from the northern part of Mexico, over Texas and Arizona, have no regular chiefs, know nothing of manufactures or agriculture, but devote their lives to war, theft and treachery. They and the Comanches are the best horsemen in the world, and they now use firearms with great precision. They are of slight build, very agile, of low stature, ugly features, and of a somewhat Mongolian cast. They fight more like assassins and murderers than warriors, and will lie in ambush many days, in order to surprise an enemy. None but the Catholic missionary can ever hope to civilize and convert this fierce tribe, which is still the terror of the traveller.

18. The First American Cardinal.—In the year 1875, Pius IX., of blessed memory, manifested his interest in, and his appreciation of, the American Church, by creating the first American Cardinal. This dignity was conferred upon the venerable John McCloskey, Archbishop of New York.

The event was hailed with joy throughout the country; and on the occasion of the conferring of the emblems of the Cardinalate, St. Patrick's *old Cathedral*, New York, was the scene of ceremonies surpassing in grandeur anything heretofore seen on this continent.

In May, 1879, St. Patrick's new Cathedral was solemnly dedicated to God by His Eminence, Cardinal McCloskey.

19. **The Third Plenary Council of the Church in the United States** was convened at Baltimore, in the fall of 1884, Archbishop Gibbons presiding as Apostolic Delegate. Cardinal McCloskey was prevented by illness, from attending. Thirteen Archbishops, sixty Bishops, seven Mitred Abbots, eleven Monsignori, twenty-three Superiors of Religious Orders, seven Rectors of Seminaries, and ninety theologians assisted at its deliberations.

20. **In the Fall of 1885,** the venerable Cardinal McCloskey peacefully expired; and the following Spring Archbishop Gibbons was created Cardinal by the reigning Pontiff.

CARDINAL McCLOSKEY,
(Born 1810; Died 1885.)

21. The Catholic Centennial.—In November, 1889, in Baltimore, was celebrated the first Centennial of the establishment of the hierarchy in this country.

22. At the same time, the first Catholic lay Congress in the United States was assembled. It numbered about 1,500 delegates from the various dioceses, men by birth and descent of different nationalities, including Indians and negroes. All joined in perfect harmony and with one common purpose.

The objects of the Congress, as set forth by Henry Brownson, were: a closer union of all the members of the Catholic body in this country; an increased activity on the part of the laity in aid of the clergy in religious work; a declaration of their views on the important questions of the hour; and the assistance and relief of the poorer classes of society.

23. Statistics of Catholicity.—The Catholic Church in the United States now numbers fourteen Archbishops, one being a Cardinal, seventy-three Bishops, more than nine thousand priests, over twelve thousand churches and chapels, fifty-four theological seminaries, one hundred and thirty-eight colleges, more than six hundred academies, three thousand six hundred parish schools, and six hundred and fifty charitable institutions. The Catholic laity include about ten million.

* At the beginning of this century, the principal Protestant sects in this country were the Episcopalians, Methodists, Presbyterians, and Baptists.

At the present day, American Protestants number in their ranks: Associate Presbyterians, Baptists, Baptist Brethren, Calvinists, Congregationalists, Cumberland Presbyterians, Dutch Reformed, Episcopal Methodists, Evangelists, Finders, Free-Will Baptists, Friends, German Reformed, German Seventh-day Baptists, Hard-Shell Baptists, High-Church Episcopalians, Low-Church Episcopalians, Latter-Day Saints, Lutherans, Mennonites, Methodists, Millenarians, Moravians, New Jerusalemites, New Presbyterians, Old Presbyterians, Protestant Episcopalians, Protestant Methodists, Puseyites, Quakers, Reformed Mennonites, Reformed Methodists, Reformed Presbyterians, Restorationists, Ritualists, Schwenkfelders, Second Advent Men, Seekers, Seventh-day Baptists, Shakers, Shouting Baptists, Society Methodists, Soft-Shell Baptists, Spiritualists, Spiritists, Swedenborgians, Theosophists, Tunkers, Unitarians, United Brethren in Christ, United Presbyterians, Universalists, Welsh Methodist Calvinists, Wesleyan Methodists, etc., etc.

BIOGRAPHICAL SKETCHES

OF DISTINGUISHED PERSONAGES MENTIONED IN THE PRECEDING SECTION.

Bragg, Braxton, (1815-1876), an American general. He gained distinction at the battle of Buena Vista ; and in the Civil War, fought on the Confederate side at Shiloh, Perryville, Murfreesboro, Chickamauga, and Chattanooga.

Buchanan, James, (1791-1868), the *"bachelor President,"* was born in Pennsylvania. He was sixty-six years old when called to the executive chair, and had just returned to his native country, after an absence of four years as minister to England. Previously to that he had been well known in public life, as Congressman, Senator, and as Secretary of State under President Polk. Much was hoped from his election, as he avowed the object of his administration to be *" to destroy any sectional party, whether North or South, and to restore, if possible, that national fraternal feeling between the different States that had existed during the early days of the Republic."* But popular passion and sectional jealousy were too strong to yield to pleasant persuasion, and when Buchanan's administration closed, the fearful conflict was close at hand. He retired to his estate in Pennsylvania, where he died.

Burnside, Ambrose E., (1824-1881), a Union general in the Civil War. He was at the battles of South Mountain, Antietam, Fredericksburg, Knoxville, Wilderness, Spottsylvania Court-House, and Cold Harbor. He was Governor of Rhode Island in 1866-67-68.

Calhoun, John C., (1782-1850), a Southern statesmen, celebrated for his advocacy of the doctrine of "State rights." As a speaker, he was noted for forcible logic, clear demonstration, and earnest manner. He rejected ornament, and rarely used illustration. Webster, his political antagonist, said of him, *" He had the indisputable basis of all high character, unspotted integrity, and honor unimpeached. Nothing groveling, low, or meanly selfish came near his head or his heart."* He was twice elected Vice-President of the United States.

Cass, Lewis, (1782-1866), an American patriot and statesman. He became governor of Michigan Territory in 1814, and was henceforth prominently connected with its early history. He is said to have negotiated nineteen treaties with the Indians. The Baltimore Convention of 1848 nominated him as the Democratic candidate for the Presidency, but he was defeated by General Taylor. Under President Buchanan, he served as Secretary of State.

Clay, Henry, (1777-1852), the first of American orators and statesmen, whose whole life was devoted to the preservation of the Union and to offices of good-will and peace. With Webster, Calhoun, Benton, Seward, and others, he adorned the political annals of the first half of the nineteenth century.

Respected by opponents, he was almost idolized by his friends. In this, he somewhat resembled Jefferson; but, unlike him, he had not in his early years the advantages of a liberal education. His father, whose means were limited, died when Henry was five years old, and at fifteen he was left to support himself. Meantime he had received some little tuition, in a log-cabin school-house, from very indifferent teachers. With a rare tact for making friends, ready talent waiting to be instructed, and a strong determination seeking opportunities, he soon began to show the dawnings of the power which afterward distinguished him. He has said: "*I owe my success in oratory to one single fact, namely, that at an early age I commenced, and continued for some years, the practice of daily reading and speaking the contents of some historical and scientific book. These off-hand efforts were sometimes made in a corn-field; at others, in the forest; and not unfrequently in some distant barn, with the horse and ox for my only auditors.*" Rising rapidly by the force of his genius, he soon made himself felt in State and nation. An eminent and stern political antagonist once refused an introduction to him expressly on the ground of a determination not to be magnetized by personal contact, as he "had known other good haters" of Clay to be. United with this suavity was a remarkable strength of will and an inflexible honor. His political adversary, but personal admirer, John C. Breckinridge, in an oration pronounced at his death, uttered these words: "If I were to write his epitaph, I would inscribe as the highest eulogy on the stone which shall mark his resting-place : '*Here lies a man who was in the public service for fifty years, and never attempted to deceive his countrymen.*"

Davis, Jefferson, (1808-1889), an American statesman and military leader, was born in Kentucky. He gained distinction in the Mexican War. Having been elected to the Senate in 1847, he became prominent in advocating the doctrine of State rights and the defence of slavery. John Quincy Adams, on hearing Davis's first speech in Congress, remarked : "*That young man, gentlemen, is no ordinary man; he will make his mark yet.*" He resigned his seat in Congress to become the head of the Confederate Government. After his capture at the close of the Civil War, he was confined in Fortress Monroe, but was released on bail, Horace Greeley becoming one of his sureties. The General Amnesty of December, 1868, included Mr. Davis with the others who had before that been refused pardon.

Douglas, Stephen A., (1813-1861), an American politician and a popular Democratic orator, known as the "Little Giant," in allusion to his small stature. He is famous as the author of the doctrine of "Popular Sovereignty."

Farragut, David G., (1801-1870), a celebrated American sea-captain, was the son of a Spaniard who fought for the United States during the American Revolution. At the breaking out of the Civil War, he had been in the United States Navy forty-eight years, having been commended for his bravery on board of the *Essex*,—a famous ship of Revolutionary times,—when too young for promotion. He gained great credit at the capture of New Orleans, at Port Hudson, Vicksburg, and Mobile. The office of Vice-Admiral was created for him, and afterward that of Admiral.

Fulton, Robert, (1765-1815), a celebrated American engineer. He was born in Lancaster County, Pennsylvania. In 1786, he went to England and studied painting under the famous Benjamin West. Later he abandoned that pursuit and became a civil engineer. Henceforward his name is associated with the growth of steam navigation,—an idea to which he devoted the whole energy of his life. Others had conceived the thought, but he, in his little vessel the *Clermont*, first made it practicable. In the midst of his triumph and the height of his prosperity, he died in New York.

Grant, U. S., (1822-1885), was born at Mount Pleasant, Ohio. He was very unwilling to follow his father's trade, that of a tanner; and, at seventeen, an appointment was secured for him at West Point. His name having been incorrectly registered, Grant vainly attempted to set the matter right, but finally assumed the change thus forced upon him, and thenceforth signed himself "*Ulysses Simpson*," the latter being his mother's family name. Two years after the completion of his four years' course as cadet, the Mexican War broke out, in which Grant conducted himself with great gallantry, receiving especial mention and promotion. After this, he retired to civil life, where he remained until the opening of the war in 1861, when he immediately offered his services in behalf of the Union. His modesty and diffidence delayed their acceptance, and Governor Yates, of Illinois, was the first to avail himself of them. Grant finally took the field as colonel of the *Twenty-first Regiment Illinois Volunteers*. His subsequent military history has been narrated in the text. He died July 23, 1885.

He was the republican candidate for the Presidency in 1868. His letter of acceptance ended with the words, "*Let us have peace,*" which became the motto of the campaign. He was elected as the eighteenth President of the United States, over Horatio Seymour of New York, the Democratic candidate. After the completion of his second term of office, he spent several years in visiting the countries of the Old World and the East. Everywhere he was received with the greatest enthusiasm, and his dignified bearing and wise conduct reflected honor on the American name.

Greeley, Horace, (1811-1872), an American journalist, distinguished as an opponent of slavery, was a native of New Hampshire. He early showed remarkable talent, and at the age of fifteen he entered the office of the *Northern Spectator*, at East Poultney, Vt., as printer. His wages were $40 a year, the greater part of which was saved and sent to his father, then struggling in poverty upon a farm in Pennsylvania. The *Spectator* having failed, in 1831 Greeley went to New York. He landed with ten dollars and a scanty outfit tied in a handkerchief. Franklin-like, he traversed the streets in search of work. As he had no friends or acquaintances in New York, and his dress was very odd and shabby, he met with many repulses; but he at last obtained employment, and then diligence, integrity, and ability won him a ready rise. Ten years later he founded the New York *Tribune*. He served in Congress in 1848-'49, where he was known for his opposition to the abuses of the mileage system. When civil war seemed imminent, he advocated a peaceable division of the country; but after it opened, he urged a vigorous prosecution of hostilities. At the close of the war, he pleaded for immediate conciliation, and was a signer of the bail-bond which restored Jefferson Davis to liberty, after two years imprisonment in Fortress Monroe.

Horace Greeley was pure, simple, and conscientious in character. He had a peculiar disregard for dress, and neglected many of the courtesies of society; but he was a true gentleman at heart, and possessed rare gifts in conversation. He was fond of agriculture, and spent his leisure days on his farm at Chappaqua. Just before the close of the Presidential canvass, his wife died, and this, together with the desertion of friends and the excitement of the contest, unsettled his mind. He was carried to a private asylum, where he died November 29, 1872.

Houston [*hu'-ston*], **Sam,** (1793-1862), was governor of Tennessee in 1827, but resigned his office, and abandoning civilized society, went among the Cherokee Indians. He finally emigrated to Texas, where he took a prominent part in the war against Mexico. After the annexation of Texas, he was chosen to the United States Senate. His life was full of incident and romantic adventures.

Hughes, Most Rev. John, (1797-1864), the first Archbishop of New York, and one of the most illustrious prelates the American Church has produced, was born in Ireland. Having emigrated to this country about the year 1817, he pursued his theological studies at Mt. St. Mary's, Emmittsburg, and was ordained in 1826.

His pecuniary means being limited, he, in the beginning of his collegiate career, took charge of the college garden, in return for his board and tuition,—a lesson and an encouragement to the young. After his ordination, he labored on various missions for several years, and at length became pastor of St. John's Church, Philadelphia. Already had he begun to manifest that strength of character and that magnetic personality which, joined to a spotless and holy life, gave him so remarkable an influence over the minds and hearts of men. He was skilled in controversy; and more than once was called upon to show, in public, his ability in this respect.

In 1838, he was made the Coadjutor Bishop of New York; and in 1841, succeeded Bishop Dubois in that See. In 1840, he founded St. John's College, Fordham; and in the fall of the same year, occurred that memorable debate before the Common Council of New York, in which he discussed the Public School system, and opposed alone the eminent counsel arrayed against him. Though his demands were rejected by the Common Council, he did not dismiss the matter, but recommended the Catholics to nominate independent candidates at the ensuing elections. This movement brought to view such unexpected strength that a modification of the school system was soon afterward effected. The present New York system, though an improvement on that which preceded it, is still false in principle, and affords to Catholics no immunity from *double taxation* for the education of their children.

Bishop Hughes also dealt the death-blow to the Church trusteeism. "*Those only*," says Archbishop Bayley, "*who have carefully studied the history of the Church can form any idea of the amount of undeveloped evil that lay hid within that system of uncontrolled lay administration of ecclesiastical property*." In 1850, he was raised to the dignity of Archbishop, and in 1858 he laid the corner-stone of St. Patrick's Cathedral, New York. He established schools, founded many churches and charitable institutions, and introduced into the diocese various religious orders.

His last attempt at public speaking was made during the draft riots of 1863. His health was already much enfeebled, and it now continued steadily to decline until his death. When informed that he could not recover, he received the intelligence with perfect calmness and resignation, and spent his remaining days in communion with God and preparation for eternity. In him, the Church lost a zealous and laborious prelate, and an able and devoted champion.

BIOGRAPHICAL SKETCHES.

Jackson, Thomas J., (1824-1863), a distinguished Confederate general, commonly known as "*Stonewall Jackson*," was born in Virginia. He gained distinction in the Mexican War, and in 1852 became professor in the Military Institute at Lexington, Va. He served at the battles of Bull Run, of the Shenandoah Valley, the Seven-Days battles before Richmond, and the battles of Cedar Mountain, Antietam, Fredericksburg, and was killed at Chancellorsville. He was remarkable for his calm, indomitable courage, the remarkable influence he exercised over his soldiers, and his earnest piety and deep religious convictions.

Johnston, Joseph E., (1809-1891), a distinguished Confederate general, was born in Virginia. He won considerable credit in the Mexican War, and in 1861 resigned the rank of brigadier-general in the Union army, to take part with the South. He gained great reputation for his promptness at the battle of Bull Run; he was wounded at Seven Pines; he resisted Sherman's advance upon Atlanta in a series of desperate battles, and was finally recalled to prop up the fading energies of the Confederacy in North Carolina, after Sherman began to move northward from Savannah. With Lee and Jackson he shared the honor of the first position among the Southern generals.

Kearney, Philip, (1815-1862), an able Union general, was born in New York. He served with great credit in the Mexican War, losing an arm at Chepultepec. He participated in the battles of Williamsburg, Fair Oaks, the Seven-Days fight, and was killed at Chantilly (Sept. 1, 1862). Kearney was devotedly loved by his soldiers.

Lee, Robert E., (1806-1870), a distinguished Confederate general, the son of General Henry Lee (Light Horse Harry), of Revolutionary fame, was born in Virginia. He was graduated at the head of his class, at West Point, in 1829; and in 1832 he married a daughter of George Washington Parke Custis, the adopted son of Washington. He served with great credit in the Mexican War as chief engineer of the army of General Scott. In March, 1861, he was appointed Colonel of Cavalry, but in April he resigned his commission, writing thus to General Scott:

"My resignation would have been presented at once but for the struggle it has cost me to separate myself from a service to which I have devoted all the best years of my life."

After the war, General Lee became President of Washington College, Lexington, Va. Here he died in 1870. In appearance General Lee was tall, erect, and handsome; in manner, dignified and gracious; in character, upright, honorable, and pious.

He was devotedly loved, and with reason, by his soldiers and by the Southern people. After the war this feeling seemed intensified, and he could not move abroad without receiving demonstrations of respect and affection that deeply touched his generous heart.

Lincoln, Abraham, (1809-1865), the sixteenth President of the United States, was born in Kentucky. His father was unable to read or write, and Abraham's education consisted of only one year's schooling. When he was eight years old his father moved to Indiana, the family floating down the Ohio on a raft. At eleven, he met with a severe loss in the death of his mother. Under her care he had learned to read, and to her influence is due much that was good in his character. When nineteen years of age, the future President hired out as a hand on a flat-boat at $10 per month, and made a trip to New Orleans. On his return, he accompanied the family to Illinois, driving the cattle on the journey, and on reaching their destination helped them to build a cabin, and to split rails to enclose the farm. He was now in succession a flat-boat hand, clerk, captain of a company of volunteers in the Black Hawk War, country store-keeper, postmaster, and surveyor; yet he managed to get a knowledge of law by borrowing books at an office, before it closed at night, and returning them at its opening in the morning. On being admitted to the bar, he rapidly rose to distinction. At twenty-five he was sent to the Legislature, and was thrice re-elected. Turning his attention to politics, he soon became a leader. After his accession to the Presidency, his history is identified with that of his country. He was a tall, ungainly man, little versed in the refinements of society, but gifted by nature with great common sense, and everywhere known as "*Honest Abe.*" Kind, earnest, sympathetic, faithful, democratic, he was only anxious to serve his country. His wan, fatigued face, and his bent form, told of the cares he bore, and the grief he felt. His only relief was, when tossing aside for a moment the heavy load of responsibility, his face would light up with a humorous smile, while he narrated some incident whose aptness to the subject at hand, and irresistible wit, convulsed his hearers, and rendered "*Lincoln's stories*" household words throughout the nation.

Madison, James, (1751-1836), the fourth President of the United States, was born in Virginia. Entering Congress in 1789, he became one of the strongest advocates of the Constitution, and did much to secure its adoption. From his political principles, he was obliged, though reluctantly, to oppose Washington's administration, which he did in a courteous and temperate manner. After his Presidential services, he retired from public station. In disposition he was very pacific; and he hesitated so long in declaring war against Great Britain as to cause one of the federalists to declare in Congress that "*Madison could not be kicked into a fight.*" This expression passed into a proverb. It has been said of him: "*It was his rare good fortune to have a whole nation for his friends.*"

Maury, Matthew F., (1806–1873), an American scientist and naval officer. He is most generally known for his admirable work connected with the coast survey, and his book entitled "*The Physical Geography of the Sea.*" On the outbreak of the Civil War, he resigned his post at Washington and was appointed a commander in the Confederate navy. He died Feb. 1, 1873.

McClellan, George B., (1826–1885), a distinguished American general. He served with honor in the Mexican War, and on the retirement of General Scott, was appointed general-in-chief of the armies of the United States. He participated in most of the great battles of the army of the Potomac, until after the engagement at Antietam. He was the democratic nominee for the Presidency in 1864, but was defeated by Lincoln. Of the popular vote he received 2,228,085, Lincoln 1,811,754. In 1864 he resigned his commission as major-general of the regular army, and started on a European tour, from which he returned in 1868. In 1877, he was elected Governor of the State of New Jersey. His death occurred in 1885.

McCloskey, His Eminence, John, Cardinal, (1810–1885), the son of Irish parents, was born in Brooklyn, N. Y., March 20, 1810. At the age of twelve, he entered Mount St. Mary's College, Emmittsburg. Here he remained until he had completed his classical and theological studies. He was ordained priest in 1834; and soon afterwards, proceeded to the Eternal City, where, for three succeeding years, he followed the courses of the Roman College, laying up a store of theological learning.

Having returned to his native land (1837), he devoted himself with great zeal to his priestly duties; and in 1844, at the early age of thirty-three, was made coadjutor to Bishop Hughes, of New York. Three years later, he was appointed to the new See of Albany. Seventeen years of devoted, self-sacrificing labor were given to this diocese, until in 1864, upon the death of Archbishop Hughes, he was promoted to the See of New York. Here for twenty-one years, he continued the work of his predecessors, completing and dedicating the grand Cathedral, and administering the diocese with marvellous success.

In 1875, he was elevated to the dignity of Cardinal priest, his title being derived from the Church "Sancta Maria Supra Minervam." (See page 377.) His advancing years and failing health soon made it necessary that he should have a helper. The zealous and youthful Bishop Corrigan, of Newark, was accordingly promoted to the See of Petra, and made coadjutor to His Eminence (1880).

Thus relieved of much of the burden of his office, Cardinal McCloskey prepared for the last great hour, and with the Hail Mary on his lips, calmly expired, Oct. 10, 1885. His name will ever be held in benediction.

McCulloch, Benjamin, (1814–1862), an American general. He served in the Mexican War (1846–47) and took up arms in the Confederate cause (1861). He commanded at the battle of Wilson's Creek, Missouri (Aug. 10, 1861), and was killed at the battle of Pea Ridge, March, 1862.

McDonough, Thomas, (1784–1825), an American Commodore, born in New Castle County, Delaware. As commander of the American fleet on Lake Champlain, he gained a splendid and decisive victory over the British in September, 1814, in an action of little more than two hours. For this service, he was promoted to the rank of captain. He died in 1825.

Meade, George G., (1815–1872), served in the Mexican War, and, in 1861, became a brigadier-general of volunteers. He was at the battles of Gaines's Mill, Malvern Hill, Antietam, Fredericksburg, and Chancellorsville. Just before the engagement at Gettysburg, he was entrusted with the direction of the Union army. During the battles before Richmond in 1864–5, he was second in command of the Army of the Potomac, under Grant, and shared with him the honors of those campaigns. He died Nov. 6, 1872.

Monroe, James, (1758–1831), the fifth President of the United States, was born in Virginia. As a soldier under General Washington, he bore a brave record, and especially distinguished himself in the battles of *Brandywine, Germantown,* and *Monmouth.* Afterward, he studied law, and entered political life. Having been sent by Washington as Minister to France, he showed such marked sympathy with that country as to displease the President and his cabinet, who were just concluding a treaty with England, and wished to preserve a strictly neutral policy. He was therefore recalled.

Under Jefferson, who was his warm friend, he was again sent to France in 1803, when he secured the purchase of Louisiana. He is said always to have taken particular pride in this transaction, regarding his part in it as among the most important of his public services. Soon after his inauguration as President, he visited all the military posts in the north and east, with a view to thorough acquaintance with the capabilities of the country in the event of future hostilities. This tour was a great success. To remind the people of his former military services, he wore a blue military coat of homespun, light-colored breeches, and a cocked hat, this being the undress uniform of a Revolutionary officer. This, with his plain and unassuming manners, completely won the hearts of the nation, and brought an overwhelming majority to the support of the administration. Monroe was a man more prudent than brilliant, and who acted with a single eye to the welfare of his country. Jefferson said of him: "*If his soul were turned inside out, not a spot would be found on it.*" Like that loved friend, he passed away on the anniversary of the independence of the country he had served so faithfully.

Rosecrans, William S., (1819-), an able American general of the Union army, was born in Ohio. He graduated at West Point, and from 1844 to 1847, was professor of engineering at that institution. In 1854, he resigned his commission; but at the breaking out of the Civil War he became voluntary aide-de-camp to General McClellan, and was soon made brigadier-general. He participated in the battles of Rich Mountain, Iuka, Corinth, Murfreesboro, and Chickamauga. He resigned his commission in the United States army in 1867.

Scott, Winfield, (1786-1866), one of the most distinguished of American generals. In the War of 1812-14, he won a great reputation for his gallantry at Queenstown Heights; and at the capture of Fort George, he was the first to enter the fortifications, and tore down the enemy's flag with his own hands. At Lundy's Lane, two horses were shot under him and he was twice wounded. "*For his distinguished services,*" Congress passed him a vote of thanks, and requested the President to confer upon him a gold medal. In the Nullification difficulties with South Carolina, Scott displayed his usual zeal and inflexible firmness in the execution of his official duty. The war with Mexico illustrated his military abilities and won him a place among the great generals of history. In 1852 he was nominated by the whigs for the Presidency, but was beaten by General Pierce. In 1861, he resigned his active duties and retired to private life.

Seward, William H., (1801-1872), an American statesman. He became governor of New York in 1838-1842, and was elected to the United States Senate in 1849. Here he persistently opposed the extension of slavery, and every measure like the compromise of 1850. In one of his speeches he declared that there is a "*Higher Law than the Constitution.*" This became an electioneering by-word, and Seward himself was denounced as a "*seditious agitator.*" He was a prominent republican candidate for the Presidency in 1860, and on the election of Lincoln was appointed Secretary of State. His ability in the conduct of the foreign affairs of the United States, saved the country from European entanglements.

Sheridan, Philip H., (1831-1888), an American general who gained great renown during the Civil War. He participated in the battles of Perryville, Murfreesboro, Chickamauga, and Chattanooga, and was afterwards appointed to the command of the cavalry in the army of the Potomac. His Shenandoah campaign and his attack upon Five Forks before Richmond, were the most noted of his achievements. His famous ride from Winchester to Cedar Creek has been embalmed in Buchanan Read's well-known verses. In 1869, he was raised to the rank of lieutenant-general.

Sherman, William Tecumseh, (1820-1891), a distinguished American general, was born in Ohio. He received a commission as colonel in the Union army, June, 1861, and was at the battle of Bull Run. At Shiloh, "*his individual efforts*" won the Federals the victory, according to Grant's report. In this battle, three horses were shot under him and he was wounded. In the campaign against Vicksburg, the battle of Chattanooga, the advance upon Atlanta, and the famous March to the Sea, his exploits are matters of history. When General Grant became President in 1869, Sherman succeeded him as general and commander-in-chief of the army. In October, 1874, he removed his headquarters from Washington to Missouri.

Sherman, Thomas W., (1818-1879), an American general who served at Bull Run and was in command of the troops in the expedition against Port Royal in 1861.

Smet, Father Peter de, (1801-1872), "*the Apostle of the Rocky Mountains,*" and the greatest Indian missionary of our age, was a native of Belgium. At an early age he entered the Episcopal seminary at Mechlin. While there his zeal was fired by accounts of the missions in the New World, and, with five companions, he offered himself to the Society of Jesus for the American mission (1821). Having spent a short time at the Novitiate in Maryland, he proceeded to Missouri, and there, at Florissant, pronounced his first vows. For some years after this he was professor in the University of St. Louis. At length, in 1838, to his great joy, he was sent to found a mission among the Pottowatomies at Sugar Creek, Kansas; and two years later, at the earnest entreaty of the Flatheads, he visited and preached to the Indians of the Rocky Mountains. In two months his preaching was rewarded by the conversion of six hundred, including two chiefs. On his return, in conjunction with his superiors, he planned a series of missions among the Western Indians, reserving to himself the general superintendence and the duty of providing funds. From this period until his death he was devoted to the service of the red men. For them he journeyed, labored and prayed. For their welfare no sacrifice seemed too difficult to him, no hardship too severe. In return, he won from the Indian that. confidence, reverence and love, which a *Black Robe* alone can inspire in these untutored yet wary children of the forest. The United States government, conscious of his wondrous influence, on more than one occasion employed his intervention to put a stop to Indian hostilities. Would that such mild and gentle measures had always been adopted! The blood of the Indian would not then, as now, cry to Heaven for vengeance. Father de Smet was joined by many zealous laborers in the field, and the harvest proved abundant. The missions still continue to flourish, except where the government has withdrawn them from Catholic care.

After more than forty years of incessant toil, the venerable missionary's once powerful frame began to succumb, and in the month of May, 1872, he yielded up to God his beautiful soul. His remains were carried to his early home at Florissant, where they now lie entombed. The spirit that animated a Las Casas in the sixteenth century, a Jogues, a Marquette and a Brebœuf in the seventeenth, a Gravier and a Rasle in the eighteenth, found new life in the breast of *Peter de Smet* in the nineteenth.

Taylor, Zachary, (1784–1850), the twelfth President of the United States, was born in Virginia. While he was still an infant, his parents removed to Kentucky. His means of education were of the scantiest kind, and until he was twenty-four years of age, he worked on his father's plantation. Madison, who was a relative, and at that time Secretary of State, then secured for him an appointment in the army as lieutenant. From this he rose, by regular and rapid degrees, to a major-generalship; and his triumphant battles at *Palo Alto, Resaca de la Palma, Monterey,* and *Buena Vista,* won great applause. He was the popular hero of a successful war, and the soldiers admiringly called him "*Old Rough and Ready.*" Having been offered the nomination for President, he published several letters defining his position as "*a whig, but not an ultra-whig,*" and declaring that he would not be a party candidate or the exponent of party doctrines. Many of the whig leaders violently opposed his nomination. Daniel Webster called him "*an ignorant frontier colonel.*" The fact that he was a slaveholder was warmly urged against him. He knew nothing of civil affairs, and had taken so little interest in politics that he had not voted in forty years. His nomination caused a secession from the whigs, resulting in the formation of the *free-soil party.* He felt his want of qualifications for the position, and sometimes expressed his regret that he had accepted it. Yet he maintained as President the popularity which had led to his election, and was personally one of the most esteemed who have filled that office.

Thomas, George H., (1816–1870), gained some reputation for his valor in the Mexican War. On the breaking out of the Civil War, though born in Virginia, he remained loyal to the Union. His conduct at Murfreesboro and Chickamauga, are matters of history. When in command at Nashville, in 1864, he was engaged in organizing his forces for the field, and delayed so long in moving out of his intrenchments against Hood, that General Grant issued positive orders for an advance, and had started to take charge of the troops in person, when he learned of the victory his slow but sure general had achieved. In 1868, President Johnson offered him the brevet rank of lieutenant-general, but he declined, saying that he had done nothing since the war worthy of the honor.

Webster, Daniel, (1782–1852), the great American statesman and jurist, was fourteen years old before he first enjoyed the privilege of a few months schooling at an academy. The man whose eloquence was afterward to stir the nation, was then so shy that he could not muster courage to speak before the school. He says, "*Many a piece did I commit and rehearse in my own room, over and over again; yet when the day came, when my name was called, and I saw all eyes turned toward me, I could not raise myself from my seat.*" In other respects, however, he gave decided promise of his future eminence. One year after, his father resolved to send him to college,—a dream the boy had never dared to cherish. "*I remember the very hill we were ascending through deep snow, in a New England sleigh, when my father made known this purpose to me. I could not speak. How could he, I thought, with so large a family, and in such narrow circumstances, think of incurring so great an expense for me? A warm glow ran all over me, and I laid my head on my father's shoulder and wept.*"—Having finished his collegiate education and entered his profession, he at once rose to eminence. Elected to Congress, in his maiden speech he "*took the House and country by surprise.*" By rapid strides he placed himself at the head of American orators. His next famous parliamentary struggle was in the debate upon the subject of State Rights in 1830. His speech in reply to Hayne of South Carolina, contained those memorable words, familiar to every school-boy, "*Liberty and Union, now and forever, one and inseparable.*" Webster's speeches are masterpieces, and may well be the study of every aspirant for distinction. It was a disappointment to many of his friends, as it is said to have been to himself, that he was never called to the Presidential chair. But, like Clay, although he might have honored that position, he needed it not to enhance his renown. His death called out, it is said, a greater number of orations than had any other since that of Washington.

CHRONOLOGICAL REVIEW.

NINETEENTH CENTURY.

1800.—The Capital removed from Philadelphia to Washington. Treaty with France, (Sept. 30).

1801.—**Thomas Jefferson** (III.) inaugurated. War declared against Tripoli, (June 10).

1802.—*Ohio* admitted to the Union, (Nov. 29).

1803.—A fleet sent against Tripoli. Louisiana purchased, (April 30).

1804.—Lieut. Decatur destroyed the frigate *Philadelphia*, (Feb. 15). Hamilton killed by Burr, (July 11).

1805.—The Jesuits restored in the United States. Treaty of peace with Tripoli, (June 3).

1806.—The Dominicans founded a house in Kentucky.

1807.—The *Chesapeake* fired into by the *Leopard*, (June 22). Fulton's first steamboat, "*The Clermont*," on the Hudson, (Sept. 14). The embargo on American ships, (Dec. 22).

1809.—**James Madison** (IV.) inaugurated. Mother Seton established the Sisters of Charity at Emmittsburg.

1811.—Action between the "*President*" and the "*Little Belt*," (May 16). Battle of Tippecanoe, (Nov. 7).

1812.—*Louisiana* admitted to the Union, (April 8). War declared against England, (June 19). Detroit surrendered by General Hull, (Aug. 16). The *Constitution* captured the *Guerriere*, (Aug. 19). The *Wasp* captured the *Frolic*, (Oct. 13).

1813.—Perry's victory on Lake Erie, (Sept. 10).

1814.—Battles of Horse-shoe Bend, (Mar. 27), Chippewa, (July 5), and Lundy's Lane, (July 25). Washington captured by the British, (Aug. 24). The Hartford Convention, (Dec. 15). *Treaty of Peace*, (Dec. 24).

1815.—Battle of New Orleans, (Jan. 8). War with Algiers. Death of Archbishop Carroll.

1816.—*Indiana* admitted to the Union, (Dec. 11).

1817.—**James Monroe** (V.) inaugurated. *Mississippi* admitted to the Union, (Dec. 10). The Ladies of the Sacred Heart in New Orleans.

1818.—*Illinois* admitted to the Union, (Dec. 3).

1819.—Florida purchased. (Feb. 22). *Alabama* admitted to the Union, (Dec. 14).

1820.—The *Missouri Compromise Bill* passed, (Mar. 3). *Maine* admitted to the Union, (Mar. 15).
1821.—*Missouri* admitted to the Union, (Aug. 10).
1823.—The Western Indian missions renewed under the Jesuits.
1824.—The visit of La Fayette, (Aug. 15).
1825.—**John Quincy Adams** (VI.) inaugurated.
1826.—Jefferson and the elder Adams died, (July 4).
1829.—**Andrew Jackson** (VII.) inaugurated.
1832.—The Black Hawk War.
1835.—The Seminole War begun.
1836.—*Arkansas* admitted to the Union, (June 15).
1837.—*Michigan* admitted to the Union, (Jan. 26). **Martin Van Buren** (VIII.) inaugurated. Battle of Okeechobee. The Seminoles routed by Taylor, (Dec. 25).
1837-8.—The "Patriot War," Canada.
1840.—*Father De Smet* went on the Indian Mission.
1841.—**Wm. H. Harrison** (IX.) inaugurated, (Mar. 4), and died, (April 4). **John Tyler** (X.) inaugurated.
1842.—The *Dorr Rebellion* in Rhode Island.
1845.—*Florida* admitted to the Union, (Mar. 3). **James K. Polk** (XI.) inaugurated. *Texas* admitted to the Union, (Dec. 27).
1846.—The Mexican War begun. *Iowa* admitted to the Union, (Dec. 28). Oregon City made a metropolitan See.
1847.—The City of Mexico taken by General Scott.
1848.—The *Treaty of Peace* with Mexico, (Feb. 2). Gold discovered in California, (Feb.). *Wisconsin* admitted to the Union, (May 29).
1849.—**Zachary Taylor** (XII.) inaugurated.
1850.—President Taylor died, (July 9). **Millard Fillmore** (XIII.) inaugurated, (July 16). *California* admitted to the Union, (May 29).
1852.—*First Plenary Council of Baltimore.*
1853.—**Franklin Pierce** (XIV.) inaugurated.
1854.—Commodore Perry's treaty with Japan, (March). The Missouri Compromise Bill repealed.
1857.—**James Buchanan** (XV.) inaugurated.
1858.—*Minnesota* admitted to the Union, (May 11).
1859.—*Oregon* admitted to the Union, (Feb. 14).
1860.—*Secession Ordinance passed by South Carolina*, (Dec. 20).
1861.—*Secession Ordinances passed by ten other States.* *Kansas* admitted to the Union. **Abraham Lincoln** (XVI.) inaugurated. Beginning of the great *Civil War.* First battle of Bull Run.
1862.—New Orleans taken by the Union forces. The Seven Days' Battles. Union victory at Antietam.

CHRONOLOGICAL TABLE. 395

1863.—The Emancipation Proclamation. Union victory at Murfreesboro. Union defeat at Chancellorsville. *West Virginia* admitted to the Union. Union victory at Gettysburg. Capture of Vicksburg by Grant. Draft riot in New York city. Death of Archbishop Kenrick.

1864.—Death of Archbishop Hughes, (Jan. 3). Campaign of Grant in Virginia. Petersburg besieged. Atlanta taken by Sherman. *Nevada* admitted to the Union.

1865.—Petersburg and Richmond taken. Surrender of General Lee. *End of the Civil War.* Assassination of Lincoln. **Andrew Johnson** (XVII.) inaugurated. Slavery abolished.

1866.—*The Second Plenary Council of Baltimore.*

1867.—*Nebraska* admitted to the Union. The Reconstruction and Tenure-of-office bills passed. Alaska purchased.

1868.—Johnson impeached by the House of Representatives, (Feb. 24); acquitted, (May 26). The seceded States admitted, (June 24). *The Fourteenth Amendment* declared, (July 28).

1869.—**Ulysses S. Grant** (XVIII.) inaugurated.

1870.—*The Fifteenth Amendment* declared, (Mar. 30).

1871.—The Treaty of Washington, (May 8).

1875.—The Centennial anniversaries. **Archbishop McCloskey created Cardinal**, (April 27).

1876.—*Colorado* admitted, (Mar. 3) The Centennial Exhibition at Philadelphia, (May 10 to Nov. 10).

1877.—**Rutherford B. Hayes** (XIX.) inaugurated (Mar. 5). The Custer massacre, (June 25). The Railroad Strike.

1878.—The Bland Silver Bill, (Feb. 21).

1879.—The Fishery Award.

1880.—Treaty with China.

1881.—**James A. Garfield** (XX.) inaugurated.

1881.—President Garfield shot (July 2).

1881.—**Chester A. Arthur** (XXI.) inaugurated (Sept. 20).

1884.—*The Third Plenary Council of Baltimore.*

1885.—**Grover Cleveland** (XXII.) inaugurated.

1885.—Death of U. S. Grant.

1885.—Death of Cardinal McCloskey (Oct. 10).

1886.—**Archbishop Gibbons created Cardinal.**

1889.—**Benjamin Harrison** (XXIII.) inaugurated.

1889.—*N. Dakota, S. Dakota, Washington, and Montana* admitted

1889.—*The Centennial of Washington's Inauguration.*

1889.—*The Centennial of the American Hierarchy.*

1891.—Death of General W. T. Sherman.

1893.—**Grover Cleveland** inaugurated.

1893.—The World's Fair opened at Chicago.

CONTEMPORARY CHRONOLOGY.

1800.—Napoleon I, Consul of France. Order of the Ladies of the Sacred Heart founded.
1801.—Legislative Union of Great Britain and Ireland.
1804.—Napoleon Emperor.
1809.—Napoleon excommunicated. Pius VII. made prisoner.
1812.—Burning of Moscow.
1815.—Napoleon an exile at St. Helena.
1820.—George IV. King of England.
1829.—Emancipation of British Catholics.
1830.—Second French Revolution. William IV. King of England.
1832.—Poland incorporated with the Russian Empire.
1833.—Accession of Isabella, Queen of Spain.
1837.—Accession of Victoria, Queen of England.
1848.—Third French Revolution. Louis Napoleon President.
1849.—Accession of Victor Emmanuel, King of Sardinia.
1853.—The Crimean War.
1855.—Accession of Alexander II., Emperor of Russia.
1860.—Insurrection in Italy under Garibaldi.
1861.—Victor Emmanuel assumed the title of King of Italy.
1866.—Austrian and Prussian War.
1868.—Revolution in Spain. Queen Isabella dethroned.
1869.—**The Council of the Vatican.**
1870.—Victor Emmanuel seized Rome. Alphonso II. King of Spain.
1870-1.—Franco-German War.
1872.—Suppression of Religious orders in Germany.
1873.—MacMahon President of France.
1878.—Death of Victor Emmanuel. Russian-Turkish War.
1879.—Resignation of President McMahon.
1881.—Alexander II. of Russia assassinated.
1885.—Death of Alphonso II. of Spain.
1888.—Resignation of President Grévy.

CONTEMPORARY POPES.

Pius VII., (1800-1823); Leo XII., (1823-1829); Pius VIII., (1829-1831); Gregory XVI., (1831-1846); Pius IX., (**1846-1878**); Leo XIII., (1878-   ).

GEOGRAPHICAL TABLE NO. 5,

OF PLACES MENTIONED IN THE PRECEDING SECTION.

(1.) **Alaska,** a territory of the United States, formerly known as Russian America.

(2.) **Antietam Creek** rises in the southern part of Pennsylvania, and flowing south into Maryland, empties into the Potomac River.

(3.) **Appomattox,** a railroad station twenty-four miles east of Lynchburg.

(4.) **Atlanta,** the capital of Georgia, and an important railroad center.

(5.) **Ball's Bluff** is on the southern bank of the Potomac, thirty-three miles above Washington.

(6.) **Baltimore,** the largest city in Maryland, from the number and prominence of its monuments called the "*Monumental City,*" is situated on a small bay which extends from the north side of the Patapsco River.

(7.) **Belmont,** a town of southeastern Missouri, on the bank of the Missouri River.

(8.) **Bermuda Hundred,** a peninsula lying between the James and the Appomattox Rivers.

(9.) **Big Bethel,** a hamlet on the peninsula north of Fortress Monroe.

(10.) **Boonville,** the county seat of Cooper County, Missouri, on Missouri River.

(11.) **Bull Run,** a small stream in Virginia, twenty-five miles south of Washington.

(12.) **Carthage,** the county seat of Jasper County, Missouri, on Spring River.

(13.) **Cedar Creek** rises in Shenandoah County, Virginia, and empties into the Shenandoah River.

(14.) **Cedar Mountain** is about six miles south of Culpepper Court-House, in North Central Virginia.

(15.) **Chancellorsville,** a village of Spottsylvania County, Virginia.

(16.) **Chattanooga, Tenn.,** on the Tennessee River, one hundred and forty miles southeast of Nashville.

(17.) **Chickamauga Creek** of Georgia and Tennessee, enters the Tennessee River near Chattanooga. In the Indian tongue it is called "*River of death.*"

(18.) **Cold Harbor** is ten miles northeast of Richmond.

(19.) **Corinth,** a village in the northeast corner of Mississippi.

(20.) **Dallas,** Paulding County, Georgia.

(21.) **Ellsworth,** an important commercial town of Maine, situated on both sides of the Union River, which is here spanned by four bridges.

(22.) **Emmittsburg,** a post-village of Frederick County, Maryland, fifty miles northwest of Baltimore. It is surrounded by a fertile and populous country.

(23.) **Fair Oaks,** a railroad station seven miles east of Richmond.

(24.) **Five Forks** is situated twelve miles southwest from Petersburg.

(25.) **Fort de Russy, La.,** on the Red River.

(26.) **Fort Donelson,** on the Cumberland River, Tennessee.

(27.) **Fort Fisher,** on the Cape Fear River at its mouth.

(28.) **Fort Henry,** on the Tennessee River, Tennessee.

(29.) **Fort Jackson,** on the Mississippi River, eighty miles below New Orleans.

(30.) **Fort Macon,** at the entrance of Beaufort Harbor, South Carolina.

(31.) **Fort McAllister,** (or McAlister), near the mouth of the Ogeechee River.

(32.) **Fort Pillow,** on the Mississippi River, north of Memphis.

(33.) **Fort Pulaski,** at the entrance to Savannah River.

(34.) **Fortress Monroe,** at the entrance to Hampton Roads, Virginia.

(35.) **Fort Sumter,** at the entrance to Charleston Harbor, South Carolina.

(36.) **Fredericksburg, Va.,** on the Rappahannock River, sixty-five miles north of Richmond.

(37.) **Gaines's Mill,** ten miles northeast of Richmond.

GEOGRAPHICAL TABLE. 399

(38.) **Galveston, Texas,** the largest and most commercial city of that State.

(39.) **Gettysburg, Penn.,** 36 miles southwest of Harrisburg.

(40.) **Ghent,** a famous fortified city of Belgium. It stands on twenty-six islands, connected by one hundred bridges. The extent to which the cotton manufacture is carried on in this city has procured it the name of the "Belgium Manchester."

(41.) **Hampton Roads,** an arm of Chesapeake Bay, lying between Hampton and Norfolk, Va., forming the estuary of James River. It is commanded by Fortress Monroe, situated on a point of land on the north shore, near the entrance.

(42.) **Harper's Ferry,** a village of West Virginia, situated at the junction of the Shenandoah and Potomac Rivers. The scenery in the vicinity is in the highest degree beautiful and picturesque.

(43.) **Heart's Content,** a bay on the east side of Trinity Bay, Newfoundland.

(44.) **Holly Springs,** a railroad station in the northern part of Mississippi.

(45.) **Knoxville, Tenn.,** beautifully situated on the Holston River.

(46.) **Lexington, Mo.,** on the Missouri River.

(47.) **Lost Mountain,** near Dallas, Ga.

(48.) **Memphis,** a flourishing city of Tennessee, beautifully situated on the Mississippi River, 420 miles below St. Louis.

(49.) **Mobile,** a city of Alabama, situated on Mobile River, just above its entrance into the bay of the same name.

(50.) **Murfreesboro,** a village of Tennessee, thirty miles southeast of Nashville. It was the capital of the State from 1817 to 1827.

(51.) **Nashville,** the capital of Tennessee.

(52.) **Newbern** (or New Bern), a port of entry of North Carolina.

(53.) **Norfolk,** on Elizabeth River, is the second city of Virginia. It has a fine harbor and is noted for its commerce.

(54.) **Pea Ridge,** a post-office of Burton County, Mo.

(55.) **Petersburg, Va.,** a handsome town on the Appomattox River.

(56.) **Philippi,** on the Monongahela River, W. Va.

(57.) **Pittsburg Landing,** on the Tennessee River, Tenn.

(58.) **Port Hudson,** on the Mississippi River, above Baton Rouge.

(59.) **Port Royal, S. C.,** the channel by which the Broad River communicates with the ocean.

(60.) **Richmond,** the capital of Virginia, situated on the James River, one hundred miles from its mouth.

(61.) **Sabine Cross Roads,** a locality in the western part of Louisiana.

(62.) **San Francisco,** the commercial metropolis of California, and the western port of the United States, is situated on the magnificent bay from which it takes its name.

(63.) **Shenandoah,** a county in the northeast central part of Virginia. It is drained by the North Fork of the Shenandoah River, from which its name is derived.

(64.) **Shiloh,** a post village of Gibson County, Tennessee.

(65.) **Spottsylvania Court-House,** a village about sixty-five miles north of Richmond.

(66.) **Vera Cruz,** a seaport town of Mexico, on the Gulf coast. It was founded in the latter part of the sixteenth century, near the spot on which Cortez first landed.

(67.) **Vicksburg,** the largest city of Mississippi, on the left bank of the Mississippi River, four hundred miles from New Orleans.

(68.) **Washington,** the capital of the United States, is situated in the District of Columbia. It is a splendid city, adorned with some of the grandest specimens of architecture in the world.

(69.) **West Point,** on the Hudson River, N. Y.

(70.) **Wilderness, The,** a jungle of scraggy trees, intersected only by narrow roads and paths, in Northern Virginia, south of the Rapidan River.

(71.) **Williamsburg, Va.,** a city six miles from the James River, and sixty miles east of Richmond.

(72.) **Winchester,** Frederick County, Va., a thriving town seventy miles northwest of Washington.

REVIEW QUESTIONS.

SECTION I.

I. Who were the earliest inhabitants of America? What memorials have they left? Mention some of the contents of these mounds. Are these works of great antiquity? Give from Bryant an extract concerning the Mound-builders. Is anything definite known of the fate of the Mound-builders? Who succeeded the Mound-builders? Had the Indians any written language? How did they regard women? What were their religious ideas? Give in this connection an extract from *Hiawatha*. What European nations visited America in the ninth century? When and where did Catholic missionaries first labor on this continent? Did the Northmen confine their explorations to Greenland? Where are remains of their works to be seen? What happened to these early colonists? Who was Prince Madoc? (pp. 1-8.)

II. What was the state of our country four centuries ago? Give Mrs. Sigourney's lines on Indian names. What was the extent of the known world four centuries ago? What of maritime science at that time? Who were the precursors of Columbus? To whom did Columbus apply for aid? Give some account of the kindness of Father Perez to Columbus. What can you say of Isabella's generosity? How did the mariners prepare for the voyage? Describe the voyage. Describe their landing. What prayer did Columbus say? How did the natives regard the Spaniards? (pp. 9-17.)

III. What further discoveries were made by Columbus? Describe his return home. His reception in Spain. Give the incident concerning the egg. Give an account of the *second voyage* of Columbus. Of his other voyages. Give an account of the *Cabots*, their voyages and the results thereof. What was the origin of the name America? By what spirit was Columbus animated? (pp. 18-21.)

IV. Give a biographical sketch of John Cabot. Of Sebastian Cabot. Of Columbus. Of Cardinal D'Ailly. Of Bishop Eric. Of Vasco da Gama. Of Prince Henry of Portugal. Of Isabella of Spain. Of Father Perez. Of Toscanelli. Of Amerigo Vespucci. Mention some of the principal European events of the fifteenth century. Name the Popes who reigned during the latter part of the fifteenth century. (pp. 22-25.)

SECTION II.

I. Upon what sad scene did the sixteenth century open? What did Columbus reply to the commander of the vessel? What occurred on his arrival in Spain? What lands were occupied by the Spaniards, as early as 1500? What expedition was now sent out by the king of Portugal? When did Las Casas come to America? When and by whom was Darien settled? When and by whom was Florida discovered? When and by whom was the Pacific discovered? What did Cordova and Grijalva discover? By whom was Mexico conquered? Give an account of the expedition of Narvaez. Give an account of Verrazani's expedition. Describe Cartier's first voyage. His second voyage. What was the result of Cartier's second voyage? Give an account of Cartier's third voyage. Give an account of De Soto's discovery of the Mississippi. What was his fate? What happened to the remnant of De Soto's expedition? (pp. 28–35.)

II. Give some account of the *Franciscan Missions* in New Mexico in the sixteenth century. Of the *Dominican Missions* in Florida. Give an account of Ribaut's and Laudonnière's attempts at settlement. When did Melendez arrive? When was *St. Augustine* founded? Give an account of the early *Jesuit Missions* in Florida. Give an account of Father Segura's journey north to Maryland and its results. What other missionaries arrived in Florida towards the close of the sixteenth century? Give an account of the death of Father Da Corpa. Give further account of the Franciscan Missions in New Mexico. What can you say of these early missionaries? (pp. 36–41.)

III. Who was Frobisher, and what was the result of his voyages? Who was Sir Francis Drake, and for what is he remarkable? What was the fate of Sir Humphrey Gilbert? Give an account of Sir Walter Raleigh's first attempt at colonizing Virginia. How did Raleigh first gain the favor of Queen Elizabeth? Give an account of Raleigh's second attempt at colonization. What tradition lingers among the Hatteras Indians? Did Raleigh immediately give up hope? Which were the only permanent settlements in North America at the close of the sixteenth century? (pp. 42–46.)

IV. Give a biographical sketch of Balboa. Of Father Cancer. Of Cartier. Of Cordova. Of Coronada. Of Cortereal. Of Cortez. Of Father Da Corpa. Of De Soto. Of Sir F. Drake. Of Sir Humphrey Gilbert. Of Grijalva. Of Bishop Juarez. Of Father Las Casas. Of Father Mark. Of Father Martinez. Of Melendez. Of Narvaez. Of Ojeda. Of Father Olmas. Of Sir Walter Raleigh. Of Ribaut. Of Father Roger. Of Father Segura. Of St. Francis Borgia. Of St. Pius V. Of Verrazzani. Mention some of the principal European events of the sixteenth century. Name the Popes who reigned during the sixteenth century. (pp. 47–56.)

SECTION III.

I. Give an account of Gosnold's voyage. Of Pring's voyage. When was Jamestown settled? What was the character of the colonists? Who was the leading spirit in the colony? Recount some of his adventures. What was the *Starving Time?* What did the colonists at last determine to do? Of what treachery was Argall guilty about 1613? Whom did Pocahontas marry? When did she die? Mention some other exploits of Argall. When was he made Governor of Virginia, and how did he act in office? When was the cultivation of tobacco commenced, and with what results? (pp. 59-65.)

II. When did the first colonial assembly meet? When was *slavery* introduced? How did the Virginia colonists obtain wives? What was the cause of the Indian war that followed the death of Powhattan? When did Virginia become a *Royal Province*, and how did it gain the title of *Old Dominion?* What did the Navigation Acts require? What was the cause of Bacon's Rebellion? Were there any *white slaves* in Virginia? What says Bancroft on this subject? What says Thébaud? Describe the manners of the early Virginians. What is to be said concerning education in Virginia at that time? What of religion? (pp. 66-71.)

III. When were the first settlements made in Maine? Give some account of the explorations of De Monts and Champlain along the New England coast. Give the history of St. Saviour's mission on Mt. Desert Island. Describe the arrival of the Puritans. What can you say of their first winter? How did the Indians act? What can you say of the progress of the colony? When was the *Massachusetts Bay Colony* founded? Were the Puritans tolerant in religious matters? Give an account of Roger Williams. When was Rhode Island founded? Give an account of Mrs. Hutchinson. When was New Hampshire founded? How were Quakers treated in Massachusetts? What Jesuit missionaries established themselves in Maine about the middle of the seventeenth century? Have the Abnaki been true to the Faith? (pp. 71-79.)

IV. What was the origin of King Philip's War? Describe the Swamp Fight. Describe Winslow's raid into the territory of the Narragansetts. What says Bancroft on this subject? When and why was the charter of the New England Colonies abolished? Give an account of the *Salem Witchcraft Delusion.* What impression did this make upon the Indians? What was the character of the Puritans? Describe the dwellings of the Puritans. What were their occupations? What was the prescribed religion in New England? How were Roman Catholics treated? (pp. 80–86.)

V. By whom was the coast of Connecticut first explored? By whom were Hartford and Wethersfield settled? Give an account of the Pequod War. Give an account of the *Blue Laws*. (pp. 87–90.)

VI. What can you say concerning the Catholic missionaries on this continent? What explorations were made by them? What discoveries and improvements? Give an account of the Franciscan missions in Canada. When did the Jesuits arrive? What is the origin of the name Sault au Récollet? What was the grand mission centre of Canada in those early times? Which three Jesuits commenced missions in the Huron country in 1633? What can you say of Brebœuf? When did Father Jogues and Raymbault visit Michigan? Who were the Iroquois? Give an account of Father Jogues' captivity among the Mohawks. What says Bancroft on this subject? By whom was Jogues ransomed? What missionary went to the Abnaki in 1646? Describe the death of Father de Noué. Of Father Daniel. Of Father Brebœuf. Name some of the other missionaries who met death this same year. What effect in Europe had the news from the American missions? Give Bancroft's description of the arrival of the Ursulines at Quebec. (pp. 91–101.)

VII. What followed among the Iroquois after the death of Father Jogues? What did Father Le Moyne discover? Who, in 1660, went westward to the Algonquins of Michigan? What was his fate? What Father established a mission at the western end of Lake Superior in 1664? Whom did he meet there? By whom was he soon joined? What did they together found? By whom was the Mississippi explored in 1673? Describe his route. (*Trace it on the map*.) What was the character of the Illinois Indians? Give a quotation from *Hiawatha* descriptive of the Illinois greeting to Marquette. How long did Marquette remain among the Illinois? When did he turn northward? When he again reached Green Bay, how long a voyage had he made? Describe Marquette's last days. Name the next great explorer of the Mississippi. Describe his voyage. What was his fate? Give from McGee a quotation concerning him. Who continued the missions commenced by Marquette? What other missions followed? (pp. 102–110.)

VIII. By whom was New York Bay visited in 1524 and 1609, respectively? Describe Hudson's voyage up the North River. Who in consequence claimed the adjacent territory? Who were the *Patroons?* Name the four Dutch governors, and give some account of their rule. What was the character of Stuyvesant? When was New Amsterdam surrendered to the English? Why was the name changed? Name the first two English governors. What was the character of Andros? For what was the rule of Thomas Dongan noted? What was the religious condition of the Iroquois about the year 1688? What effect upon the American colonies had the English Revolution of 1688? Give an account of Leisler's usurpation. Where was the first settlement made in New Jersey? What can you say of the manners of the Dutch in New York? What was the style of their dwellings? What was the religion of the colony? (pp. 111-120.)

IX. By whom was Maryland settled? Describe the landing of the Maryland pilgrims. How did the colony progress? How did the Maryland colonists treat the Indians? Who paid the colonists a visit soon after their arrival? What was the distinctive feature of the Maryland Colony? Give some account of Clayborne? What was the *Toleration Act?* When was it repealed? What was the result? What happened on the dethronement of James II.? What can you say of the manners of the Maryland colonists? What was their mode of travel? What can you say of their hospitality? What of their dwellings? What was the religion of the Maryland colonists? (pp. 121-126.)

X. When was the first settlement made in Delaware? In Pennsylvania? When and by whom was the colony of Pennsylvania founded? Give some account of William Penn. Give some account of the founding of Philadelphia. How did Penn treat the Indians? When did Penn return to England? What happened in the colony during his absence? Give some account of Penn's last years? What is meant by *Mason and Dixon's line?* Into whose possession did the colony pass after Penn's death? What were the occupations of the Pennsylvania colonists? What can you say of their manners? Of their religion? (pp. 126-129.)

XI. What was the origin of the *Albemarle Colony* in Carolina? Of the *Clarendon Colony?* Of the *Carteret Colony?* What was the *Grand Model*, and what were its results? Give some account of Archdale. Under what circumstances was rice introduced into the Carolinas? What were the principal occupations in the Carolinas? (pp. 130-132.)

XII. What was the consequence of the accession of William of Orange? Give an account of the *Massacre of Lachine*. Who was Frontenac? What did he plan? Where was blood first shed in the East? Give an account of the *Massacre of Schenectady*. What were now the feelings of the English? By whom was Acadia reduced? Describe Phipp's attack on Quebec. Was the expedition against Montreal successful? What was the result of these two failures? When was peace declared? What other settlements not previously mentioned had been made, before the close of the seventeenth century? (pp. 133–136.)

XIII. Give a biographical sketch of Father Allouez. Of Andros. Of Argall. Of Nathaniel Bacon. Of the first Lord Baltimore. Of the second Lord Baltimore. Of Sir Wm. Berkeley. Of Leonard Calvert. Of Father Charlevoix. Of Champlain. Of Gov. Dongan. Of Frontenac. Of Joliet. Of La Salle. Of Leisler. Of Father Marquette. Of Wm. Penn. Of Sir Wm. Phipps. Of Peter Stuyvesant. Of Father White. Of Roger Williams. Mention some of the principal European events of the seventeenth century. Name the Popes who reigned during the seventeenth century. (pp. 136–148.)

SECTION IV.

I. What *Penal Laws* were passed in New York in 1700? In 1701 and 1702? What can you say of Queen Anne's War? How were the English colonies situated? What hostilities took place at the *South?* Where was the greatest blow struck? Describe the hostilities at the *North.* By whom was Acadia reduced? What expeditions were undertaken against Canada, and with what result? What massacre occurred in North Carolina? When was *peace* declared? What was the state of feeling between the Indians and the Abnaki? Describe the death of Father Rasle. Describe the Natchez massacre. What was the fate of the children? Give an account of the *Mississippi Scheme.* By whom was *Georgia* settled? Why was it called Georgia? Who came to Savannah in 1636? What was the cause of the *Spanish War?* How long did it last? When was Georgia made a royal province? Give an account of the *Negro Plot.* Give an account of *King George's War.* (pp. 151–158.)

II. What region was claimed alike by France and England, and why? What grant brought matters to a crisis, and how? Give an account of Washington's embassy to St. Pierre. Describe his return. Give an account of the opening of the *French and Indian War.* Which were the five *objective points?* What region fell into the hands of the English, almost as soon as the war had commenced? Give a quotation from *Evangeline,* descriptive of the peaceful life of the Acadians. Describe their expulsion. Give an account of *Braddock's Defeat.* Of the *Battle of Lake George.* Of the capture of *Fort William Henry.* Who was William Pitt, and what influence had he on the affairs of this country? Give an account of the campaign of 1758. Describe the capture of Quebec. The last hours of Wolfe and Montcalm. When was *peace* signed? What was the result of the *Treaty of Paris?* Give an account of *Pontiac's War.* Name the principal battles of the French and Indian War. (pp. 159–169.)

III. What were the remote causes of *the Revolution?* How did England treat the colonies? What were *Writs of Assistance?* What

REVIEW QUESTIONS. 407

was the *Stamp Act*? What occurred at this time in the Assembly of Virginia? What was ordered by the *Mutiny Act*? What effect had these measures? Which act in particular excited indignation? When was the *Stamp Act* repealed? Give an account of the Boston Massacre. Of the "*Boston Tea Party*." What action did England now take? What action did the Colonies take? When and where was the first *Continental Congress* held? What was granted by the *Quebec Act*? Give an account of the *Battle of Lexington*. What were the *effects* of this battle? Give an account of the capture of *Fort Ticonderoga*. Of the *Battle of Bunker Hill*. Who was chosen commander-in-chief of the American forces? Give an account of the expedition against Canada. From what Indian tribe did we receive special aid? What does John Gilmary Shea remark in this connection? Why were commissioners sent to Canada, and who were they? When was Boston evacuated? Give the anecdote concerning the Boston boys (*note*). Give an account of the attack on Fort Moultrie. When did the DECLARATION OF INDEPENDENCE take place? By whom was the *Declaration* signed? What remarks were made on the occasion? (pp. 170–184.)

IV. What warlike preparations were now made on both sides? Describe the *Battle of Long Island*. Describe Washington's retreat. His flight into New Jersey. The battle of *Trenton*. What was the effect of this feat? Give an account of *Burgoyne's Invasion*. Of *St. Leger's Expedition*. Of the two battles of Saratoga. What was the result of these battles? Give an account of the battle of *Brandywine*. Of the battle of *Germantown*. Of the capture of the forts on the Delaware. Of the winter at *Valley Forge*. (pp. 185–194.)

V. What characterizes this period of the war (1777)? What help was early given by France? What distinguished French nobleman came to our aid? What effect had his departure from France (*note*)? What Polish nobles gave us their services? When was the French alliance made? How was the news of this alliance received in this country? At this juncture what proposals were made by England? What results immediately followed the French alliance? Describe the *Battle of Monmouth*. The attack on *Newport*. During the fall of 1778 what change was made in the theatre of the war? Describe the *Massacre of Wyo'ming*. The conquest of Georgia. The French-American attack on Savannah. The capture of Charleston. What can you say of the partisan corps of the South? Describe the battle of *Camden*. The battle of *Cowpens*. What effect had this defeat on Tarleton? Give an account of *Greene's defeat*. What incident occurred during this retreat (*note*)? Give an account of the close of the war at the South. What incident occurred during the British retreat from *Eutaw Springs* (*note*)? What aid did we receive from Spain? How did Bernardo de Galvez, the governor of Louisiana, serve us? (pp. 195–206.)

VI. How was the Northwest secured for the American cause? Describe the capture of *Stony Point*. How were the Indians in the Wyoming and Mohawk Valleys quelled? Describe the winter of 1779–'80. What can you say of the depreciation of currency about this time? In this crisis how did Robert Morris serve his country? Give an account of the *treason of Arnold*. What was his fate? What can you say of the navy at this time? What was the first capture on the seas in the name of the United Colonies? Who was the Father of the American navy? Give some account of Paul Jones' exploit with the *Bon Homme Richard*. What further aid did France send in 1780? In the summer of 1780, what attack was planned by Washington and Rochambeau? Just at this period, whose arrival proved of considerable importance to the Americans? Describe the *siege of Yorktown*. Describe the surrender of Cornwallis. What was the effect of this surrender? What was the condition of the United States immediately after the war? What proposal was made to Washington? How were the troubles concerning the soldiers' pay adjusted? When was the treaty of peace signed? What was remarked by Archbishop Hughes concerning Washington's abdication? Name the principal battles of the Revolution. (pp. 207–217.)

VII. What can you say of the *Articles of Confederation?* What Convention was called at Philadelphia? When was the new *Constitution* adopted? How was the new Constitution received? What were the principles of the *Federalists?* Of the *Anti-Federalists?* Who was elected *first President* of the United States? Name the principal events of *Washington's Administration*. Whom did he select for his *Cabinet?* With what difficulties had the new government to contend? How were the finances put in order? What was the *Whiskey Rebellion?* What *Indian wars* occurred during Washington's administration? What troubles with England? What treaty was made with Spain? With Algiers? What States were admitted into the Union? What troubles with France occurred? What political parties had arisen? How many terms did Washington serve? What can you say of his *Farewell Address?* By whom was Washington succeeded? Mention the principal events of *Adams' Administration*. What were the *Alien and Sedition Laws?* During Adams' Administration, what trouble occurred between France and the United States? By whom was Adams succeeded? What mournful event marked the close of the century? (pp. 218–226.)

VIII. What was the principal occupation of the people up till the time of the Revolution? What can you say of manufactures and commerce? Of the fisheries? How were the houses furnished? Was the *spinning-wheel* much in vogue? How were the houses lighted? Describe the dress of the colonial gentry. Of the ladies. What was the usual mode of travel? Describe Washington's receptions. What discovery was made in 1752? In 1791? In 1792? What can you say concerning our literature at this time? Mention the most noted prose writers of this period and their principal works. Mention the poets. When was the first permanent newspaper commenced, and what can you say of it? (pp. 227-231.)

IX. What can you say of the patriotism of Catholics during the Revolution? What brought about a kindlier feeling? How did Catholics distinguish themselves during the war? How did Washington express himself in his reply to the Address of the Roman Catholics? Who was our *first Bishop*, and when was he appointed? To what did Bishop Carroll immediately turn his attention? What spiritual aid did France now give to the United States? What says Archbishop Spaulding on this subject? How did Bishop Carroll feel with regard to the Indians? What deputation waited on him soon after his consecration? Where did Catholics assemble in New York during the last year of the war? Where had churches been established in Pennsylvania, before the close of the Revolution? When and by whom was the Holy Sacrifice first offered in Western Pennsylvania? What can you say of Catholicity in the West, at this period? In California? What can you say of *old prejudices?* (pp. 227-231.)

X. Give a biographical sketch of John Adams. Of Ethan Allen. Of Arnold. Of Commodore Barry. Of Charles Carroll. Of Archbishop Carroll. Of Benjamin Franklin. Of Prince Gallitzin. Of De Grasse. Of Hamilton. Of Patrick Henry. Of Jefferson. Of Paul Jones. Of Kosciusko. Of Lafayette. Of Richard Lee. Of Henry Lee. Of Marion. Of Morris. Of Moylan. Of William Pitt. Of Pulaski. Of Putnam. Of General Sullivan. Of Sumter. Of George Washington. Mention some of the principal European events of the eighteenth century. Name the Popes who reigned during the eighteenth century. (Pp. 232-250.)

SECTION V.

I. What event took place in the year 1800? Mention the principal events of *Jefferson's Administration.* When and for how much was Louisiana purchased? What remark was made on this occasion by Napoleon? Give an account of the death of Hamilton. What was the after-fate of Burr? What was the cause of the war with Tripoli? How did it end? What was the cause of the difficulty with England during Jefferson's Administration? What was the *Embargo Act?* Which was the first State carved out of the Northwest Territory? Mention the principal events of *Madison's Administration.* Give an account of the Battle of

Tippecanoe. What was the cause of the Anglo-American War of 1812? Give an account of the *Surrender of Detroit.* Of the Battle of Queenstown Heights. Of the contest between the *Constitution* and the *Guerriere.*. Between the *Frolic* and *Wasp.* (pp. 250-262.)

II. What was the plan of the campaign for 1813? What were the operations of the *Armies of the Centre and the North?* Of the *Army of the West?* Describe the encounter between the *Chesapeake* and the *Shannon.* Give an account of *Perry's Victory* on Lake Erie. Of the Battle of the Thames. What Indian War occurred in 1813-14? Describe the operations of the British along the Atlantic coast (1813). Why was the campaign of 1814 more energetically prosecuted by the British? Describe the Battle of Lundy's Lane. The Battle of Lake Champlain. What happened on the Atlantic coast this year (1814)? What occurred during the bombardment of Fort McHenry? Give an account of the *Hartford Convention.* When was the *Treaty of Peace* signed? Give an account of the *Battle of New Orleans.* What were the results of the War of 1812? What occurred between Barbary and the United States? Name the principal battles of the War of 1812. (pp. 263-272.)

III. Name the principal events of Monroe's Administration. What was the *Slavery Question?* The *Missouri Compromise Bill?* How was Florida obtained? What is the *Monroe Doctrine?* Describe Lafayette's visit. Name the principal events of *John Q. Adams' Administration.* After the war to what did the nation apply itself? Give some account of the *Erie Canal.* Of the first railroad in the United States. What secret societies had been formed about this time? What was the *American Tariff System?* Name the principal events of *Jackson's Administration.* What was the *Nullification Ordinance?* The *Tariff Compromise Bill?* During Jackson's Administration, what happened concerning the United States Bank? Give an account of the *Black Hawk War.* What was done with the Cherokees? What was the cause of the *Seminole War?* Who was the leading Indian warrior? What was his fate? How was the war concluded? (pp. 273-281.)

IV. Name the principal events of *Van Buren's Administration.* Give an account of the *Crisis of 1837.* What was the *Patriot War?* How long did *Harrison* continue in office? Name the principal events of *Tyler's Administration.* Why were the *Whigs* disappointed? What was the *Dorr Rebellion?* What were the *Anti-rent* difficulties? Give an account of the *Mormons.* Name the principal events of *Polk's Administration.* Describe *Taylor's Campaign* in Mexico. Describe the Battle of Buena Vista. Give an account of *Scott's Campaign* in Mexico. Of the capture of the City of Mexico. Who particularly distinguished themselves during this war? What did the United States gain by the *Treaty of Guadaloupe Hidalgo?* What discovery was made in 1848? What was the result? What can you say concerning Irish immigration? Name the principal battles of the Mexican War and the victors. (pp. 283-291.)

V. How long did Taylor fulfil the duties of President? Name the principal events of *Fillmore's Administration.* What about the *Slavery Question* at this time? What was the *Omnibus Bill?* Give some account of the invasion of Cuba. Who was Kossuth? Who succeeded Fillmore? Name the principal events of *Pierce's Administration.* When was the *Missouri Compromise Bill* repealed? Give an account of the civil war in Kansas. What was the *Know-Nothing* movement? What was the *Gadsden Purchase?* By whom was the *Treaty with Japan* negotiated? Who succeeded Pierce? Name the principal events of *Buchanan's Administration.* On the opening of this *Administration,* what was the state of feeling concerning *Slavery?* What was the *Dred Scott* Decision? Give an account of *John Brown's Raid.* Who succeeded Buchanan? What effect did Lincoln's election have upon the South? Which States seceded? Who was chosen President of the *Confederate States?* What took place at Fort Sumter in December, 1860? (pp. 291-299.)

VI. Name the principal events of *Lincoln's Administration.* Describe the capture of Fort Sumter, and the effect. What State became the chief battle-field of the war? What were the operations in the East? Describe the battle of *Bull Run.* What was the *effect* of this battle? Which was the only operation in the East during the remainder of 1861? What were the movements of the armies in the East? What were the naval operations of 1861? What was the *Trent affair?* What mission did Archbishop Hughes accept? Give a summary of the *first year of the War.* (pp. 300-305.)

VII. What was the state of affairs in the hostile armies at the beginning of 1862? What were the military movements at the West? Which two forts were captured early in the year? What was the effect of these victories? Describe the battles of Shiloh and Corinth, and the capture of Island No. 10. What took place in Missouri during this year (1862)? What battles took place in Tennessee at the close of 1862 and the beginning of 1863? Describe the first *Vicksburg Expedition.* Describe the *Capture of New Orleans.* What were the movements on the Atlantic coast during 1862? Describe the contest between the *Merrimac* and *the Monitor.* What was the effect? Give an account of *McClellan's Peninsular Campaign.* The Siege of Yorktown. The Battles of Williamsburg and Fair Oaks. Give an account of Stonewall

Jackson's movements in the *Shenandoah*. Of the *Seven Days' Battles*. What was the effect of the Peninsular Campaign? Describe Lee's Invasion of the North. Give the incident concerning *Barbara Frietchie*, and the quotation from Whittier. Who was killed at Chantilly? Give an account of the battles of *Antietam* and Fredericksburg. Give a summary of *the second year of the War*. (pp. 306–318.)

VIII. What was issued *New Year's Day, 1863*? Describe the operations in the East during this year. What General was killed in the battle of Chancellorsville? Describe the *battle of Gettysburg*. Give an account of the siege of *Vicksburg*. Of Rosecrans' Campaigns. Who is styled the *Rock of Chickamauga*? Give an account of the "*Battle above the Clouds.*" Give an account of the war in Tennessee during 1863. Describe the attack on Charleston. Give an account of the *Draft Riots*. What Indian troubles broke out during this year? Give a *summary of the third year of the War*. (pp. 319–325.)

IX. At the beginning of 1864, what were the relative situations of the two armies? Give an account of Grant's *Overland Campaign*. What siege was commenced during the summer of this year? Describe the *Mine Explosion*. The siege of Washington. Describe *Sheridan's Campaign*. *Sherman's Campaign*. The capture of Atlanta. The Battle of Nashville. *Sherman's March to the Sea*. What was the effect of this march? Describe the *Red River Expedition*. What were the *Naval Operations* of this year (1864)? What about the *Blockade?* Confederate Cruisers? *The Alabama?* In the elections of 1864, what candidate opposed Lincoln? Give a *summary of the fourth year of the War*. (pp. 326–338.)

X. Describe Sherman's *March through the Carolinas*. Describe the operations of *Sheridan, Wilson*, and *Stoneman*. Describe the attack on Fort Steadman. Describe the final campaign. Give an account of the surrender of the Confederate generals. What were the losses of the war? What was the Union debt? What can you say of female patriotism during the war? What of the charity manifested throughout the country? What of the Sisters of Charity and Mercy? What of the army chaplains? Name the principal battles of 1861. Name the *Union* victories of 1862. The *Confederate* victories. In the *Seven Days' Battles*, what was the loss on each side? Name the Union victories of 1863. The Confederate victories. What was the loss on each side in the battle of *Gettysburg?* Name the *Union* victories of 1864. The *Confederate* victories. What was the loss, on each side, in the battle of the *Wilderness?* Name the Union victories of 1865. The Confederate victories. Describe the assassination of Lincoln. Give some account of his obsequies. Did the death of Lincoln produce any

disorder? Name the principal events of *Johnson's Administration.*
What was the *reconstruction policy* of the President? Of Congress?
What was the *Freedmen's Bureau Bill?* The *Civil Rights Bill?* The
Tenure-of-office Bill? Which of the seceded States was first admitted?
What other States were admitted, June 1868? What was meant by
the iron-clad oath? (*note*). When was the *Thirteenth Amendment*
adopted? The *Fourteenth?* Give an account of the impeachment of
the President. What Indian war occurred in 1865–'66? Give some
account of Maximilian's brief reign in Mexico. When was Alaska
purchased? What was the *Fenian excitement?* In 1868, what
treaty was made with China? By whom was Johnson succeeded?
(pp. 339–352.)

XI. Mention the principal events of *Grant's* Administration. When
was the *Fifteenth Amendment* adopted? What can you say of the
state of the country after the war? What was shown by the *census* of
1870? What great fires occurred in 1871–'72? Give an account of the
Treaty of Washington. What can you say concerning the proposed
annexation of Santo Domingo? What of Santo Domingo? (*note*).
What was the affair of the "*Virginius*"? How many *terms* did Grant
serve? What was the *Crédit Mobilier?* What panic occurred in 1873,
and with what result? What anniversaries were celebrated in 1875?
What exhibition took place in 1876? Which nations were represented?
Give an account of the *Sioux war.* What troubles occurred during the
fall elections of 1876? By whom was Grant succeeded? Mention
some of the events of Hayes' Administration. What was Hayes' Southern policy? Give an account of the railroad strike of 1877, and its
results. In what did the *Nez Percé War* originate? Where had the
Nez Percés long dwelt? What can you say, in general, of the conduct
of the whites towards the Indians? Give an extract from the first
report of Indian commissioners appointed by Grant, (*note*). Who
succeeded President Hayes? How long had Garfield been in office,
at the time of his death? By whom was he succeeded? Name the
Presidents who have held office since Arthur. (p. 852.)

XII. What can you say of the increase of population in the United
States during the present century? What are the principal occupations in this country at present? What can you say of the inventive
genius of the Americans? By whom was the *magnetic telegraph*
invented? When was the *Atlantic Cable* laid? By whom was the
sewing machine invented? The telephone and phonograph? When
was steam first practically applied to navigation? What can you say
of America with regard to railroad construction? Give some account
of the Pacific Railroad. What can you say of American literature
during the nineteenth century? Name the most noted American

prose writers and their principal works. Name the best known American Catholic prose writers. Name the most noted American poets. (pp. 362-367.)

XIII. What occurred before the death of Archbishop Carroll? What can you say of the growth of the Catholic Church in the United States? Mention the Religious Orders established in this country in the early part of this century. What peculiar case concerning the *Confessional* occurred in New York City in 1813? When was the *First Provincial Council* held? What can you say of Archbishop Hughes? What of the anti-Catholic feeling evinced at various epochs? Mention an act of the Sixth Council of Baltimore, held in 1846. About the same time, who were appointed Chaplains to the American army then invading Texas? When was held the *First Plenary Council* of the Church in the United States? What can you say of Catholics during the *civil war?* When was the *Second Plenary Council* held? What were its objects? What can you say of its decrees? How many American prelates assisted at the *Council of the Vatican?* What can you say of the Indian missions? To whom were they confided in 1835? Give from *Evangeline* a quotation describing a mission scene. What plan with regard to the Indians was devised by Grant? What honor was conferred upon the American Church in 1875? Who became the second American Cardinal? When was held the *Third Plenary Council* of the Church in the United States? Give the present statistics of Catholicity. Name some of the various Protestant sects (*note*). (pp. 368-378.)

XIV. Give a biographical sketch of Braxton Bragg. Of Buchanan. Of Burnside. Of Calhoun. Of Lewis Cass. Of Henry Clay. Of Jefferson Davis. Of Stephen A. Douglas. Of Farragut. Of Fulton. Of U. S. Grant. Of Horace Greeley. Of General Houston. Of Archbishop Hughes. Of Stonewall Jackson. Of General Johnston. Of General Kearney. Of President Lincoln. Of Gen. Lee. Of Madison. Of Maury. Of General McClellan. Of Cardinal McCloskey. Of General Meade. Of Monroe. Of General Rosecrans. Of General Scott. Of Governor Seward. Of General Sheridan. Of General W. T. Sherman. Of General T. W. Sherman. Of Father de Smet. Of Zachary Taylor. Of General Thomas. Of Daniel Webster.

Mention some of the principal European events of the present century.

Name the Popes of this century. What is there remarkable with regard to the length of the reign of Pius IX.? Who is the reigning Pontiff? (pp. 370-400.)

DECLARATION OF INDEPENDENCE.

THE following preamble and specifications, known as the Declaration of Independence, accompanied the resolution of Richard Henry Lee, which was adopted by Congress on the 2d day of July, 1776. This Declaration was agreed to on the 4th, and the transaction is thus recorded in the Journal for that day:

"*Agreeably to the order of the day, the Congress resolved itself into a committee of the whole, to take into their further consideration the Declaration: and, after some time, the president resumed the chair, and Mr. Harrison reported that the committee have agreed to a Declaration, which they desired him to report. The Declaration being read, was agreed to as follows:*"

A DECLARATION BY THE REPRESENTATIVES OF THE UNITED STATES OF AMERICA, IN CONGRESS ASSEMBLED.

When, in the course of human events, it becomes necessary for one people to dissolve the political bands which have connected them with another, and to assume, among the powers of the earth, the separate and equal station to which the laws of nature and of nature's God entitle them, a decent respect to the opinions of mankind requires that they should declare the causes which impel them to the separation.

We hold these truths to be self-evident—that all men are created equal; that they are endowed by their Creator with certain inalienable rights; that among these are life, liberty, and the pursuit of happiness. That, to secure these rights, governments are instituted among men, deriving their just powers from the consent of the governed; that, whenever any form of government becomes destructive of these ends, it is the right of the people to alter or abolish it, and to institute a new government, laying its foundations on such principles, and organizing its powers in such form, as to them shall seem most likely to effect their safety and happiness. Prudence, indeed, will dictate that governments long established should not be changed for light and transient causes; and, accordingly, all experience hath shown that mankind are more disposed to suffer, while evils are sufferable, than to right themselves by abolishing the forms to which they are accustomed. But when a long train of abuses and usurpations, pursuing invariably the same object, evinces a design to reduce them under absolute despotism, it is their right, it is their duty, to throw off such government, and to provide new guards for their future security. Such has been the patient sufferance of these colonies, and such is now the necessity which constrains them to alter their former systems of government. The history of the present king of Great Britain is a history of repeated injuries and usurpations, all having in direct object the establishment of an absolute tyranny over these States. To prove this, let facts be submitted to a candid world.

1. He has refused his assent to laws the most wholesome and necessary for the public good.

2. He has forbidden his governors to pass laws of immediate and pressing importance, unless suspended in their operations till his assent should be obtained; and, when so suspended, he has utterly neglected to attend to them.

3. He has refused to pass other laws for the accommodation of large districts of people, unless those people would relinquish the right of representation in the Legislature—a right inestimable to them, and formidable to tyrants only.

4. He has called together legislative bodies at places unusual, uncomfortable, and distant from the repository of their public records, for the sole purpose of fatiguing them into compliance with his measures.

5. He has dissolved representative houses repeatedly, for opposing, with manly firmness, his invasions on the rights of the people.

6. He has refused, for a long time after such dissolutions, to cause others to be elected, whereby the legislative powers, incapable of annihilation, have returned to the people at large for their exercise; the State remaining, in the mean time, exposed to all the dangers of invasions from without, and convulsions within.

7. He has endeavored to prevent the population of these States; for that purpose obstructing the laws for the naturalization of foreigners; refusing to pass others to encourage their migration hither, and raising the conditions of new appropriations of lands.

8. He has obstructed the administration of justice, by refusing his assent to laws for establishing judiciary powers.

9. He has made judges dependent on his will alone for the tenure of their offices, and the amount and payment of their salaries.

10. He has erected a multitude of new offices, and sent hither swarms of officers to harass our people and eat out their substance.

11. He has kept among us in times of peace, standing armies, without the consent of our Legislatures.

12. He has affected to render the military independent of, and superior to, the civil power.

13. He has combined with others to subject us to a jurisdiction foreign to our constitutions, and unacknowledged by our laws; giving his assent to their acts of pretended legislation:

14. For quartering large bodies of armed troops among us;

15. For protecting them, by a mock trial, from punishment for any murders which they should commit on the inhabitants of these States;

16. For cutting off our trade with all parts of the world;

17. For imposing taxes on us without our consent;

18. For depriving us, in many cases, of the benefits of trial by jury;

19. For transporting us beyond seas, to be tried for pretended offences;

20. For abolishing the free system of English laws in a neighboring province, establishing therein an arbitrary government, and enlarging its boundaries, so as to render it at once an example and fit instrument for introducing the same absolute rule into these colonies;

21. For taking away our charters, abolishing our most valuable laws, and altering, fundamentally, the forms of our governments;

22. For suspending our own Legislatures, and declaring themselves invested with power to legislate for us in all cases whatsoever.

23. He has abdicated government here, by declaring us out of his protection, and waging war against us.

24. He has plundered our seas, ravaged our coasts, burned our towns, and destroyed the lives of our people.

25. He is at this time transporting large armies of foreign mercenaries to complete the works of death, desolation, and tyranny, already begun with circumstances of cruelty and perfidy scarcely paralleled in the most barbarous ages, and totally unworthy the head of a civilized nation.

26. He has constrained our fellow-citizens, taken captive on the high seas, to bear arms against their country, to become the executioners of their friends and brethren, or to fall themselves by their hands.

27. He has excited domestic insurrection among us, and has endeavored to bring on the inhabitants of our frontiers the merciless Indian savages, whose known rule of warfare is an undistinguished destruction of all ages, sexes, and conditions.

In every stage of these oppressions we have petitioned for redress in the most humble terms; our repeated petitions have been answered only by repeated injury. A prince whose character is thus marked by every act which may define a tyrant, is unfit to be the ruler of a free people.

Nor have we been wanting in our attentions to our British brethren. We have warned them, from time to time, of attempts by their legislature to extend an unwarrantable jurisdiction over us. We have reminded them of the circumstances of our emigration and settlement here. We have appealed to their native justice and magnanimity, and we have conjured them by the ties of our common kindred to disavow these usurpations, which would inevitably interrupt our connections and correspondence. They, too, have been deaf to the voice of justice and of consanguinity. We must, therefore, acquiesce in the necessity which denounces our separation, and hold them as we hold the rest of mankind—enemies in war; in peace, friends.

We, therefore, the representatives of the United States of America, in general Congress assembled, appealing to the Supreme Judge of the world for the rectitude of our intentions, do, in the name and by the authority of the good people of these colonies, solemnly publish and declare that these united colonies are, and of right ought to be, free and independent States; that they are absolved from all allegiance to the British crown, and that all political connection between them and the state of Great Britain is, and ought to be, totally dissolved, and that, as free and independent States, they have full power to levy war, conclude peace, contract alliances, establish commerce, and do all other acts and things which independent States may of right do. And for the support of this Declaration, with a firm reliance on the protection of Divine Providence, we mutually pledge to each other our lives, our fortunes, and our sacred honor.

ADAMS, JOHN,
ADAMS, SAMUEL,
BARTLETT, JOSIAH,
BRAXTON, CARTER,
CARROLL, CHARLES, of Carrollton,
CHASE, SAMUEL,
CLARK, ABRAHAM,
CLYMER, GEORGE,
ELLERY, WILLIAM,
FLOYD, WILLIAM,
FRANKLIN, BENJAMIN,
GERRY, ELBRIDGE,
GWINNET, BUTTON,
HALL, LYMAN,
HANCOCK, JOHN,
HARRISON, BENJAMIN,
HART, JOHN,
HEYWARD, THOMAS, Jr.,
HEWES, JOSEPH,
HOOPER, WILLIAM,
HOPKINS, STEPHEN,
HOPKINSON, FRANCIS,
HUNTINGTON, SAMUEL,
JEFFERSON, THOMAS,
LEE, FRANCIS LIGHTFOOT,
LEE, RICHARD HENRY,
LEWIS, FRANCIS,
LIVINGSTON, PHILIP,

LYNCH, THOMAS, Jr.,
M'KEAN, THOMAS,
MIDDLETON, ARTHUR,
MORRIS, LEWIS,
MORRIS, ROBERT,
MORTON, JOHN,
NELSON, THOMAS, Jr.,
PACA, WILLIAM,
PAINE, ROBERT TREAT,
PENN, JOHN,
READ, GEORGE,
RODNEY, CÆSAR,
ROSS, GEORGE,
RUSH, BENJAMIN, M.D.,
RUTLEDGE, EDWARD,
SHERMAN, ROGER,
SMITH, JAMES,
STOCKTON, RICHARD,
STONE, THOMAS,
TAYLOR, GEORGE,
THORNTON, MATTHEW,
WALTON, GEORGE,
WHIPPLE, WILLIAM,
WILLIAMS, WILLIAM,
WILSON, JAMES,
WITHERSPOON, JOHN,
WOLCOTT, OLIVER,
WYTHE, GEORGE.

CONSTITUTION OF THE UNITED STATES.

WE, the People of the United States, in order to form a more perfect union, establish justice, insure domestic tranquillity, provide for the common defence, promote the general welfare, and secure the blessings of liberty to ourselves and our posterity, do ordain and establish this CONSTITUTION for the United States of America.

ARTICLE I.

SECTION 1. All legislative powers herein granted shall be vested in a Congress of the United States, which shall consist of a Senate and House of Representatives.

SECTION 2. The House of Representatives shall be composed of members chosen every second year by the people of the several States, and the electors in each State shall have the qualifications requisite for electors of the most numerous branch of the State Legislature.

No person shall be a representative who shall not have attained to the age of twenty-five years, and been seven years a citizen of the United States, and who shall not, when elected, be an inhabitant of that State in which he shall be chosen.

Representatives and direct taxes shall be apportioned among the several States which may be included within this Union, according to their respective numbers, which shall be determined by adding to the whole number of free persons, including those bound to service for a term of years, and excluding Indians not taxed, three-fifths of all other persons. The actual enumeration shall be made within three years after the first meeting of the Congress of the United States, and within every subsequent term of ten years, in such manner as they shall by law direct. The number of representatives shall not exceed one for every thirty thousand, but each State shall have at least one representative: and until such enumeration shall be made, the State of New Hampshire shall be entitled to choose three; Massachusetts, eight; Rhode Island and Providence Plantations, one; Connecticut, five; New York, six; New Jersey, four; Pennsylvania, eight; Delaware, one; Maryland, six; Virginia, ten; North Carolina, five; South Carolina, five; and Georgia, three.

When vacancies happen in the representation from any State, the executive authority thereof shall issue writs of election to fill such vacancies.

The House of Representatives shall choose their Speaker and other officers; and shall have the sole power of impeachment.

SECTION 3. The Senate of the United States shall be composed of two senators from each State, chosen by the Legislature thereof, for six years; and each senator shall have one vote.

Immediately after they shall be assembled in consequence of the first election, they shall be divided as equally as may be into three classes. The seats of the senators of the first class shall be vacated at the expiration of the second year; of the second class, at the expiration of the fourth year; and of the third class, at the expiration of the sixth year, so that one-third may be chosen every second year; and if vacancies happen by resignation, or otherwise, during the recess of the Legislature of any State, the executive thereof may make temporary appointments until the next meeting of the Legislature, which shall then fill such vacancies.

No person shall be a senator who shall not have attained to the age of thirty years, and been nine years a citizen of the United States, and who shall not, when elected, be an inhabitant of that State for which he shall be chosen.

The Vice-President of the United States shall be president of the Senate, but shall have no vote, unless they be equally divided.

The Senate shall choose their other officers, and also a president *pro tempore*, in the absence of the Vice-President, or when he shall exercise the office of President of the United States.

The Senate shall have the sole power to try all impeachments: When sitting for that purpose, they shall be on oath or affirmation. When the President of the United States is tried, the Chief-Justice shall preside: and no person shall be convicted without the concurrence of two-thirds of the members present.

Judgment in cases of impeachment shall not extend further than to removal from office, and disqualification to hold and enjoy any office of honor, trust, or profit under the United States; but the party convicted shall nevertheless be liable and subject to indictment, trial, judgment, and punishment, according to law.

SECTION 4. The times, places, and manner of holding elections for senators and representatives shall be prescribed in each State by the Legislature thereof; but the Congress may at any time, by law, make or alter such regulations, except as to the places of choosing senators.

The Congress shall assemble at least once in every year, and such meeting shall be on the first Monday in December, unless they shall by law appoint a different day.

SECTION 5. Each house shall be the judge of the elections, returns, and qualifications of its own members, and a majority of each shall constitute a quorum to do business; but a smaller number may adjourn from day to day, and may be authorized to compel the attendance of absent members, in such manner, and under such penalties, as each house may provide.

Each house may determine the rules of its proceedings, punish its members for disorderly behavior, and, with the concurrence of two-thirds, expel a member.

Each house shall keep a journal of its proceedings, and from time to time publish the same, excepting such parts as may in their judgment equire secresy, and the yeas and nays of the members of either house on any question shall, at the desire of one-fifth of those present, be entered on the journal.

Neither house, during the session of Congress, shall, without the consent of the other, adjourn for more than three days, nor to any other place than that in which the two houses shall be sitting.

SECTION 6. The senators and representatives shall receive a compensation for their services, to be ascertained by law, and paid out of the treasury of the United States. They shall in all cases, except treason, felony, and breach of the peace, be privileged from arrest during their attendance at the session of their respective houses, and in going to and returning from the same; and for any speech or debate in either house, they shall not be questioned in any other place.

No senator or representative shall, during the time for which he was elected, be appointed to any civil office under the authority of the United States, which shall have been created, or the emoluments whereof shall have been increased, during such time; and no person holding any office under the United States, shall be a member of either house during his continuance in office.

SECTION 7. All bills for raising revenue shall originate in the House of Representatives; but the Senate may propose or concur with amendments as on other bills.

Every bill which shall have passed the House of Representatives and the Senate, shall, before it become a law, be presented to the President of the United States; if he approve, he shall sign it, but if not, he shall return it, with his objections, to that house in which it shall have originated, who shall enter the objections at large on their journal, and proceed to reconsider it. If after such reconsideration, two-thirds of that house shall agree to pass the bill, it shall be sent, together with the objections, to the other house, by which it shall likewise be reconsidered, and if approved by two-thirds of that house, it shall become a law. But in all such cases the votes of both houses shall be determined by yeas and nays, and the names of the persons voting for and against the bill shall be entered on the journal of each house respectively. If any bill shall not be returned by the President within ten days (Sunday excepted) after it shall have been presented to him, the same shall be a law, in like manner as if he had signed it, unless the Congress by their adjournment prevent its return, in which case it shall not be a law.

Every order, resolution, or vote to which the concurrence of the Senate and House of Representatives may be necessary (except on a question of adjournment) shall be presented to the President of the United States; and before the same shall take effect, shall be approved by him, or being disapproved by him, shall be repassed by two-thirds of the Senate and House of Representatives, according to the rules and limitations prescribed in the case of a bill.

SECTION 8. The Congress shall have power to lay and collect taxes, duties, imposts, and excises, to pay the debts and provide for the common defence and general welfare of the United States; but all duties, imposts, and excises shall be uniform throughout the United States;

To borrow money on the credit of the United States;

To regulate commerce with foreign nations, and among the several States, and with the Indian tribes;

To establish an uniform rule of naturalization, and uniform laws on the subject of bankruptcies throughout the United States;

To coin money, regulate the value thereof, and of foreign coin, and fix the standard of weights and measures;

To provide for the punishment of counterfeiting the securities and current coin of the United States;

To establish post-offices and post-roads;

To promote the progress of science and useful arts, by securing, for limited times, to authors and inventors the exclusive right to their respective writings and discoveries;

To constitute tribunals inferior to the Supreme Court;

To define and punish piracies and felonies committed on the high seas, and offences against the law of nations;

To declare war, grant letters of marque and reprisal, and make rules concerning captures on land and water;

To raise and support armies, but no appropriation of money to that use shall be for a longer term than two years;

To provide and maintain a navy;

To make rules for the government and regulation of the land and naval forces;

To provide for calling forth the militia to execute the laws of the Union, suppress insurrections and repel invasions;

To provide for organizing, arming, and disciplining the militia, and for governing such part of them as may be employed in the service of the United States, reserving to the States respectively the appointment of the officers, and the authority of training the militia according to the discipline prescribed by Congress;

CONSTITUTION OF THE UNITED STATES. 421

To exercise exclusive legislation in all cases whatsoever over such district (not exceeding ten miles square) as may, by cession of particular States, and the acceptance of Congress, become the seat of the government of the United States, and to exercise like authority over all places purchased by the consent of the Legislature of the State in which the same shall be, for the erection of forts, magazines, arsenals, dockyards, and other needful buildings;—And

To make all laws which shall be necessary and proper for carrying into execution the foregoing powers, and all other powers vested by this Constitution in the government of the United States, or in any department or officer thereof.

SECTION 9. The migration or importation of such persons as any of the States now existing shall think proper to admit, shall not be prohibited by the Congress prior to the year one thousand eight hundred and eight, but a tax or duty may be imposed on such importation, not exceeding ten dollars for each person.

The privilege of the writ of habeas corpus shall not be suspended, unless when in cases of rebellion or invasion the public safety may require it.

No bill of attainder or ex-post-facto law shall be passed.

No capitation or other direct tax shall be laid, unless in proportion to the census or enumeration hereinbefore directed to be taken.

No tax or duty shall be laid on articles exported from any State.

No preference shall be given by any regulation of commerce or revenue to the ports of one State over those of another; nor shall vessels bound to, or from, one State, be obliged to enter, clear, or pay duties in another.

No money shall be drawn from the treasury but in consequence of appropriations made by law; and a regular statement and account of the receipts and expenditures of all public money shall be published from time to time.

No title of nobility shall be granted by the United States: And no person holding any office of profit or trust under them, shall, without the consent of the Congress, accept of any present, emolument, office, er title, of any kind whatever, from any king, prince, or foreign state.

SECTION 10. No State shall enter into any treaty, alliance, or confederation; grant letters of marque and reprisal; coin money; emit bills of credit; make anything but gold and silver coin a tender in payment of debts; pass any bill of attainder, ex-post-facto law, or law impairing the obligation of contracts, or grant any title of nobility.

No State shall, without the consent of the Congress, lay any impost or duties on imports or exports, except what may be absolutely necessary for executing its inspection laws; and the net produce of all duties and impost, laid by any State on imports or exports, shall be for the use of the treasury of the United States; and all such laws shall be subject to the revision and control of the Congress.

No State shall, without the consent of Congress, lay any duty of tonnage, keep troops, or ships-of-war, in time of peace, enter into any agreement or compact with another State, or with a foreign power, or engage in war, unless actually invaded, or in such imminent danger as will not admit of delay.

ARTICLE II.

SECTION 1. The executive power shall be vested in a President of the United States of America. He shall hold his office during the term of four years, and, together with the Vice-President, chosen for the same term, be elected, as follows:

Each State shall appoint, in such manner as the Legislature thereof may direct, a number of electors, equal to the whole number of senators and representatives to which the State may be entitled in the Congress: but no senator or representative, or person holding an office of trust or profit under the United States, shall be appointed an elector.

[The electors shall meet in their respective States, and vote by ballot for two persons, of whom one at least shall not be an inhabitant of the same State with themselves. And they shall make a list of all the persons voted for, and of the number of votes for each; which list they shall sign and certify, and transmit sealed to the seat of the government of the United States, directed to the president of the Senate. The president of the Senate shall, in the presence of the Senate and House of Representatives, open all the certificates, and the votes shall then be counted. The person having the greatest number of votes shall be the President, if such number be a majority of the whole number of electors appointed; and if there be more than one who have such majority, and have an equal number of votes, then the House of Representatives shall immediately choose by ballot one of them for President; and if no person have a majority, then from the five highest on the list the said house shall, in like manner, choose the President. But in choosing the President, the votes shall be taken by States, the representation from each State having one vote; a quorum for this purpose shall consist of a member or members from two-thirds of the States, and a majority of all the States shall be necessary to a choice. In every case, after the choice of the President, the person having the greatest number of votes of the electors shall be the Vice-President. Bu if there should remain two or more who have equal votes, the Senate shall choose from them by ballot the Vice-President.]

The Congress may determine the time of choosing the electors, and the day on which they shall give their votes; which day shall be the same throughout the United States.

No person except a natural-born citizen, or a citizen of the United States at the time of the adoption of this Constitution, shall be eligible to the office of President; neither shall any person be eligible to that office who shall not have attained to the age of thirty-five years, and been fourteen years resident within the United States.

In case of the removal of the President from office, or of his death, resignation, or inability to discharge the powers and duties of the said office, the same shall devolve on the Vice-President, and the Congress may by law provide for the case of removal, death, resignation, or inability, both of the President and Vice-President, declaring what officer shall then act as President; and such officer shall act accordingly until the disability be removed, or a President shall be elected.

The President shall, at stated times, receive for his services a compensation which shall neither be increased nor diminished during the period for which he shall have been elected, and he shall not receive within that period any other emolument from the United States, or any of them.

Before he enter on the execution of his office, he shall take the following oath or affirmation:—" I do solemnly swear (or affirm) that I will faithfully execute the office of President of the United States, and will, to the best of my ability, preserve, protect, and defend the Constitution of the United States."

SECTION 2. The President shall be commander-in-chief of the army and navy of the United States, and of the militia of the several States, when called into the actual service of the United States; he may require the opinion, in writing, of the principal officer in each of the executive departments, upon any subject relating to the duties of their respective offices; and he shall have power to grant reprieves and pardons for offences against the United States, except in cases of impeachment.

He shall have power, by and with the advice and consent of the Senate, to make treaties, provided two-thirds of the senators present concur; and he shall nominate, and by and with the advice and consent of the Senate shall appoint ambassadors, other public ministers and consuls, judges of the Supreme Court, and all other officers of the United States, whose appointments are not herein otherwise provided for, and which shall be established by law: but the Congress may by law vest the appointment of such inferior officers, as they think proper, in the President alone, in the courts of law, or in the heads of departments.

The President shall have power to fill up all vacancies that may happen during the recess of the Senate, by granting commissions which shall expire at the end of their next session.

SECTION 3. He shall from time to time give to the Congress information of the state of the Union, and recommend to their consideration such measures as he shall judge necessary and expedient; he may, on extraordinary occasions, convene both houses, or either of them, and in case of disagreement between them with respect to the time of adjournment, he may adjourn them to such time as he shall think proper; he shall receive ambassadors and other public ministers; he shall take care that the laws be faithfully executed, and shall commission all the officers of the United States.

SECTION 4. The President, Vice-President, and all civil officers of the United States, shall be removed from office on impeachment for, and conviction of, treason, bribery, or other high crimes and misdemeanors.

ARTICLE III.

SECTION 1. The judicial power of the United States shall be vested in one Supreme Court, and in such inferior courts as the Congress may from time to time ordain and establish. The judges, both of the Supreme and inferior courts, shall hold their offices during good behavior, and shall, at stated times, receive for their services a compensation which shall not be diminished during their continuance in office.

SECTION 2. The judicial power shall extend to all cases, in law and equity, arising under this Constitution, the laws of the United States, and treaties made, or which shall be made, under their authority;—to all cases affecting ambassadors, other public ministers, and consuls;—to all cases of admiralty and maritime jurisdiction;—to controversies to which the United States shall be a party;—to controversies between two or more States;—between a State and citizens of another State;—between citizens of different States;—between citizens of the same State claiming lands under grants of different States, and between a State, or the citizens thereof, and foreign states, citizens or subjects.

In all cases affecting ambassadors, other public ministers and consuls, and those in which a State shall be party, the Supreme Court shall have original jurisdiction. In all the other cases before mentioned, the Supreme Court shall have appellate jurisdiction, both as to law and fact, with such exceptions and under such regulations as the Congress shall make.

The trial of all crimes, except in cases of impeachment, shall be by jury; and such trial shall be held in the State where the said crimes shall have been committed; but when not committed within any State, the trial shall be at such place or places as the Congress may by law have directed.

SECTION 3. Treason against the United States shall consist only in levying war against them, or in adhering to their enemies, giving them aid and comfort.

No person shall be convicted of treason unless on the testimony of two witnesses to the same overt act, or on confession in open court.

The Congress shall have power to declare the punishment of treason, but no attainder of treason shall work corruption of blood, or forfeiture, except during the life of the person attainted.

ARTICLE IV.

SECTION 1. Full faith and credit shall be given in each State to the public acts records and judicial proceedings of every other State. And the Congress may by general laws prescribe the manner in which such acts, records, and proceedings shall be proved, and the effect thereof.

SECTION 2. The citizens of each State shall be entitled to all privileges and immunities of citizens in the several States.

A person charged in any State with treason, felony, or other crime, who shall flee from justice, and be found in another State, shall, on demand of the executive authority of the State from which he fled, be delivered up, to be removed to the State having jurisdiction of the crime.

No person held to service or labor in one State, under the laws thereof, escaping into another, shall, in consequence of any law or regulation therein, be discharged from such service or labor, but shall be delivered up on claim of the party to whom such service or labor may be due.

SECTION 3. New States may be admitted by the Congress into this Union; but no new State shall be formed or erected within the jurisdiction of any other State; nor any State be formed by the junction of two or more States, or parts of States, without the consent of the Legislatures of the States concerned as well as of the Congress.

The Congress shall have power to dispose of and make all needful rules and regulations respecting the territory or other property belonging to the United States; and nothing in this Constitution shall be so construed as to prejudice any claims of the United States, or of any particular State.

SECTION 4. The United States shall guarantee to every State in this Union a republican form of government, and shall protect each of them against invasion, and on application of the Legislature, or of the executive (when the Legislature cannot be convened) against domestic violence.

ARTICLE V.

The Congress, whenever two-thirds of both houses shall deem it necessary, shall propose amendments to this Constitution, or, on the application of the Legislatures of two-thirds of the several States, shall call a convention for proposing amendments, which, in either case, shall be valid to all intents and purposes, as part of this Constitution, when ratified by the Legislatures of three-fourths of the several States, or by conventions in three-fourths thereof, as the one or the other mode of ratification may be proposed by the Congress; provided that no amendment which may be made prior to the year one thousand eight hundred and eight shall in any manner affect the first and fourth clauses in the ninth section of the first article; and that no State, without its consent, shall be deprived of its equal suffrage in the Senate.

ARTICLE VI.

All debts contracted, and engagements entered into, before the adoption of this Constitution, shall be as valid against the United States under this Constitution, as under the confederation.

This Constitution, and the laws of the United States which shall be made in pursuance thereof; and all treaties made, or which shall be made, under the authority of the United States, shall be the supreme law of the land; and the judges in every State shall be bound thereby, anything in the Constitution or laws of any State to the contrary notwithstanding.

The senators and representatives before mentioned, and the members of the several State Legislatures, and all executive and judicial officers, both of the United States and of the several States, shall be bound by oath or affirmation to support this Constitution; but no religious test shall ever be required as a qualification to any office or public trust under the United States.

ARTICLE VII.

The ratification of the conventions of nine States shall be sufficient for the establishment of this Constitution between the States so ratifying the same.

Done in convention, by the unanimous consent of the States present, the seventeenth day of September, in the year of our Lord one thousand seven hundred and eighty-seven, and of the Independence of the United States of America the twelfth.

In witness whereof, we have hereunto subscribed our names.

GEORGE WASHINGTON,
President, and Deputy from Virginia.

NEW HAMPSHIRE.
JOHN LANGDON,
NICHOLAS GILMAN.

MASSACHUSETTS.
NATHANIEL GORHAM,
RUFUS KING.

CONNECTICUT.
WILLIAM SAMUEL JOHNSON,
ROGER SHERMAN.

NEW YORK.
ALEXANDER HAMILTON.

NEW JERSEY.
WILLIAM LIVINGSTON,
DAVID BREARLEY,
WILLIAM PATERSON,
JONATHAN DAYTON.

PENNSYLVANIA.
BENJAMIN FRANKLIN,
THOMAS MIFFLIN,
ROBERT MORRIS,
GEORGE CLYMER,
THOMAS FITZSIMONS,
JARED INGERSOLL,
JAMES WILSON,
GOUVERNEUR MORRIS.

DELAWARE.
GEORGE READ,
GUNNING BEDFORD, Jr.,
JOHN DICKINSON,
RICHARD BASSETT,
JACOB BROOM.

MARYLAND.
JAMES M'HENRY,
DANIEL OF ST. THOMAS JENIFER.
DANIEL CARROLL.

VIRGINIA.
JOHN BLAIR,
JAMES MADISON, Jr.

NORTH CAROLINA.
WILLIAM BLOUNT,
RICHARD DOBBS SPAIGHT,
HUGH WILLIAMSON.

SOUTH CAROLINA.
JOHN RUTLEDGE,
CHARLES C. PINCKNEY,
CHARLES PINCKNEY,
PIERCE BUTLER.

GEORGIA.
WILLIAM FEW,
ABRAHAM BALDWIN.

Attest: WILLIAM JACKSON, *Secretary*

AMENDMENTS

TO THE CONSTITUTION OF THE UNITED STATES, RATIFIED ACCORDING TO THE PROVISIONS OF THE FIFTH ARTICLE OF THE FOREGOING CONSTITUTION.

ARTICLE THE FIRST.—Congress shall make no law respecting an establishment of religion, or prohibiting the free exercise thereof; or abridging the freedom of speech, or of the press; or the right of the people peaceably to assemble, and to petition the government for redress of grievances.

ARTICLE THE SECOND.—A well-regulated militia, being necessary to the security of a free State, the right of the people to keep and bear arms shall not be infringed.

ARTICLE THE THIRD.—No soldier shall, in time of peace, be quartered in any house, without the consent of the owner, nor in time of war, but in a manner to be prescribed by law.

ARTICLE THE FOURTH.—The right of the people to be secure in their persons, houses, papers, and effects, against unreasonable searches and seizures, shall not be violated, and no warrants shall issue, but upon probable cause, supported by oath or affirmation, and particularly describing the place to be searched, and the persons or things to be seized.

ARTICLE THE FIFTH.—No person shall be held to answer for a capital, or otherwise infamous crime, unless on a presentment or indictment of a grand jury, except in cases arising in the land or naval forces, or in the militia, when in actual service in time of war and public danger; nor shall any person be subject for the same offence to be twice put in jeopardy of life or limb; nor shall be compelled in any criminal case to be a witness against himself, nor to be deprived of life, liberty, or property, without due process of law; nor shall private property be taken for public use, without just compensation.

ARTICLE THE SIXTH.—In all criminal prosecutions, the accused shall enjoy the right to a speedy and public trial, by an impartial jury of the State and district wherein the crime shall have been committed, which district shall have been previously ascertained by law, and to be informed of the nature and cause of the accusation; to be confronted with the witnesses against him; to have compulsory process for obtaining witnesses in his favor, and to have the assistance of counsel for his defence.

ARTICLE THE SEVENTH.—In suits at common law, where the value in controversy shall exceed twenty dollars, the right of trial by jury shall be preserved, and no fact tried by a jury shall be otherwise re-examined in any court of the United States than according to the rules of common law.

ARTICLE THE EIGHTH.—Excessive bail shall not be required, nor excessive fines imposed, nor cruel and unusual punishments inflicted.

CONSTITUTION OF THE UNITED STATES. 427

ARTICLE THE NINTH.—The enumeration in the Constitution of certain rights, shall not be construed to deny or disparage others retained by the people.

ARTICLE THE TENTH.—The powers not delegated to the United States by the Constitution, nor prohibited by it to the States, are reserved to the States respectively, or to the people.

ARTICLE THE ELEVENTH.—The judicial power of the United States shall not be construed to extend to any suit in law or eqrity, commenced or prosecuted against one of the United States by citizens of another State, or by citizens or subjects of any foreign state.

ARTICLE THE TWELFTH.—The electors shall meet in their respective States, and vote by ballot for President and Vice-President, one of whom, at least, shall not be an inhabitant of the same State with themselves; they shall name in their ballots the person voted for as President, and in distinct ballots the person voted for as Vice-President; and they shall make distinct lists of all persons voted for as President, and of all persons voted for as Vice-President, and of the number of votes for each, which lists they shall sign and certify, and transmit sealed to the seat of the government of the United States, directed to the president of the Senate;—the president of the Senate shall, in the presence of the Senate and House of Representatives, open all the certificates, and the votes shall then be counted;—the person having the greatest number of votes for President, shall be the President, if such number be a majority of the whole number of electors appointed; and if no person have such majority, then from the persons having the highest numbers not exceeding three on the list of those voted for as President, the House of Representatives shall choose immediately, by ballot, the President. But in choosing the President, the votes shall be taken by States, the representation from each State having one vote; a quorum for this purpose shall consist of a member or members from two-thirds of the States, and a majority of all the States shall be necessary to a choice. And if the House of Representatives shall not choose a President whenever the right of choice shall devolve upon them, before the fourth day of March next following, then the Vice-President shall act as President, as in the case of the death or other constitutional disability of the President. The person having the greatest number of votes as Vice-President. shall be the Vice-President, if such number be a majority of the whole number of electors appointed; and if no person have a majority, then from the two highest numbers on the list, the Senate shall choose the Vice-President; a quorum for the purpose shall consist of two-thirds of the whole number of senators, and a majority of the whole number shall be necessary to a choice. But no person constitutionally ineligible to the office of President shall be eligible to that of Vice-President of the United States.

ARTICLE THE THIRTEENTH.—*Section* 1. Neither slavery nor involuntary servitude, except as a punishment for crime, whereof the party shall have been duly convicted, shall exist within the United States, or any place subject to their jurisdiction.

Section 2. Congress shall have power to enforce this article by appropriate legislation.

ARTICLE THE FOURTEENTH.—*Section* 1. All persons born or naturalized in the United States, and subject to the jurisdiction thereof, are citizens of the United States and of the State wherein they reside. No State shall make or enforce any law which shall abridge the privileges or immunities of citizens of the United States; nor shall any State deprive any person of life, liberty, or property, without due process of law, nor deny to any person within its jurisdiction the equal protection of the laws.

Section 2. Representatives shall be appointed among the several States according to their respective numbers, counting the whole number of persons in each State, excluding Indians not taxed. But when the right to vote at any election for the choice of electors for President and Vice-President of the United States, representatives in Congress, the executive or judicial officers of a State, or the members of the Legislature thereof, is denied to any of the male inhabitants of such State, being twenty-one years of age, and citizens of the United States, or in any way abridged, except for participation in rebellion or other crime, the basis of representation therein shall be reduced in the proportion which the number of such male citizens shall bear to the whole number of male citizens twenty-one years of age in such State.

Section 3. No person shall be a senator or representative in Congress, or elector of President and Vice-President, or hold any office, civil or military, under the United States, or under any State, who, having previously taken an oath as a member of Congress, or as an officer of the United States, or as a member of any State Legislature, or as an executive or judicial officer of any State, to support the Constitution of the United States, shall have engaged in insurrection or rebellion against the same, or given aid or comfort to the enemies thereof. But Congress may, by a vote of two-thirds of each house, remove such disability.

Section 4. The validity of the public debt of the United States, authorized by law, including debts incurred for payment of pensions and bounties for services in suppressing insurrection or rebellion, shall not be questioned. But neither the United States nor any State shall assume or pay any debt or obligation incurred in aid of insurrection or rebellion against the United States, or any claim for the loss or emancipation of any slave; but all such debts, obligations, and claims shall be held illegal and void.

Section 5. Congress shall have power to enforce, by appropriate legislation, the provisions of this article.

ARTICLE THE FIFTEENTH.—*Section* 1. The rights of citizens of the United States to vote shall not be denied or abridged by the United States, or by any State, on account of race, color, or previous condition of servitude.

Section 2. Congress shall have power to enforce this article by appropriate legislation.

TABLE OF THE PRESIDENTS.

NO.	PRESIDENT.	STATE.	BORN.	DIED.	TERM OF OFFICE.	BY WHOM ELECTED.	VICE-PRESIDENT.	SECRETARY OF STATE.
1	George Washington	Virginia	1732	1799	Two terms; 1789–1797.	Whole people	John Adams	Thomas Jefferson, Edmund Randolph, Timothy Pickering.
2	John Adams	Massachusetts	1735	1826	One term; 1797–1801.	Federalists	Thomas Jefferson	Timothy Pickering, John Marshall.
3	Thomas Jefferson	Virginia	1743	1826	Two terms; 1801–1809.	Republicans	Aaron Burr, George Clinton.	James Madison.
4	James Madison	Virginia	1751	1836	Two terms; 1809–1817.	Republicans	George Clinton, Dan'l D. Tompkins.	Robert Smith, James Monroe.
5	James Monroe	Virginia	1759	1831	Two terms; 1817–1825.	All parties	Dan'l D. Tompkins.	John Quincy Adams.
6	John Quincy Adams	Massachusetts	1767	1848	One term; 1825–1829.	House of Reps.	John C. Calhoun.	Henry Clay.
7	Andrew Jackson	Tennessee	1767	1845	Two terms; 1829–1837.	Democrats	John C. Calhoun, Martin Van Buren.	Martin Van Buren, Edward Livingston, Louis McLane.
8	Martin Van Buren	New York	1782	1862	One term; 1837–1841.	Democrats	Rich'd M. Johnson.	John Forsyth.
9	William H. Harrison	Ohio	1773	1841	One month; 1841.	Whigs	John Tyler	John Forsyth.
10	John Tyler	Virginia	1790	1862	3 yrs. and 11 months; 1841–1845.	Whigs		Daniel Webster, Hugh S. Legaré, Abel P. Upshur.
11	James K. Polk	Tennessee	1795	1849	One term; 1845–1849.	Democrats	George M. Dallas	John C. Calhoun. James Buchanan.
12	Zachary Taylor	Louisiana	1784	1850	1 yr. and 4 months; 1849, 1850.	Whigs	Millard Fillmore.	John M. Clayton.
13	Millard Fillmore	New York	1800	1874	2 yrs. and 8 months; 1850–1853.	Whigs		Daniel Webster, Edward Everett.
14	Franklin Pierce	N. Hampshire	1804	1869	One term; 1853–1857.	Democrats	William R. King.	William L. Marcy.
15	James Buchanan	Pennsylvania	1791	1868	One term; 1857–1861.	Democrats	J. C. Breckinridge	Lewis Cass, Jeremiah S. Black.
16	Abraham Lincoln	Illinois	1809	1865	1 term and 1 month; 1861–1865.	Republicans	Hannibal Hamlin, Andrew Johnson.	William H. Seward.
17	Andrew Johnson	Tennessee	1808	1875	3 yrs. and 11 months; 1865–1869.	Republicans		William H. Seward.
18	Ulysses S. Grant	Illinois	1822	1885	Two terms; 1869–1877.	Republicans	Schuyler Colfax, Henry Wilson.	Elihu B. Washburne, Hamilton Fish.
19	Rutherford B. Hayes	Ohio	1822		One term; 1877–1881.	Republicans	Wm. A. Wheeler	Wm. M. Evarts.
20	James A. Garfield	Ohio	1831	1881	6 months, 15 days; 1881.	Republicans	Chester A. Arthur.	James G. Blaine.
21	Chester A. Arthur	New York	1830	1886	3 yrs., 5 months, 15 days; 1881–'85.	Republicans		F. T. Frelinghuysen.
22	Grover Cleveland	New York	1837		One term; 1885–1889.	Democrats	Thos. A. Hendricks	Thos. F. Bayard.
23	Benjamin Harrison	Indiana	1833		One term; 1889–1893.	Republicans	Levi P. Morton	James G. Blaine.
24	Grover Cleveland	New York	1837			Democrats	Adlai E. Stevenson	Walter Q. Gresham.

TABLE OF STATES.

NO.	STATES	ORIGIN OF NAME	DATE OF ADMISSION INTO THE UNION	SETTLEMENT When	SETTLEMENT Where	SETTLEMENT By whom	AREA, SQ. MILES	POPULATION 1870	ORIGINAL NAMES, OR TERRITORY FROM WHICH DERIVED
1	Delaware	In honor of Lord Delaware	*1787	1638	Wilmington	Swedes	2,120	125,015	New Netherland. The three Lower Counties on the Delaware.
2	Pennsylvania	Latin, meaning Penn's Woods	*1787	1682	Philadelphia	English	46,000	3,521,951	
3	New Jersey	In honor of Sir George Carteret, governor of Jersey Island	*1787	1664	Elizabethtown	"	8,320	906,096	New Netherland
4	Georgia	In honor of George II	*1788	1733	Savannah	"	58,000	1,184,109	North Va., New England.
5	Connecticut	Indian, meaning Long River	*1788	1635	Windsor	"	4,674	537,454	"
6	Massachusetts	The place of Great Hills	*1788	1620	Plymouth	"	7,800	1,457,351	"
7	Maryland	In honor of Queen Henrietta Maria	*1788	1634	St. Mary's	"	9,356	780,894	"
8	South Carolina	In honor of Charles II	*1788	1670	Ashley River	"	29,385	705,606	Carteret colony.
9	New Hampshire	Hampshire county, England	*1788	1623	Portsmouth	"	9,280	318,300	North Virginia, New England, Laconia.
10	Virginia	In honor of Elizabeth, the "Virgin Queen."	*1788	1607	Jamestown	"	38,629	1,225,163	South Virginia.
11	New York	In honor of the Duke of York	*1788	†1613	New York	Dutch	47,000	4,382,759	North Virginia, New Netherland.
12	North Carolina	In honor of Charles II	*1789	†	Albemarle Sound	English	45,500	1,071,361	Albemarle colony
13	Rhode Island	Red Island	*1790	1636	Providence	"	1,306	217,356	North Va., New England, Aquiday, Providence and R. I. Plantations.
14	Vermont	French, meaning Green Mountain	1791	1724	Fort Dummer	"	10,212	330,551	New Netherland, New Hampshire Grants.
15	Kentucky	Indian, meaning Dark and Bloody Ground	1792	1775	Boonesboro'	"	37,680	1,321,011	Virginia.
16	Tennessee	Indian, meaning River with the Great Bend	1796	1757	Fort London	"	45,600	1,258,520	Kentucky Territory.
17	Ohio	Indian, meaning Beautiful River	1802	1788	Marietta	"	39,964	2,665,260	Northwest Territory.

TABLE OF STATES. 431

#	State	Meaning	Settled	Date	Capital	By whom	Pop. prev.	Pop.	Formed from
18	Louisiana	In honor of Louis XIV	Biloxi	1819	1559	French	46,431	726,915	Louisiana. Territory of Orleans.
19	Indiana	Indian's Ground	Vincennes	1816	†		63,509	1,680,637	Northwest Territory. Indiana Territory.
20	Mississippi	Indian, meaning Great Father of Waters	Natchez	1817	1716		47,156	827,922	Louisiana, Georgia, Mississippi Territory.
21	Illinois	Indian, meaning River of Men	Kaskaskia	1818	†1683		55,405	2,530,891	Northwest Territory, Illinois Territory.
22	Alabama	Indian, meaning Here we Rest	Mobile	1819	1702		50,722	996,992	Louisiana, Florida, Georgia, Mississippi Territory.
23	Maine	The main land	Bristol	1820	1625		81,766	626,915	New England, Laconia, Massachusetts.
24	Missouri	Indian, meaning Muddy Water	St. Genevieve	1821	1755		67,380	1,721,295	Louisiana, Missouri Territory.
25	Arkansas	From a tribe of Indians	Arkansas Post	1836	1685		52,198	484,471	Louisiana, Missouri Territory, Arkansas Territory.
26	Michigan	Indian, meaning Great Lake	Detroit	1837	1701		56,243	1,184,059	Northwest Territory, Indiana Territory, Michigan Territory.
27	Florida	Spanish, meaning Blooming	St. Augustine	1845	1565	Spaniards	50,298	187,748	Florida.
28	Texas	†	†	1845	†		287,321	818,579	New Philippines.
29	Iowa	Indian, meaning Drowsy Ones	Burlington	1846	1833	English	50,914	1,194,020	Louisiana, Louisiana Ter., Missouri Ter., Michigan Ter., Wisconsin Ter.
30	Wisconsin	Indian, meaning Gathering of the Waters	Green Bay	1848	1745	French	53,924	1,054,670	Louisiana, Illinois Territory, Michigan Territory
31	California	A character in an old romance	San Diego	1850	1769	Spaniards	160,000	560,247	New Albion, Upper California.
32	Minnesota	Indian, meaning Cloudy Water	St. Paul	1858	1846	Americans	95,274	439,706	Louisiana, Minnesota Territory.
33	Oregon	Spanish, meaning Wild Marjoram	Astoria	1859	1811		100,000	90,923	Louisiana, Oregon Territory.
34	Kansas	Indian, meaning Smoky Water	Leavenworth	1861	1854		78,418	364,399	Louisiana, Kansas Territory.
35	West Virginia	From Virginia	Upshur Co.	1863	1784		23,000	442,014	South Virginia, Virginia.
36	Nevada	Spanish, meaning Snow covered	Genoa	1864	1850		112,000	42,491	Upper California.
37	Nebraska	Indian, meaning Water valley	Bellevue	1867			75,000	122,993	Louisiana, Nebraska Territory.
38	Colorado	Spanish, meaning Red or Ruddy	Denver	1876			104,500	39,864	Louisiana, Mexican Cession.

* Date of ratifying the Constitution. † Doubtful or unknown.
‡ The blue hills south-west of Boston, the highest land in the eastern part of the State.

TABLE OF STATES.—Continued.

NO	STATES	ORIGIN OF NAME	DATE OF ADMISSION INTO THE UNION	SETTLEMENT			AREA SQ. MILES	POPULATION 1870	ORIGINAL NAMES, OR TERRITORY FROM WHICH DERIVED
				When	Where	By whom			
39	Washington	Named after Geo. Washington, first Pres. U.S.	1889	1811	Columbia River	English and Americans	69,180	349,390	Louisiana, Oregon Ter., Washington Ter.
40	Montana	Spanish *montaña*, a mountain	1889	1809	Yellowstone River	Americans	146,080	132,159	Louisiana, Missouri Ter., Nebraska Ter., Dakota Ter.
41	North Dakota	Indian, allied	1889	1812	Pembina	English	70,795	182,719	Louisiana, Minnesota Ter., Dakota Ter.
42	South Dakota	" "	1889	1859	S.E. part	Americans	77,650	328,806	Louisiana, Minnesota Ter., Dakota Ter.
43	Idaho	Indian, gem of the mountain	1890	1842	Cœur d'Alène	"	84,800	84,385	Oregon Ter., Washington Ter., Idaho Ter.
44	Wyoming	Indian, an extensive plain	1890	1867	Cheyenne	"	97,890	60,705	Louisiana Ter., Nebraska Ter., Dakota Ter., Idaho Ter., Wyoming Ter.

www.ingramcontent.com/pod-product-compliance
Lightning Source LLC
Chambersburg PA
CBHW022113300426
44117CB00007B/700